A WICKED COMPANY

A WICKED COMPANY

The FORGOTTEN RADICALISM *of the* EUROPEAN ENLIGHTENMENT

Philipp Blom

McCLELLAND & STEWART

Simultaneously published in the United States of America by Basic Books,
A member of the Perseus Books Group

Library and Archives Canada Cataloguing in Publication

Blom, Philipp, 1970-
A wicked company : the forgotten radicalism of the European Enlightenment / Philipp Blom.

ISBN 978-0-7710-1635-6

1. Holbach, Paul Henri Thiry, baron d', 1723-1789.
2. Salons--France--Paris--History--18th century. 3. Paris (France)--Intellectual life--18th century. 4. Enlightenment.
5. Radicalism--Europe--History--18th century. 6. Philosophy, French--18th century. I. Title.

B2056.B56 2010 194 C2010-905369-9

We acknowledge the financial support of the Government of Canada through the Book Publishing Industry Development Program and that of the Government of Ontario through the Ontario Media Development Corporation's Ontario Book Initiative. We further acknowledge the support of the Canada Council for the Arts and the Ontario Arts Council for our publishing program.

Printed and bound in the United States of America

McClelland & Stewart Ltd.
75 Sherbourne Street
Toronto, Ontario
M5A 2P9
www.mcclelland.com

1 2 3 4 5 14 13 12 11 10

After a seminar I gave in 2007 in Bogotá, Colombia,
I was approached by a boy of fourteen or fifteen years of age who
wanted to know, then and there, everything about Diderot,
Holbach, Rousseau, and the radical Enlightenment.
I was not able then to give him the reply he was looking for,
but this book is partly an attempt to answer him now.

I dedicate this book to him and to all those of his age
who are curious enough to question who we are and
courageous enough to imagine who we might become.

O you whom the itch to write torments like a demon and who would give all the mines of Peru for a grain of reputation: abandon that vile herd of vulgar authors who run after the others or who root in the dust of erudition, abandon the fastidious savants whose works are like endless plains without flowers and without end. Either don't write at all, or take another way: be great in your writings, as in your actions, show the world a soul that is lofty, independent.

JULIEN OFFRAY DE LA METTRIE,
Discourse on Happiness

CONTENTS

THE ISLAND OF LOVE

INTRODUCTION

You can lose for all sorts of reasons—because you are not determined enough or because you are too fanatical, not flexible enough or too indifferent, not sufficiently strong, simply unlucky, too immersed in the details or too ignorant of them, too far behind your time or too far ahead of it. You can be a coward in victory and a true hero in defeat.

What is true for the living also holds for the dead. There is something like a stock market for reputations, which is watched anxiously by big investors in the prevailing version of history and with amusement by gamblers taking a punt on an obscure poet or a forgotten musician or philosopher trying to reestablish or tarnish his or her reputation. The workings of this marketplace are important to our present, because those whose stocks are highest, those with the most powerful and most numerous investors behind them, determine the ways we think about ourselves, the stories we tell about our world, the repertoire of our ideas. If Plato's stock is riding above that of Aristotle and completely obliterating the value of Epicurus, then we are more likely to translate Plato's thinking into our language, to tell our own stories along the lines he marked out for us.

On a sweltering summer's day in Paris I went looking for two men who had triumphed in a historic battle but lost their very last. Once they had held in their hands the keys to a society that might have been freer and more just, less repressed and happier. They fought for this vision courageously and at great risk to themselves, but their ideas fell from grace, were deluged by the roaring tide of the French Revolution, and were eventually all but written out of history. They had lived magnificently, but after their death more than two hundred years ago, they had lost the battle for posterity, for the memory of future generations.

Today one of these men, Baron Paul Thiry d'Holbach (1723–1789), is forgotten by all but a few specialized scholars, while the other, Denis Diderot (1713–1784), is known mainly as the editor of the great *Encyclopédie* and the author of a handful of innovative works of fiction. And yet Holbach was not only host to some of the most brilliant minds of the century but also an important philosophical writer in his own right, author of the first uncompromisingly atheist books published since antiquity. His work is ignored, while Diderot has been reduced to the role he most despised: that of collator of other people's articles and ideas. His own philosophy—so fresh, so humane, so liberating—does not even appear in many histories of philosophy. His message was too disquieting, too anarchic, too dangerous to be released into the world at large.

Walking through the streets of Paris, I wanted to visit the places they had known, the houses in which they had lived, and especially the house at which Holbach had held his then-legendary salon. The circle of friends around Baron d'Holbach and his close friend and collaborator Diderot remains a kind of phantom ship in the history of philosophy to which rumors and legends have attached themselves like barnacles. Its members were part of a vast conspiracy that planned the French Revolution under the guise of debating questions of economics, some said; they were operating a factory for illegal books, which were written, revised, and disseminated by the thousands to bring down the monarchy, others believed. Most of their contemporaries agreed that Holbach and his cohorts were vile atheists who should be burned at the stake.

Sometimes historical reality is more rewarding and more exciting than even legend. Baron d'Holbach's salon and its principal protagonists did foment revolutionary ideas, but it was more than a mere political revolution they were thinking about; they did write and publish subversive books, but they wanted to bring down something infinitely more vast than the monarchy or even the Catholic Church. The vision they discussed around the baron's dinner table was one in which women and men would no longer be oppressed by the fear and ignorance instilled by religion but could instead live their lives to the full. Instead of sacrificing their desires to the vain hope of reward in the afterlife, they would be able to walk freely, to understand their place in the universe as intelligent machines of flesh and blood and pour their energies into building individual lives and communities based on their inheritance of desire, empathy, and reason. Desire, erotic and otherwise, would make their world beautiful and rich; empathy would make it kind and livable; reason would allow an understanding of the world's immutable laws.

Before this paradisiacal and remote vision could be reached, the enemies of reason and of desire had to be defeated. The church condemned desire as lust and reason as pride—mortal sins both—and perverted empathy into the practice of making people suffer now so that they could reap rewards after their death. The Enlightenment radicals saw it as their duty to convince their contemporaries that there is no life after death, no God and no Providence, no divine plan, but only a physical world of life and death and the struggle to survive—a world of ignorant necessity and without higher meaning, into which kindness and lust can inject a fleeting beauty. During the eighteenth century, when such thoughts were regarded as heretical and punishable by death, defending these ideas was a truly herculean challenge.

Back in modern-day Paris, I faced a challenge of my own. Finding Holbach's town house proved more difficult than I had anticipated. I knew that it was in what was once the rue Royale Saint-Roch (pronounced "rock"), but the modern map diverges from the eighteenth-century city. The modern rue Saint-Roch is not identical with the previous one, which was renamed. The whole layout of the city had been changed during the nineteenth century, when Baron Hausmann realized his plans for a new Paris and demolished thousands of buildings and streets to create wide avenues (ideal for using artillery to crush the revolutions and popular uprisings for which the city was so famous) and spectacular visual axes throughout the city.

"If you want to know which street used to be the rue Royale Saint-Roch you need to ask the parish priest," someone had told me. "He knows everything about the history of the *quartier*." The priest was easy to find: a very elegant, elderly gentleman, white hair combed back, wearing an ecclesiastical collar under a fine suit, sitting on a small café terrace directly beside his church, the *église* Saint-Roch. With exquisite politeness he explained to me that yes, he had heard about a Baron d'Holbach living in this part of town during the eighteenth century, but no, he had no idea where the street I was looking for was, and no, he could not tell me anything else about the baron. "*Au revoir, Monsieur*," he said to me, leaving no doubt that he had no desire whatsoever to see me again.

Not willing to give up so easily, I continued my research in the area. After several false starts, I found the street and, indeed, the house in which Holbach had lived and received his guests. The street is now called rue des Moulins, and his house is not even five hundred meters from the terrace on which I met the priest. Obviously, the baron's atheism was not yet forgotten. Then I discovered something else: Both Holbach and Diderot had been interred in the very church of Saint-Roch, whose knowledgeable parish priest knew nothing about their whereabouts. They are resting in unmarked graves, under the well-worn stone slabs in front of the main altar.

On a later visit to Paris, I took the opportunity to visit the *église* Saint-Roch once again, this time with the objective of locating the exact graves of Diderot and Holbach. The priest I had met previously had since retired, and I introduced myself to his successor, a man with a finely drawn face and also an enthusiast for the history of his church. Of course he knew where Diderot lay buried, he said. There was an ossuary underneath the altar. Unfortunately it had been desecrated twice, he added, once during the Revolution and a second time in 1871, during the Paris Commune. Bones and skulls of the people buried there were now strewn randomly on the floor, "and nobody knows what's whose," he added, with a tinge of amusement. He regretted that it would be impossible to visit the room. It awaited restoration, which was a matter for the state. "But Diderot is not alone down there," he informed me cordially. "Many important artists were buried in this church. André le Notre is there, too, and Pierre Corneille, and the great *salonière* Madame Geoffrin . . . " "And the Baron d'Holbach," I added. The priest looked surprised. "Who did you say?" I repeated his name, this time in full: Baron Paul Thiry d'Holbach. "Now, I'm not sure about that," he replied, in a cool and official voice. "A lot of people had masses read here but were never interred in these walls."

I did not insist, but the priest's reaction is a good indication why Diderot and Holbach lost the battle for posterity: They have still not been forgiven for their unpalatably radical ideas. Both men believed that there is nothing in the world but atoms organized in countless and complex ways, no inherent meaning, no higher purpose than life itself. While more moderate Enlightenment thinkers such as Voltaire believed that there must be a God, a supreme watchmaker who had created the mechanism of the world, the friends at Holbach's salon (or most of them) were already convinced that the world had not been created but had evolved through chance and natural selection, without any guiding intelligence, any higher being.

Their philosophy provoked strong reactions from the very first. In the ancien régime, before the French Revolution, it was dangerous to speak one's mind. Those opposed to the teachings of the church were threatened with prison and even public execution. It was important to know whom one could trust and in front of whom you could speak freely. Holbach's salon, open to like minds every Thursday and Sunday, offered ideal conditions for the Enlightenment radicals. He was wealthy and employed an excellent chef; his cellar and his library were equally well stocked.

In these congenial surroundings in which everybody knew everybody else, Holbach's friends could test their ideas, debate philosophical and scientific questions, read and criticize new work. Diderot, one of the greatest conversationalists of the century, was at the center of every discussion—to the admiration and occasionally also the acute frustration of the other guests. The ultimate goal of these discussions was not personal enjoyment but philosophical and political influence. The thinkers of the radical Enlightenment wanted to change the general way of thinking, and to do this they had to intervene in the public discussion. This they did indirectly through Diderot's *Encyclopédie*, a twenty-eight-volume Trojan horse, carrying a cargo of subversive ideas into the homes of unsuspecting readers, and directly through a stream of books and pamphlets they had to publish clandestinely and anonymously. They were printed abroad, then smuggled back into the country and sold in strict secrecy.

The friends' evolutionist conception of nature and of humanity had momentous consequences. Without a Creator who had revealed his will to his creatures through the Bible, ideas of good and evil had to be rethought. In the brave new world envisaged by Diderot, Holbach, and their like-minded friends, there was suddenly no sin anymore and no reward or punishment in the afterlife; instead, there was only the search for pleasure and the fear of pain. Diderot and friends went further than traditional philosophy, which considered human beings as inherently rational and reason, being the closest approximation of the divine accessible to humans, the supreme faculty. Therefore, other Enlightenment philosophers replicated the Christian disdain for the passions and based their ideas about a better future for humanity on an exclusively rationalist utopia in which there was little space for irrational impulses such as passion, instinct, or the yearning for beauty.

The radicals argued that human nature was exactly the opposite. Nature expressed itself through individuals in the form of strong and blind passions, the real driving forces of existence. They could be directed by reason much as the sails of a ship may allow sailors to navigate the storms, the waves and currents of a mighty ocean. Nevertheless, reason is always secondary, always weaker than the basic reality of passion.

Religious critics threw up their hands in horror. All this was nothing but a license for wickedness and debauchery, they wrote. Without God's law, there was no goodness in the world; without divine reason, there was no reason to exist. But the Enlightenment radicals had a clear answer to these charges. Their morality was not one of wild orgies, unrestrained greed, and heedless indulgence, but of a society based on mutual respect, without masters and slaves, without oppressors and oppressed.

While in a godless universe there is no transcendental yardstick of an absolute, revealed Truth and Goodness, it is perfectly easy to see what is beneficial and what is harmful to people here and now. This insight alone should be the principle of all morality. It was a dangerous idea, because a moral code based on the pursuit of happiness in this life had truly revolutionary implications. Without a God who has set some people above others, everybody—regardless of social station, sex, race, and creed—has an equal right to seek pleasure and, ultimately, happiness. A duchess has no higher claim to happiness than the humblest peasant, and a society in which happiness is possible not just for the privileged few can be achieved only through solidarity and cooperation. There was no place in this vision for an aristocracy, for birthright, or for social hierarchy. In ancien régime France, an absolute monarchy, this was tantamount to treason, but it also attracted an array of exceptional and courageous people to Holbach's salon.

Even today, this vision has lost none of its persuasiveness and appeal.

During their lifetime, Holbach and Diderot were equally feted and reviled, fixed stars in the intellectual universe even of those who wanted to see them burned at the stake (and there were many). Today, however, if you consult any Paris tour guide or ask any educated person where to visit the graves of two important eighteenth-century philosophers whose work changed the world, you will not be sent to the *église* Saint-Roch but to the Panthéon, close to the Jardins du Luxembourg. There, in the crypt, you will find the sarcophagi of Voltaire and Jean-Jacques Rousseau, two of the first famous dead to be accorded the honor of having their remains transferred here. With revolutionary pomp and ceremony, Voltaire was reinterred in the crypt of the Panthéon in 1791, Rousseau in 1794. Upstairs, in the nave of the building, there is a monument dedicated to Diderot, installed, as an afterthought, in 1925.

The Panthéon is official history cut in stone. There is something deceptively plausible about this version. You have to make an effort to remember that the fabric of the present has not grown as it had to grow, simply and organically, but is the result of countless decisions and acts of violence, forcing each present moment to conform to the dreams and nightmares of those in power. So why is it that Voltaire and Rousseau are lying in state in the central, secular sanctuary of the French Republic, dedicated to the *grands hommes* of France (Marie Curie, the first *grande femme,* was allowed in only in 1995), while their contemporaries Diderot and Holbach are in unknown graves in a church whose priest disclaims all knowledge of them to a casual visitor?

One answer might be, of course, that Voltaire and Rousseau simply were better, more original philosophers who were more deserving of this special honor. Voltaire was, after all, the great champion of human rights and Enlightenment ideas, the very embodiment of the battle between reason and superstition. Rousseau is still revered as the voice of human freedom and radical personal honesty, a wise friend leading societies to freedom, a pioneer of the unconscious, and a tireless investigator of the emotional dimension of life.

Without a doubt Voltaire was the most influential and best-known figure of the Enlightenment, but his philosophical contribution does not go much beyond solid common sense liberally sprinkled with ironic wit. His political activities reveal him to be a shrewd operator interested mainly in his own reputation and his financial fortune. As for Rousseau, he is altogether more original and important as a thinker, but also in possession of a far more sinister, self-serving, and self-consuming mind. Moreover, he was a compulsive liar, which makes for compelling biography but not for great philosophy.

Rousseau and Diderot had been close personal friends once, but they fell out very publicly and very spectacularly. Their friendship ended not only because of Rousseau's paranoia, but more significantly because he came to hate the Enlightenment Diderot stood for, a life free from fear of the unknown and from self-disgust, a clear-eyed and serene acceptance of our place in the world as highly intelligent, morally conscious apes.

Profoundly disgusted with himself as well as fearful of his own desires, Jean-Jacques Rousseau became the avowed enemy of those he had previously loved. In the nineteenth century, the art historian John Ruskin coined the term "pathetic fallacy" for the error of imputing intentions to inanimate objects—leaves that dance, books waiting to be read, nature being alternately kind and cruel. Rousseau's pathetic fallacy was to believe the entire world was united to ruin him. Out of this fear he formulated a philosophy suggesting at first glance a defense of freedom and human dignity, while actually laying the foundation for a deeply oppressive, intensely pessimistic view of life. The ideal society he advocated was based on ideological manipulation, political repression, and violence, and on a philosophy of guilt and paranoia that turned out to be ideally suited to justifying totalitarian regimes of all stripes. It is no accident that Rousseau was the philosophical idol of Maximilien Robespierre, the most terrifying of all leaders of the French Revolution, whose favorite political instrument was the guillotine.

What makes the thinking of the radical Enlightenment so essential today is its power, its simplicity, and its moral courage. What makes it more important than ever is the fact that it is Rousseau, not Diderot, who has won the battle for posterity, and his influence is continuing to cloud our debates and our societies. Rousseau rediscovered religion for himself, though not a religion of the institutional kind. He believed in an afterlife, he wrote, because this life was simply too awful to be all he could hope for—a classic case of the wish being father of the thought. He was an intensely religious man at war with the world at large and with himself, and his philosophy reflected his situation by taking Christian concepts out of their religious context and making them accessible in a not explicitly religious, philosophical context. During the nineteenth century, in a world still smarting from the decline of religion, this offer was gratefully accepted. Rousseau showed how it was possible to incorporate originally Christian feelings and beliefs into a modern worldview without having to speak the language of theology.

Even today, the public discussion about moral and political issues is no longer framed in an explicitly religious context, but the change in terminology only conceals the all-pervasive influence of the unexamined theological ideas underlying it. Our vocabulary has changed, of course: We no longer speak about the soul but about the psyche; we have exchanged original sin for inherited, psychological guilt. But the cultural soil on which these ideas flourish has remained the same, and all too often our worldview is inherently religious without our even realizing it.

When we look into the future, we instinctively fear the Apocalypse and fully expect either paradise or purgatory. Next to the beatific vision of a perfect market, a science-fiction future without wars and energy problems, a perfect Socialist society, or whatever other dreams we happen to subscribe to is the looming prospect of an overheating planet, a nuclear World War Three, collapsing ecosystems, wars about water and other natural resources, destructive asteroids on a collision course with Earth—an ultimate, murderous clash of civilizations. The possibility of humanity's simply muddling through for millennia to come (the most likely scenario by far), avoiding some catastrophes while suffering others (some of them self-inflicted), is simply less instinctive to our theologically conditioned brains than the thought of salvation or damnation, of heaven or hell.

So deeply ingrained are these cultural instincts that Rousseau's totalitarian utopia can seem more natural and sensible than Holbach's utilitarian tinkering. Utopians are always religious at heart, and it comes as little surprise that Rousseau was a direct inspiration not only for Robespierre but also for Lenin and Pol Pot. The latter studied Rousseau's works in Paris during the 1950s, before his murderous campaign forced Cambodia back into the Iron Age, under the guise of creating a society of virtuous peasants isolated from the corrupting influences of higher civilization.

Not only are our utopias theological in nature, but our relation to desire and passion bears the same religious imprint, as the map of every city will show. The red light districts in our cities bear witness to a very Christian revulsion toward physical pleasure. They are situated on the periphery (though nowadays cities have often sprawled around them, putting them close to the center of a seemingly endless conurbation) and in less desirable areas; they are seedy and depressing, vulgar and cheap. They serve a shameful desire, guiltily satisfied in dim and grubby corners or by the lurid light of neon signs.

Sex itself is dirty, and women willing to sleep with men are often still referred to as "sluts," "whores," or worse. Not for us the celebration of physical beauty of antiquity or the joyful erotic ornaments and amulets adorning everyday life in ancient Rome or decorating Indian temples. We are still ashamed of ourselves, and we have internalized this shame in our popular culture: In the Hollywood blockbusters washing across our movie screens, a glimpse of a naked body is deemed offensive and obscene, but the gratuitous and pornographically detailed depiction of extreme violence is not.

There is a direct line from this seemingly ultra-secular world of seamy seduction to Puritan preachers invoking hellfire against lust and to self-hating hermits. One could be forgiven for thinking that the endless images of beautiful people being young, slim, rich, and irrepressibly happy owe more to Epicurus than to Ecclesia, but in fact their unachievable perfection makes them essentially religious.

Believers in the Western gospel of earthly bliss must detest their bodies and their actual lives just like the nuns and monks of old. Pious Christians used to chastise themselves by fasting, by denying themselves everyday pleasures, by stifling their desires and crushing their self-respect, by starving their bodies and their desires to gain the life eternal. Their modern, secular opposites no longer fast to save their immortal souls, but they diet, curbing their desires, forever chasing after a youthful body that will never again be theirs, forever feeling guilty about being too old, too flabby, insufficiently fit. The icons of our day may be fashion models instead of saints, but they still function by making us suffer. They instill guilt, humiliate us, and spur us to emulate an impossible ideal, as we vainly hope for a better afterlife, a remote vision of being wealthy, tanned, and cool that has replaced the beatitudes of the church.

Christianity is the religion of the suffering God. Christ was made flesh and had to die, to be tortured to death, thus allowing God the Creator to forgive humanity for its wickedness. Holbach and Diderot wrote all there is to be written about the perversity of this argument, but even the most irreligious of Westerners still believe in the positive, transformative value of suffering. We have all internalized the Romantic stereotype of the solitary, suffering genius (a figure almost single-handedly invented by Rousseau in his *Confessions*). We love stories in which people triumph over adversity, in which they are almost crushed by wickedness or misfortune, only to emerge again, to be resurrected. This kind of story is found in many cultures, but not in all. The ancient Greeks attached no moral value to suffering: After journeying around the

Mediterranean for twenty years and surviving many dangers, Homer's Odysseus is older—but not a wiser or a better man.

For the many who opt out of this very religious game of guilt and suffering, of responsibility and striving for a better afterlife (and, possibly, of hope), there is nothing left but a void to be filled by entertainment and indulgence, an endless presence punctuated by gadgets, accessories, and conspicuous consumption. The Enlightenment radicals were adamant that society and individuals must build on education and solidarity. Those in our society who feel they cannot or do not want to aspire to the secular ideals of our church of brand-name canonization have made a choice: Instead of chasing after an unattainable ideal, they have let go of all aspirations and replaced all hope of a better tomorrow with a supersized helping of instant satisfaction.

A religious matrix—theology in secular clothes—permeates our lives, and theological preconceptions continue to confuse many of the debates that will shape our future. Arguments put forward in the ongoing debate about genetic research and its possibilities show how much we still regard ourselves as beings endowed with a soul and a destiny by a Creator. Cloning of animals is controversial, the mere thought of human cloning makes us deeply uneasy, stem cell research causes virulent debate, and the only reason to oppose abortion in the very early stages of pregnancy must be the idea that even a cluster of as yet unspecialized cells already has a human soul attached to it, that it is already a full person in the eyes of God.

The legacy of nineteenth-century Idealism and Romanticism has created our intellectual world, ruled not by the secularized, scientific mind many historians have written about but, on the contrary, by a fundamentally Christian worldview that has merely been stripped of its outward signs and rituals. This is why the work of the radical authors who came together in Holbach's salon has lost very little of its freshness, its capacity to shock, and its ability to inspire constructive reflections about our own cultural, scientific, and political landscape. We are still grappling with many of the questions Diderot, Holbach, and their friends wrote about, and we still have not learned their lesson that any philosophical or moral debate must start from the scientific facts.

Beginning with the idea, so brilliantly exposed by Holbach, that it is simply narcissistic to believe that there must be a Providence, a higher intelligence, because otherwise life would be meaningless, the thinkers of the rue Royale believed we must accept the meaninglessness of the existence of *Homo sapiens*. Only then can each individual's quest to seek pleasure and flee pain become the beginning of a common story. The realization that no one is completely autonomous, coupled with our strong feeling of empathy, leads directly to a morality of mutual solidarity, to social meaning.

Diderot and Holbach may appear to have lost the battle for posterity, but they have not yet lost the war, still raging, for our civilization and its dreams, which could be so much more generous, more lucid, and more humane than they are now. Their works still richly repay rereading, and their careers can serve as both an inspiration and a warning to us. They demonstrate both what we have gained since their day and what we are in danger of losing once again, as we are faced not only by threats from the outside but also by our own laziness, indifference, and muddled thinking.

FATHERS AND SONS

CHAPTER I

CITY OF LIGHTS

Paris is a metropolis to which the bright and ambitious have been drawn for centuries. The lives of the protagonists of this story unfolded on its streets—in its parks, cafés, salons, and bedrooms (and, occasionally, in the country estates dotted around the capital or on a voyage abroad to England, Italy, or even Russia). But far-reaching as they are, the events and ideas that made up this great moment in the history of Western thought have a very clear center, a definitive address, a house number: in the center of the City of Lights, at 10, rue des Moulins, just a stone's throw from the Louvre and the beautiful colonnades of the Jardin Royal. There stands a handsome seventeenth-century house that was once inhabited by Paul Thiry, Baron d'Holbach, and his wife, and that was for a time the epicenter of intellectual life in Europe. Some of the most exciting minds of the Western world came to Holbach's salon to partake of sumptuous dinners and discuss dangerous ideas far from the public eye. It is hard to imagine another room that has seen so many brilliant people, heard so many spirited exchanges.

The building breathes quiet confidence and comfort without being demonstratively ornate or flashy. The staircase is still exactly as it was during the eighteenth century: wooden steps framed by elegant, cast-iron railings with gilt flower decor, leading to landings with black-and-white tiles and to the salon on the first floor, a generous room overlooking the street. Here, guests were received and dinners held. The room is in no way ostentatious but spacious enough to accommodate a good dozen people around a large dining table and still leave space for servants to pass behind the diners. The wooden floors are of the period, the ceiling high, and the large bay windows flood the room with light, giving it a gracious, elegant air.

"Elegance" was a watchword in this part of town even two and a half centuries ago, when the adjoining street to the south, the rue Saint-Honoré—with its innumerable tailors and couturiers and the wig makers, coiffeurs, shoemakers, glovers, and others who went with them—was the mecca of the fashion-conscious throughout the Western world. Luxury merchants had been drawn to the area by the huge, looming, eternally unfinished Louvre, the royal palace at the heart of the capital, directly by the banks of the Seine. Courtiers needed to be presentable, and they constantly needed to show off new clothes, setting the tone for the rest of the country and for Europe. But the palace had been practically empty ever since the beginning of Louis XIV's personal rule in 1661, when the young Sun King, suspicious of the subversive undercurrent of city life, had displaced his court out of the city and eventually to the palace of Versailles. A monstrous construction project in the swamps, its drainage and conversion into the world's most spectacular park had cost hundreds of workers' lives, swallowed endless millions, and eventually ruined the kingdom. The Louvre was deserted by the court for most of the year: empty ceremonial halls echoing with the footfall of occasional servants; exquisitely carved furniture covered up, its delicate fabrics (often made from last season's silk court robes) hidden from view; chandeliers tinkling softly in the breeze as the rooms were aired and cleaned periodically. Only the countless workshops of tradesmen and craftsmen on the ground floor and in the courtyards filled the site with life.

The rue Saint-Honoré, however, continued to do brisk business. As far as fashion was concerned, it was the only place to go. But Holbach had not chosen this part of Paris for its fashionable or royal associations. He was not very interested in his appearance and was an instinctive republican. But the house was convenient, right in the middle of things yet quietly situated in a side street, within easy reach of all amenities. For this part of town was a center not only of fashion but also of intellectual life. Several of his wealthier friends and other salon hosts lived around the corner, and there were bookshops and art dealers. The enclosed universe of the leafy Jardin Royal nearby (lovingly described in Diderot's novel *Rameau's Nephew*) tempted with cafés and chess tables as well as gambling and altogether more carnal pleasures in the shape of gaudily made-up prostitutes in low-cut dresses sauntering past gentlemen in powdered wigs—a theatre of vanities that the baron, by all accounts a model husband, was content to observe from a distance.

Less than a mile farther east, past the graceful, circular Place de Victoires dominated by a statue of Louis XIV, the world became even more carnal. Heaving with countless porters, grocers, butcher boys, flower sellers, fishmongers, spice dealers, and sausage sellers; ringing with their market cries and warning shouts from dawn to dusk; and reeking to high heaven during the summer months, the Les Halles markets were the stomach of Paris, the source for the ingredients of the baron's famous twice-weekly dinners.

The area's other landmark, the magnificent Place Vendôme, originally a speculation scheme that had almost broken the back of its investors and had stood like a huge theatre set as an assembly of empty facades for years, was one of the capital's preeminent addresses, a place that smelled of money as much as Les Halles did of pickled herring on a warm August day. Ostentatious to the point of vulgarity, it could be reached on foot from the baron's house within a few minutes, and yet it was a different universe. The stars of Holbach's intellectual salon were not financiers but writers, scientists, and philosophers.

Several great salons vied for the attention and the presence of the city's brightest and most fashionable intellectuals. Each of these houses had a distinctive character and orientation, both artistically and politically. Just around the corner in the rue Sainte-Anne, the baron's friend Claude-Adrien Helvétius regularly welcomed progressive philosophers and writers, but even if Holbach and Helvétius were famous for their hospitality, they were exceptional in a salon landscape dominated by distinguished ladies. Indeed, keeping a salon was the only way for a woman to make her mark on the still overwhelmingly male literary world. At the rue Saint-Honoré, no more than a few minutes from Holbach's doorstep, the sexually voracious novelist Claudine Guérin de Tencin had welcomed some of the nation's most powerful and witty men into her salon—and frequently her bed. "One can see that God is a man by the way he treats us women," she famously sighed, but even divine negligence did not deter her from enjoying life to the full. In 1717 she had given birth to an illegitimate son, whom she had promptly laid on the steps of the Church of

Jean-le-Rond. He would grow up to become Jean d'Alembert, one of this century's most eminent mathematicians and coeditor, with Diderot, of the great *Encyclopédie*.

After Madame de Tencin's death in 1749, Marie-Thérèse de Geoffrin (1699–1777), reputedly the greatest hostess of all, held court at the rue Saint-Honoré. No one could dream of making a literary career without her approval, and an invitation to read at her house from a manuscript was not only a mark of recognition but practically a guarantee of success. Voltaire had been a regular here before his exile; government ministers, scientists, poets, and wits mingled here and could speak with a freedom impossible at court or in public. Here, introductions could be made, alliances forged, literary destinies determined. Among the many whose path to later glory led through Madame de Geoffrin's salon was the young Diderot, who made the acquaintance of a number of writers who would later contribute to his *Encyclopédie*.

As the example of Madame de Geoffrin indicates, salons fulfilled an important function in eighteenth-century Paris. The usual networking was and still is such an important feature in literary circles—replete with young hopefuls, freshly arrived in the city and eager to make themselves known, and the old, established names wanting to shine and enjoy their growing reputation. But the salons served as much more than just a vehicle for vanity. In an intellectual environment controlled by harsh censorship laws, it was not easy to find places allowing a free exchange of ideas. In eighteenth-century France, no work could legally appear in print without a royal privilege indicating that it had gone through the hands of church censors and been approved. The penalties for contravening these laws were stiff and applied strictly at the discretion of the authorities, such as the chief censor and the mighty Paris *parlement*, though powerful courtiers were also known to use their influence against books and their authors. Punishments ranged from a symbolic tearing and burning of the book by the hangman of Paris to a few weeks in the Bastille to backbreaking forced labor on the galleys of the French navy (a virtual death sentence) or outright public torture and execution.

Ideas depend on gregariousness and exchange to flourish, but public places, the parks, the many cafés and taverns were too insecure to meet in. The person at the next table could be a police spy, and the merest accusation could suffice to ruin one's career or force the accused into exile. Even the great Voltaire had found that his considerable wealth did not protect him from prosecution; in 1728, having made one disrespectful quip too many, he had been obliged to leave Paris and eventually France, retiring to a pretty country estate at Ferney, near Geneva and close to the French border.

Salon hostesses had a very specific and strictly circumscribed function. The writer and salon regular Jean-François Marmontel praised their "grace of the mind, the mobility of their imagination, the ease and natural flexibility of their ideas and their language" and described their conversation as necessary training for writers: "He who wants to write only with precision, energy and vigor must live only with men; but whoever wants style with suppleness, ease, connectedness and a certain *je ne sais quoi* which is called charm would do well, I believe, to live with women."[1]

There was no thought, however, of the women themselves appearing as authors or as philosophers. The natural flexibility and delicacy with which their male contemporaries believed them to be endowed rendered them inspired mediators and facilitators, but little more than that. While the limitations of their role were no doubt intensely frustrating for many of the women concerned, playing hostess was nevertheless the only way open to them of participating in literary society, and it allowed them to influence intellectual life by promoting some authors and artists more than others.

Every salon had its own temperament, its own cast of characters, and its own philosophical or even political orientation. But the salons all shared the invaluable function of giving visitors an opportunity to speak, to listen, to read their works to an appreciative and critical audience, to forge alliances, to find a powerful patron, and just to escape the drudgery and boredom of their working days. Those who were lucky enough to be received at all the great houses could count their weekdays in salons: Mme Geoffrin on Monday, then on Tuesday the home of the philosopher Helvétius, the next day Mme Geoffrin again, then Holbach, and finally the home of Mme Necker. For Saturdays, there were minor salons, but on Sundays several great houses threw open their doors, including Holbach's, of course.

The glittering world of the salons was nothing but a distant dream for the adolescent Denis Diderot when he set foot in Paris for the first time in 1728, at age fifteen, a pious provincial boy admitted to one of the city's great schools in preparation for becoming a priest. His father, a master cutler, had accompanied him to oversee his first days in the capital, a dazzling spectacle very far from the quiet surroundings of their home.

Diderot had been baptized on October 6, 1713, in the small town of Langres, in northern Champagne. Eleven months earlier his mother had given birth to another boy, only to lose him days after his birth. She was thirty-four when she married, uncommonly old for the time. The couple would have three more surviving children, whose lives illustrate the family's devout background. A second son, Didier, would become a thorny priest and forever quarrel with his notorious atheist brother; Angélique, the older sister, became an Ursuline nun against the wishes of her family and apparently died from overwork in the convent at the age of twenty-eight. Only the youngest sister, Denise, would remain a lifelong friend and confidante for her brother.

The Diderots were a prosperous family. The father's workshop occupied the ground floor of their handsome house, while the family's living quarters on the higher floors overlooked the cathedral square of the proud town of Langres. Their oldest son was baptized Denis after the sainted missionary beheaded in Paris around the year 250 (but unwittingly also after Dionysus, the Greek god of wine and ecstasy). He quickly grew into a bright, personable child, fast-witted and outgoing. The father decided that Denis would continue the family tradition and become a priest, so he sent the child to the local school, where he excelled not only at the basics but also at Latin.

But Denis was no bookish boy. When he was about ten years old, he enthusiastically participated in a protracted and at times bloody war between two rival gangs of children, during which two armies of up to a hundred boys squared off with sticks and stones. A childhood memory (described, as so often with Diderot, in dialogue form, and this time directed at a boy from a richer family) paints a no doubt tendentious but highly revealing portrait of the young warrior, as well as of the man he would become. The mature author remembers himself as a Spartan, fierce and proud, and superior in his simplicity to the effeminate Athenian manners of his rival: "You recoil at the sight of the disheveled hair and torn clothes. Yet I was that way when I was young and I was pleasing—pleasing to even the women and girls in my home town in the provinces. They preferred me, without hat and with my chest uncovered, sometimes without shoes, in a jacket and with the feet bare, me, son of a worker at a forge, to that little well-dressed monsieur all curled and powdered and dressed to the nines, the son of the presiding judge."[2] A portrait of the artist as a young man and as a writer: his rebellious spirit, his entertaining vanity, and his—at times exasperating—stylization as a man of the people. Even in later life he would not wear a wig, and portraits show the mature man with short hair and simple clothes, an honest worker like his father, not some grandee dressed after the latest fashion.

When the boy entered his teenage years, he sought out the most intellectual branch of the church. Young Diderot wanted to become a Jesuit, but his father would not hear of it, especially as Denis' uncle had already indicated that the position of canon at Langres Cathedral would be open to Denis once his education was completed. Much better to have a decent sinecure at home than to enter an order where one might be sent anywhere and lead an uncertain life.

When it became clear that the Langres schoolmasters had little left to teach young Denis, his parents decided to invest in his future and send him to Paris, where he could study at one of the great colleges—a sure first step for a career in the ecclesiastical hierarchy. In 1728 the boy and his father boarded a slow coach for an uncertain but exciting future in the capital. Before setting off, the fifteen-year-old, intellectually restless boy formally entered the church. Having been tonsured by the bishop, he now had to be addressed not by his first name but as *abbé* Diderot.

Around the time when the lanky *abbé* Diderot was on the road to the capital, the much younger Holbach also arrived there. He had been born in the little town of Edesheim in the German Palatinate in 1723; his father was a well-to-do wine grower. Young Dietrich spent his first years in a handsome manor among vineyards and wood-framed houses. He might have become a wine grower himself, but his future was transformed by a recently ennobled uncle, Baron Franz Adam d'Holbach. The uncle had emigrated and made his fortune in Paris. He had even bought the title of baron from the imperial court in Vienna. Now, in 1728, he decided to adopt his lively nephew, take him to the greatest of all cities, and give him the best education money could buy. Renamed Thiry d'Holbach, the boy proved a voracious reader, fascinated by the sciences, by experiments and the natural world. We know little about his early years beyond this outline. Holbach never appears to have been sufficiently interested in himself to talk about his youth at length, and his home schooling means that no documents about his education survive in school archives.

Ten years separated Diderot and Holbach, a huge gulf during their early years, which they spent in the capital. Other things also differentiated them. The schoolboy Thiry lived in a grand house with servants and was schooled at home, by tutors. Denis, now in his late teens, would have lived in a garret or a frugal lodger's room, and received only a meager allowance from home—too meager, in any case, to live comfortably. Most of his time outside of class was spent immersing himself in literature: Roman authors as well as some Greek, which he never read as fluently. He attended an ecclesiastical school, most likely the famous Jesuit college Louis-le-Grand, where Molière, Cyrano de Bergerac, and Voltaire had been pupils before him.

We know next to nothing about what the schoolboy Denis was thinking apart from the fact that he had already acquired a strong taste for the authors of Roman and Greek antiquity, so much freer in their ideas than later European authors, and that he liked to play tricks on his teachers by uttering apparently outrageous thoughts and then innocently demonstrating that he had only quoted from the works of great Roman authors. But if this seems little to go on, it is possible to draw inferences about his intellectual world by looking at the country during the 1720s and 1730s, its culture, and its preoccupations.

Diderot attended the Collège Louis-le-Grand, named, of course, after Louis XIV, who had died two years after Diderot's birth, in 1715. At the height of his fifty-four-year reign, the glorious Sun King had created a courtly culture that was the envy of the world. But eventually time had turned against him, and as an old man, the king had grown jealous of his own former greatness. Two hugely expensive wars (one on the northeastern border in the Netherlands from 1772 to 1778; the other, the 1701–1714 War of the Spanish Succession, fought practically everywhere but in Spain) had all but bankrupted the state. The erstwhile splendid style of the court appeared rigid and old-fashioned to a new generation of artists. Even Versailles, situated miles away from the capital and still a ruinously expensive building site after so many years, had lost much of its luster and appeal in an intellectual and cultural climate slowly moving away from the celebration of absolute monarchs and towards a more Enlightened model of rule and a more urban culture.

The royal ballet was a good example of the changes taking place. An accomplished dancer in his youth, Louis himself had starred in many court productions, written for him by his court composer, the brilliant and irrepressible Jean-Baptiste Lully. In accordance with the king's taste, most of the works (excepting dance interludes for the comedies of Molière) featured classical gods and mythical heroes, choirs singing effusive praise to absolute rule, and spectacular music to support stage effects such as maritime battles with model ships on moving seas and gods apparently floating through the air. It was all very splendid, very formal, and very festive, much like the giant park extending behind the palace. But after Lully's disgrace in 1685 on account of his same-sex love affairs carried on too flagrantly even for Versailles (the king's brother was a cross-dresser), there was nobody to continue this tradition. Lully died two years later from an infection sustained when he accidentally pierced his foot with his conductor's baton. The fashion was changing. Younger composers such as Jean-Philippe Rameau and Marain Marais sought a more emotional, more internal style and often turned to chamber music, reflecting a stronger call for music to be performed and listened to at home by the rising bourgeoisie.

When the king died in 1715, Philippe, Duke of Orléans, son of the king's cross-dressing brother and the wonderfully candid German princess Liselotte, became regent of France and promptly moved the court back to Paris. Philippe was an avowed atheist who had the works of the scandalous François Rabelais bound into his Bible so that he could read them privately during Mass. He was a cultured and progressive man who attempted to move the impoverished country towards a modern, constitutional monarchy by giving more power to the local *parlements*, but his liberal style of ruling (to say nothing of his decidedly liberal private life) did little more than confuse a country used to the most rigid, absolutist government. Amidst the squabbling of rival political parties, the country effectively ground to a standstill. In retrospect, the luckless Philippe would have done better as a benevolent dictator.

In one area at least, the liberal regent did have some success. With a great sigh of relief, the metropolis rediscovered its literary and intellectual life. Philippe had loosened censorship and encouraged intellectuals. One man in particular made this new, more modern, and freer tone his own: François-Marie Arouet, born in 1694, was a young, well-to-do man about town. He soon attracted attention, and trouble, with his sharp pen, writing satirical verses about some of the grandest grandees in the land, aristocrats who did not appreciate such an uncommon lack of respect. Arouet was banned from Paris in 1716 after making fun of the regent's supposed incestuous relationship with his daughter, then allowed back, only to publish a second satire on the duke, who by this time had had enough. In 1717, he had the impertinent scribbler imprisoned in the Bastille, where the young man began writing for the stage. After almost a year Arouet was freed and, after the performance of his tragedy *Oedipe*, famous. He frequented the most aristocratic salons and could have settled down nicely, were it not for his spirit of mockery.

Upon his release from prison, the fledgling star dramatist began calling himself "Voltaire" (an anagram of Arouet Le Jeune, treating *u* and *v* and *j* and *i* as interchangeable, as they are in Latin). An aging and childless aristocrat challenged him on his name change, and the town wit could not resist the jibe "*Je commence mon nom, monsieur, vous finissez le vôtre*" (I am the first of my name, monsieur, you are the last of yours), whereupon the nobleman had him beaten by his servants and thrown into the Bastille a second time. Now the condition of his release was that he would leave the country, and so he did, heading for London, the capital of pragmatic reason and free enterprise. There he immersed himself, among other things, in the writings of Newton and Locke.

By 1728, he was back in France but banned from Paris in perpetuity. Voltaire nonetheless made himself the voice of the most progressive tendencies in society. When the great actress Adrienne Lecouvreur died in 1730, her body was refused a Christian burial on account of her decidedly impious lifestyle and had to be interred in the swampland outside Paris (today the Champ-de-Mars). Voltaire wrote a bitter poem on the matter, asking himself, or rather God, why his country was the home no longer of talent and glory but of bigotry. The urbane wit was becoming an important and acerbic critic of the influence of religion on politics and of cruelty in the name of Christianity.

Voltaire was hardly a born revolutionary, however. He simply wanted people to be reasonable, not to topple the existing order. He limited his criticism of religion to exposing superstition and narrow-mindedness, and his jibes against the powerful became markedly more moderate as the years progressed. No doubt his reticence was due in part to his financial and professional position. He had become a very wealthy man after he had realized, in 1728, that the first prize of the state lottery was many times the sum of the price of all tickets combined. Together with some friends he formed a syndicate that had bought up all the tickets, shared the huge winnings, and allowed Voltaire to live wealthily ever after, multiplying his money by lending large sums to European princes, who used them to finance their autocratic rule. Effectively the banker of several absolute monarchs, he was simply not in a position to attack religion or absolute rule, the foundations of their authority.

Voltaire and other Enlightened authors, such as the wonderfully urbane Charles de Montesquieu, represented one side of the new flowering of intellectual life during the regency. But this strand of Enlightenment was limited to high culture, to the few people actively interested in these debates. Another, more popular strand of intellectual life took place within the context of the church. Louis XIV had left his country a poisonous legacy. Increasingly concerned about his undying soul and the possibility of eternal damnation, the formerly voracious bon vivant and serial seducer had by the 1680s turned pious. He had tried to please the Lord by banning the frivolous entertainments he had loved as a young man; marrying his main mistress, Madame de Maintenant; and persecuting Protestants, the largest religious minority in the country, by revoking the Edict of Nantes, which had effectively granted French Protestants freedom of conscience and religious toleration. His cruel policy caused an exodus of some 400,000 men, women, and children, many highly skilled laborers—silk weavers, engineers, tradesmen, and merchants—to the great detriment of France but to the considerable benefit of more tolerant destinations such as the Netherlands, Britain, and Prussia.

France had become a less liberal, more restrictive country in this process. The power behind the throne lay in the hands of the church, and its direction depended on which of the two dominant factions inside Catholicism could secure the most important posts. The church was internally divided between two warring parties, one buoyed by the Counter-Reformation, spearheaded by the Jesuits and influential at court, while the other side, the Jansenists, relied more strongly on the values of the urban bourgeoisie. Jansenism drew its theological inspiration from a Dutch cleric, Cornelis Jansen (1585–1638), and defended a theological view that shared key aspects with Protestant thought. Instead of emphasizing the authority of the pope and the role of the priest and the holy sacraments in the salvation of the soul, Jansenist thought stressed the idea of human depravity and the reliance on divine grace, without which, Jansen had argued, there was no redemption, not even through repentance and good works. Effectively, those who were damned already by divine Providence could not redeem themselves through piety, while those who lived in divine grace needed no pope to tell them what to do. Jansenism took control and power out of the hands of the church and made each individual's conscience the ultimate authority.

While these theological issues may appear arcane, the ensuing political and very worldly power struggles were all too real, particularly as the Jansenists were in control of the *parlement* of Paris, an ancient administrative body that was part high court and part lawgiving assembly, a mixture of competences that set it on a collision course with the royal claim to absolute power. In this context it is also significant that according to some sources the young *abbé* Diderot changed colleges halfway through his schooling from the Jesuit college Louis-le-Grand to the Jansenist college Harcourt, indicating that his sympathies and convictions might have been beginning to shift away already from the scholastic subtleties of Jesuit thinking and towards a more ethics-based approach.

Whether or not Diderot changed colleges, his religious ideas were certainly affected by another phenomenon, a popular religious frenzy that soon grew into a serious threat to public order. Centered on the cemetery of the city parish of Saint-Médard, only a mile or so from the colleges, the clamor reached its height during Diderot's school days. A quiet cult had developed at the grave of a former parish priest, François de Pâris, who had lived a life of pious deeds and charity and had died in 1727. Accounts of mysterious healings at his graveside had been making the rounds for some years, but in 1731 the stories about miraculous incidents appeared to intensify, often backed up by signed affidavits. Huddled hopefuls and quiet prayers by the graveside were replaced by the astonishing spectacle of trancelike convulsions followed by healing, and soon the graveyard drew spectators, who loved miracles not for spiritual reasons but for their entertainment value. Ever larger crowds had been attracted and were soon jostling in the surrounding streets to get a place close to the grave and witness the excited faithful—particularly attractive young women—fall into mysterious and ecstatic convulsions before getting up, apparently healed of all afflictions. The police viewed the goings-on with increasing suspicion. "What is most scandalous," wrote one informer, "is to see pretty young girls in the arms of men, who, while holding them, could be aroused to certain passions, because [the girls show themselves for] two or three hours, neck and breasts uncovered, skirts low, and arms in the air."[3]

The real scandal, however, was not in the supposed immorality of the often raucous miracle healings, but in their popular appeal. The dead priest on whose grave the miracles were said to be taking place had been a Jansenist himself and had therefore believed that miracles were one of the ways God chose to indicate his grace to the uncertain faithful, who pursued these miracles enthusiastically. Gripped by religious ecstasy, some of the cult's most zealous women would have themselves beaten with clubs or even literally nailed to a wooden cross as proof of their limitless devotion. A popular site of pilgrimage to a Jansenist sanctuary or even the chance of a Jansenist on his way to canonization—ideas such as these presented a real and potentially politically divisive threat to the power of Rome and of the king. Only eighteen years earlier, in 1709, the royal party had hit their opponents in the capital by forcing the closure of the convent Port-Royal, which had become an intellectual center of Jansenist thought. A miracle-working saint belonging to the other party would not be tolerated, and on January 27, 1732, the cemetery was closed by royal order, effectively putting an end to the healings at the priest's graveside and to the crowds.

As a young student, the curious Denis witnessed these orgiastic goings-on in the name of religion, and he was revolted by the spectacle, which he would later describe as hysteria. But while the bloody and superstitious excesses of popular miracle cults nauseated the young man, he found his spiritual peace troubled by his very own sensual disorder, which severely tested his desire to spend his life contemplating divine truths. The City of Lights intruded with its worldly temptations, both intellectual and sensual—too sensual for a young mind focused on divine commandments. Conscientiously, the young *abbé* took up the fight against the stirrings of his unruly body by using the arsenal his faith put at his disposal: praying, wearing hair shirts, fasting, and sleeping on straw to ward off the evil powers. Later in life, he saw his fervor with the detached irony of a psychologist. At some point, he wrote, almost every growing girl or boy was likely to fall into melancholy, seek solitude, and be attracted by the peaceful calm of religious surroundings: "They mistake the first manifestations of a developing sexual nature for the voice of God calling them to Himself; and it is precisely when nature is inciting them that they embrace a fashion of life contrary to nature's wish."[4]

Despite his initial best efforts, nature's wish prevailed, and Diderot, who would even towards the end of his life confess to feeling moved to tears by the pomp and circumstance of a religious procession, felt irresistibly drawn to another kind of spectacular ritual: the theatre. To the mature man it would later seem that not only his own imagination had been set aflame during these performances: "People had come with ardour, they left in a state of intoxication: some went to visit the girls, others scattered themselves in society."[5]

Like a new gospel, the voice of literature was resonating in the young mind, sense and sensibility mingling in its echoes. On long, solitary walks he read and recited his favorite plays over and over, crying at the sad scenes and declaiming the great monologues as he went along. From the cheapest seats, high up in the gods, he would watch performances of his favorite plays, blocking his ears and reciting the text quietly to himself—only allowing himself to hear the actors' voices when their mouth movements and gestures diverged from the lines he had memorized.

The youthful fascination rapidly became something more like a vocation: "What did I have in mind? to be applauded? Perhaps. To live on familiar terms with the women of the theatre whom I found infinitely lovable and whom I knew to be a very easy virtue? Assuredly."[6] No profession seemed more wonderful to him than that of a playwright, and before long he was head over heels in love not only with the pretty actresses but with the words they spoke, the sentiments they embodied, and the ideas they brought to the stage. The world of Voltaire began to exert its steady pull on the pious boy from the provinces.

CHAPTER 2

JOURNEYS

By the time Diderot finished his schooling around 1732, it was already clear to his father that his nineteen-year-old son would not become a man of the church. Through family connections he arranged a position in a lawyer's office for Denis and pressed him to take up either law or medicine himself, but Denis refused, pointing out that the law was far too boring and that he could never bring himself to become a doctor because he did not like the thought of killing anybody.

Diderot père implored, cajoled, threatened, and for a long time resisted the obvious conclusion that his boy would not in fact return to Langres to live a quiet and respectable life there. In a last attempt to bring him into line he did what fathers of wayward children have done for centuries: He cut off his allowance. Denis appeared indifferent; he valued his freedom over anything else and was willing to live precariously and even go hungry in order to preserve it. His decision caused him some years of hardship, but he remained firm in his resolve to remain independent. Many were the days on which he did not have a decent meal. Only once did he relent, accepting an easy and relatively well-paid position as personal tutor to the children of a rich Parisian. But he resigned his lucrative post after only a few weeks. His employer was so satisfied with him that he offered to double his salary and give him a larger, more comfortable apartment, but characteristically the young man replied, "Monsieur, look at me; a lemon is less yellow than my face. I make men out of your children, but every day I become a child with them. I am a thousand times too rich and too comfortable in your house, but I simply have to leave; what I really want is not to live better, but not die."[1]

Diderot would have had a much easier time if he had been content, as many others were, with his position of *abbé*. He could have accepted a life of independent scholarship funded by a church sinecure or the generosity of a rich patron and made more agreeable by a succession of discreet affairs or even a quiet cohabitation with a de facto wife. As the *abbés* at Holbach's salon would later demonstrate, he could within such a role even have written skeptical and critical works. But a life within the church was no longer an option for the young man. He had let his hair grow back (and indeed he was proud of his blond locks); he no longer wore the distinguished cassock of an *abbé*; he had renounced the life of an *abbé* for good.

Trying to survive by his wits alone, he was not always fussy about his methods. He borrowed money from visitors to Paris from his hometown, assuring them that his father would repay his debts (which his father duly did); he wrote sermons for a missionary who was preparing to go abroad, loading them with the very teachings he was himself coming to reject; and he even conned a credulous monk into believing that he would enter his order if only all his worldly affairs were settled, which included a one-off payment of 1,200 *louis* to an imaginary mistress who was expecting a child by him, or so he said. The monk paid up, only to be informed that the desirable novice had decided against ecclesiastical life after all.

If such schemes were hardly up to the moral standards of the later philosopher, they were indicative not only of his need for money but also of the milieu he had entered as an aspiring author. Beginning a career as a writer has always been an uncertain business, but trying to become the philosopher in a country whose censorship laws were a constant source of disruption and even threat presented additional challenges and uncertainties. Even the well-connected and popular Voltaire had had to leave town, after all, and other authors were dealt with far less decorously. It was no rarity for a writer not only to spend time under constant supervision by spies and informers but to be arrested and imprisoned without trial for an indefinite period.

Unknown, poor, and poorly dressed, an aspiring writer with nothing but his wits to live on would have no access to the great salons in which literary reputations were made. Instead, his world was that of taverns and cafés such as the café Procope on the left bank, close to the old Comédie Française. Here he would dive into the literary demimonde of long discussions fueled by the old triad of literary drugs—coffee, alcohol, and tobacco—and here he could make a name for himself. After a night spent in a freezing garret or a small, unheated rented room, he could warm his stiff limbs by a stove that was searing hot to the touch but left most of the room almost as cold as it had been before, and he could stoke his mind with newspapers featuring a quick flow of puns and sarcastic remarks.

This was the universe of hack writers and clandestine authors that Diderot inhabited for years. Like many others, he longed to make a name for himself. And also like them, he almost certainly would have earned himself a few *louis* by writing pornographic stories and clandestine pamphlets attacking the political circumstances and the power of the church. These publications were printed under the cover of night by mobile printing presses hastily set up in a basement or in the multistory piles of firewood situated close to the Seine, fuel for a voracious city whose labyrinthine byways and canals provided countless hiding places. The pamphlets were then sold *sous le manteau* (under the cloak), as secretly and often as expensively as hard drugs today, and with the same risk of being arrested and imprisoned. This is where the Jesuit-trained *philosophe* learned his craft.

Even this underworld had its hierarchy, of course. The café Procope and the grand Régence were the meeting places of the most able and ambitious writers, while hacks with more modest talents drifted into the taverns, and the lowest orders spent their time in anonymous cafés whose clientele consisted of "swindlers, recruiting agents, spies, and pickpockets . . . pimps, buggers, and faggots."[2] The police kept tabs on this world, of course, as well as meticulous records. Police spies drew up descriptions such as these of the participants in this literary netherworld:

> GORSAS: Proper for all kinds of vile jobs. Run out of Versailles and put in [the notorious jail] Bicêtre by a personal order of the King for having corrupted children whom he had taken in as lodgers, he has withdrawn to the fifth floor on the rue Tictone. Gorsas produces *libelles*. He has an arrangement with an apprentice printer of the Imprimerie Polytype, who has been fired

from other printing shops. He is suspected of having printed obscene works in there. He peddles prohibited books.

MERCIER: Lawyer, and fierce, a bizarre man; he neither pleads in court, nor consults. He hasn't been admitted to the bar, but takes the title of lawyer. He has written the *Tableaux de Paris*, in four volumes, and other works. Fearing the Bastille, he left the country, then returned and wants to become attached to the police.

CHENIER: Insolent and violent poet. He lives with Beauménil of the Opéra, who, in the decline of her charms, fell in love with him. He mistreats her and beats her—so much that her neighbours report that he would have killed her had they not come to her rescue. She accuses him of having taken her jewels; she describes him as a man capable of any crime and doesn't hide her regrets at having let herself be bewitched by him.[3]

Two of the three men treated like criminals here, Sébastien Mercier and André Chenier, would later become known as major writers, while the third, the violent and apparently pedophiliac Antoine Joseph Gorsas, would eventually have a minor role to play in the Revolution and would die under the guillotine.

Scandalmongering and pornography were dependable sources of income for many of these marginal writers. Unable to participate in the lives of the rich, whose footmen would shoo them away from their doorstep, they got their revenge by peddling the same purple prose that would later become the stock-in-trade of the tabloid press: scandalous tales of homosexual escapades and adultery, of lecherous old counts running after their lackeys or after a pretty chambermaid, of cuckolded dukes, impotent princes, and nymphomaniac princesses.

While many of the clandestine pamphlets attacked the rich by questioning their morals, other authors followed more directly revolutionary goals, for this vast underground literature was also the period's great laboratory of political and philosophical ideas. In the pages of pamphlets, every intellectual experiment could be conducted—from political revolt to biological evolution, from critique of religious doctrine to hard-core atheism. In short tracts, so short that they comprised only a few pages and could easily be slipped into a discreet pocket or under the floorboards to hide them during a police raid, every possible seditious and subversive idea was aired and discussed.

Many of the fiercest debates of our own age were already rehearsed in these early eighteenth-century texts. Advocates of "intelligent design" argue today that mere chance could not have created the complexity of life on earth, any more than a monkey hitting random typewriter keys could produce a perfect copy of the complete works of Shakespeare. In the eighteenth century, creationists argued that no random scattering of a typesetter's lead characters would ever happen to compose Homer's *Iliad*, and that therefore a higher intelligence must have informed creation.

Secularists today will respond to the example of the typing monkey by pointing out that evolution does not start from scratch every time a mutation occurs but builds from the last step already in existence, and so the monkey at the typewriter would not have to start the complete works of Shakespeare all over again. If a correct letter remained on the page while a wrong one simply vanished, a hardworking primate could write Shakespeare's works in less than forty years. During the eighteenth century, a pamphleteer likewise answered the *Iliad* example by pointing out that if each new letter of the *Iliad* were determined by throwing dice, one could calculate how long it would take to finish the epic poem, especially if the random typesetter had eternity to play with.

Of course, these ideas were far more dangerous in eighteenth-century France than they are today. The anonymous pamphleteer went on to write: "Our earth, our skies, everything contributes to the formation of species. The uniformity of organisms is not surprising, because all animals and plants are formed under the same circumstances; but it must be true that in the same measure as our knowledge of mechanics will increase, the necessity of metaphysics will diminish and when one is perfect the other will be zero, that is to say nil."[4] Philosophy as a mere stopgap until a better kind of knowledge comes around? A world made exclusively of material principles and forces? Arguments such as these could have brought the author to the gallows.

Many of these philosophical and theological questions would have been little more than intellectual boys' games to some of the Jesuit-educated authors, but they retained their explosiveness in society. A steady stream of clandestine tracts declared, for instance, that free will and divine omniscience were mutually exclusive, because a free act is necessarily one that will alter the future and God can only be all-knowing if he already knows everything that will happen. If astronomers could confidently predict astronomical events centuries before they occur, the future was predetermined, and there was obviously no free will. The concepts of personal responsibility and of sin were thus meaningless. Without responsibility, however, there could be no way in which an individual could be said to have sinned and to need forgiveness and redemption; no divine punishment could be justified if the sinner could not be held to account, heaven and hell thus collapsed into the mechanistic certainty of the clockwork world, and God was no more than a cuckoo on a cuckoo clock—a trick to disguise the unfailing precision of the machine.

Many of the clandestine tracts published during the mid-eighteenth century took a determinedly and angrily antireligious position. One classic of the genre, the *Treatise of the Three Imposters*, argued passionately that the founders of the three great monotheistic religions, Moses, Jesus, and Mohammed, were impostors who had tricked their fellow humans into believing in a world beyond their senses. If only people would follow common sense, the anonymous author concluded, they would throw off the yoke of superstition, as reason would always lead to the truth. Such seditious talk established reason as the enemy of faith. Anonymous authors pitted themselves (and, presumably, their readers) against despotism, against the worldly and spiritual powers, and explored other forms of governance. Some attacked the suspicious union between church and throne and even called for overthrowing the monarchy, arguing that all human beings were born equal. Reason was by its nature subversive and could lead to revolution—many writers demanded nothing less.

We know very little about the years Diderot spent in this marginal world, a time covering most of the 1730s, between the end of his formal education and his emergence into the literary world. Only a handful of his letters from these years have survived, all of them to his future wife, Anne-Toinette Champion. His daughter's memoirs about her father only give a very sketchy outline, no doubt based on anecdotes he used to tell himself.

The most personally revealing episode of these is his courtship of Anne-Toinette, a girl from a respectable family fallen on hard times, who was living with her mother and working as a seamstress and lace maker. Around 1742, Diderot had taken lodgings with Madame Champion. He had immediately fallen in love with her daughter and set about seducing her—without luck, as it turned out, because she was not available for casual affairs. His own recollection of his courtship contains a surprising reference, indicating that in 1743 he was still considering a career as a theologian:

> I was going to take the fur [by obtaining a doctorate in theology] and install myself among the doctors of the Sorbonne. On my way I meet a woman beautiful as an angel; I want to sleep with her, and I do; I have three children by her and am forced to abandon my mathematics, which I loved, my Homer and Virgil, which I always had in my pocket, the theatre, for which I had a taste, and was only too happy to undertake the *Encyclopédie*, to which I devoted twenty-five years of my life.[5]

It was not quite as simple as that, of course. To request his father's permission to marry a penniless girl, Diderot had traveled to Langres, only to learn that Diderot père, who had hoped for a much better match for his Paris-educated son, would not hear of him marrying a seamstress. Denis proved stubborn as ever, and his father even went so far as to have him incarcerated in a monastery to make him come to his senses. The rebellious son climbed out of a window and walked the 230 miles back to Paris, where he married Toinette some months later. He might have taken some time weighing his decision, as his marriage closed off the possibility of becoming a theologian, but in October 1743 he finally stepped in front of the altar of the *église* Saint-Pierre-aux-Boeufs, a small parish church specializing in midnight wedding ceremonies. He was thirty years old, and his life had taken a new turn.

Even if he was now a married man, Diderot was in no way ready to settle down to a life of quiet domesticity, especially as he soon found, once the first erotic infatuation had subsided, that he and his "Nanette" had very little in common. Used to living hand to mouth during his bachelor days, Diderot now had to look after his young family, and he did so in a way he was to maintain until the end of his life. He looked after them financially as well as he could, and he was careful not to create open scandal, but he did not spend much time at home, and already in 1745, barely two years after his wedding, he had a regular mistress, a lady by the name of Madame de Puisieux, for whom he even penned an erotic novel, *The Indiscreet Jewels*.

His marriage, meanwhile, appeared to exist under an unhappy star—and not only because of his infidelities. The couple's first three children, Angélique (born in 1744), Francois-Jacques-Denis (1746), and Denis (1750), died in infancy. The pace of the births slowed over time, a possible reflection of increasing marital difficulties. Anne-Toinette Diderot had little education and was very pious. She had married her husband when he was still an aspiring theologian, a handsome young man with every chance of having a respectable career. Initially, she saved money by eating less herself to allow him to go to the cafés with his literary friends, but eventually his infidelities, her grief over her dead children, and his increasing notoriety as a heretic estranged her from her husband. She became cantankerous and bitter, as her only surviving child, Diderot's beloved daughter, another Angélique (born 1753), would later testify.

Providing for his wife and children was not easy for the young author, who was always careful to protect his independence and had not found and perhaps not even tried to find a powerful sponsor. An excellent linguist and already an experienced author, Diderot turned his hand to translation, which offered him a modest and reasonably regular income. During the 1740s, he published two French versions of works by English philosophers, one of them the Earl of Shaftesbury, whose empirical, utilitarian point of view seems to have resonated with the young philosopher. Diderot added his own observations to the text, and these commentaries, known as the *Pensées philosophiques*, offer a first glimpse of Diderot as an emerging thinker in the midst of his momentous transformation from *abbé* to atheist. His commentary shows him as a believer inclined to skepticism and equally critical of intolerance and of unbelief, a position familiar from Voltaire's writings. Even in the very first sentence of the *Pensées*, the first words published under his name, Diderot reveals himself: "The passions are endlessly reviled; one accuses them of every evil in man, and one forgets that they are also the source of all his pleasures . . . and yet, only the passions, the great passions, can lift the soul to the greatest things."[6]

The young philosopher's God is a reasonable God, and certainly not the Lord of the established church, which he attacks with great flair, in one instance conjuring up a vision of hell in which damned souls are tortured: "Some of them are beating their own chest with rocks; others tear apart their bodies with iron hooks; all have remorse, pain and death in their eyes. Who has condemned them to all these torments?—The God they have offended against.—And who is this God?—The God of loving kindness."[7] This contradiction between divine love and extravagantly cruel divine punishment was an old theological staple. If God had fashioned his creatures in such a way that they would sin, why was he then angry at them? And if it was not God but chance that had cast the lots of each individual life (as the believers in empiricism held), then why did the Creator blame his creatures for their sins? The problem of evil, that most stubborn of all theological problems, was exploited with relish by the young philosopher, who did not yet reject the existence of God but had already turned decisively against the doctrines of the church and had reached a position not unlike the rational deism professed by Voltaire.

Portrait as a literary artisan: Denis Diderot in simple clothes, and already without the golden locks of his youth. Drawing by Jean-Baptiste Greuze, circa 1766.

THE PIERPONT MORGAN LIBRARY / ART RESOURCE, NY

Throughout the next works, and the next years, Diderot's position evolved further. In his short *De la suffisance de la religion naturelle* (*Of the Sufficiency of Natural Religion*) he still argues for a reasonable deity who instructs his creatures in the use of their faculties: "the end of a religion which comes from God can only be the knowledge of essential truths."[8] But which essential truths? Not the truths of revealed religion, he argues, for these can never be proven to be true. Instead, the only essential truths are those derived from empirical observation and logical deduction, the truths of science. In 1747, only four years after his *Pensées philosophiques*, the author has made a decisive step towards intellectual emancipation, or, rather, he has entered into an active dialogue with other opinions.

Throughout his life, the passionate theatregoer, dramatist, and conversationalist Diderot found it easiest and most satisfying to put his thoughts in dialogue form. In his *La Promenade du sceptique* (*A Skeptic's Walk*, 1747) he lets the arguments for and against God appear as characters walking through an allegorical landscape. One of them, significantly called "Atheos," is given many of the best lines. In the style of a fairy tale, the narrator describes a landscape and its godlike prince. His soldiers (the believers) are described as wearing blindfolds and believing that "the less you see, the better you can go straight ahead." Diderot felt that he had taken off that blindfold. He was moving away from the faith of his fathers—and headed for trouble.

Much of Diderot's transformation was due to the books he read, to his interest in the sciences, and to the friends he made during this time. Among his friends was a man who was to play a fundamentally important role in Diderot's future, one of the army of young men who arrived in Paris in search of fame and fortune, a Genevan by the name of Jean-Jacques Rousseau.

Rousseau was born on June 28, 1712, to a watchmaker and his wife in the proudly independent, Calvinist city republic of Geneva, just beyond the French border. Nothing in his early life seemed to indicate that he would become one of the most influential philosophers in Western history, but some key episodes and experiences of his childhood and apprenticeship years clearly inform his later thinking.

As the newborn Jean-Jacques was baptized on July 4, his mother, Suzanne, was at home, already at death's door. She did not recover from giving birth and from the fever that followed, and she died nine days after his birth. "I cost the life of the best of mothers," he reflected ruefully in his famous *Confessions*, often thought to be the first autobiography in the modern sense. It promises great, unsparing candor, and it is as fascinating as it is treacherous.

Having lost their mother, the boy and his elder brother were brought up by their father, Isaac, who was by all accounts emotionally unstable and economically stressed; his watchmaking workshop did not go well, and he was liable to fly into terrible rages and severely beat the boys, occasionally accusing the younger of having caused his mother's death, an accusation terrible enough to scar any child. The irascible nature of the father would determine Jean-Jacques' childhood in many ways. In 1722, father and sons had to flee the city after Isaac had a violent altercation with an officer. To avoid being tried and sentenced in Geneva, Isaac took his two sons to live in the village of Bossey, outside of the city's jurisdiction. Here the young Jean-Jacques lived a life he would later hold up as ideal, a "country idyll," as he put it, of simple pleasures, simple needs, and virtuous people to whom he "opened his heart to the joys of friendship."

Jean-Jacques now received his education at the house of Pastor Lambercier, whose unmarried sister was also the local schoolmistress. The boy enjoyed his lessons with Mlle Lambercier, but he enjoyed being corrected for misbehaving even more: He loved being spanked. "I had found in that pain, in that shame even, an element of sensuality which left me desiring rather than fearing to experience it again from the same hand," he later confessed, adding that his predilection had helped to make him a more moral man in later life. "I devoured beautiful women with an ardent eye; my imagination conjured them up endlessly, only to put them into action in my own way, and turn them into so many Mlle Lamberciers. Even after reaching maturity, this bizarre and ever-persistent taste preserved in me the sound morals of which it might have robbed me."[9]

When it was time for the boy to learn a trade, he was sent to live with an uncle in Geneva. There he was eventually apprenticed to an engraver, who proved a hard taskmaster, especially with a dreamy adolescent given to staring out of the window and secretly devouring books whenever his employer was not looking. The books were impounded and burned, and Jean-Jacques was whipped for his laziness. Life in the city had turned bitter after the glorious freedom of a childhood in the country.

The end of this phase of Rousseau's life was as abrupt as it was characteristic. One day in the spring of 1728, after the fifteen-year-old Jean-Jacques and some friends had made an outing into the countryside, they found the city gates already closing as they approached. They were forced to sleep in front of the city, and the adolescent engraver's apprentice knew that he would be beaten once again on his return to work in the morning. He decided then and there that he would not go back to that unloved life and would not even set foot again in Geneva. Having spent a clammy night under the stars, Jean-Jacques sent word to a friend inside the city as soon as the gates opened in the morning, asking the friend to bring him a few personal effects. The boy then stormed off with his bundle, intending never to return.

Rousseau's flight from Geneva was more than just an attempt to get away from an unloved master and a father whose bouts of temper were difficult to bear. The young lad went to pursue a dream. Inspired by the romantic novels he had read at his workbench, he had decided that he wanted to live at a castle "where I could be the favourite of the Lord and Lady, the love of their daughter, the friend of the brother and the protector of their neighbours." For a Protestant boy from a modest background this was an ambition difficult to achieve in Catholic France, but Jean-Jacques already had a plan. He approached a priest, telling him that he intended to convert. The churchman, excited at the prospect of saving a soul, gave him a letter of introduction to a baroness in the town of Annecy. Françoise-Louise de Warens, a young woman who had only recently converted herself, was known to offer asylum to young Protestant men running away from home and about to embrace the True Faith—and perhaps not just the faith.

Quickly gaining Mme de Warens' patronage, Jean-Jacques became part of the household. He was close to achieving his dream, even if there was no lord of the manor whose favorite he could have become, as the baroness's husband, a Protestant, lived apart from his apostate wife. The boy now had a protectress, a childless noblewoman only too eager to assume the role of the mother he had never known.

But before he could settle fully into his new role, there was business to attend to. The young convert-to-be had to be instructed in the faith, and it was decided that he should travel to Turin, where he could be taught at a hospice specializing in conversions. Here, as so often, the evidence is at odds with Rousseau's own account. According to the *Confessions*, he stayed at the hospice for two months, tenaciously debating with the priests, showing himself an able theologian and challenging them to justify Catholic doctrine, before finally taking the momentous step of conversion. According to the hospice registers, however, "Rosso, Gio Giacomo, di Geneva, Calvinista" was baptized two days after his arrival, hardly a period long enough for epic disputes and vigorous soul searching.

There was, however, some turmoil of a different kind. This trouble involved one of Rousseau's fellow lodgers, whom he describes as a "Moor." Abraham Ruben, a Levantine Jew, was a conversion tourist who made a living by having his soul saved, and his life paid for, by missionaries and monks in many cities. By the time he met Rousseau he had been baptized already at least twenty times.

Ruben was obviously an old hand at life in religious institutions and the pleasures that could be found there. He propositioned and groped the adolescent Jean-Jacques and, having being repulsed by the shocked boy, masturbated in front of him. Sickened and bewildered by what he had seen, but also fascinated and unable to understand it, Rousseau talked to anyone who would listen about the man "manipulating himself" and spurting "a white and sticky substance" into the fireplace. Despite some discreet hints by the monks that it would be better to keep quiet, he continued to recount his strange experience. Rousseau was sixteen years old and obviously quite ignorant about his own physical development. Finally, one of the monks took him aside and explained the facts of life. In the course of the conversation, Rousseau learned a surprising truth about the celibate life: The old monk told him that there was no reason to be alarmed by being approached by another man and that after the first shock was over, he would find it was neither painful nor frightening to exchange caresses with him. This advice disgusted his troubled listener even more.

Rousseau's stay in Turin was a journey of sexual self-discovery, even if his own erotic adventures were more quixotic than anything else. Having finally understood the crude mechanics of lust but unsure about how to engineer an encounter with a suitable woman and desperate to be spanked once again as he had been by his schoolmistress, he hung around in an alleyway and exposed his bottom at female passersby in the vain hope that they might understand and hit him. But they did nothing of the kind. They laughed, ran away, and came back in the company of women carrying broom handles and accompanied by an armed policeman. Once again, Jean-Jacques was deeply humiliated.

After several months of living and doing odd jobs in Turin, the newly baptized substitute son returned to Annecy and to *maman*, as he had taken to calling Mme de Warens. The volatile baroness was passionately interested in philosophy, and she could drive her young protégé to distraction at dinner by discussing metaphysics between courses, delaying the arrival of the next dish far too long for his adolescent appetite. At the same time, however, the young man took to reading philosophical books and familiarized himself with aspects of Western thought as well as with the foundations of musical theory and composition.

After an unsuccessful and probably halfhearted attempt at becoming a priest, Jean-Jacques decided to try his luck at music and became a music teacher, an occupation he enjoyed because it brought him into contact with pretty young girls whom he could admire without being required to act on his feelings. Unable to live out his masochistic fantasies, he sought refuge in a love that was childlike and pure. He was deeply in love with *maman* without ever wanting to become intimate with her. Instead, he almost literally worshipped the ground she walked on, kissing the bed, the furniture, even the curtains she had used when she was not looking.

While Rousseau immersed himself in an ardor that was deep and intense but unsullied by the physical passion he had always regarded as dirty, he was soon to find out that *maman*'s love for him was not as motherly as he had imagined. The baroness, after all, was only in her early thirties herself. Apparently frustrated by her young friend's shyness, she gave him an ultimatum, and he eventually became her lover. It was his first experience of physical love, and it was not a happy one: "I had tasted the pleasure, but some strange invincible sadness poisoned its charm for me. I felt as if I had committed incest." Rousseau was twenty-one years old.

In 1740, after twelve years with Mme de Warens, the time had come for the young man to move on. The generous baroness arranged a position as tutor for him, a professional change that would take him to the household of a powerful and well-educated man, Monsieur de Malby, the police chief of the thriving city of Lyon and the surrounding provinces. Having arrived at his new place of employment, the young teacher quickly found out that his employer was not only a high civil servant but also one of the chief exponents of Enlightenment thinking in his city. Malby welcomed intellectuals at his dinner table; the conversation was peppered with names such as Francis Bacon, Voltaire, Isaac Newton, and Montesquieu. Rousseau was entranced, as dinner guests discussed the importance of science and reason or the advantages of ancient Sparta and the Roman republic over the modern monarchy.

Dressed in his best coat and condemned to silence by his relative ignorance and his lowly station as a tutor, Rousseau sat and listened while the worldly intellectuals discussed philosophy and history. He had not yet turned to philosophy himself, trying instead to establish himself as a composer of operas, a curious if ambitious choice for a man who had encountered the art of playing and writing music in his late teens and not, as most musicians did, as a child. But his passion for writing arias and recitatives obviously distracted him from his primary duties as a teacher, and when his contract expired after one year, it was not renewed.

Once again, Jean-Jacques was on his own, without attachment, without concrete plans, and without an income. He decided to go to Paris and to establish himself there as an artist in his own right. Having arrived in the capital, he attempted to convince the French Academy of Sciences to adopt a newly devised system of musical notation, which substituted numerals for conventional notes, only to find it damned by faint praise and effectively rejected. He fared no better with his comedy *Narcisse*, in which a young aristocrat falls deeply in love with a portrait of himself in woman's clothes and breaks off the engagement to his angelic fiancée until he finally realizes his error. It is not a particularly original play but an intriguing study in psychology—and one that perhaps reveals more about its author than he intended.

A new arrival in the capital, Rousseau was eager to make friends. In or around early 1743, a mutual acquaintance introduced him to a writer and translator who was also languishing in the shadows of the literary establishment and trying to make a name for himself: Denis Diderot. The two had much in common: They were born only one year apart, both had fathers who were proud craftsmen, both had enjoyed a sheltered upbringing, both had left home at fifteen, both were passionate about philosophy and art, and both had come to Paris to make a new life for themselves. One of the most influential philosophical friendships of the eighteenth century was born.

While Diderot and Rousseau were precariously making their way up in the world, young Thiry d'Holbach pursued his studies with more ease. He did not have to earn a living, and supported by his uncle's generosity, he could choose the best place to continue his education. For Holbach, always fascinated by science and empirical knowledge, this place was the university of Leiden, in the Netherlands, where the great philosopher Baruch Spinoza had studied almost a century before.

During the Dutch golden age in the seventeenth century, Leiden had been the second city of the United Provinces, after nearby Amsterdam. In addition to its graceful canals and arched bridges, two beautiful Gothic churches jutted into the grey sky far above the gables of the brick houses along the waterways, testimonies to a proud merchant class whose wealth was based mainly on cloth production and dyeing. Prosperous and self-confident, the city looked to its famous university, founded by William of Orange in 1575, to crown its commercial success with intellectual glory.

And indeed, the university rose swiftly to become one of Europe's greatest centers of learning. By the beginning of the eighteenth century it had established itself as Europe's most important educational institutions—far ahead of Oxford and Cambridge, which were then, if we are to believe Samuel Johnson, mainly places where the sons of the rich got drunk. At Leiden, students had at their disposal a great library; graceful botanical gardens receiving plants from all corners of the Dutch trading empire; cabinets of curiosities filled with strange artwork, unknown plants, exotic animals, and mineral samples; and a theatre for public dissections of corpses (usually of executed criminals or paupers drowned in the canals).

The atmosphere here was notably different from other universities. While the Sorbonne still exclusively taught theology and law, Leiden offered a wide choice of subjects, excellent libraries funded by civic wealth, and a culture of free speech based on the great Dutch tradition of pragmatic tolerance. Leiden attracted some of Europe's best scientists, whose presence transformed a community built on cloth and Protestant devotion into a city filled with bookshops, coffeehouses, and lively debate—a student town, alive with young men from England, Germany, France, and even Italy, who had come to study with renowned scholars and taste a freedom of ideas beyond anything they could enjoy at home. Outwardly graceful but unassuming, Leiden had a reputation for being a city of international camaraderie and intellectual revolt.

By the time young Thiry d'Holbach put his name down in the university's register in 1744, the city had experienced a period of genteel decline, as its cloth industry had come under pressure from competition from abroad. But the lecture halls had lost none of their buzz. The university had even extended its reputation for innovative teaching and research, particularly in the physical sciences. One generation earlier, the great doctor Herman Boerhaave, holder of the chairs of both medicine and botany, had given new luster to the faculty and its fame, and in the second year of Holbach's studies, Professor Pieter van Musschenbroek proudly announced to the world the discovery of a device capable of storing electric charges, later named the Leyden jar, which he used for demonstrations of electrical phenomena during his classes.

Demonstrations of the mysterious powers of static electricity were hugely popular and were soon on offer throughout Europe's cities. The Amsterdam diarist Jakob Bicker Raye described one such sensation in 1745, a glass globe charged with static electricity until it caused "sparks to fly in all directions from the body of anyone who touches it. I myself have stood there with a spoonful of brandy in my other hand which ignited. I did the same thing [ignited the brandy] with a sword in my hand. Someone whose finger came close to my leg caused electrical sparks to fly out of my shin, through two pairs of socks, without my being burnt or causing any pain. . . . Thousands of people go daily to see this machine and be electrified."[10]

Science was often spectacular, always disquieting, and fascinating to the new arrival from Paris, then twenty-one years old. In vigorous debates with theologians, Leiden scientists such as Boerhaave and Musschenbroek had worked to emancipate scientific research from merely speculative thinking. Physics, as Musschenbroek noted with evident satisfaction, "makes new conquests every day, and is insensibly spreading into most professions."[11]

While the young Holbach encountered a new universe of scientific learning and innovation, he also relished making the acquaintance of other students from across Europe. His closest personal friend during these years was another student, the nineteen-year-old John Wilkes (1725–1797), the son of a London distiller. Later to become one of Britain's most notoriously radical politicians and journalists, a member of the Hellfire Club, known for its members' loose talk and equally flexible morals, Wilkes also enjoyed the intellectual freedom at the university and was already experimenting with many of the ideas that would later make him such a notorious figure in Britain, a courageous champion of free speech, and an open supporter of American independence. As young students are wont to do, he would discuss the great questions of the world with his French friend Holbach, often going for long walks through the reliably flat countryside. When Wilkes returned to Britain in 1746, Holbach wrote to him, in English, how he dreamed of being reunited with his friend

> in one of those delightfull evening walks at Leyden. It is a dream, I own it, but it is so agreeable to me that nothing in reality could be compared to the pleasure I feel: let me therefore insist a little more upon't and travel with my Letter, we are gone! I think to be at Alesbury! there I see my Dear Wilkes! What a Flurry of Passions! Joy! fear of a second parting! what charming tears! What sincere Kisses!—but time flows and the end

> of this Love is now as unwelcome to me, as would be to another to be awaken'd in the middle of a Dream wherein he is going to enjoy a beloved mistress; the enchantment ceases, the delightfull images vanish, and nothing is left to me but friendship, which is of all my possessions the fairest, and the surest,
>
> I am most sincerely Dear Wilkes,
>
> De Holbach.[12]

One other Frenchman living in Leiden was to become an important inspiration for Holbach's thinking, though it is not clear whether the two ever met during their time in that city: the French philosopher Julien Offray de la Mettrie (1709–1751), who had taken refuge in the Netherlands and who was then working on his most important work, *L'Homme machine* (*Man a Machine*, published anonymously in 1748).

The Breton La Mettrie lived the unsteady life of the born radical. Originally interested in theology, La Mettrie had, like Diderot, come to Paris to study at one of the famous colleges there, only to find that his interests drew him away from the church and into the world. He turned to medicine and went to Leiden to study with Herman Boerhaave before returning to his hometown of Saint-Malo, where he set up a medical practice. He soon found that he was not cut out for the tranquil life of the country doctor; leaving his young family behind, he moved back to Paris, became an army surgeon, and began to write philosophical essays.

Having noticed during a bout of fever that his mental activity had showed a clear correlation to his pulse, he had become interested in the interaction between body and mind, which he, like Spinoza, took not to be two different things but merely two aspects of the same, physical phenomenon. This line of argument, which later would be adopted by both Holbach and Diderot, led to troubling conclusions. If a bodily state, having a fever, could be translated into a clear mental reality such as a hallucination, then mental activity could be seen as merely an aspect of physical activity, not something existing separately. But if our minds are merely extensions of our body, then what of our souls? Once again, philosophical argument led straight into an attack on religion and a denial of the immortal soul, the afterlife, heaven and hell, and therefore divine laws. When he published, in 1746, the result of his reflections, the *Histoire naturelle de l'âme* (*A Natural History of the Soul*), the book was condemned and burned by court order. La Mettrie fled France and once again moved to the more tolerant climate of Leiden.

Persecution breeds radicalism. In his previous works, La Mettrie had adopted a moderately materialist position. Now, however, he embraced a darker materialism, possibly also a reflection of his own reduced situation. "It is not enough for a scholar to study Nature and Truth," he wrote at the very beginning of his great work, *L'Homme machine*. "He must also have the courage to say it to the small number of those who want to think and are able to think; as for the others, who voluntarily are slaves to their prejudices, they can no more attain the Truth than frogs can fly."[13]

La Mettrie was a stylish writer as well as a courageous one. Human beings, he argued, are biological machines regulated to seek pleasure and flee pain—not the summit of creation but part of the natural world and different from other animals by degree, not by kind. Sober and clear-eyed, the author had no intention of building a great metaphysical system, as was customary among ambitious philosophers. The more valuable work, he believed, was to accommodate the mind in what a human could know, and not waste time with what he would never be able to grasp. Don't look for the meaning of life, La Mettrie advised. After all, human existence is governed not by reason but by natural laws. We can never know why we are here, but we must simply live and die, no different from and hardly more lasting than mushrooms appearing after a rainfall or spring flowers by the roadside. We must simply learn to live with our urge for ultimate meaning and accept that it cannot be satisfied. La Mettrie wrote, "Let's not lose ourselves in infinity, we are not fashioned in a way to have the smallest idea of it; it is absolutely impossible to us to go back to the origin of things. . . . What madness to torture oneself so much over something which to know is impossible, and which would not even make us happy if we could penetrate to the end!"[14] Philosophy becomes an exercise in intellectual modesty, even humility.

An advocate of realistic hopes, La Mettrie was nevertheless a man of great intellectual ambitions. He wanted to reimagine what it meant to be human. There is no immortal soul, he argued, no spiritual substance, but only different functions depending on the proper functioning of the human body, which is nothing but a well-tuned machine. People might talk of the immortal soul, but they are incapable of defining what exactly they mean, making talk useless or even harmful.[15] If there is no soul, no Providence, and no possibility of finding out whether there is a God, only our sensations remain, pulling us towards pleasure and away from pain, and entirely independent of vice or virtue. As a result, La Mettrie concluded that "happiness is, like lust, within reach for everyone; the good as the wicked, and that the most virtuous are not the happiest: or if they are, it is simply because they take delight in their manner of existing & of acting."[16]

This time, even the liberal Dutch were outraged at La Mettrie's godlessness. Within only a few months of the publication of *Man a Machine*, the author was obliged to move once more, this time to Potsdam, to the court of Frederick II of Prussia. Frederick the Great liked to think of himself as a philosopher king, and he was either tolerant or cynical enough to appoint as his personal physician a man reviled just about everywhere else in Europe. But the newly minted courtier had little time to glory in his new position and unaccustomed wealth. He died in 1751, allegedly from food poisoning from a game pie but possibly simply from overeating. The cause of his death delighted La Mettrie's many philosophical enemies, who henceforth portrayed him as prophet of mindless gluttony caught by his own vice.

Thiry d'Holbach thoroughly absorbed the atmosphere of vigorous discussion and empirical science in Leiden, and he enjoyed the student life—the friendships, the chance encounters, and the long, well-lubricated lunches, dinners, and parties, during which friends from various countries and in possession of diverse views talked and debated, as do all students, into the small hours of the morning.

When Holbach returned to Paris in 1748 or 1749, he brought with him not only a robust, radical cast of mind and a solid scientific education but a vivid desire to reproduce the wonderful times he had known at university. He decided to hold dinners of his own, intellectual get-togethers for friends and their friends, and unlike Diderot, whom he was yet to meet, he was ready to settle down. In 1749 he married Basile-Geneviève d'Aine, his second cousin, to whom he was devoted and who was also glad to escape the tedium of domestic life, embroidery, and social calls. On Sundays and Thursdays, the Holbachs received guests on the first floor of their elegant but unassuming town house in the rue Royale Saint-Roch, today rue des Moulins, a short walk away from the graceful Palais Royale and the bustle of the Louvre. The stage was set for what was to be the greatest intellectual enterprise of the eighteenth century.

CHAPTER 3

ENCYCLOPÉDIE: GRAND AMBITIONS

On the morning of July 24, 1749, Denis Diderot received two visitors. They informed him that they were policemen and had come to arrest him. Diderot calmly asked for a little time to get dressed. He went to see his wife and child to tell them that he had to step out on literary business and might be delayed for a while, and then followed the two officers down the steep stairs. He was driven to the fortress of Vincennes, on the outskirts of the city, where he was placed in solitary confinement. His jailer brought him two candles and two more the next day. When the prisoner lightly remarked that one would be quite enough because the summer evenings were long and bright, he was told that it would be wise to accept them and to save them—for the winter. Diderot, the gregarious, intellectual rabble-rouser, began to realize that he might spend a long time in his solitary cell.

The reasons for his sudden arrest lay in his intellectual jealousy and in the great project with which he had become involved, the most important publishing venture of the eighteenth century, which became known simply as the *Encyclopédie* of Diderot and d'Alembert. It was this wording that had stoked the jealousy, a simple matter of precedence: Next to the young scientific star Jean Le Rond d'Alembert, Diderot, who had not yet made a name for himself, felt small and overlooked. This, he had decided, would change.

It had all begun with a modest translation job. The young author, struggling to feed his family, had been commissioned to translate a two-volume

English encyclopedia, the *Cyclopaedia* by Ephraim Chambers. Other translators had come and gone, and the project was in the doldrums, when the booksellers (who during the eighteenth century also published books themselves) decided to entrust the work to Diderot, who had already translated Shaftesbury and other English works. It was a modest task and would not have taken longer than a year or two, had not Diderot decided that a mere translation would not be enough. Supported by influential friends who were watching the young man's career, he had resolved to revise and expand the work. He was a persuasive talker, and he had convinced a syndicate of three booksellers to finance a much larger collective work, which had very little to do with Chambers's.

Diderot had resolved to do nothing less than unite all the knowledge of his time. A multivolume work, the *Encyclopédie* would be written by the finest experts in each particular field and financed by subscription. It would be the definitive reference source for all conceivable subjects and more than that: It would be a veritable school of skeptical thinking.

From an *abbé* and aspiring Jesuit, Diderot had turned skeptic, anti-Christian, and even atheist, believing that the facts of science, not the scriptures, should be yardsticks of knowledge. He would provide that knowledge, from architecture to zoology, lavishly illustrated in several volumes of detailed engravings, and he would disseminate Enlightened ideas, stressing the precedence of reason over faith, celebrating humanity's potential for delivering itself from evil, opening and explaining the great book of nature.

The concept was bold and had to remain largely secret, because any frank discussion of editorial policy was likely to land Diderot and his colleagues in prison. Under the guise of unobjectionable, factual information, the *Encyclopédie* would be used to disseminate dangerous ideas. Even the very form of the *Encyclopédie* would be subversive. Unlike other dictionaries, which listed entries by subject and piously gave precedence to topics like theology, church history, and aristocratic houses, this work would be organized strictly alphabetically—a planning nightmare in an age before computers, but a phenomenally potent method. Now all subjects would be mixed, the hierarchies of society (both socially and conceptually) toppled from the outset. Princes and pimps, counts and cabbages would be sharing the same letter, the same space. The entire map of knowledge would be redrawn.

Unsurprisingly, the nature of Diderot's project brought him in conflict with the censor's office, which had to pass every volume, every page, and every article of the *Encyclopédie* for it to be published with royal privilege. Most of the censors were theologians, and it was clear that the entries relating to Christianity and implicitly questioning the holy scriptures would receive the closest attention.

Helping Diderot deal with close and largely hostile attention of this kind was a man who had died seven years before Denis' birth: Pierre Bayle (1647–1706), a French Protestant and himself the author of an important and revolutionary dictionary, which not only was one of the greatest achievements of seventeenth-century scholarship but also became one of the best sellers of its time. To understand the *Encyclopédie*, its methods, and its greatness, we need to have a sense of Bayle and his solitary, staggering project.

Pierre Bayle's *Dictionnaire historique et critique* was in four volumes, published from 1695 to 1702. Bayle came from a Huguenot (Protestant) family in southern France. Born and raised at a time of intense religious persecution, he led an itinerant life before accepting, in 1681, a position as professor at a college in tolerant Rotterdam, where he remained until his death.

Hailed by Voltaire as the greatest master of the art of reasoning who ever wrote, Bayle was more influential than any other thinker of the early Enlightenment, despite or because of the fact that the true nature of his great work remained enigmatic. Superficially, Bayle's *Dictionnaire* is a kind of biographical digest, an overview of important philosophers and historical figures, compiled with stupendous erudition. The greatest part of the text, however, some 90 percent, lies in the footnotes, in which Bayle comments on the entries themselves and marshals an enormous range of sources quoted at length, both supporting and refuting the arguments discussed. The notes, which often cover entire pages and commonly reduce the main text to a few lines at the top of the page, open up a panorama of debate, dissent, and anecdote, a plethora of annotations from theology to obscenity, complete with exact bibliographic reference in the margins. It is, in other words, a delight to read.

Unable and perhaps unwilling to show his hand, Bayle plays a constant game of hide-and-seek with the reader, disguising his own opinions and putting skeptical ideas into the mouths of famous scholars. His strategy is to appear as an innocent bystander, the honest compiler of opinion and debate—the oldest trick in the book, since a good memory and a keen eye will always be able to find an appropriate quote. From the very beginning, Bayle forces his readers to read between the lines, search alternate meanings, and duck and weave in and out of ancient debates to arrive at troubling conclusions.

Bayle practices this prudent duplicity from the very beginning. In a footnote to the article "Abimelech" he berates the ancient Jewish historian Flavius Josephus for claiming that his sources were "better than Moses" and for suggesting that the account of Genesis may not be literally true. The author ends with a somewhat unsettling reflection on how historical sources had been dealt with since time immemorial: "I believe that all the ancient historians have exercised the same license with regard to the old memoirs they consulted. They have tacked on supplements, and, not finding facts developed and embellished according to their fancy, they have enlarged and dressed them up as they pleased and today we take this for history." This learned insight might have been directed at his contemporaries, but at the same time, if "all the ancient historians" were liars, then how do we know which sources to believe?

In a footnote to an article about the courtesan Ariosta, Bayle quotes another author's musings about the absurdity of the institution of marriage, or rather the singular power of the Latin liturgical formula "*ego conjugo vos*" (I unite you in marriage). Uttering them, a priest "makes a young fellow lie with a girl in the sight of, and with the consent of the whole world," but the same action without these three words "is an enormous crime which dishonours a poor woman. . . . The father and the mother, in the first case, rejoice, dance, and themselves conduct their daughter to the bed. And in the second case, they are in despair. They have the daughter shaved, and they put her in a convent. One must admit that the laws are very amusing." Deftly choosing the famously worldly and acerbic writer Roger de Bussy Rabutin, Bayle introduces a note of wry amusement into the discussion of a sacrament, a skeptical half smile that is all his own.

"What a man says, he does not necessarily believe," Bayle writes, quoting Aristotle. Like Montaigne, Bayle ultimately was a skeptical humanist and a humane skeptic. Outwardly, however, he was a regular churchgoer—a stalwart member of the Rotterdam French Protestant community—and always defended his faith. Nobody could take him for an atheist, even if in his *Dictionnaire* all questions remained open. Lengthy entries are devoted to Greek and Roman atheist and materialist philosophers, such as Epicurus or Lucretius, and to modern ones, such as Thomas Hobbes and Baruch Spinoza. While their work is always subjected to critical appraisal and even refuted, this skeptical approach does not prevent Bayle from giving a thorough exposition of their ideas. Different and often contradictory interpretations are at war with one another in the footnotes, and the reader is never treated to anything so convenient as what to think about any given theme. He has to make up his own mind, find his own way among the multitude of intellectual paths meandering in front of him.

Bayle's work is a school of critical thought as well as a master class in disingenuous deception and disguise. He writes that it is all very well to decree that historians must speak the truth at all times, as the Italian Traiano Boccalini had done, but like the Ten Commandments this law is almost impossible to live by. Indeed, Boccalini had lost his life because he offended those in power. "Eternal life is the fruit of obedience to the Decalogue; but temporal death is the almost inevitable consequence of obedience to the lawgiver of the historians."[1] Saying the truth too directly, the refugee Bayle warns his readers, can be fatal.

The *Dictionnaire* was the main conduit through which several generations of French and other European intellectuals learned about dissident currents of thought and forbidden thinkers such as Spinoza and a whole procession of skeptical and atheist philosophers, from Muslim and Chinese sects to Epicurus, Lucretius, and Johann Bredenburg (a Rotterdam wine merchant turned philosopher and critic of Spinoza) and the notorious treatise *The Three Impostors*. All dissenting voices are heard at length, even if the author's comments often express shock at so much impiety.

While this loving care lavished on freethinkers might have merited the suspicion that Bayle himself harbors some sympathies for such heretical points of view, he also rigorously criticizes Spinoza's "ridiculous" and "absurd" doctrines. He holds in particular contempt the philosopher's claim that creation is perfect and any perceived imperfection is nothing but an imperfection of the human mind. How can it be true that the human mind, part of God's perfect creation, is capable of thinking imperfect thoughts, of perceiving things in an imperfect way? Does not the entire system collapse once this imperfection is admitted?

But what of Bayle himself? Was he protesting too much in order to protect himself? Was he the pious Protestant he claimed to be? Once again, the reader is abandoned to his own thoughts, aided, if at all, by the bibliographical notes, which are an invitation to investigate the problem further.

There are, in fact, good indications of what Bayle really believed, even if the central enigma—whether or not his religiosity was more than a facade—remains intact. In his role as marshal of European thought, the scholar took great care not to appear as a thinker in his own right and preferred to confine himself to critical remarks, letting others express conflicting points of view, which were judiciously arranged by him. In an earlier work he was much clearer about his views. His *Pensées diverses écrites à un docteur de Sorbonne à l'occasion de la Comète qui parut au mois de décembre 1680* (*Miscellaneous Reflections, Occasion'd by the Comet which Appear'd in December 1680: Chiefly Tending to Explode Popular Superstitions Written to a Doctor of the Sorbonne*) was published in 1682. Bayle, who hardly ever left his study and whose immense reading list meant that he could hardly have found the time to lift his nose out of his books and towards the stars, was not particularly interested in comets. What interested him about the appearance of Halley's comet in 1680 was the hysterical, superstitious fascination it had aroused. Prophets and doomsday merchants had treated the phenomenon as a divine portent, a warning of the approaching end of the world. Nonsense, writes Bayle to his (possibly fictitious) correspondent, a doctor at the Sorbonne, confessing his surprise that "you, who ought to be convinced that these are bodies subject to the normal laws of nature & not miracles, which follow no rule; have allowed yourself to be carried with the current & imagine with the rest of the world . . . that the Comets are similar to heralds at arms, which come to declare war on humankind on God's behalf."[2]

Ordinary people will believe anything, Bayle argues, because they are lazy and unwilling to analyze their beliefs, but even his learned correspondent apparently prefers the authority of poets and historians over the evidence of his eyes. The poets, however, will make us believe that "Heaven and Earth move at their orders,"[3] that the world is full of monsters, and that comets are portents of events the poets will invent if they cannot find them. And while the poets see a hidden intention everywhere and invent meaning where there is none, the reports of historians are no better: They are only too pleased "to compile everything that smells of miracles" to make their dry histories more interesting and inflate their pretensions to philosophy. They should stay in their archives and interpret documents. When it comes to the workings of nature, "*Messieurs* the Historians have no authority and must be regarded as simple privateers who hazard a conjecture."[4] As for the wisdom of tradition, it is altogether worthless in this respect. If historians have no expertise on the subject, it does not matter how many of them have been of the same ignorant opinion. The crowd will uncritically believe whatever others hold to be true and will be careful not to contradict received wisdom.

An uncompromising champion of skepticism, Bayle attacks the beliefs about the supernatural qualities of comets, using arguments from science as well as philosophy and literary history, and discrediting any reliance on the philosophers of antiquity to explain natural phenomena. The authority of ancient accounts is portrayed as especially unreliable because it is, after all, nothing more than a plebiscite of the past, and truth is found not in the number of believers but in the facts alone. "I say it once again; it as an illusion through and through to assume that a sentiment which has passed from century to century, & from generation to generation, could not be entirely false."[5] In a world in which the authority of an ancient book, the Bible, reigns supreme and its theological interpreters are said to possess the sole key to the truth handed down through the ages, this viewpoint is radical. Faith might be important in God's realm, but in the physical world, only skeptical reason and empirical inquiry could and should determine the nature and significance of physical phenomena. Religion is dethroned.

In the philosophical context of the time, any argument about truth and history is necessarily an argument about the truth of religion, for if the ancients are not to be relied on, divine revelation itself becomes uncertain. This is dangerous, theologians repeated over and over again, for only faith in God and his laws elevates humans above animals and saves their immortal souls. Bayle is not convinced. As far as the soul is concerned, he does not doubt its existence, of course; he simply regrets that the many excellent people who had died in the past had not troubled to make themselves known from beyond the grave to allay all doubts of their living friends.

The question of faith is more complicated. Citing abundant contemporary examples of pious but corrupt and cruel princes and lecherous priests, Bayle concludes that simply being a Christian does not necessarily lead to a virtuous life. As the apocalyptic hysteria surrounding Halley's comet showed, religious people can be superstitious and even downright immoral; their faith does not elevate them over pagans. But what about unbelievers? Orthodox opinion and popular stereotype use "atheist" synonymously with "scoundrel," but, writes Bayle, there is no reason to suppose that a commonwealth of atheists, a society of unbelievers, could not be as just as any other society, as long as it respects the principles of justice and virtue. Virtuous living, Bayle argues, is based on just laws and principles, not on religion, and it is therefore possible to be at the same time atheist and virtuous. As long as it gave itself clear moral rules, a society of atheists could function just as well as any other, its citizens just as trustworthy, charitable, passionate for justice, and loyal to their friends as any other.

There is one final step implicit in this argument, but never spelled out: If religion serves to explain the world and to organize society, yet it is unable to offer adequate explanations and is thus useless for a life well lived, then what use is it? Bayle leaves it to the reader to arrive at this question and draw the inevitable conclusions for themselves.

It is tempting to imagine young Denis Diderot poring over Bayle's *Dictionnaire*, his face flushed with excitement. After all, no work was reprinted more often and disseminated more widely around the beginning of the eighteenth century than this one, and no self-respecting library, certainly not a Jesuit library, would be without it. At his Paris college, the teenage Denis would have been expected to consult it regularly. Now, fifteen years later, Bayle's strategies of dissimulation became a model for the great project of the *Encyclopédie*, as well as one of its resources for articles about philosophy and history.

Previously, in his 1743 *Pensées philosophiques*, Diderot had made it clear how much he owed to the Huguenot scholar. Mentioning him in the august company of Descartes, Montaigne, and Locke (three other great skeptics), the young philosopher had promptly attached a "profession of faith" that began in disingenuously fulsome tones, only to end in a skeptical flourish: "I am born in the Catholic Apostolic and Roman Church, and I submit to its decisions with all my strength. I want to die in the religion of my fathers, and I believe it is right as far as it is possible to believe for someone who has never had any direct commerce with the Deity and who has never been witness to any miracles."[6] Could a conscientious intellectual be expected to say more? And yet did this profession of piety not contain the possibility of pure unbelief? As Diderot commented about the expected response of his dogmatic opponents, "they won't be satisfied with this, even if not one of them may be able to make a better one." Honesty—a dangerous game, as Bayle had taught him—was often tantamount to open dissent.

Bayle's lesson was valuable to the editors of the *Encyclopédie* in their planning of the great enterprise, for which they would have to write or commission and coordinate thousands of articles from hundreds of authors. While Chambers's *Cyclopaedia* gave the impetus for the project and suggested an alphabetical order from the start, reading Bayle had lent the enterprise its intellectual weight, its method, and its true, subversive potential. In addition to a detailed survey of the natural world as well as of arts and crafts, it would be a panorama of philosophical dissent—always cushioned by careful and carefully orthodox refutations, enough to placate the censors or at least to make it impossible for them to object.

Nor could the censors take issue with the fact that some biblical themes were treated to loving, detailed, and literal examination, none more so than the story of Noah's ark. In his article on the subject, the *abbé* Edme Mallet, an obscure author (either a pious blockhead or a revolutionary genius), calculated exactly how many species of animals there were on earth; how much water, hay, and sheep (for the carnivores) would have to be taken on board; how much mucking out there would have been every day (the only men on board were Noah and his two sons); how the animals would have to be distributed so that the vessel would not capsize; how the ventilation of the stables would have to be organized; and so forth. Needless to say, the measurements and numbers he came up with were grotesquely large. Even if one assumed that the carnivores would eat no more than 27 wolves and the herbivores were no more hungry than 208 head of cattle, Mallet calculates that the ark would have to load 9.6 million gallons of water, 47,000 cubic meters of hay, and so on. The mythical story evaporates under the microscope of literal-minded piety.

If the stories of the Bible could be turned against themselves, pagan rituals could also be used to reflect back on Christianity. In principle, attacking paganism was a perfectly respectable thing to do—but in the *Encyclopédie*, many of these cults seem to overlap suspiciously with certain Christian rituals and beliefs. A Roman cult featuring a dove? Ludicrous! Virgin birth in Egyptian myth? Preposterous! The ruse is transparent but effective. The cross-references also have a sting in their tail. The entry "Eucharist" contains the reference "see: Cannibalism," and other references are similarly barbed.

While the duplicity of many of the articles dealing with religious themes was designed to introduce an element of doubt in the most pious of minds, other tactics ensured that the world according to the *Encyclopédie* was populated not by saints and kings but by honest, hardworking folk, by the largely anonymous, decent workers in the streets and in the fields—an unusually democratic vision for the eighteenth century, valuing facts and productive work over everything else. Diderot decided not to include biographical entries, so that the emphasis lay not on great men but on ideas, objective knowledge, and manual work. The *Encyclopédie* would literally lavish far more attention on the manufacture of a pin than on the rituals of the coronation. Decent, industrious people are the heart of society, these entries insinuate, while the article on bees suggests, if only implicitly, that the unproductive, useless drones (who are killed by the worker bees) are remarkably like aristocrats.

The project of the *Encyclopédie* was to be a battering ram, shaking the foundations of the age. Diderot could not yet know that it would occupy most of his working life for more than a quarter of a century and would eventually span seventeen volumes of text running to 18,000 pages, more than 20 million words, and eleven volumes containing some 1,900 lavish and detailed engravings, but he was already aware that it was an ambitious idea, one that could decide his literary fate.

The booksellers, meanwhile, wanted to secure their investment. The *Encyclopédie* was a huge undertaking, involving scores of specialist authors and correspondents and thousands of detailed illustrations of the arts, crafts, and sciences, as well as typesetters, paper merchants, printers, and bookbinders. It represented a very substantial initial great investment. Diderot could not carry it off alone, and the book dealers insisted on taking on board a coeditor well-known and respected as a man of science. Diderot might be brilliant, they appear to have argued, but nobody had ever heard of him.

A brilliant mind: The mathematician Jean Le Rond d'Alembert was appointed coeditor of the Encyclopédie, *but he was unable to grasp the project's full political implications. Pastel portrait by Maurice-Quentin de la Tour, circa 1750.*

RÉUNION DES MUSÉES NATIONAUX / ART RESOURCE, NY

The booksellers needed a name, and they found one in none other than Jean-Baptiste d'Alembert (1717–1783), the illegitimate son of the great salon hostess Mme de Tencin. D'Alembert was a brilliant mathematician who was already a member of the Academy of Sciences, a man with connections at court, the young star of scientific France. Always a woman with a great zest for life, Mme de Tencin had decided not to keep her newborn and had left him, in a space provided for such occasions, on the steps of the Chapel of Saint Jean-le-Rond. The boy had been adopted by a glazier and his wife, but it appears that his biological parents (his father was an officer and a count) made sure that the child would want for nothing and gave him the protection he needed to get a good education and start his career. Prodigiously gifted and extremely ambitious, the young man had soon made a name for himself in the scientific community. He was a star, and Diderot was not.

In 1748–1749, as the publication of the first volume of the *Encyclopédie* was drawing near, Diderot decided to raise his own profile. He needed d'Alembert, but he was also jealous of the younger man, who was, partly through protection but undoubtedly also through dazzling intellectual achievements, already famous. Diderot needed a striking, important work of his own that would finally secure his reputation and ensure that the names Diderot and d'Alembert could be printed in the same large letters on the title page of the great *Encyclopédie*, whose first volume was planned for 1750.

It was here that Diderot overplayed his hand. In the wake of a sensational case of a cataract operation that succeeded in restoring the sight of a girl who had been blind from birth, he published—anonymously of course—a short book entitled *Lettre sur les aveugles à l'usage de ceux qui voient* (*Letter on the*

Blind for the Benefit of Those Who See), rather disingenuously pretending to explore how the world might appear to those who are born blind. Relating a conversation with a blind man in Paris, the author writes that sightless people have moral ideas that are different from those of the sighted. To the blind the worst crime is theft, to which they are terribly vulnerable, while the idea of public indecency simply has no meaning to them at all. They wear clothes not out of modesty or fashion, but simply to cover themselves against the elements. Morality, therefore, is not universal or revealed but must depend on the physical constitution and social context of each individual. Moral ideas are specific to a particular place or time, not the product of divine revelation.

Diderot then turned to the case of the blind Cambridge mathematician Nicholas Saunderson (1682–1739), who was rather ironically an authority on the laws of optics. In an imaginary deathbed conversation with a priest, who praises the beauty of nature as a proof for God's existence, the mathematician explains that references to physical beauty accessible to sight only are useless to him: "If you want me to believe in your God, you must let me touch him." The priest tries to make him see the ineffable mystery of creation, but this argument, too, fails to convince the sightless scholar. People will see God's work behind all things they do not understand, he says, a case of simple vanity and a wonderful excuse for ignorance, but "if nature presents us a knot which is difficult to untangle, let us leave it as it appears and let us not cut it with a hand of a being which will afterwards become a knot even more impossible to untangle than the first."[7]

Assuming a Creator, Diderot argued, did not solve the problem at hand; it merely veiled it behind a cloud of incense. If one admits that one cannot explain the origin of the universe and the significance of its existence with physical laws alone, then positing the solution "therefore it must be God's work" is simply lazy and even narcissistic. The knot of nature may be impossible to disentangle, but introducing the idea of a being who does not obey laws such as cause and effect and who cannot even be perceived, an uncreated Creator, simply makes the knot more complicated. The existence of the universe can be attributed to God's ineffable will, but assuming something so contrary to experience and common sense causes logic to collapse and marks the end of rational thought, our only trustworthy guide in this world. To a person blind since birth, the only reality comes by hearing and by touch or smell, while the rest is hearsay and therefore unreliable. It can be talked about by inference, even if people who are trustworthy in other ways vouch for the fact that they themselves have perceived it. Those who are in command of all their senses may have a larger reality, but they have no way of talking sensibly about anything that lies beyond the senses, a reality vouchsafed by no one's direct experience and yet apparently the most important reality of all. A realm of meaning beyond our sensual experience is like the beauty of a sunset to a blind eye: a story, a metaphor, nothing more. The deist who had flirted with atheism had finally taken sides.

The authorities were fooled neither by the subject nor by the anonymity of its author. They saw the book for what it was: a thinly veiled sensualist attack on the idea of a Creator who is invisible and indeed unperceivable. In 1747 Diderot had been denounced by his parish priest, Hardy Levaré, who had described Denis' scandalous views to the police:

> The remarks that Diderot sometimes makes in his household clearly prove that he is a deist, if no worse. He utters blasphemies against Jesus Christ and the Holy Virgin that I would not venture to put into writing. . . . It is true that I have never spoken to this young man and do not know him personally, but I am told that he has a great deal of wit and that his conversation is very amusing. In one of his conversations he admitted being the author of one of the two works condemned by the *Parlement* and burned about two years ago. I have been informed that for more than a year he has been working on another work still more dangerous to religion.[8]

This work, which was reputedly Diderot's most dangerous to date, was the *Lettre sur les aveugles*, and this time he had gone too far. He was arrested, imprisoned, and awaited an uncertain fate. After several weeks of solitary confinement, during which he felt that he was almost driven insane by fear and loneliness, the conditions of his imprisonment were eased somewhat, and he could even receive visitors.

His most faithful caller was his closest friend, Jean-Jacques Rousseau, who had finally settled in the French capital after having spent some months as a minor diplomat in Venice and then as private secretary and scientific factotum

The Bear: Even as a young man, Jean-Jacques Rousseau was a restless spirit. His initial close friendship with Diderot was later destroyed by Rousseau's paranoia.
BRIDGEMAN-GIRAUDON / ART RESOURCE, NY

to another wealthy lady. Having left the service of this second protectress, he was now making a very modest living as a music copyist while working on another opera. Denis and Jean-Jacques had forged a strong bond. They had met with a group of like-minded young men every week for evenings of discussions and music. Rousseau had played the harpsichord during the long sessions in his lodgings. He and Diderot had shared their ambitions and their dreams of recognition, and now Jean-Jacques walked two hours to Vincennes and back to be with his unhappy friend in the prison yard.

For Rousseau, these acts of kindness to a friend turned into one of the most fruitful periods of his life. During one of his visits, he had talked of plans to enter an essay competition on the role of the arts and sciences in improving the lot of humanity. According to his memoirs, the *Confessions*, Diderot advised him not to argue the obvious line in celebration of the arts but to strike a paradoxical note, showing how increasing civilization had made humans more decadent and corrupted their morals. Rousseau took the advice, submitted the essay, and won the competition, a feat that made him a minor literary celebrity. The fame he craved so much finally seemed within his reach.

The paradoxical method Diderot had suggested worked wonderfully in the hands of Rousseau, who was a contrarian by nature. His essay, entitled "Discourse on the Arts and Sciences," already contains key elements of his later thinking. Instead of freeing humanity of the immediate necessities and perils of a life in nature, the arts and sciences had in fact enslaved civilized societies: "They stifle in men's breasts that sense of original liberty, for which they seem to have been born; cause them to love their own slavery, and so make of them what is called a civilised people."[9] Before becoming the "happy slaves" they were now, humans had a morality that was "crude but natural" and based exclusively on immediate desires and needs. People may not have been better at heart, but they were not yet spoiled by the decadent and perverse pleasures of civilization.

Rousseau's argument, that the luxurious life of civilized peoples ultimately makes them decadent, had been familiar since antiquity, but it was a daring move to apply the idea to a civilization that regarded itself as the greatest the world had ever seen, and naturally the highest because of its Christian faith. The Greeks might have had virtue and high achievements, but they had been pagans after all, as were the Romans. Even the great Italian poet Dante had placed the most noble souls from the ancient world in purgatory because they had not yet partaken of the revealed Truth. Rousseau, however, claimed that far from being great, the arts and sciences did nothing but make people weak, vain, and idle and sap their virtues.

The "Discourse" made Rousseau famous as a courageous thinker willing to question what others took for granted, and it was also his first appearance as a philosopher in his own right. With the essay's publication, he was set on a course that would eventually turn him against all society—and even against his friends.

While Jean-Jacques and his embattled friend Denis were debating philosophical questions in the courtyard of the fortress of Vincennes, the associated booksellers who were to publish the *Encyclopédie* were pleading with the chief of police and the ministry of the interior for Diderot's release. Their main argument was not the right to due process or freedom of speech, but the simple fact that the great publishing project helped to secure French jobs, which might otherwise all too easily be lost to foreign cities like Amsterdam, Geneva, or Berlin. Eventually, this pragmatic argument convinced the relevant authorities, and the editor was set free—though not without having first signed a letter in which he promised never again to write and publish anything blasphemous, on pain of returning to prison with no hope of release. For those who wonder why Diderot never produced a substantial philosophical work, it may be instructive to recall this letter. Throughout his life, the letter lay in some ministerial drawer, a continuous threat at a time when long periods of imprisonment and even executions were still common for all works contradicting the teachings of the church.

For Diderot, who was now thirty-five, the release brought the approbation he had sought: He was hailed as a martyr for the cause of the Enlightenment and even received the official blessing of the movement's father figure, Voltaire, who wrote to the former prisoner, congratulated him on his liberation, and referred to him as a modern Socrates. He invited Diderot to visit his castle, an honor bestowed only on the most skilled and important men of letters. Diderot acknowledged congratulations in an effusive letter of thanks but excused himself from traveling to see the great man. He preferred to keep his distance from Voltaire, whom he suspected of playing his own game and using and even sacrificing his friends to further his own reputation. In later years, it would become apparent how wise Diderot's caution had been.

Published in 1751, the first volume of the *Encyclopédie*, covering "A" to "Azymites," was a great critical success, though it was by no means perfect. Diderot himself was the first to acknowledge that it was almost impossible to maintain an equal level of quality and expertise throughout a work to which so many authors had contributed. In the entry "*Encyclopédie*" he would later impart to his readers a sense of the frustrations of his daily work of commissioning and editing individual texts:

> Here we are swollen and exorbitant, and there meagre, small, paltry, and emaciated. In another place we looked like skeletons; in another, we have appeared inflated; we are alternatively dwarfs and giants, colossi and pygmies; straight, well proportioned; humpbacked, limping and malformed. Add to all these grotesque forms a discourse that is now abstract, obscure or far-fetched; but more often sloppy, long-winded and its lack; and you had to compare as the monsters appearing in poetry. . . . But these faults are inseparable from the first attempt . . . and later centuries will correct them.[10]

Later centuries have corrected many of the mistakes contained in this magnificent work, but these corrections have taken away nothing from the overall achievement. In the end, it was not so much the intellectual quality or factual

ENCYCLOPÉDIE,

OU

DICTIONNAIRE RAISONNÉ

DES SCIENCES,

DES ARTS ET DES MÉTIERS.

A A

A & *a*, ſ. m. (*ordre Encyclopéd. Entend. Science de l'homme, Logique, Art de communiquer, Gramm.*) caractere ou figure de la premiere lettre de l'Alphabet, en latin, en françois, & en preſque toutes les Langues de l'Europe.

On peut conſidérer ce caractere, ou comme lettre, ou comme mot.

I. A, en tant que lettre, eſt le ſigne du ſon *a*, qui de tous les ſons de la voix eſt le plus facile à prononcer. Il ne faut qu'ouvrir la bouche & pouſſer l'air des poumons.

On dit que l'*a* vient de l'*aleph* des Hébreux: mais l'*a* en tant que ſon ne vient que de la conformation des organes de la parole; & le caractere ou figure dont nous nous ſervons pour repréſenter ce ſon, nous vient de l'*alpha* des Grecs. Les Latins & les autres peuples de l'Europe ont imité les Grecs dans la forme qu'ils ont donnée à cette lettre. Selon les Grammaires Hébraïques, & la Grammaire générale de P. R. p. 12. l'*aleph ne ſert* (aujourd'hui) *que pour l'écriture, & n'a aucun ſon que celui de la voyelle qui lui eſt jointe*. Cela fait voir que la prononciation des lettres eſt ſujette à variation dans les Langues mortes, comme elle l'eſt dans les Langues vivantes. Car il eſt conſtant, ſelon M. Maſclef & le P. Houbigant, que l'*aleph* ſe prononçoit autrefois comme notre *a*; ce qu'ils prouvent ſurtout par le paſſage d'Euſebe, *Prép. Ev.* liv. X. c. vj. où ce P. ſoutient que les Grecs ont pris leurs lettres des Hébreux: *Id ex Græcâ ſingulorum elementorum appellatione quivis intelligit. Quid enim aleph ab alpha magnopere differt? Quid autem vel betha a beth?* &c.

Quelques Auteurs (Covarruvias) diſent, que lorſque les enfans viennent au monde, les mâles font entendre le ſon de l'*a*, qui eſt la premiere voyelle de *mas*, & les filles le ſon de l'*e*, premiere voyelle de *femina*: mais c'eſt une imagination ſans fondement. Quand les enfans viennent au monde, & que pour la premiere fois ils pouſſent l'air des poumons, on entend le ſon de différentes voyelles, ſelon qu'ils ouvrent plus ou moins la bouche.

Tome I.

On dit *un grand A, un petit a*: ainſi *a* eſt du genre maſculin, comme les autres voyelles de notre alphabet.

Le ſon de l'*a*, auſſi bien que celui de l'*e*, eſt long en certains mots, & bref en d'autres: *a* eſt long dans *grâce*, & bref dans *place*. Il eſt long dans *tâche* quand ce mot ſignifie un ouvrage qu'on donne à faire; & il eſt bref dans *tache*, *macula*, ſouillure. Il eſt long dans *mâtin*, gros chien; & bref dans *matin*, premiere partie du jour. *Voyez l'excellent Traité de la Proſodie de M. l'Abbé d'Olivet.*

Les Romains, pour marquer l'*a* long, l'écrivirent d'abord double, *Aala* pour *Ala*; c'eſt ainſi qu'on trouve dans nos anciens Auteurs François *aage*, &c. Enſuite ils inſérerent un *h* entre les deux *a*, *Ahala*. Enfin ils mettoient quelquefois le ſigne de la ſyllabe longue, *āla*.

On met aujourd'hui un accent circonflexe ſur l'*a* long, au lieu de l'*ſ* qu'on écrivoit autrefois après cet *a*: ainſi au lieu d'écrire *maſtin*, *blaſme*, *aſne*, &c. on écrit *mâtin*, *blâme*, *âne*. Mais il ne faut pas croire avec la plûpart des Grammairiens, que nos peres n'écrivoient cette *ſ* après l'*a*, ou après toute autre voyelle, que pour marquer que cette voyelle étoit longue: ils écrivoient cette *ſ*, parce qu'ils la prononçoient; & cette prononciation eſt encore en uſage dans nos Provinces méridionales, où l'on prononce *maſtin*, *teſte*, *beſte*, &c.

On ne met point d'accent ſur l'*a* bref ou commun.

L'*a* chez les Romains étoit appellé *lettre ſalutaire*: *littera ſalutaris*. Cic. Attic. ix. 7. parce que lorſqu'il s'agiſſoit d'abſoudre ou de condamner un accuſé, les

A

Victory! Pictured here is the first page of the first volume of the Encyclopédie. *When the first volume was published in 1751, the progressive faction had won an important battle against the church and censorship.*

reliability of the entries but the sheer perseverance of the project and the fact that it was published against the massed opposition of all conservative factions in the land, both at court and in the church, where the Jesuits could not forgive the Encyclopedists for fishing in their scholarly waters, while the Jansenist parliamentarians saw it as a threat to their authority and to the piety of the people. Despite all of this enmity, the *Encyclopédie* was a publishing success and stands as a defining moment in the intellectual history of Europe, a point at which skeptical reason won over orthodoxy, and an important inspiration to the next generation—the generation of the Revolution.

Around the year 1750, this achievement was a glorious but distant prospect for the embattled editors. The project was desperately in need of competent authors, and Diderot was therefore more than pleased when one of his friends introduced him to a wealthy and knowledgeable young man who had just returned from his studies in the Netherlands, one Paul Thiry d'Holbach. Because the correspondence between Diderot and Holbach has been lost, it is not possible to say who brought the two together. Holbach's salon was beginning to attract like-minded people, and on his release from Vincennes Diderot had become a minor celebrity, a man about whom Voltaire had written many flattering things. It is therefore likely that Holbach invited the courageous philosopher to dinner, prompted, perhaps, by Rousseau, who appears already to have been in Holbach's circle.

The exact circumstances of their encounter are unknown, but Holbach did not contribute to the first volume, which appeared in 1751 and would have been ready to go to press when the two men first met in late 1749 or early 1750. When the second volume appeared in 1752, the editors noted in the preface: "We particularly are indebted to one person, whose mother tongue is German, and who is very well versed in the matters of mineralogy, metallurgy and physics; he has given us a prodigious amount of articles on different subjects, of which already a considerable number is included in this volume." Thiry d'Holbach had officially joined the encyclopedic endeavor.

CHAPTER 4

CHEZ M. HOLBACH

When Thiry d'Holbach returned to Paris from the Netherlands in 1748, he brought with him new ideas and a great hunger for intellectual discovery. Possessing an independent income from his uncle, the young baron hesitated for a while, unsure what to do with himself. He married and acquired a license to practice law, but he never worked as a lawyer. Instead, he acquired a fine scientific library, collected works of art and thousands of mineralogical specimens, and tried to find a way into the scientific establishment. When he heard of the *Encyclopédie*, he did not hesitate to offer his services to its editor. He would write more than three hundred articles on scientific themes as well as translating a whole shelf full of scientific and philosophical books (most importantly the great poem *De rerum natura* by the Roman philosopher Lucretius).

Holbach knew how to keep himself busy and use his wealth to a constructive end, but he still felt unsuited to a life of a private scholar, sitting at home and studying rock samples. He craved company and new ideas, the cut and thrust and challenge of open debate. Apart from the different academies and other scientific establishments, the intellectual meeting places of Paris were the great salons, but these were not meant for intense philosophical discussions. Respectable ladies moderated polite conversation and readings from new literary work; open controversy was largely avoided.

Pining for something more substantial, akin to the all-night student dinners of his Leiden days, Holbach decided to revive them by himself. Essentially, it

Baron Paul Thiry d'Holbach was called "master of the Café de l'Europe." Secretly he was also an important atheist author. Anonymous engraving after a drawing by Charles-Nicholas Cochin, circa 1758.

was the combination of Holbach's gracious and generous hospitality and Diderot's connections that made the salon such an important meeting place. From the beginning of his association with the *Encyclopédie*, the baron contributed hundreds of articles to the project, initially on scientific questions such as geology and mineralogy, but later also on topics such as priests and theocracy. His involvement made it natural for other Encyclopedists to frequent his house, where the more radical-minded among them could say openly what they could never commit to print, and so Holbach received a steady stream of freethinking and knowledgeable guests, first and foremost Denis Diderot, who was delighted to find a place where he could indulge his greatest passion: talking with his friends, provoking his opponents, and entertaining those who were as yet undecided.

Among Holbach's regular guests who also contributed to the *Encyclopédie* during the early 1750s were Jean-Jacques Rousseau, who wrote on music; the literary critic Jean-François Marmontel; the ebullient Charles-Georges Le Roy, the lieutenant of the Royal Hunt, whose contributions included entries on deer, hunting, and instinct; the career officer Jean-François de Saint-Lambert, who was also an accomplished poet; and the engineer and historical scholar Nicolas-Antoine Boulanger. An evening would typically have consisted of a reading of a new piece written by one of the guests and a discussion of politics, philosophy, or history. Sharing gossip mingled with ideas, guests from abroad would bring foreign news, which would immediately be compared with the situation in France, while scientists came with new experiments and half-thought-out theories or with stories gleaned from colleagues—all this in an atmosphere that was both freer and less deferential than at the other Parisian salons. After all, this was not a debate supervised by a grand hostess (Mme d'Holbach was tactful enough not to insist on this role). Instead, the host was a scientist himself, and his opinions were likely to be more radical than those of his most daring guests.

The unique character of Holbach's salon, as well as his chef's enviable reputation and his particularly good wine cellar, soon attracted some of the city's most brilliant minds and most discerning diners, and while there is no surviving menu detailing what exactly was served on a particular evening, we get a fair idea of the dishes prepared for the table of a wealthy man from Vincent de la Chapelle's famous cookbook *Le Cuisinier moderne* (1735), which helpfully supplies a sample menu for *une bonne table bourgeoise*, a dinner for fourteen to twenty people at a town house not of a great aristocrat, but of a wealthy man like Holbach, who loved his food and was renowned for his hospitality. La Chapelle makes the following suggestion for a dinner:

A MENU

For fourteen diners, & which can serve twenty for dinner

FIRST COURSE

For the centerpiece one dish for all which stays during the entire course

AT TWO ENDS, TWO SOUPS

1 CABBAGE SOUP

1 CUCUMBER SOUP

4 ENTRÉES FOR THE 4 CORNERS OF THE CENTERPIECE

1 PIGEON TART

1 DISH OF TWO *POULETS À LA REINE*, WITH AN APPETIZING SAUCE

1 VEAL BREAST IN CHICKEN FRICASSEE

1 OXTAIL IN HOTCHPOTCH

6 HORS-D'OEUVRES FOR THE TWO SIDES AND THE 4 CORNERS OF THE CENTERPIECE

1 DISH OF GRILLED MUTTON

1 OF OX PALATES IN SMALL STRIPS

I RABBIT BLACK PUDDING

I CAULIFLOWER IN BREAD

2 HORS-D'OEUVRES OF LITTLE APPETIZING PÂTÉS
FOR THE TWO FLANKS OF THE CENTERPIECE

SECOND COURSE

2 additions for the two soups

I PIECE OF BEEF

I OF VEAL GRILLED ON A SPIT

THIRD COURSE

Roasts and side dishes together

4 ROAST DISHES AT THE 4 CORNERS OF THE CENTERPIECE

I OF CHICKEN

I OF THREE PHEASANTS

I OF EIGHTEEN LARKS

I OF ONE ROUEN DUCK

2 SALADS

2 SIDE DISHES FOR BOTH ENDS

I MEAT PIE

I COLD PÂTÉ

4 SMALL SIDE DISHES FOR THE FOUR CORNERS

I OF CREAM FRITTERS

I OF SMALL GREEN BEANS

I OF TRUFFLES IN BOUILLON

I OF RASPBERRY GELÉE

{ FOURTH COURSE }

Dessert

FOR THE TWO ENDS OF THE CENTERPIECE

2 LARGE BOWLS OF FRUIT

FOR THE TWO SIDES

2 BOWLS OF WAFFLES

FOR THE 4 CORNERS

4 COMPOTES OF VARIOUS FRUITS

4 DISHES OF DIFFERENT JAMS[1]

Add to this the appropriate wines—Holbach was fond of good burgundy, and his cellar was as famous as his table—and it is not surprising that Diderot constantly complained of indigestion. Indeed, his letters are full of references to overindulgence: "I'm growing round like a ball, how you are going to detest me!" (October 20, 1760); "my gallbladder is swollen, I have taken to moralizing" (September 22, 1761); "I have eaten like a wolf cub. . . . I drank wines with all sorts of names; a melon of incredible perfidy was waiting for me; and do you think that it was possible to resist the enormous ice cream? And then the liqueurs; and then the café, and then an abominable digestion which has kept me on my feet all night, and which made me pass the morning between the tea pot and another vessel, which decency forbids me to name" (June 5, 1765); "my stomach and my intestines are in a miserable state" (July 25, 1765)[2]—the list goes on.

The earliest guests at Holbach's table would remain regulars for a quarter of a century, helping shape what was to become a pivotal moment of Western intellectual history. Their biographies provide a sense of the atmosphere of the salon.

Perhaps the grandest among the guests those first years was Georges-Louis Leclerc de Buffon (1707–1788), the famous director of the Royal Botanical Gardens as well as main author of the *Histoire naturelle, générale et particulière, avec la description du Cabinet du Roy*, in thirty-six volumes (*Natural History,*

General and Particular, with a Description of the Royal Collections, 1749 to 1789), and general science genius extraordinaire, who attended for several years before quietly drifting on to the salon of Mme de Geoffrin.

As director of the Royal Botanical Gardens, one of Europe's foremost scientific establishments, Buffon conducted his project of enlarging the collection and gathering specimens from all over the known world with single-minded energy. His real passion, though, was the *Histoire naturelle*, nothing less than a compendium of all knowledge about the natural world, for which he, aided by several assistants, measured, classified, described, reclassified, and redescribed tirelessly. Like many great scientists he believed that knowledge must be built up from observation: "It is only through refined, reasoned and coherent experience that one forces nature to uncover its secrets; all other methods have never been known to work."[3] Such insistence on observation and due care might be expected from a man whose professional life consisted of comparing skulls and leaf shapes, but this comparative method also bore surprising and even humbling revelations. The human being, he wrote, must take his place "in the class of animals, whom he resembles in everything material."[4] Far from being the crown of creation, humans are a part of nature, different from all other animals by degree, but not by kind, only a few nuances away from monkeys, dogs, and horses. La Mettrie had already suggested this, but it was still heresy.

Buffon was careful to sugar the pill for his readers, but it was bitter nonetheless. They could set themselves at the head of creation and look down, but what they saw from there gave scarce comfort. The human being an animal? Humans, the zoologist implied, were mere apes, distinguished from those hairy creatures in the cages of the *jardin du roi* not by kind, but merely by degree, by "imperceptible nuances." Despite the fact that he invoked the Creator every now and then in a show of outward piety, the consequences of his work were there for everyone to see. Buffon worked right at the cutting edge of the science of his day. Drawing on the observations and theories of the French mathematician and explorer Pierre Louis Maupertuis, who also defended the idea that species could mutate and develop over time, Buffon roundly rejected the belief that the earth could have been created in six days and that there was a fixed pyramid of species with humans on top, an immutable natural order. The fossil record suggested otherwise; indeed, it suggested not only that a human was an animal among others, but that all animals continued to change in patterns much like in a game of chance (an image often employed by Diderot) and in all possible different ways, developing in response to pressures in the world around them.

Buffon found an eager audience for his ideas, particularly in Holbach and Diderot, who wrote: "It appears that nature took pleasure in varying the same mechanism in an infinity of different ways. She never abandons one kind of production until she has multiplied individuals of all possible kinds."[5] Nature was in permanent flux, and humans were part of this great change. "Who knows which races of animals have preceded us? Who knows the animal races which will succeed ours?" Diderot was later to write, "Everything changes, everything passes, only the whole remains constant. The world begins and ends without cease. . . . In this immense ocean of matter, no molecule resembles another. . . . There is nothing dependable but drinking, eating, living, loving and sleeping."[6]

The influence exercised by the naturalist Buffon on the friends of the rue Royale was profound, but he himself eventually retreated from the salon. Despite his intellectual radicalism, his well-known gregariousness, and his love of good food—even during his journey to Italy his letters told of great meals enjoyed, not great cultural sites visited—he was only an infrequent guest at Holbach's table and eventually ceased attending altogether. In his memoirs, the salon habitué Jean-François Marmontel gave two unflattering reasons for the count's sudden disappearance. First, Marmontel suggested, Buffon was too much of a careerist to associate himself with so controversial and precarious an enterprise as the *Encyclopédie*. Second, he was used to being surrounded by flatterers and toadies and to being the center of attention. At Holbach's, however, "he had the vexation of seeing that the mathematicians, the chemists, the astronomers, granted him but a very inferior rank among them; that the naturalists themselves were but little disposed to put him at their head, and that, among men of letters, he obtained only the slender praise of an elegant writer, and a great colorist."[7] Surrounded by other stars, his sun shone less brightly.

It was no easy thing to retain the upper hand in the company of brilliant minds; eventually the mutual respect between the eminent botanist and the other guests became eroded, and Buffon hardly ever appeared at the gatherings.

In 1760, when he put in an exceptional visit to the rue Royale in the company of his wife, an acerbic Diderot wrote, "M[onsieur] and M[adame] de Buffon arrived. I have seen Madame. She no longer has a neck. Her chin has made half of the way, her tits the other half; now her three chins are resting on two well-stuffed pillows."[8] To Diderot's malicious eye, the great man's wife herself had become evidence of her husband's theory of the changeability of all organic things.

Jean-François Marmontel (1723–1799), the one who so perceptively analyzed Buffon's reasons for staying away from Holbach's salon, also wrote an affectionate—if remarkably tame—portrait of the baron's dinners:

> We were no longer led and held by leading strings, as at Madame Geoffrin's. But this liberty was not license, and there are revered and inviolable objects that were never submitted to the debate of opinions. God, virtue, the holy laws of natural morality, were never subjected to doubt, at least in my presence; this I can attest. . . . It was there that Baron D'Holbach, who had read everything, and forgotten nothing interesting, poured out abundantly the riches of his memory; it was there above all, with his mild and persuasive eloquence, and his face sparkling with the fire of inspiration, that Diderot spread light into every mind, and his warmth into every heart. He who has only known Diderot by his writings has not known him.[9]

This chaste portrait of literary gentlemen politely conversing about the mysteries of nature without ever calling into question "God, virtue, the holy laws of natural morality" is a classic case of protesting too much: At the time he wrote these lines, Marmontel was no longer a young radical but a pillar of society, permanent secretary of the Académie Française as well as royal historiographer to Louis XVI, not a man eager to advertise his erstwhile membership in a group of atheists and troublemakers. As the official chronicler implied in his defense, he was once surrounded by the air of freedom but did not inhale.

Marmontel was known as a bit of a pedant, as Diderot reported to his long-term mistress, Sophie Volland, in 1762: "Last Thursday I dined with the baron. Marmontel was there. . . . Nobody has more wit, more knowledge, and more logic than Marmontel; but why spoil all that with a self-importance and a hard-headedness that nobody can stand?"[10]

Among the other regulars were several *abbés*, particularly André Morellet and Guillaume-Thomas Raynal, both clergymen by title only. It was common then for scientists and private scholars to become *abbés* and to continue holding this title even if their work and their thinking had taken them far from the teachings of the church. The caustic and witty André Morellet (1727–1819), or *Abbé Mords-les* (bite them) as Voltaire had dubbed him, also ceased regular attendance, and for reasons similar to Buffon's. Constantly frustrated in his efforts to outshine the effusive Diderot, he was once heard protesting that one "simply couldn't get a word in edgewise" when the philosopher was in full flight.

Guillaume-Thomas Raynal (1713–1796), on the other hand, was never lost for words, and his wit was a foil even for Diderot. Having started his career as a Jesuit priest in Toulouse, he had left the Society in 1747 and become chaplain of Saint-Sulpice in Paris. He obviously failed to take his duties and obligations seriously, because very shortly after his arrival he was accused of burying Protestants in hallowed ground for sixty livres apiece, a nice little supplementary income for a priest always in need of money. He tried to support himself as a tutor and ghostwriter of sermons, but eventually he drifted into literary journalism and began to frequent the most exclusive salons, particularly that of Mme Geoffrin and soon also that of Holbach. Rousseau writes about having met him in 1748, and he can therefore be regarded as a friend of the first hour.

Polite, intelligent, and always well informed, Raynal knew how to navigate Parisian society and not only was able to get some lucrative pensions but also became editor of the famous *Mercure de France*, an influential intellectual journal. Eventually he would turn his hand to political philosophy and write a major work, *Voyage aux deux Indes*, on France's dealings with its colonies and on intercultural trade in general. Diderot collaborated on the volume and was inspired to write one of his most important essays.

None of the salon regulars, however, was more important for Diderot, for the *Encyclopédie*, and very probably for the entire radical Enlightenment than the

Friedrich Melchior Grimm was German by birth and a close friend of Diderot, as well as the editor of the subversive Correspondance littéraire. *Drawing by Louis Carmontelle, 1758.*

RÉUNION DES MUSÉES NATIONAUX / ART RESOURCE, NY

one member who did not write original works, limiting himself instead to report on the works of others. Friedrich Melchior Grimm (1723–1807) was a lifelong outsider and self-made man. A German like Holbach, he had set out to conquer the French capital. In the process he became one of the most fascinating and ultimately elusive personalities of the ancien régime.

Born in the south German town of Regensburg, Grimm had come to Paris in the service of a nobleman and had chosen to stay. He had arrived in January 1749 and met Rousseau, who introduced him to Holbach and to his best friend, Diderot, after he had been liberated from prison in November.

Possessing neither an independent income nor powerful friends, Grimm transformed himself into a purveyor of literary news and gossip to the more enlightened princely houses of Germany, which he supplied not only with opinions and news from France but also, if necessary, with life-sized fashion dolls wearing the newest Parisian dresses for the edification of provincial German princesses and even with useful contacts to other noble houses with offspring of marriageable age—making him effectively a high-class marriage broker for the German aristocracy. Grimm was a one-man public relations office and would become in great part responsible for the fame of the salon and its members, even if he began to keep a cautious personal distance from the meetings themselves as his career progressed.

His public influence stemmed mainly from his literary magazine, *Correspondance littéraire*, which was by far the most forthright and candid source of intellectual news in France. All printed materials were subjected to censorship, but Grimm had his journal copied out by hand and could therefore avoid the censor's office. From Naples to London and St. Petersburg, the *Cor-*

respondance reached the more progressive European courts by diplomatic mail and became an important mouthpiece for the radical Enlightenment and its protagonists. Then as now, publicity could act as a protective shield, and as the fame, or notoriety, of the group increased, Grimm's dispatches played a major role in ensuring their personal and collective safety. Also, as is often true today, it was more difficult to arrest and imprison or even execute a person living in the limelight and applauded throughout Europe.

A man with a strong though inscrutable personality, Grimm often polarized his contemporaries. He spoke excellent French (according to Goethe, he was the only German ever to have truly mastered the language) and was a fastidious dresser, insisting on coats after the newest fashion, powdered wigs (much in contrast to Diderot, who refused to wear wigs), and white face powder. Because he looked like a rococo fob, he was easily underestimated. Although he earned his money as a servant to German princes, he was nevertheless very much his own man and would be dictated to by no one.

The white facade of the international power broker hid an intensely passionate interior man. He once rather melodramatically almost starved himself to death out of grief when a female star of the Opéra rejected him (Diderot nursed him back to health), and he would later share the house and the bed of the fascinating Louise d'Epinay, a novelist and one of the few women to take an active role (as anonymous contributor) in both the *Encyclopédie* and Grimm's *Correspondance littéraire*.

Grimm was Diderot's close friend, too, linked to him by a band of mutual affection such as perhaps only new arrivals can form in a foreign city. Indeed, their friendship had some perplexing aspects. Contemporaries unanimously described Grimm as a cool and calculating careerist, determined to be the voice of Enlightened reason in the ear of Europe's princes, and perpetually in thrall to the grandeur and power of titles and courtly life. In many ways, the emotionally effusive Diderot, with his enthusiasm and unguarded generosity, was the very opposite of Grimm's circumspect character. Yet Diderot sang the praises of his friendship in tones usually reserved for lovers, recounting how an emotional reunion after one of his friend's journeys was accompanied by warm hugs, palpitations, speechless joy, and silently gazing at each other, holding hands. Writing to the sculptor Falconet, Diderot declared, "He whom I love, who has the softness of contours of a woman, and, when he wants to, the muscles of a man; this rare composite of the Medici Venus and the Gladiator, my hermaphrodite, you have guessed it, is Grimm."[11]

This overly suggestive portrait appears to speak of a love that was more than just platonic, especially if one takes into account that both the Medici *Venus* and *The Gladiator*, celebrated classical sculptures (one a Roman bronze copy, one a Greek original in marble), were housed in the Louvre and held respectively to be the ideal of female and male beauty. Diderot certainly knew the sculptures, as well as another figure he mentioned in his letter: *The Hermaphrodite*, part of the same collection in the Louvre, a voluptuous girl's body, naked and languidly resting as if from great exertion, with testicles and an erect penis clearly visible between the delicate thighs.

Always a good source for malicious gossip, Rousseau in his *Confessions* suggests that Grimm, his former friend, was "false" and had in fact been in love with Rousseau just as he had been the lover of his first employer in Paris, the Count de Friese, though he adduces no evidence for this. This explanation would fit the ambivalent image of the enigmatic German, but it was put forth by a man convinced that Grimm had usurped his place in Diderot's heart and had done everything to ruin his life and reputation and alienate him from his friends. Rousseau was notorious for his creative and self-serving unreliability.

If Grimm had homosexual leanings, he was careful to conceal them. He lived with Mme d'Epinay and was by all accounts her lover. At any rate, it is unlikely that Diderot and Grimm were sexually intimate. The all-knowing Paris rumor machine and the police spies who hung around wherever Diderot went would have been only too delighted to record any such stories, but no such record exists. Apart from Rousseau, nobody claimed or implied that he was romantically attached to men.

Indeed, both Diderot and Grimm had more than just an eye for the ladies, a fact that also complicated Rousseau's response to the group, as despite his own private life (he was living with his mistress, Thérèse Levasseur), he held decidedly prudish views about the sexual morality of others. Diderot's infidelities were known to his friends, and his writings show an active and roving erotic imagination—stretching from a conventional erotic novel to a highly charged tale set in a nunnery. In his letters to Sophie, there are strong intimations of affairs—not only with her but also with her two sisters. He would frequently wax lyrical in his praise of female beauty, while his appreciation for men seems to have been limited to an admiration of moral fortitude and nobility of mind.

If Diderot's protestations of eternal love and physical attachment to Grimm sound like more than just strong feelings of friendship to us today, it is also because our rhetoric of personal affection has changed—supercharged emotional intensity was commonplace in the literature of the time, and Denis was never reticent about his emotions. Indeed, his always effusive rhetoric abounds with sensual images, almost regardless of subject, and the erotic and the intellectual are frequently intertwined: "the spectacle of justice fills me with a sweetness, inflames me with such ardor and enthusiasm that life would mean nothing to me if I had to yield it up," he wrote to his mistress, Sophie Volland. "Then it seems to me that my heart expands beyond me, that it swims; an indescribably delicious and subtle sensation runs through me; I have difficulty breathing; the whole surface of my body is animated by something like a shudder; it is marked above all on my forehead, at the hairline; and then the symptoms of admiration and pleasure come to mingle in my face with those of joy, and my face with tears."[12] This was a man who really *loved* the truth.

To the philosopher who was acutely attuned to the importance and paradoxical power of the passions, every attachment was ultimately erotic. Even so, his contemporaries were bemused by the *philosophe*'s devotion to his friend, whose public persona was at odds with the image of the tender brother projected by Diderot. There were those who thought the philosopher naïve for not seeing that he and his reputation were being used to further Grimm's own literary reputation. Diderot, however, remained enthusiastically and demonstratively attached to his friend. Several acquaintances wondered why a philosopher who celebrated frank and honest emotions and who had always scrupulously stayed away from the corrupting influence of aristocratic protection would be entranced by a professional toady to provincial princes who wanted nothing more ardently than a title for himself. Rousseau began to suspect his former friend Grimm of dark machinations in keeping with his growing reputation for diplomatic backroom deals. The entire group began to acquire a different, sinister aspect for the struggling author, whose growing

Diderot called Louise d'Epinay "the very image of tenderness and voluptuousness." Her own literary work remained unknown until after her death.

RÉUNION DES MUSÉES NATIONAUX / ART RESOURCE, NY

suspicions of Grimm were complicated by the fact that he was living rent-free in a cottage on the estate of Grimm's lover, the extraordinary Louise d'Epinay.

Even if she was probably never present at Holbach's soirées, Mme d'Epinay was a considerable presence in the circle, both in Paris and at her country seat, La Chevrette at Grandval, home to Grimm and for several years also to Rousseau. La Chevrette was frequently the scene of visits from Diderot and others.

Born Louise Florence Pétronille Tardieu d'Esclavelles in 1726 to an impoverished aristocratic family, she had been educated in a convent (at fourteen she had been deeply devout) and as a poor relative in the house of a wealthy aunt. When she turned nineteen, she was married off to a marquis who was also her cousin. Louise soon learned that her husband was a philanderer, a gambler, and a spendthrift. They began to live separate lives: he in the capital, close to his mistress and the whores at the Jardin Royal; she at La Chevrette, their estate outside the capital. There she began a relationship with the witty and cultivated Louis Dupin de Francueil, himself a married man, by whom she had one daughter.

Still only in her early twenties, a mother of three children, and free from both financial worries and a husband she had grown to detest, Louise discovered the life of the mind. She read voraciously and gathered around herself the most interesting men of letters she could find. She had admirers. She was no conventional beauty, perhaps, but her big, black eyes captivated her male friends; Diderot once described a portrait of her as "the very image of tenderness and voluptuousness."

Among the striving authors and men of letters who came to see her was one who particularly captivated her attention: Jean-Jacques Rousseau. Her lover, Francueil, had introduced them. Louise and Jean-Jacques shared an interest in theories of education; perhaps the two also discovered in each other an active but insecure mind without formal training, eager to discover, discuss, and learn. Some biographers assume that the two also had an affair, but there is no evidence for this.

Louise was fascinated by the Genevan philosopher, but she was still in love with Francueil. The two staged and starred in amateur theatricals at La Chevrette, often in plays written by Jean-Jacques. The plays themselves have not survived and were by all accounts not the most outstanding feature of those evenings; judging by Rousseau's libretto to his opera *The Village Soothsayer*, their disappearance is not a great loss to literary history.

When Louise finally met Grimm in 1754, it was under dramatic circumstances, at least according to her fictionalized autobiography, *Histoire de madame de Montbrillant,* a nuanced and lively work based in large part on correspondence and not published in its original form until 1818. Without the heroine's knowledge, and without his ever having met her, a German cavalier had been wounded in a duel fought against another man who had called her a loose woman. She visited her injured hero on his sickbed to thank him for his valor. Acquaintance deepened into friendship, gratitude into affection, and soon Grimm spent most of his free time at La Chevrette. Through him, Louise discovered Plutarch, Locke, Montaigne, Montesquieu—a little library of intellectual ancestors of the radical thinking that so attracted her and had already made her an ardent admirer of Diderot, whom she had, however, never dared to approach. Grimm encouraged his companion to improve not only her active mind but also her perception of herself, which had been withered by a strict convent and a disdainful aunt. Under Grimm's tutelage, the young woman thrived. She noted to an acquaintance:

> The great mistake I had been making with my friends and myself was always to give preference to *their* fancies, with no thought of what *I* might be wishing. Owing to that little system, I found that half of my "friends" were in fact my masters. To have a will of my own seemed to me a crime. I was doing a thousand unsuitable things with a willingness that was equally unsuitable. I was a perpetual victim, inspiring gratitude in no one. I examined myself closely. I began to dare to be myself. Now I have no

> regard for the caprices of others. I do only what I prefer, and feel marvelously the better for it.[13]

Word spread about the well-read and arresting young woman who kept an open house for writers and their friends. By 1755 several of Holbach's regulars would also be found at her estate. Diderot was skeptical at first. He had heard and obviously believed rumors about her easy virtue from an earlier lover, and he did not want Grimm to have another unhappy love affair. He may actually have been jealous of this woman, who was stealing so much of Grimm's attention from him. It took him several years to overcome his reservations about the woman who was monopolizing his bosom friend, but eventually Diderot consented to meet her. Soon he developed a warm friendship with her, perhaps aided by the fact that visiting her also meant seeing Grimm. Louise was thrilled. She had long admired the famous *philosophe*, and she felt inspired by him: "he has come to see me every day," she wrote about their first meeting. "His conversation is ravishing: his confidence, his self-possession, an inspiration. He has stirred my mind and my soul; he—how shall I express it? It is not that he has made me happy, precisely, but he has given me a new capacity to enjoy all my advantages."[14]

With Grimm for her lover and Diderot as well as other luminaries as her regular guests, Louise d'Epinay was finally able to live the life of intellectual exhilaration and personal intimacy of which she had dreamed, and the image might have seemed utterly perfect when, in 1756, she invited Jean-Jacques, the writer who had captivated her the most, to live in a cottage in her park, and he accepted. In fact, his proudly grudging acceptance of her offer was a portent of great trouble.

It had all begun four years earlier, in 1752, when Jean-Jacques added to the laurels he had won as prizewinning author of a controversial philosophical essay another success, this time as composer of the opera *Le Devin de village* (*The Village Soothsayer*), to which he had written both the libretto and the music and which was performed in front of Louis XV by royal command. The aesthetically and musically unambitious monarch liked the profoundly conservative tale of a country lad who finds the love of a charming shepherdess a more appropriate ambition than the embrace of a countess. He liked it so much that he decided to offer its composer a royal pension. Jean-Jacques, who was still struggling to support himself, his mistress, and her mother by copying out musical parts for paying customers, would finally be able to devote all energy to his writing, both musical and philosophical. The only thing he would have to do in return was to accept the royal gift from the royal hand.

Rousseau refused. He would not hear of traveling out to the palace of Fontainebleau, despite the fact that he had attended not only the dress rehearsal of his opera there but also the first performance—unshaven and in an unkempt wig in the box opposite the king's. (He hoped his appearance would be interpreted as evidence of simple virtue and manly courage.) But attend a royal audience? He was too shy, Jean-Jacques claimed; all the great personages would only intimidate him. His friends beseeched him to change his mind. It was the fulfillment of his ambition for recognition and of his wish to work, they argued, and if not for himself, he should accept the pension for the sake of his Thérèse, a washerwoman, who had never known material comfort in her life. He did not budge.

Perhaps Rousseau's reluctance to appear in front of the king and the assembled court was more than a tantrum by an artist looking for attention. One of the factors that certainly contributed to his distaste for social life was a closely guarded secret: a painful and nagging urinary complaint that meant he could never be far from a chamber pot and occasionally resulted in incontinence. For a man with low confidence at the best of times, the terrible embarrassment of such an incident looming at any moment may have been enough to drive him away from the society of his urbane acquaintances, not to mention the presence of great ladies. It may also have been enough to affect his thinking about society itself.

Whether or not he knew about Rousseau's condition, and it is almost certain that he did, Diderot regarded his friend's decision as incomprehensible and selfish. Surely an afternoon's discomfort was a small price to pay for a lifetime's security for himself and the two women dependent on him. Soon, Rousseau's sullen intransigence clashed with the moral grandstanding of the *philosophe* in full flight. The two friends quarreled, and Rousseau retreated into himself. If he would not receive a royal pension, it was by his own free choice, he noted in 1753: "I do not give a damn for any of the people at Court; today all the kings of the world, with all their arrogance and their titles and their gold put together, would not make me move one step."[15]

When a mind drifts away from reality as perceived by others, its greatest efforts go into reimagining the world according to its needs and emotional certainties. Rousseau was beginning to sense a hostility towards him among his friends, and he attributed it not to his own eccentricity but to some dark plot on their part. He was a successful composer now, after all. Grimm and Diderot, especially, but also the genial baron were obviously jealous of his success, he convinced himself. "Since my success," he reported, he no longer found "that friendliness, that openness, that pleasure to see me which I had believed to find in them up to that point."[16]

It is certain that the relationship between the friends changed around 1753. In his literary journal, the *Correspondance littéraire*, Grimm began writing more critically about Jean-Jacques, who was then involved in a highly publicized attack against French musical taste and in favor of Italian music. How strange such an attack was, Grimm commented acerbically, coming from a man who had just raked in a great success with a French opera from his own pen—a not entirely fair criticism, as Rousseau had tried to write an opera in French but in the Italian style. Still, it was true that he claimed that French was simply "unsingable" as a language, which was a curious statement for the author of a French libretto. Others, however, went considerably further in their criticism and their anger: Orchestra musicians of the Paris Opéra publicly hanged a life-sized dummy bearing Rousseau's features.

Irritated by criticism, defensively proud of his own success, and hypersensitive to social slights, Rousseau began to feel ill at ease in Paris, among his friends, and at Holbach's house. He switched salons and attended the house of the former actress Jeanne-Françoise Quinlault, where, he wrote, "I received all the attention, consideration and favor that I had found lacking at M. D'Holbach's."[17] But it was not enough. Soon Rousseau decided to leave the bustling capital altogether and return home. He would find tranquility by returning to his native Geneva, he decided, where the strict and sober Calvinism was closer to his moral convictions. In 1754, he finally made the journey back, stopping on the way to see *maman*, as he still called Mme de Warens in his letters.

In Geneva, Rousseau converted back to Protestantism and tried unsuccessfully to settle back into life in the city he had sworn never to enter again. His fame was not the same here as it was in Paris—a prophet, after all, has no honor in his own country. Just over a year later, having refused a post as a librarian, Jean-Jacques was back in Paris, where he had alienated most of his old friends, not least by his entirely unphilosophical conversion. Once again, he decided he could not stay in the capital, and when Louise d'Epinay invited him to stay at her cottage on her estate at Montmorency, to the north of the city, he saw her offer as the answer to his problems.

Not that Jean-Jacques made this decision easily, of course. Louise had badgered him into accepting, he grumbled; he had finally conceded much against his better judgment, but he should have never gone along with it. Still, in spring 1756, he left Paris, "city of noise, smoke and mud, where women no longer believe in honor nor men in virtue,"[18] to become a country dweller. Accompanied by his long-suffering companion Thérèse and her mother, he moved into self-imposed exile, hours on foot away from the salons, the cafés, and the public places that had been his life. To the friends of the rue Royale, who lived close to one another, met frequently, and thrived in this atmosphere of mutual solidarity in an otherwise hostile world, Jean-Jacques' withdrawal seemed like a reproach of everything they stood for. The real conflict between them was only just beginning.

CHAPTER 5

AUDACITY

"*Sapere aude!*" the Latin poet Horace had demanded—Dare to know! A considerable number of the men assembling around Holbach's table had in common not only opinions but also intellectual audacity. Many also shared aspects of a certain kind of life story: They had left their homes, defied their fathers, constructed their own lives far away. Holbach was an exception; he had been too small to choose emigration when he was taken to Paris as a young schoolboy, and he had never broken with his paternal uncle, who had eventually done him the favor of dying and leaving him a large fortune. The nephew put to good use supplying his friends the best wines and food, buying works of art and books in great quantities, and discreetly supporting authors in need. Diderot, however, had openly defied his father and left the career chosen for him for a forbidden marriage and a scandalous life of godlessness. Grimm had left his native Germany to make it in the French capital and was living openly with his mistress, Mme d'Epinay. Rousseau had run away from his watchmaker father to become a great man. Raynal had left the Society of Jesus to make a secular life for himself. Other, less famous friends had similar tales to tell.

There was, then, a certain animus against the idea of the powerful father at the baron's table, a reckless quality to their discussions that had an air of defiance. Undoubtedly this spirit of opposition spurred on the friends to attack the religion they had all grown up with. It may also have given Holbach the courage to publish these views, anonymously but very openly, in an atheist manifesto, the first one published at such length since antiquity. *Le Christianisme dévoilé* (*Christianity Unveiled*, 1761, 1767) was condemned, burned publicly by the hangman (a common substitute for burning an unknown author), and angrily attacked in a wave of violent rebuttals and condemnations.

With his first major work, Holbach had taken sides in a war that had broken out a century earlier, a war for nothing less than the soul of humankind. He had become an active combatant in the epic struggle between the Christian, hierarchical order of the old world and another, exciting, but threatening way of seeing the world. It was a battle waged by philosophers but all too often carried into the streets in the form of repression of dissent and executions of dissidents.

The two greatest leaders in this war had themselves felt the power of this repression: The Dutch-Jewish thinker Baruch de Spinoza had lost his community and many of his friends because of his ideas, while the Frenchman René Descartes (1596–1650) spent much of his life fleeing from the authorities and living in exile. Their crime had been to admit radical doubt into philosophy—even if the conclusions they drew from their doubt differed greatly from each other. For freethinkers such as Holbach and Diderot, these predecessors were heroes, eagerly read and discussed passionately. They were men to admire, to think of in moments of hardship, to dispute and refute, shining beacons of inspiration in an intellectual history dominated by theological thought.

At the dawn of the seventeenth century, the stirrings of this new way of thinking had come not from philosophy but from what was then called "natural philosophy": empirical science. Astronomers, mathematicians, experimental scientists, and explorers produced a flood of new discoveries and facts, all of which could be verified or refuted by reason, observation, and experiment alone.

In Britain, Isaac Newton revolutionized science by formulating basic laws about the physical world. It was not his intention to demolish religion—towards the end of his career he spent much of his time pondering theological and even mystical questions—but its effect was devastating. Newtonian physics opened up a new understanding of the world resting on nothing but observation and inference, predicting how physical objects would behave—an entirely new appreciation of the universe.

At around the same time, astronomical observation and calculation had turned the order of the cosmos upside down by demonstrating that the earth revolved around the sun. Galileo Galilei had not only argued this case before the Inquisition (and was condemned to lifelong house arrest) but published research in astronomy and gravity, while Dutch lens cutters created microscopes enabling scientists to see bacteria and individual sperm cells, prompting new ideas about the origin of life.

Science was undeniably changing the world, and it did not need theology to do it. With every new discovery or theory, the domain of empiricism was enlarged, and God's realm made a little smaller. These incursions were as yet small in scale but devastating in principle: If there was well-founded knowledge that was possible without God, if the world and its workings could be understood without recourse to a Creator, then the fundamental role of God's Word was cast in doubt.

During the seventeenth century, France was at the forefront of the great debate raging between science and theology. All philosophy was based, officially at least, on the teachings of the church. After 1600, however, as the empirical, observation-based approach to the world yielded more and more results, the defenders of faith became increasingly embattled.

The rescuer of a science that could still be called Christian, the reconciler of God and empiricism, was a man who called himself a skeptic. As a young soldier in the Thirty Years War, René Descartes had visited the workplaces of the astronomers Johannes Kepler and Tycho Brahe, whose discoveries had proved instrumental in the revolution of cosmology at the beginning of the seventeenth century. A gifted mathematician, Descartes had become fascinated with the idea of a universal method for investigating and discovering truth, a hard kind of truth that would stand the test of both logic and observation.

The skeptical method used by Descartes became synonymous with the most radical doubt and made the philosopher wanted for heresy in his native France. He took refuge first in the Netherlands (which he detested on account of the bad weather) and then, on the personal invitation of the bluestocking Queen Christina, the Athena of the North, in Stockholm. There the portly thinker rapidly succumbed to a bout of pneumonia contracted while teaching the young monarch one freezing winter morning in an unheated library.

Descartes set out to do nothing less than create a new basis for philosophy. If one questions even the most elemental certainties, how is it possible to arrive at absolute certainty about anything at all? What can we be sure of? Descartes offered an answer so simple and so strikingly effective that it became legendary: *Cogito ergo sum.* Even in the act of tearing down all certainty and in radical questioning, there is no denying that the doubting mind itself exists. Doubt's presence is proof of a mind doubting. This elegant argument allowed Descartes to find an entirely new basis for philosophizing, but it immediately landed him with another problem: While it is true that I can be certain of my existence through the very act of thinking, how can I be certain about the existence of anything I am thinking about? How can I possibly know that my senses do not lie to me, that there is a world of objective fact outside my mind? Waking up in the morning after having had a dream in which I was a butterfly, how can I know that I am a man who dreamed he was a butterfly, and not a butterfly dreaming it is a man?

We *can* know this for certain, answered the philosopher; we can know the world as it really is, not just as it appears to our senses. Our knowledge of things outside ourselves can be a faithful representation of these things. His proof of this assertion was the following: We have in our minds the idea of perfection, and as existence is necessary to perfection (because any being that is nonexistent is, by definition, imperfect), the very idea implies that a Perfect Being must exist. And because this Being, God, is perfect, he cannot deceive his creatures—because deception itself is a diminution of perfection, and a perfection diminished is no longer perfect. A truthful God, therefore, shows his creatures His creation as it really exists, so our perception is a faithful representation of external reality.

The external, material reality perceived by the mind is fundamentally different from the mind itself. In fact, wrote Descartes, the world is made up of two different kinds of "substances": mind and matter. While matter is extended in space but has no self-awareness, the mind is self-aware—but not extended—and is eternal. The realms of the unextended mind and of extended matter intersect, but they are, in fact, two quite separate realities. While the realm of matter is subject to empirical observation and scientific explanation, the domain of the mind is purely rational and spiritual.

This little exercise in definition and sophistry was, in fact, profoundly important for Descartes' philosophical system, which now appeared to reconcile science and religion under the authority of philosophical doubt. By marking out two distinct territories—matter and mind—the philosopher had created the impression that skeptical reason need not be a threat to the existence of

God but on the contrary leads to a necessary proof of his existence and perfection, and that material reality is quite different from spiritual reality. Therefore, scientific, empirical judgments about the material world are possible without affecting the spiritual realm. You could be a scientist and a pious Christian after all.

Descartes' reconciliation of empiricism and faith came at a price: The duality of the world, which he had deduced from his investigations, was essentially Platonist, determined by the assumption that the world is made of two substances—and that ultimately the material world is the lesser one. But this dualist definition also intensified one of the oldest debates in philosophy: If it is true that mind and body are quite separate substances, how is it then possible that one can act upon the other? How can a thought result in a turning of the head, an impulse of will in the lifting of an arm? How exactly can the immortal soul act upon the mortal body? This so-called mind-body problem had exercised philosophers for centuries, but now oil had been poured on the flames of debate. Anatomists dissected the corpses of executed criminals in search of the seat of the immortal soul; philosophers sought ways of resolving the puzzle of how substances of different kinds can interact. The investigation of the object world had acquired a new—or newly mysterious—aspect.

Although Diderot wrote of Descartes that he had launched only "impotent shots" against materialism, he conceded that he regarded Descartes as a rare genius. By the eighteenth century, Jesuit schools had steeped their pupils in the principles and apparent resolution of Cartesian doubt and dualism, a method that had gradually become accepted as the most powerful weapon against the troubling implications of the scientific method. In the face of the great leaps made by science, this weapon was desperately needed. "Natural philosophers" (i.e., scientists) made new discoveries almost daily, rendering literal interpretation of the Bible impossible. Critical minds were discussing the implications of these findings for philosophy and for faith itself, and for theologians it seemed safest to take the realm of the spiritual entirely out of the increasingly quantifiable world of matter. The defenders of biblical truth claimed that a spiritual substance as a "thinking matter" was entirely unaffected by what science was saying and discovering about mere "extended matter."

As the philosopher who had made doubt—not faith or revelation—the foundation of all rational inquiry, Descartes was a direct inspiration for the *philosophes* at Holbach's table, most of whom (excepting the Calvinist Rousseau) would have been educated and trained according to the Cartesian method. They followed him by declaring rational doubt to be the bedrock of all philosophy and by applying strictly empirical explanation to all investigations of the physical world. But instead of following his second step, the supposedly inescapable logical proof of a separate realm of the mind and of God, they refused to follow Descartes into the trap of the mind-body problem, which has caused so many fine intellects to founder. They simply did not accept the existence of two distinct "substances" or that there was anything at all beyond the realm of the material.

To circumvent Descartes' dualism, and the existence of a distinct realm of the mind, the friends of the rue Royale turned to one of his most penetrating critics.

Almost a century after his death, Baruch Spinoza (1632–1677) was still perceived as a danger to the Christian faith and an enemy of public order. At one time he had been a meek, soft-spoken lens maker in the Netherlands. There was nothing in the first half of his life to indicate that he would revolutionize European philosophy. It is very possible that we owe the revelation of his genius to piracy and to the activities of the British Royal Navy off the French coast.

Spinoza was born in Amsterdam into the Portuguese-Jewish community, a close-knit group of refugees from persecution. He was educated in the traditional Jewish way, studying rabbinic scriptures and performing religious duties. When his elder brother died, it was expected that Baruch would take over the family trading house led by his father, Miguel. But it was a difficult time for trade. Britain was at war with the Netherlands, and from 1650 onwards, several ships carrying sugar from Brazil, as well as wine, olives, and almonds—cargoes Miguel Spinoza had invested in heavily—were either seized by British ships or taken by corsairs, plunging the family business into deep debt. When Miguel died four years later, he left his son Baruch, then twenty-one years old, at the head of the firm and facing insolvency.

The young and beleaguered merchant had long nurtured a private interest in philosophy, particularly in the radical possibilities arising from the hotly debated theses of Descartes. As a teenager, he had begun to take Latin lessons from an ex-Jesuit, Franciscus van Enden, who was known as a radical intellectual in Amsterdam and who acquainted his gifted pupil not only with declensions and conjugations but also with the great Latin authors, medieval Scholastic philosophy, and the discussions surrounding the new, empirical cast of mind that was on the rise in Europe. Baruch kept his thoughts about these ideas largely to himself while he was the breadwinner of his family, and he continued to live as an observant Jew and a practicing member of the community. But when the firm finally collapsed in 1655, he had to accept that there was no longer any hope of living the life of a wealthy merchant whose daytime activities could fund a private fascination with matters of the mind. He decided to hide his personal convictions no longer.

When the young scholar began to associate with known atheists outside the Jewish community, carry his convictions into the synagogue, and challenge all aspects of the religious tradition, the elders of the community tried every conceivable means of inducing him to come to a discreet arrangement. They even went so far as to promise him a regular stipend if he agreed to keep quiet, but Spinoza was resolved to burn his bridges. His banishment from the community was unavoidable. The formal decree was issued in 1656 with the ancient formula banning the young man from the community and branding him a heretic and a damned soul. While Romantic biographers have seen this as evidence of the community's inexplicable severity towards a pure mind and a young genius, Spinoza had, in fact, left his elders very little choice.

Financially ruined and cut off from the friends and acquaintances of his childhood, Spinoza probably went to study at nearby Leiden University, a place known throughout Europe as a haven of freethinkers and science-oriented radicals. He also appears to have lived in the town of Rijnsburgh, where he made a precarious living as a lens cutter producing microscopes and telescopes, an occupation that allowed him to make use of his fascination with mathematics (it also ruined his eyesight and very probably led to his early death, most likely from tuberculosis exacerbated by the inhalation of glass dust).

During the latter part of his life, Spinoza courted admiration and trouble in equal measure. Living in a modest house in The Hague, close to his native city, he surrounded himself with other philosophical radicals and devoted his intellectual energies to elaborating and writing a systematic exposition of his views. His greatest work, the *Ethica ordine geometrico demonstrata* (*Ethics Demonstrated in Geometrical Order*), was deemed too radical for publication even by the author himself and was circulated only in manuscript to a small number of friends. Spinoza's attempt at publishing it in 1675 was abandoned because of pressure by the authorities, and the work only appeared posthumously, in 1677.

What, then, was so scandalous about Spinoza's thought? At first glance, his philosophy is nothing but a closely argued, rationalist defense of God's infinite greatness and perfection. What turned this defense into a shattering blow against theology was a unique cultural cross-fertilization combining seventeenth-century skepticism, thirteenth-century Scholastic thought, and traditional Jewish teaching.

During his teenage years, Baruch Spinoza, the first Jew to participate directly in the European philosophical debate, had been sent to Amsterdam's Talmud Torah school, in which bright boys were introduced to the writings of the Jewish tradition with a view to making them scholars or even rabbis. During these lessons, he would have encountered an argumentative method that became critically important for his own work. In order to reconcile the primitive morality of a Bronze Age society as reflected in the injunctions of the Bible with the very different ethical ideas of later centuries, the rabbinical scholars had found a multitude of ways of dramatically reinterpreting biblical passages without ever contradicting them. To do this, they turned the meaning of scripture against itself, reading or misreading rules under impossibly restrictive criteria or playing off quotations from different biblical books (and centuries) against one another, all with the goal of making it appear as if the values of community in, say, thirteenth-century France, home to the great rabbinical scholar Rashi, were in fact exactly identical with those of Palestine, 2000 BCE.

The young Baruch Spinoza was a better pupil than his masters realized. He found a way of transferring this rabbinical ruse to the Western tradition of philosophy. Later, having left the religion of his fathers, he continued to write about God, but with an interest very different from that of the religious debates he had grown up with and from the Christian theology he had encountered during his later studies. Instead, he now used the arguments of the Scholastic thinkers of the church and of Descartes against themselves. Like Descartes' ideas, his own arguments were clothed in the language of mathematics and geometry, which made them appear unassailably logical, but Spinoza wanted to do more than just tinker with the Cartesian system of metaphysics. He wanted nothing less than to remold philosophy itself. His investigation of the mind-body problem did not openly contradict religion but instead smashed its theoretical foundations. For the friends of the rue Royale, this became an indispensable philosophical armor for their own struggle with religious concepts.

Choosing a mathematically inspired way of constructing his argument with numbered definitions, axioms, and propositions, Spinoza argued that only a single substance could exist, a substance infinitely modified to create the world in all its variety. In his *Ethics*, he states that "God, or substance, consisting of infinite attributes, of which each expresses eternal and infinite essentiality, necessarily exists," coming to the conclusion that "besides God no substance can be granted or conceived." So far, so good for the theologian, who could appreciate that a series of strict definitions and logical conclusions had led Spinoza to proving the necessity of God's existence.

Spinoza followed Descartes and the Scholastic tradition in defining God as necessarily existing, but he contradicted Cartesian dualism by saying that nothing could exist outside or independently of God, so, by implication, there could not be two realms of the world, mind and matter, but only one single substance of divine origin, infinitely moderated into material and mental phenomena. This not only reversed Descartes' rescue of theology but also paved the way for the eighteenth-century materialists, who would argue that the mind is a mere function of the body, not an independent entity.

But Spinoza's logical rigor had even more troubling implications for theology, particularly, and notoriously in Chapter VI of his *Tractatus*, in which he wrote about miracles. God, Spinoza held, exists by necessity, is substance, and is perfect. His will is the law of the universe, and his inherent perfection means that the world as such is perfect, since no imperfection can come out of perfection without rendering the originator imperfect. It is therefore impossible that God could will anything to be less than perfect without perverting the very nature of his being. If humans do not perceive the world as perfect—if they point to death, putrefaction, and suffering as evident imperfections—it is only because these things are not understandable to them as they are understandable to God. Things may seem imperfect from a person's limited perspective, but they are necessarily perfect in the eyes of God, who created them as expressions of his own perfection.

From this seemingly abstract and pious analysis, Spinoza drew a scandalous conclusion: Stories of divine miracles, he wrote, must be born out of ignorance or even conscious deception but cannot possibly be used to infer the existence of God. God's perfection means that the laws of nature must themselves be perfect, too, and it would be impossible for God to intervene in the course of natural events, because any alteration of the course of the universe would mean introducing imperfection, which is incompatible with God's own perfection. The laws of nature—that is, God's laws—cannot be contravened, even by God himself.

Here the circle of Spinoza's virtuoso argument closes. He makes out God to be a being so perfect, so universal, so necessary that this being could not possibly intervene in the course of nature—indeed, can no longer act at all. Miracles are nothing but misunderstood natural occurrences, he argues. The laws of the universe are synonymous with God's will and intelligence; God himself becomes a metaphor for necessity, for natural laws.

This is a crucial point. Many interpreters have made Spinoza out to be a pantheist, who sees God's will, love, and Providence in every leaf of grass and every dewdrop, but this is a fundamental misunderstanding. As his contemporary followers and enemies immediately understood, Spinoza's God is nothing but a particular way of referring to the laws governing the physical world, the only world. One might praise the absolute perfection of this God, but it is soon revealed that no entity, no Creator, no loving or angry Father, no God who saves or punishes is designated by this name. There is only impersonal necessity in a material world; there is no one left to pray to. Spinoza had done nothing less than praise God out of existence.

The sober and closely argued works in which the Dutch-Jewish philosopher had laid out his conception of the world carried a charge of almost infinite potential for European thought. They were immediately recognized as oxygen for dissidents and freethinkers, as dangerous heresy. The philosophical tradition, Spinoza had shown, could be turned against itself and made to prove what it had long served to refute. His contemporaries were not slow to respond. A professor at Utrecht University called the *Tractatus* a "*liber pestilentissimus*" (a most pestilential book), while the South Holland synod ranked it among "all kinds of foul and godless books . . . as vile and blasphemous as any that are known of."[1] It was banned in the Netherlands in 1674, four years after its publication. It continued to be printed, often with false title pages in an attempt to fool the authorities.

To the generation that would reach maturity around 1750—including the friends who were to assemble at Holbach's salon—Spinoza symbolized the allure of freethinking. His appeal increased with every official condemnation, with every angry refutation of his thought. His works were forbidden in France, and only a few precious copies were in circulation. Revealingly, Diderot hardly ever refers to Spinoza, and while it seems perilous to interpret "the silence in the text," this is a glaring omission. Having encountered Descartes at school, it is likely that Diderot found Spinoza later in his life, after completing his first philosophical work, the *Pensées philosophiques*, published in 1745, which shows no awareness of Spinoza's thought. Already two years later in *Promenade du sceptique*, however, one of the protagonists clearly represents Spinozan ideas, which would mean that his encounter with the Jewish philosopher coincided with and in all likelihood played a role in Denis' own skeptical change of mind, helping him to make the transition to a clear atheist stance.

While Diderot chose not to be candid about Spinoza's influence on his thinking, Holbach based his own philosophical ideas much more clearly on Spinozan concepts. His own radical materialism, as well as his ideas on human psychology and the perceived need for religious faith as a consequence of ignorance about nature, were based on them. At the same time, however, Holbach made very little explicit reference to Spinoza and never quoted him, as he did others. Is this evidence of anti-Jewish prejudice? Probably not. Instead, Holbach was careful only to quote thinkers who were generally accepted and respected, in order to make his own radical views more palatable. Openly admiring a known heretic would have done no favors to the reception of his argument.

Descartes and Spinoza formed the two poles between which philosophical debates could be conducted. If God was put at the center of the thinkable universe, then this universe must have two substances, extended matter and thinking matter, one being the realm of reason and science, the other of faith and hope. If one accepted only one substance, then there was ultimately no door left open for miracles, for eternal souls, for faith itself—the world had become material, rational, entirely here and now. It was only one step to give this argument a political slant and to pit the world of science and reason against the world of faith and, by implication, the power of the church, a power whose claim to legitimacy rested on the ineffable, transcendental will of God.

It is obvious why Diderot and Holbach chose not to acknowledge the notorious heretic Spinoza openly in their works. Any open association with him would have been a potential danger to them, even if Holbach's works were published anonymously. Their secretiveness extended to another thinker who was important for their own work, and particularly their critique of Christianity, a man whose ideas were so incendiary that his influence on them remained unmentioned and unmentionable.

On the face of it, Jean Meslier (1664–1729) was a highly unlikely candidate for a key atheist thinker—he spent his entire working life as a curate in the French village of Étrépigny, in the Ardennes. During his quiet life as a servant of the church, he spent countless long evenings by candlelight penning the most vituperative, most informed, and most cutting critique possible of the faith he represented to his parishioners, a five-hundred-page indictment that was discovered after his death copied out by hand and in the strictest secrecy, and circulated among trustworthy people in the literary underground in which the young Denis Diderot had been moving. Meslier's *Testament* became a kind of underground bible. In his *Promenade du sceptique,* Diderot likens him to an intellectual guerrilla fighter. Diderot's work portrays the subjects of a legendary king (God) as content to walk around with bandages over their eyes, until a small group of people sneak up and tear the bandages off, forcing the walkers to see reality—an image straight out of Meslier. Many of the curate's trenchant arguments can also be found almost verbatim in Holbach's later works. The baron, however, was too prudent to mention their origin by name.

Meslier's all-out attack has lost little of its force today. "Know, my dear friends," wrote the country priest to those who came after him, "that everything that is happening in the world concerning the cult and the adoration of gods, is nothing but error, abuse, illusion, mendacity, and betrayal; that all the laws and ordinances published under the authority of God or gods are nothing but human inventions, just like all the beautiful spectacles and feasts and sacrifices and all the other practices and devotions in their honor."[2]

Knowing that he himself would be speaking from the safety of his grave, Meslier lets fly the pent-up outrage of decades of secrecy about his real views of heaven and hell. The faithful are being kept ignorant by priests who tell them terrifying fables, he writes. The priests are in league with those who profit from the existing order by stealing from the poor: the magistrates, the nobility, the lawyers, the bailiffs, who know that they can keep people docile and living in effective servitude only by making them fear eternal punishment for temporal transgressions, or even for defending their own interests. According to his *Testament*, "on the one side the priests . . . command you on pain of eternal damnation to obey the magistrates, the princes and the sovereigns, because God has put them in their place to rule over others; and the princes, on the other hand, enforce respect for the priests, give them good appointments and good revenues, and maintain them in the vain function of their false ministry."[3] Once the people would be told that there was no profit to be hoped for and no harm to be feared after death, this malicious charade must surely collapse.

If there were anything to religion, its representatives would not have to rely on legends, blind faith, and trickery, Meslier argues. Why would God trouble to carved the Commandments of the law into stone tablets if he could have engraved it directly into every human heart? Where was the sense, and the humanity, in keeping his creatures ignorant about his laws (which was the case for the pagans) or in throwing temptations in their way? Could such a capricious Creator possibly be called benevolent and full of love? Of course he could not, the curate retorted angrily. A little over a decade after Meslier's death and the dissemination of his manuscript, Diderot would use this line of argument in his first work, the *Pensées philosophiques*.

A lifetime of work in a rural community had taught Meslier everything there was to know about rural poverty, daily hunger, the brutality within the family, and the violence outside. This life of toil, viciousness, and ignorance bred its own kind of cruelly diminished human beings, Meslier wrote, people whom he contemptuously dubbed *Christicoles* (pathetic little "Christlings"). The atheist curate had nothing but pity for their superstition and contempt for their cowardice.

Meslier's angrily uncompromising analysis led him to advocate an early form of communism or even anarchism in a preindustrial world, in which the working classes are represented by the rural poor, who were made to believe in fables like that of "an alleged terrestrial paradise, of a snake that talks, that argues, and which is even more intelligent and more cunning than man."[4]

Founded on greed and lies, the privileges of the rich could not be allowed to stand, Meslier concluded. Once people had come to accept that there was no god, no miracles, no heaven and hell, they would no longer obey the dictate of privilege. Instead they would take for themselves what they needed to live well and to enjoy their lives and their bodies, freed by the certain knowledge of their physical and mental annihilation in death. Necessity and empathy would replace divine commandments and create a society more equitable and more joyful than could ever be possible under the rule of a God who apparently took pleasure in human suffering and who demanded from his creatures that they chastise and diminish themselves and their lives in order not to incur his wrath.

It is clear that the authorities could never allow such a work to see the light of day, but see the light it did, or so it seemed. In 1761, the *Testament de Jean Meslier* was published, in a version printed outside France and edited by Voltaire himself. This seemed only sensible, as the original manuscript, which had been circulating in the literary underground, was full of repetitions and redundancies—unsurprisingly, perhaps, in a work written in the greatest secrecy, at night, and in a state of suppressed rage. Now the patron saint of the Enlightenment had taken it on himself to order the poor curate's thoughts and to present them to a wider reading public.

A closer reading, any reading in fact, reveals a very different truth: Far from simply organizing and tightening Meslier's radical manifesto, Voltaire had excised all atheist references and had created a mild, deist treatise against ecclesiastical abuse of power and excessive superstition on the part of the faithful. There are no more attacks on Christianity in this version, and certainly no calls to revolution or violent resistance against the aristocracy, and no utopian dreaming of a just society composed of equal, free, and informed citizens. Voltaire had castrated the author in the grave.

It is highly instructive to compare Meslier's angry, radical atheism with Voltaire's moderate and deist form of Enlightenment thought, which was to become dominant, even synonymous with "the Enlightenment."

Voltaire had become very wealthy by lending money to princes, and he was certainly no radical. He was as much the banker as the preceptor of several of Europe's nobles. His motto "*Écrasez l'infâme!*" (crush the infamous one—that is, the church) is brought up whenever his name is mentioned, but it is rarely added that Voltaire, while polemicizing against spectacular miscarriages of justice in the name of Catholicism, used most of his energies to maintain his good relations with members of the nobility and to manipulate from afar anyone he perceived as a rival pretender to the throne of philosopher king.

Unlike Meslier, who had looked at the world from the perspective of the poor, Voltaire was keenly aware of the value and the usefulness of God. When he erected a chapel on his estate, he sent a letter to the pope in which he asked to be granted a holy relic for his altar. "I want my attorney, my tailor, my servants, even my wife to believe in God, and I think that then I shall be robbed and cuckolded less often,"[5] one of his most-quoted witticisms goes. How else to stop the footmen from pinching the silverware? God had his uses, as long as faith was not taken to its superstitious extreme. "I believe! I believe in you! Powerful God, I believe!" he was once heard to shout as he observed a beautiful sunset, adding drily, "As for Monsieur the Son, and Madame His Mother, that's a different story."[6]

A sworn and famous enemy of church power, Voltaire nonetheless had no patience with unbelievers. Outright atheism not only was politically dangerous but also threatened to eclipse his own reputation as a radical and to erode his currency. "The atheist is a monster all his life," he opined, commenting that "Italy, in the fifteenth century, was full of atheists—and what was the consequence? Cases of poisoning were as common as invitations to supper; and there was no more hesitation in plunging a stiletto into the heart of one's friend than in embracing him. There were teachers of crime, just as there are now teachers of music or mathematics."[7]

It was part of Voltaire's mission to save the world from atheists and from dangerous people who, like Meslier, thought that greater social justice must be pursued, even if this pursuit involved open rebellion. This had been his reason for effectively neutralizing the curate by transforming his great atheist diatribe into an insipid deist treatise, and it would also be the motive for his changing and hardening his stance towards the Encyclopedists, and more particularly towards Holbach and his salon. Voltaire was the Enlightenment. He had a reputation to defend. As the star of the rue Royale began to rise and the members of Holbach's salon became famous far beyond their native country, he viewed them as competition, a potential threat. But he was a resourceful man—he would find a way to win.

CHAPTER 6

CHRISTIANITY UNVEILED

Sustained by copious food and fueled by fine wines, the philosophical debates in Holbach's salon followed the lead of Spinoza and Meslier. Diderot was the voluble and provocative star of these shared attempts to rethink a world without God. For him, talking was an art form and a passion, as he himself acknowledged in old age, quoting his favorite modern author and kindred spirit, Montaigne:

> When I am excited over a matter I have in hand, either by another man's resistance or by the intrinsic heat of the narration, I magnify and inflate my subject by voice, movements, vigor and power of words, and further by extension and amplification, not without prejudice to the simple truth. But I do so, however, on this condition, that for the first man who catches me up and asks me for the naked and unvarnished truth, I promptly abandon my straining and give it to him without exaggeration, without overemphasis or padding. A lively and noisy way of speaking, such as mine ordinarily is, is apt to be carried away into hyperbole.[1]

Diderot was often carried away, to the delight and exasperation of the other guests, while the host was content to watch and observe.

Holbach appears to have had no desire whatsoever to be in the limelight. He published most of his works under pseudonyms. Despite his wealth, for a long time he did not trouble to commission an oil portrait of himself from a first-rate painter. A graceful 1766 pair of pastel drawings by Louis Carmontelle shows the baron seated in an upholstered easy chair and on the other sheet his second wife at a reading table, their exquisite furniture rather pointedly plunked into a park landscape complete with garden ornaments, but these images reveal little about Holbach's character or traits. When he was finally painted by the society portraitist Alexander Roslin in 1774, the result was deeply conventional: The baron is wearing a white, powdered wig and copiously ruffled sleeves. In his left arm he holds an open book. It is tempting to assume that this book is his *Système de la nature*, but the writing remains illegible.

In a later portrait, also by Roslin, the philosopher seems strained and awkward, in spite of Roslin's usual fluency. Holbach, a gouty sixty-two years old when he sat for the painter in 1785, is looking up from his desk, but the resulting, studied pose shows a man impatient to get back to work. His right hand is framed by a coat sleeve with gold embroidery and grips the armrest of his chair; his left hand is set on the writing desk. To the modern eye it is almost necessary to cover the white, formal horsehair curls of the baron's strangely old-fashioned wig in order to concentrate on his facial traits. It is worth doing so: The facial expression reveals itself as forthright and kind, full of knowing intelligence, and entirely in keeping with the subject's character.

While there are only a few extant letters by Holbach's hand, his personality is also revealed by his own, impassioned philosophical works. His first important statement, *Le Christianisme dévoilé* (*Christianity Unveiled*), was published in 1761. Contentious and even heretical—and therefore dangerous for both author and readers—it had to be written, printed, and disseminated under strict secrecy. The manuscripts were copied by a trustworthy friend to avoid the author's handwriting being recognized in case of interception. They were then sent, probably in individual chapters, by mail carriage or in the luggage of travelers, first to Nancy, where one batch was printed in 1761, and then to Amsterdam, where the bulk followed six years later, giving a false place of publication, "*Londres*," and a false author's name. For this, Holbach had chosen "*par feu M. Boulanger*" (by the late Monsieur Boulanger), a protective measure for himself as well as a little bow to an old friend, Nicolas-Antoine, who had often attended Holbach's salon and had conveniently died two years earlier.

The books were then smuggled back, often hidden under the false bottoms of fish barrels, in bales of straw, or in the luggage of a sympathizing diplomat, to France, where they were sold at absurd prices by clandestine booksellers. Absurd they might be, but not unjustified, at least from the perspective of the dealers, who were risking everything with their merchandise. In 1768 Diderot wrote to Sophie Volland about three unfortunates, one young apprentice who had obtained two copies of *Chistianisme dévoilé*, a colporteur, and his wife: "All three were arrested. They have been pilloried, flogged, and branded, and the apprentice has been condemned to nine years on the galleys, the colporteur to five years, and the woman to the hospital [the madhouse] for her entire life."[2]

Faced with such dangers, Holbach kept the authorship of the work a closely guarded secret, even among his friends. Only a select circle knew the truth; others were left guessing and predictably came up with the most unlikely candidates. "Tell me to whom you attribute *Dévoilé*," Diderot wrote to the sculptor Falconet in May 1767. "If you only knew how much the conjectures all around me make me laugh!"[3] Meanwhile, the baron himself could for once not suppress his pride, writing full of satisfaction to a friend that *Christianisme dévoilé* had caused in Paris "a great deal of well-deserved noise."[4]

The secret around the author remained intact, but it was only part of the mysteries presented by the book. As a thinker, Holbach was more systematic than inspired, and he had the modesty to admit this and to ask the help of stylistically more adept friends, including Diderot, of whom the exact opposite was true. Diderot's quick wit and Holbach's methodical vein, the deep knowledge of theology and literature of the former and the scientific orientation and radical thinking of the latter, refracted discussions and arguments and recast them in the light of reason. The baron's sheer courage created a work of great power and integrity, if one that was likely to lurch back and forth between long and wordy expositions of systematic argument and sudden flashes of wit and razor-sharp style, which leap off the page as if printed in a different color and are obviously not the baron's own.

Diderot, in fact, was often exasperated by Holbach's ponderous and repetitive style, as he rather maliciously confided in a letter to Madame de Maux, who incidentally had a brief affair with Diderot in or about 1770. The baron had a very useful strategy of countering the effect of theological works published in foreign languages. He simply had them translated by earnest but atrociously bad translators, thus effectively destroying the market for other translations and making the work unreadable in French. What Holbach did not realize, wrote Diderot, was that he himself was having the same effect on books he approved of and therefore translated himself, "because of the long, flat and confused way in which our friend the baron has rendered them."[5]

In letters to intimate friends Diderot was chronically unable to restrain his delight in sharp characterizations. In his collaboration with Holbach, however, he invested countless hours in editing and rewriting arguments he himself approved of, but would have put so much better himself—if he had been able find the time and, after Vincennes, the audacity to put these ideas to paper. Instead, he became the baron's editor, trying to inject esprit and sharpness into texts lacking in sparkle, while at the same time continuing his toil on the *Encyclopédie*.

The argument of *Christianisme dévoilé* takes us directly into the heart of the radical Enlightenment. Holbach and his friends wanted nothing less than to construct a new way of being in the world to support a new morality, but to construct anything one first has to clear the ground, and this the baron did with the greatest possible clarity and consequence. Christianity, he believed, was not only nonsense but harmful nonsense, reducing believers to pale shadows of their human potential and turning them into slaves of an illusory power, represented by the very real interests of priests and magistrates, who had grown rich and powerful on the back of a superstitious people. The first step, therefore, was to expose the internal contradictions hidden by religious doctrine, and this Holbach did with relish. Like his precursor Meslier, Holbach attacked Christian scripture and theology simply by taking it literally and weighing its ethical implications. Having created the universe out of nothingness, God created humans, so the religious narrative went. As soon as his creatures saw the light of day, the Creator set a trap for them: "A speaking serpent seduces a woman, who is not surprised by this phenomenon at all, and, persuaded by the serpent, solicits her husband to eat a fruit forbidden by God himself."[6] By eating the wrong kind of fruit, Adam has brought death, suffering, and terrible evil over his descendants, who are additionally punished by immorality so profound that God is later compelled to drown almost all of his creatures in a deluge.

For Holbach, this God was nothing more than "a sultan, a despot, a tyrant," whose incomprehensible and inconstant actions made it impossible to please him: "This God is not always unjust and cruel, his conduct varies; now he creates all of nature for man; now he appears to have created that same man only to descend upon him with arbitrary fury; now he cherishes him, despite his faults; now he condemns the entire human race to unhappiness, for the sake of an apple. . . . For God, who is called at the same time the God of vengeance and the God of forgiveness, the Lord of Hosts and the God of peace, continuously blows hot and cold."[7] The Christian God, in fact, perversely appears to enjoy the spectacle of human suffering. How else would he have given his beloved creatures a free will, which would enable them to sin and thus condemn themselves to eternal damnation and atrocious punishments? He gives them the impulse to seek happiness, only to send them to hell if they follow it: "God . . . has made man susceptible to suffering without interruption and without term. . . . That is the idea the Christian has of the God who demands his love. That tyrant only creates him to make him unhappy."[8]

Perversity, Holbach argued, could only breed more perversity. If it was Voltaire's position that it was necessary to posit God's existence to keep down the rabble, the baron concluded the very opposite: Not only was religion a tissue of absurd stories, but it also failed to make people better, or more obedient citizens. On the contrary, it was nothing but an instrument of oppression. Pious princes begin unjust wars and make the poor poorer to finance their lives. In the name of God's plan, the powerful take from those who cannot defend themselves.

The root problem, Holbach wrote, was not Christianity per se, but the idea of a God-given religion of any kind: "All religions pretend to have emanated from heaven; all forbid the use of reason, all pretend to be the only depository of truth . . . and finally they all are false, and full of contradictions. . . . Christianity is in no way different from all other superstitions with which the universe is infected."[9]

Religion is not only logically inconsistent and morally perverse; it also diminishes and corrupts the minds of the faithful, Holbach argued. It creates sin and guilt, secrecy and deceitfulness, by condemning physical pleasure (even the mere thought of it), by making divorce impossible, and by imposing celibacy on its servants; it tortures and tyrannizes the consciousness of adults and children alike; it makes people cower in front of an illusion instead of living lives of informed choice and free morality. Most people, however, are never given the chance to think for themselves, as their indoctrination begins from birth:

> Hardly taken from its mother's breast, the priest baptizes him for money, under the pretext of washing off the stain of original sin and reconciling him with a God he has not yet had opportunity to offend; with the aid of magical incantations he removes him from the demon's realm. From earliest childhood, his education is normally entrusted to priests, whose principal object is to inculcate as soon as possible the prejudices necessary for their ends; they terrify him with a fear that will grow throughout his life; they teach him the fables of a miraculous religion, senseless dogmas, incomprehensible mysteries; in a word, they make him a superstitious Christian, but they never make him a useful citizen, an enlightened man.[10]

As long as people are unwilling or unable to use their reason, to think for themselves, and to see the blatant perversity of the beliefs preached to them, their misery is bound to continue, Holbach wrote (echoing Meslier), especially as they were faced with a conspiracy: "Most sovereigns are afraid of enlightened people; accomplices of the priest . . . [the sovereigns] ally themselves with him to extinguish reason, and to prosecute those who have the courage to speak out."[11] This courage would prevail, Holbach believed, even if it might take a revolution to rid humankind of religion, to throw off the yoke of "haughty priests and sacred tyrants" and make truth triumph over mendacity.

Holbach's moral feeling was particularly outraged by the mental and moral enslavement imposed by the church. His methodical intelligence was insulted by the fact that religion simply refused to accord with known fact. As a student, his first qualms about religion had appeared during his study of geology. The many geological layers with their different composition and fossil remains, he had concluded, could simply not be explained by the biblical account of one creation and one flood in which all living beings had been annihilated (again: a moral problem, too), but rather they pointed to a much longer, more varied history of the planet only science could unravel.

No question, Holbach concluded, could be solved by assuming the existence of God without creating more and more intractable questions. As a materialist preaching that there was no effect without cause, Holbach was also confronted with the question of the origin of the world: If the law of cause and effect was universally valid, then something must have caused the world to exist; if there is intelligence, a higher intelligence must have inspired it, the argument ran; if there was a creation, somebody must have created it.

Not so, retorted Holbach. If it is necessary to assume a Creator to satisfy the law of cause and effect, then by the same token this Creator must be created, and so on. The assumption of a Creator does not solve the mystery of creation. It simply creates an infinite regress of earlier creations lost in myth.

It is at moments such as these that we can clearly see the influence of Descartes and Spinoza. The idea of God as perfection, as a logical necessity, came from Descartes, who had used it as proof of God's existence. In theological terms, it was necessary, however, to assume that God had created the world out of nothing, by a miraculous act of his divine will. This is where Spinoza intervened by using the splendid necessity of logic to topple the theological argument without ever openly attacking it. If God is perfection, then he is also necessity, because every quality of a perfect entity is necessary to it. Subtract or add something, and the result is imperfection.

Nature is created by God and therefore a product of perfection—that is, perfect in itself. But if God himself is synonymous with nature, then he is nothing but a different way of describing the laws of nature, its underlying principles. That means that it becomes simply unnecessary to speak about God as a separate entity. It is enough to speak about nature by using not words such as "grace," "redemption," and "resurrection," but terms like "gravity," "thermodynamics," "mass," and "electricity."

To unravel the mysteries of nature, the baron argued, we need science, not theology. A powerless God, shackled by his own laws, unable to intervene in the inalterable course of history; a God without will, without purpose, without might—this was not a God worth praying to and not one remotely interested in the minute details of, say, human diet, procreation, or mythology. If the assumption of God the Creator leads to an infinite regress of creations or to an infraction of the natural law it is supposed to uphold, the idea of a God present in our daily experience is condemned to fare even worse. It may be tempting to explain natural phenomena and human suffering as God's will, but every injustice, every terrible human tragedy, challenges the assumption that God is good, all-powerful, and all-knowing.

Holbach's obvious anger against Christianity may also have been informed by a natural disaster that had become one of the most important touchstones of Enlightenment thought. On All Saints' Day 1755, the city of Lisbon was hit by a devastating earthquake. Emerging from the rubble, the survivors had assembled at the harbor when a sixty-foot-high tsunami swept away tens of thousands of victims. Within a matter of minutes, almost 100,000 people had been killed, many of them in the churches where they had attended Mass. A pious Catholic city and hardly a modern Sodom, Lisbon was razed, with only one building in ten still standing—many of them in the district housing the city's brothels and seamen's taverns. To theologians and philosophers throughout Europe, this terrible catastrophe became an object of intense debates. Was God himself unable to prevent the tragedy from killing so many innocents? Or was he momentarily distracted or simply indifferent to human suffering? Was this not, as not only Spinoza but also Scholastic theologians had claimed, the best of all possible worlds, the perfect creation of a perfect God? And if it was, how could so much apparently meaningless suffering be reconciled with the teachings of Christianity?

Some theologians declared that the earthquake was God's punishment of godless ways and proof of his active involvement in his creation; others thought that it was divine retribution for Portugal's continuing hunger for colonial gold and for centuries of mass murder among the natives in South America. Every faction within the church proclaimed its own truth. Jansenist authors pointed to the fact that Lisbon was a center of Jesuit training and that the divine choice of All Saints' Day could only indicate that the saints themselves had intervened with the Creator to put an end to the sinning in the city. The Jesuits themselves, meanwhile, saw the disaster as an indication of God's displeasure about the lax and un-Jesuitical ways of the city and promptly held an auto-da-fé, publicly burning heretics at the stake to assuage the wrath of God.

But other contemporaries felt that they themselves had been shaken out of their dogmatic slumber. The deist Voltaire was particularly disturbed by the extent of the devastation. He reacted, as he always did, by transforming it into literature. The result of his cogitations was, in addition to an occasional poem, the novel *Candide*, which is partly set in Lisbon during and after the quake. It satirizes the notion that we live in "the best of all possible worlds," a theory advanced in the novel by the fatuously overoptimistic character Dr. Pangloss, who clings to his theory despite the appalling suffering he is subjected to.

In contrast to Voltaire's intensive engagement, Holbach's friends had little to say on the matter. The baron himself, of course, was trained in geology and other sciences, wrote about them for the *Encyclopédie*, and might have had precise ideas about natural disasters, but he never explicitly referred to the Lisbon quake. The absurdity of attempting to explain a natural catastrophe in moral terms was too obvious to him. In *Christianisme dévoilé* he had argued against the folly of imputing a divine will to natural events, and at least publicly he had nothing to add to the matter.

It is possible that Holbach's atheism had not always been this uncompromising. Indeed, according to one contemporary source it had been Diderot who had made Holbach into the determined atheist he was. Having returned from Leiden with new ideas and a thorough grounding in the sciences, the young baron had nevertheless continued to be a deist in a fashion similar to Voltaire's: This was a great and marvelous world, and somebody, some power greater than mere nature, had to have made it. Diderot and Holbach had argued this point many times, and one day the baron had come to see his friend at the workshop of an engraver, where Diderot was checking the drafts for illustrations that were to be part of the *Encyclopédie*, plates dealing with botanical subjects. "But surely," the baron insisted, pointing to the intricate depiction of flowers, leaves, blossoms, and fruit stems, "all this beauty, all this ingenuity is proof of a higher intelligence?" Diderot had simply looked at him, unmoved, whereupon the baron literally broke down, weeping.[12]

If this smacks a little too much of literary invention (the bulk of the work on the volumes with illustrations was done after 1759, far too late for any such incident to have occurred), it nonetheless makes the point that Holbach might still by the early 1750s have been one of the many who had simply never bothered to examine their inherited religious beliefs for logical consistency, and who came to the realization that they could not be correct only after being confronted with a new perspective. In later life, as his perspective became fixed, the arch-atheist Holbach showed great understanding to those around him who did not share his convictions. He often had a priest stay at his country house at Grandval to say Mass for his mother-in-law, and he proudly attended church on the occasion of his daughters' weddings.

Diderot's path to atheism had been slow but purposeful, and his thinking about human rationality and human frailty was more richly layered than Holbach's eventual unblinking certainty. Denis always retained great admiration for his honest, hardworking father, for the ethos of independent craftsmanship, and for the simple values he represented, and like the baron he was willing to show his respect for this world. On a visit to his hometown of Langres after his father's death in 1759, the great atheist Encyclopedist attended church together with his siblings, sitting in the same pew as he had done as a child. "My head wants one thing, my heart another," he sighed, but in his own thought his head prevailed, much to the distress of Anne-Toinette, his deeply pious wife, who was disgusted with her husband's views and with the company he kept.

But Diderot's head did not always win over his heart. Indeed, the tension between the two, between intellectual conviction and instinctive longing, became the creative wellspring of much of his work. In his personal life, he was inclined to give the heart the precedence he refused it in intellectual matters. Estranged from his long-suffering and bitter wife, he fled into the arms of several lovers, first and foremost the educated and deeply intelligent Sophie Volland, who would remain his mistress, soul mate, and correspondent for more than two decades. Diderot had met Sophie around 1755, when she was thirty-nine years old and he himself forty-three. She had never married; she lived with her mother and her sister in the rue Vieux-Augustins, close to the Palais Royal with its beautiful formal garden and to Holbach's house in the rue Royale. There is hardly any information about the beginning of their relationship. They frequently wrote to each other, and the 187 surviving letters are models of candor and wit, an enormous pleasure to read, but they are all by Diderot, so that only his side of the story is preserved, and only part of that story, because his 134 earliest, most passionate, and possibly most indecent letters were destroyed by Sophie's mother, while all of Sophie's own letters to her lover suffered the same fate at the hand of Mme Vandeul, Diderot's own daughter.

Almost everything we know of Sophie Volland comes from Diderot's letters, an interested and tendentious witness. In fact, his lover was not even called Sophie but Louise-Henriette—her lover simply addressed her as "Sophie," which might have been a family nickname or a name he himself chose for her because he liked it better, and also because it was a sign of respect—*Sophia*, after all, is Greek for wisdom—and he greatly admired her clear, analytical mind.

Diderot would not have been the man he was had his admiration stopped at intellectual matters, however. Their affair was not the first in the years of Diderot's marriage (his daughter, who would later burn his letters, was two years old). Diderot's letters refer to the times when the lovers were separated, sometimes alluding to the good times together, always voicing his longing for Sophie. They are often filled with stories about daily life and about goings-on at Holbach's salon and the baron's Grandval country seat, gossip about friends, and accounts of what Denis was working on. They are letters written to an intellectual equal.

But in the shade of this riotous dance of detail and local color, Sophie remains barely visible, someone talked to rather than talking. Apart from a few fragments of information about her appearance (she had "dry little paws" and wore glasses), there is no record, no portrait, not even a drawing that might show what the great love of his life looked like. All we are left with is Diderot's admiration for the frankness with which she expressed her opinions, his concerned inquiries about her fragile health, and his advice to rein in her gourmandise: "You pay with 15 bad days for one little wine or one leg of pheasant too many."[13]

The relationship, of course, was a difficult one, first because the lovers thought it best to hide it, even from Sophie's mother. Denis was forced to sneak into the house by the kitchen door or meet Sophie in the gardens of the Palais Royal when a trustworthy, and no doubt well-rewarded, footman had informed him that Madame was out. But eventually the inevitable happened, and the two were discovered in flagrante delicto by Sophie's mother. The outraged Mme Volland would not have her daughter's honor besmirched and whisked Sophie, who was forty years old, to the family's country estate for an extended stay in the clean, fresh air. Sophie almost died of boredom; she always hated the countryside. Eventually, the ladies moved back to Paris, and the relationship with Diderot could resume—more discreetly this time.

Toinette Diderot took longer—almost four years—to catch on to her husband's affair. It was only when she recognized the handwriting on a letter addressed to her husband, as well as the footman who delivered it, that she drew the inevitable conclusion and raised a row that still sent sparks flying some days later, as Diderot wrote to Grimm.

Diderot's marriage had long been rocky, but now it seemed to have run aground. Often husband and wife would not speak for days on end. "After the latest domestic storm, we eat separately," he wrote to Sophie in 1761. "I am being served in my study. As long as we see each other only in passing, one can hope that we will have neither occasion nor time to quarrel further. O cruel life!"[14] But while relations between husband and wife remained alternately frosty and tempestuous, Diderot remained loyal to his Toinette. He devotedly nursed her through several serious spells of illness, often staying up all night to make compresses and comfort her. He also defended her in front of outsiders who made the mistake of taking the discord between husband and wife, and her ignorance and piety, for a license to ridicule. When one of his literary friends made fun of Toinette's lack of education and her superstitiousness, Diderot reminded him that there were several main rules of good satire, the last and most important one being that it was better to shut up than to be thrown out of the "fucking window."

But it was Sophie whom Diderot loved, with whom he wanted to be, about whom he dreamed—a dream much complicated by her mother, who appears to have gotten used to her daughter's affair with the famous atheist but remained a meddling presence in their lives. She exasperated Diderot, partly through her obtrusive presence ("How many sweet moments I sacrifice to your mother!"[15]) and partly through her determination to protect Sophie's virtue by removing her to the countryside and staying there for months on end. Between these enforced absences and Diderot's own stays outside of Paris during the summer months, there were only long and longing letters, exchanged via a reliable intermediary in town.

Eventually, the balance of the relationship shifted. Diderot, it seems, was not content with being Sophie's lover and became erotically interested in and possibly sexually involved with her two sisters, even beginning to address his letters to all of them. The hints and possibilities thrown up by the letters allow for little more than an agonizing guessing game, but it seems likely that Diderot had at least a fleeting affair with one of the other sisters Volland, who was herself at the same time sufficiently intimate with Sophie to make Diderot jealous. There are indications that Sophie was an androgynous beauty. Diderot wrote of her that "my Sophie is man and woman, whenever she likes," a remark that may lend credence to a sexual relationship between the two sisters and possibly even a brief three-way affair.

The love between Denis and Sophie did not quite recover from these complications and triangulations, and eventually Diderot's letters to Sophie assume a less ardent, less intimate tone, though it is unclear whether his or her waning interest was to blame.

To Diderot, his love for Sophie went far beyond sexual intimacy. He respected her and sought her opinion. His letters show that he made no effort to hide his convictions from her and even that he implicitly relied on her approval, particularly regarding his determined atheism. He freely told her about antireligious pamphlets being read and distributed, about discussions at the salon, and about his own work in progress.

During his hours with Sophie, the desires of Diderot's head coincided with those of his heart. But if the private and the intellectual were always intertwined for the philosopher Diderot, the resulting tensions became a source of strength for the artist. His mature views on atheism were unmistakable, as a furious 1766 letter to the engineer and writer Guillaume Vialet demonstrates. Diderot liked Vialet enough to suggest he marry his adored daughter Angélique, but when the proposed son-in-law surprisingly wrote a book in which he sang the praises of life as a monk, the philosopher replied with unconcealed scorn:

> I would say that you have committed the greatest possible abuse of the mind; to me this religion is the most absurd and the most atrocious of dogmas; the most unintelligible, the most metaphysical, the most convoluted, and therefore the most subjected to divisions, sects, schisms, heresies; . . . the most vulgar, the most depressing, the most gothic and the most sad of ceremonies; the most puerile and the most unsociable in

> its morals . . . the most intolerant of all. . . . I would say that because man, who is naturally superstitious needs a fetish, the simplest and most innocent fetish is the best of all.[16]

Diderot remained convinced that his own, clear-eyed atheism was not for all, and certainly not for the fainthearted. The "naturally superstitious," he believed, needed their fetishes: "The progress of Enlightenment is limited," he wrote to Sophie in 1759. "It hardly reaches the suburbs. The people there are too stupid, too miserable, and too busy. There it stops."[17] The problem with what Diderot and his friends perceived as a gradual hardening of minds and a rise of prejudice in the areas not illuminated by the torches of the Enlightenment was that religious feeling was so very easily converted into political oppression. If some kind of belief seemed a necessary crutch to the untutored, it was always likely to harden into dogma and persecution: "Wherever one admits God, there is a cult; wherever there is a cult, the natural order of morals is overturned, morality corrupted. Sooner or later, the moment comes where the notion that hindered people from stealing an *écu* [a French coin] leads to a hundred thousand people having their throats slashed. Some compensation!"[18]

Diderot accepted rationalism, but his sentiment bristled against its implications: "I am furious at being entangled in a confounded philosophy which my mind cannot refrain from approving and my heart from denying,"[19] he wrote to Sophie, reflecting that scientifically speaking, their love was nothing but a random encounter of atoms. Finding that his methodical thinking forced him to live in a godless universe, he faced the apparent contradictions between individual experience and universal necessity, between his love of morality and his animal existence. His writer's eye allowed him to reduce these deeply philosophical ideas to their essence as everyday situations and their implications. In a 1762 letter he reflected on sex, success, and the philosophical and scientific questions raised by both: "A post becomes vacant; a woman uses her powers of seduction; she lifts her skirts a bit; she lets them down again, and *voilà* her husband, a poor clerk with a hundred Francs a month, is suddenly *Monsieur le Directeur* with fifteen thousand Livres per year. But what is the connection between a just and generous act, and the lustful loss of a few drops of a fluid? In truth, I believe that nature is not concerned about good and evil.

She has two ends: the conservation of the individual, the propagation of the species."[20]

In this flash of insight anticipating Darwin, Diderot framed a pragmatic, scientific view of the universe. Morality may preoccupy human minds, but what counts in nature is "the propagation of the species" and by implication anything making it more likely. When an individual was faced with this fact, morality became a simple choice: "Do good, know the truth, that is what distinguishes one man from the next. The rest is nothing. The duration of life is so short, its real needs so narrow, and once one is gone, it matters so little whether one was someone or no one. In the end, one needs nothing but a dirty rag and four planks of pine."[21]

Despite such protestations of stoicism, Diderot's awareness of mortality continued to haunt him. He sought refuge and meaning in the secular religion of the humanist, in loving art, and in a continual preoccupation with posterity, his stand-in for the afterlife. Despite his own sober assessment that it would matter little "whether one has been someone or no one," the question of how he would be remembered would become central to Diderot in later life.

Much of Diderot's best philosophical work is dissimulated in his fiction, which also reveals much about his religious—or rather, antireligious—stance. In *Le Rêve d'Alembert* (*D'Alembert's Dream*, 1769) the mature Diderot dramatized current debates about the nature of matter and the purpose of life on earth by using a trick sure to raise expectations among his Paris friends, for whom the work was primarily intended. (Written for the drawer—that is, not for publication during his lifetime because of strict censorship—it was not published until 1830, seventy years after he finished it.) Not only are the characters of this fast and furious novella of ideas based on people he knew, but they also carry their names. Despite the title of the work, however, the protagonist was not Jean d'Alembert, Diderot's coeditor of the *Encyclopédie*, but his mistress, Julie de Lespinasse, who is nursing her lover through a bout of fever and is carrying on a discussion with his physician, Dr. Bordeu. Interrupted from time to time by the voice of the hallucinating mathematician, Diderot lets the doctor and the lover react to the entirely unreasonable things the fictional d'Alembert utters. As a mathematician, the famous scientist was the very embodiment of rationality. But what has happened to him? What happens to the human mind when it is housed in a feverish body? The original question was La Mettrie's, but Diderot used this situation for a wider and genuinely dramatic exploration of the nature of human rationality and consciousness.

D'Alembert's Dream reveals Diderot's fascination with the material nature of life. He shows himself to be an out-and-out materialist who qualifies humans as "thinking matter," complex organisms built out of smaller, simpler ones—akin to a cluster of bees. This material world leaves no space for anything essentially immaterial. All matter is contiguous, Bordeu explains to Lespinasse, connected to everything else like the threads in a spider's web. Nothing exists on its own terms; everything is part of the material world and subject to the law of necessity, of becoming and dying.

Bordeu claims that as there is no great difference between living and dead matter, "one makes marble out of flesh and flesh out of marble."[22] Life is movement, he states, echoing Holbach's definition. Death is inert and can only be moved by something else. The individual particles of matter, however, can bridge the gap between the two. The marble of a statue can be ground to dust and fertilize plants, which are eaten and thus become living tissue, thinking and feeling matter. Humans are simply a particular mode of organization temporarily adopted by molecules, part of an endless chain of being: "Who knows what races of animals have preceded us? Who knows which races of animals will succeed ours? Everything changes, everything passes, and the only constant thing is the totality. The world begins and ends ceaselessly, every moment is its beginning and its end."[23]

Life is a material phenomenon, a property of matter, which even creates personality and thought, argues Bordeu, quoting widely from contemporary case studies of people who suffered brain damage and lost their faculty of reflection, their memory, or their skills. The infinitely small particles making up a living body follow an organizing principle to order themselves into organs and entire individuals. And yet each of these particles has its own purpose and direction, and "while there is only one consciousness, there is an infinity of wills"[24] just as in a swarm of bees, where the individual animals retain their own sensation of pain or hunger while following a common organization.

In Bordeu's words, Diderot comes as close as he gets to finding a natural basis for internal conflict: The mind may want one thing, but the body, the nonrational part of the self, may demand quite another. Individual parts of the body will claim their share in life, as Julie de Lespinasse understands: "Would not the isolation of different parts create men with different characters? The brain, the heart, the chest, the feet, the hands, the testicles. . . . Oh! How that simplifies morality!"[25] How would a brain man, a hand man, and a testicle man act? According to the demands of their dominant organs, of course. But as all are mingled within each human being, the individual is pulled in different directions not because of any moral failing but because of his or her organic base.

Having demonstrated the biological basis of moral behavior, Diderot goes further. Birth defects have shown that each characteristic of an organism is programmed by a "filament" (*brin*), he argues, and if such a filament is missing from the sheaf of information, the resulting organism will be deformed. The filaments bearing this information may be tiny, but if they are damaged, the results can be devastating. An animal, after all, is only "a machine which advances towards its perfection by an infinity of successive developments, a machine whose regular or irregular formation depends on a parcel of fine tissues, a kind of string in which not even the finest filament may be broken, misplaced, or lacking without serious consequences for the whole."[26] There is an obvious parallel to the thin filaments of DNA here, but Diderot's strikingly modern conception of nature is also expressed in the "infinity of successive developments" by which each organism is perfecting itself. In conjunction with the "survival of the species" Diderot mentioned in his 1762 letter to Sophie, we have a natural mechanism of great power that Diderot may well have learned about during his discussions with the great zoologist Comte de Buffon during the early years of the Holbach salon: evolution *avant la lettre*.

In *D'Alembert's Dream*, the physician Bordeu is aware that a single filament cannot explain heredity. As malformed parents do not always give birth to malformed children, he speculates further that two strings of filament must be combined to make one new individual and determine its characteristics: "To make a child it needs two, as you know. Perhaps one of the agents repairs the vice of the other, and the defective tissue is not born again up to the moment at which the offspring of a monstrous race predominates and dictates the formation of the tissue." The variations of the string of filaments within one species form the monstrous varieties within that species.

When Julie de Lespinasse asks the doctor why she cannot perceive the causal links among all things in the universe, the doctor answers that the distances and the sheer multitude of stimuli are too great for any one signal to arrive. Lespinasse replies that it is a shame she cannot perceive the ultimate continuity of the universe. True, Bordeu concedes, but this would mean being God, connected to the vibrations of each atom like a spider sitting in the middle of a gigantic net, an impossibility, he argues, because in a material universe God himself "would be matter, part of the universe, subject to vicissitudes, he would age, he would die." God is a logical extrapolation of our urge to identify reasons and causes, the idea of perfect knowledge, but he cannot exist. In this radical rereading of Spinoza's God, Diderot takes the step the seventeenth-century thinker refused to make: If God is sheer necessity, the lawful course of nature, then the concept itself simply becomes superfluous. What remains is necessity itself, which inexorably rules the world but which no mind can understand fully.

In his literary works, Diderot had firmly arrived in a materialist, even evolutionist universe, just as Holbach had in his philosophical works. Together, the two men forged a coherent and forceful vision of the world and of the place humans might have within it. This uncompromisingly empirical view left no space for metaphysical speculation or divine intervention. This would have been reason enough for persecution and arrest, never mind the livid hatred of church officials and the hack writers they employed to discredit the radicals. What made the matter infinitely worse, however, was the fact that works such as *Le Christianisme dévoilé* were a direct and violent attack on Christianity itself.

Writing to Voltaire, Diderot cheerfully characterized the book's anonymous author, whose identity he rather revealingly chose not to confirm to his correspondent, as a man of great courage as well as a natural successor for the master *philosophe*: "It is a man who has taken the torch out of your hands, and who has entered proudly into their [the church's] building of straw, and has set it alight at all corners."[27]

From Diderot's perspective this may have been true, but it also coincided with Voltaire's darkest fears. Secluded in his Swiss exile but so well informed by his Paris correspondents that he might as well have attended the city's most important salon himself, Voltaire was becoming worried about his preeminence among Enlightenment thinkers.

The old sorcerer: Observing from his exile in Switzerland, Voltaire congratulated Diderot upon his release from prison but later grew increasingly critical of the atheist opinions of his former protégé. Marble bust by Jean-Antoine Houdon, 1778.

ERICH LESSING / ART RESOURCE, NY

Holbach's salon seemed beyond the reach of Voltaire's influence. None of the regular guests at the rue Royale had responded positively to his advances. Diderot had always remained polite, even effusive in his praise and prompt with his letters, but had never yet visited the great man and had only given him unimportant topics for articles in the *Encyclopédie*, an inclination that he did not entirely trust Voltaire. Holbach, too, had never made the journey to Voltaire's country estate, and neither had other, lesser luminaries such as Marmontel or the *abbé* Raynal. Only the politically naïve Jean d'Alembert, who was a leading Encyclopedist but no longer a member of Holbach's salon, was in regular contact with the master. From his vantage point in the foothills of the Alps, Voltaire began to fear that he might finally be in danger of being sidelined, eclipsed by a younger and more radical group of thinkers.

While he could not possibly disown the editors of the *Encyclopédie* and what they stood for, Voltaire was quick to realize he could not be associated with a work such as *Christianity Unveiled* and, when some suggested that he was the anonymous author, protested that the dangerous book was not his. It was simply too badly written, he declared—it did not have his elegance of style, and more importantly, it was entirely opposed to his principles. "This book leads to atheism," he wrote in a letter to a friend, "which I despise. I have always regarded atheism as the greatest confusion of reason, because it is as ridiculous to say that the arrangement of the world does not prove a supreme artisan, as it would be impertinent to say that a watch does not prove a watchmaker. I disapprove of this book as a citizen, because the author appears to be too much an enemy of the [worldly and spiritual] powers. People thinking as he does would never create anything but anarchy."[28]

In his own copy, today held at the British Museum, Voltaire scribbled angry comments in the margins. As a politician and a businessman he knew that it would not do to take too principled a stance against great powers.

Even if it was not published until a decade later, *Christianity Unveiled* gives a good impression of the arguments that ensued when Holbach's salon awoke to new life during the mid-1750s. Having buried his first wife in 1754, the heartbroken baron had spent several months traveling and attempting to forget. After this period of grief he almost abruptly decided to remarry. The woman of his choice was his first wife's half sister, Charlotte-Susanne d'Aine, an eminently sensible match, as it kept a good deal of property in the family, but apparently much more than that: They would remain happily married for more than thirty years. Initially, the close family ties had caused administrative problems, and in a procedure even an atheist could not avoid, Holbach had been forced to obtain a papal dispensation to marry. Submitting himself to the authority of the church was against his personal principles, but the baron had never believed in forcing others to live according to his ideas.

Having been in abeyance for months, "Holbach's coterie," as Rousseau now called his former friends, had resumed its regular Thursday and Sunday meetings, and its discussions. "It's raining bombs on the house of the Lord,"[29] Diderot had written to Sophie Volland with evident satisfaction when a new clutch of atheist pamphlets came on the market, and he was right. All forms of religious belief were attacked at the rue Royale. For the first time since ancient Rome, a strong philosophical alternative to religion was being formulated by a group of people debating their ideas, applying them to all aspects of life, and publishing the results. There had been isolated voices before, and the friends at Holbach's table drew on their work, even if they were sometimes reluctant to admit it, but never before in Christian Europe had there been a debate as open, as uncompromising, or as far-reaching as this discussion spinning itself out over the many Thursdays and Sundays at the rue Royale.

The spirit of opposition that animated the group, however, was only a beginning. The philosophers of the rue Royale had had the courage to reject their intellectual inheritance in favor of a different worldview; they had shown the resolve to risk their livelihoods and possibly their lives by doing everything they could to make themselves heard; they had torn down the dogma of the church and the morality of Christendom. Now they could build a better future on the ruins of the past.

CHAPTER 7

ONLY THE WICKED MAN LIVES ALONE

During the second half of the 1750s, Holbach's salon and its members were struck by a series of crises, both personal and professional. It began in 1754, when Holbach's wife, Basile-Geneviève, the gracious hostess, died in childbirth, leaving her husband bereft and disconsolate. The baron could no longer find joy in his work, in the salon, or in life itself, and his condition was so grave that Grimm decided to take his friend on an extended trip through the French provinces to distract him. The two men departed, and the gatherings at the baron's house went into abeyance for several months as he traveled the country in search of consolation.

Diderot retrenched, working on the *Encyclopédie.* It had gathered great momentum, attracting international attention and growing sales. Three thousand copies—a huge print run by the standards of the time—were printed of the fourth volume, which appeared in October. After publication, the overworked editor even took two months to visit his family in Langres, partly to patch up relations with his father, who had not approved of his marriage. On his return to Paris, the Diderot family moved to a larger flat in a building in the rue Taranne (today on the boulevard Saint-Germain), which offered more space for the growing encyclopedic business, which required hundreds of reference books, a great volume of correspondence, and the frequent visits of copyists and editors.

The next traumatic episode concerned several of the leading members of the salon and ignited a decade of frustration and histrionics. The tempest would eventually erupt into a full-scale international literary scandal: the break between the two old friends Diderot and Rousseau, or rather between Rousseau and the rest of the world. The nature of this progressive falling-out highlights not only personal but also philosophical differences between the two men, who had once been inseparable and had inspired each other's works.

Since Rousseau had moved into the hermitage at Louise d'Epinay's estate of La Chevrette, he felt increasingly ignored, marginalized, and patronized by the members of the Holbach salon, whom he no longer saw on an almost daily basis. As main editor of the *Encyclopédie*, Diderot was becoming known throughout Europe, while, despite the fact that he had a part in the success of this endeavor by contributing many articles on music, Jean-Jacques felt that he was not getting the acknowledgment he deserved. He began to suspect that he was being ill-used by the bustle of friends and acquaintances gathering around the Encyclopedists, particularly at the salon of Baron d'Holbach.

Before his departure from Paris, when Rousseau "had not yet gone savage, but was quiet and deferential,"[1] as André Marmontel put it, Jean-Jacques had already been haunted by feelings of inferiority and wounded pride. He was experiencing the anxiety many a gifted but shy person feels when amid boisterous and clever friends, especially male ones: Even if he had an argument to make, even if he knew more than the others, he would not be able to make himself heard. His idea would be dismissed, laughed at.

Rousseau was not at ease during these long evenings, and to some degree he must have felt inferior to many of the guests—he had no formal philosophical schooling, little Latin, and no Greek. He was an engraver's apprentice turned intellectual dilettante. He was surrounded by some of the sharpest and most learned minds of his century, outstanding authors, scientists, and artists; his mediocrity as a musician, his uncertain grasp of ancient literature, and his (at best) eclectic knowledge of contemporary literary life must have been obvious.

Rousseau felt upstaged and unrecognized. Denis Diderot, his Denis, was no longer his own but instead the sun around which the other, clever planets were orbiting over the empty plates and constantly refilled glasses. There was no central role for Jean-Jacques to play here, with Diderot as the undisputed heart of every discussion, Holbach as the gracious but quietly authoritative host whose scientific knowledge was second to none, and a plethora of brilliant guests and foreign visitors providing additional outside focus.

Unwilling to acknowledge that it was his own disposition that was frustrating his determination to shine and be admired, Jean-Jacques was quick to find other culprits. As he would rather snobbishly point out in his *Confessions*, Holbach was "a parvenu," recently rich and obviously far too mediocre a man to recognize Rousseau's genius, his old friend Denis Diderot possibly too callous to share the limelight with another man. The true evil genius, however, a manipulator bent on destroying his reputation, was Wilhelm Melchior Grimm, the editor of the *Correspondance littéraire* and a former friend with whom he had enjoyed singing Italian arias at the harpsichord, but now transformed into a menacing, manipulative politician. Rousseau may have had more insight into Grimm's character than Diderot would have until the end of his life—Grimm was in fact more of a careerist, more in thrall to great names and titles, and more manipulative than Denis believed—but the conclusions Rousseau drew were wildly off the mark.

With every passing day he became more convinced that he was victim of a sinister cabal dreamed up by his former friends, who had become jealous of his genius and his success. Led and egged on by the diabolical Grimm, they wanted to destabilize him, sap his strength, spread rumors about him, cause his downfall. His suspicions grew more acute and deepened into a sense of being systematically excluded and ridiculed by his former friends, as he later noted in the *Confessions*: "When I appeared the conversation ceased to be general. People huddled together in little groups and whispered in each other's ears, while I remained alone, not knowing with whom to talk. I put up for a long time with this shameful cold-shouldering; just because Mme d'Holbach who was sweet and friendly, always welcomed me, I endured the coarse humor and her insufferable husband for as long as I could."[2]

No doubt Rousseau's paranoia stemmed in part from the fact that his friendship with Diderot had lost some of its intensity. Jean-Jacques was a difficult man to deal with, and from the perspective of the men and women who had been his friends for years, he had become increasingly touchy, unpredictable, and ready to take offense. With the grand gesture of a man seeking inspiration and fleeing the moral cesspool they were all living in, he had taken himself out of their society. Moreover, Grimm not only was the main publicist of the Encyclopedists and their ideas but also had become Diderot's closest personal friend, threatening to eclipse Rousseau at the precise moment when an association with the philosopher was becoming not only a pleasure but also an asset.

One incident in Holbach's salon had particularly embittered Jean-Jacques. Diderot had been pestered by a country parson, one *abbé* Petit, a man with literary ambitions who asked the *philosophe* to read one of his poems, which ran to seven hundred stanzas. Reluctant to be impolite but equally unwilling to trawl though an endless mediocre poem, Diderot tried to buy himself some time by suggesting that the priest write a drama instead. He had underestimated the industriousness of the *abbé*, who soon returned with a play. Diderot immediately saw that the work was truly terrible and suggested with more than a little malice that the proud author read the play aloud at Holbach's salon.

What began as an unkind joke quickly became a nasty scene. Petit mistook sarcasm for admiration and proceeded to declaim his doggerel in front of Holbach, Diderot, Marmontel, Raynal, Rousseau, and others. Most of the guests tried to suppress their smirks and twitches of laughter as they watched the *abbé* enthusiastically making a fool of himself. Rousseau was incensed. He snatched the manuscript from the astonished writer's hand, flung it on the floor, and shouted: "Your play is worthless. . . . All these gentlemen are laughing at you. Go away from here; go back to your parish duties in the country!" He and the *abbé* almost came to blows, and finally Jean-Jacques angrily stormed out of the house.

The friendship between Rousseau and his former fellow travelers was deeply compromised, and when Holbach told the story to an acquaintance several years later, he commented that Rousseau's rage "has never ceased." Now the baron, too, came in for Rousseau's particular hatred and could do nothing to assuage his irrational anger. Proud but without means, Rousseau had once stated that while he was obliged to quaff local wines, fine Bordeaux was all his stomach and his fragile constitution could take. The baron quietly arranged to have fifty bottles of claret sent to his friend, only to find himself at the end of yet another first-rate temper tantrum. The rich man was mocking his poverty, the sensitive genius claimed.

For a while, both Denis and Jean-Jacques attempted to revive their flagging friendship. They wanted to meet, but Diderot claimed that he was too busy with his editing duties to make the ten-mile journey on foot (he could not afford a carriage), which was probably true, and Rousseau insisted that he would not set foot into the bad city once again. Soon the reproaches became explicit, as Rousseau sent increasingly hostile letters to Diderot, accusing him of being a bad friend. He attacked him for not visiting him in his exile, as Jean-Jacques had once visited his friend Denis in Vincennes.

Caught up in the daily grind of writing, editing, supervising typesetters and engravers, and dealing with the booksellers, Diderot failed to take these accusations seriously and responded lightheartedly. He could not imagine that he should really be expected to travel out to Montmorency just to appease the whim of a temperamental friend. He airily suggested that Rousseau come to Paris instead and stay with him, which might give them time to discuss a recent manuscript, arrange for the printing, and have dinner together, not at Holbach's salon, but at Saint-Denis.

As Rousseau's frustration grew, Diderot was becoming tired of the game of exchanging letters and implicit recriminations. Sarcastically, he wrote expressing his satisfaction that Rousseau had liked his play *Le Fils naturel*, which was currently being staged. In fact, his friend was deeply hurt because of one snippet of dialogue, which he rightly assumed was aimed at him. Diderot, the most sociable of thinkers, had a character say to another, a virtuous philosopher, in a fit of exasperation: "You have received the rarest talents, and you have to account for them in front of society. . . . You, renounce society! I appeal to your heart, ask it, and it will tell you that a good man is in society and only the wicked man lives alone."[3]

The virtuous hermit needed no one to tell him who was the target of this comment, and he was incandescent with anger about being called "wicked" by his friend. He presumably wanted Diderot to make the pilgrimage to his hermitage by way of an apology. He therefore responded vehemently to the suggestion to come and visit Denis: "I never want to go to Paris again. I will never go there. This time I am resolved!" he launched at him, accusing him once again of being unwilling to make the slightest effort for him. Diderot wrote back laconically, admitting: "It is true that fifteen years ago I had neither wife nor child, servants, or money [and could freely dispose of my time] and that now my life is full of aggravations and worries and I cannot take even some hours of happiness and relaxation. My friends joke about this or insult me, depending on their character."[4] Still, he promised Rousseau to go to see him, on foot—"my fortune does not permit me to travel otherwise."

Rousseau was apparently even more enraged by this reply than by the previous ones, because Mme d'Epinay now wrote to Diderot in an attempt to dissuade him from coming altogether, pointing out that nothing was to be gained from such a visit, which would, after all, take two or three hours each way. Now Denis was sufficiently concerned to write another note in which he implored his friend to come to his senses and remember who his true friends were, a plea culminating with an indictment: "Oh! Rousseau, you are becoming villainous, unjust, cruel, ferocious, and I cry with pain about this . . . but I fear that our most intimate links have become a matter of total indifference to you."[5]

In fact, Rousseau's feelings for Diderot had become a matter not of indifference but of pathological suspicion and simmering outrage, and he retreated into hostile isolation from his former friends, whose very passion for culture, discussion, and knowledge appeared to bear out his most pessimistic ideas about the corruption inherent in society. He had become convinced that all the world's ills—wickedness, cruelty, greed, mendacity, and debauchery—came from the conventions of established society, which alienated a person from the state of grace and made him deaf to the voice of nature.

That same voice of nature was also calling Jean-Jacques away from his mistress, Thérèse, and towards the dashing Countess d'Houdetot, Mme d'Epinay's sister-in-law. In fact, he had admired the countess from afar for some time and wanted to be closer to her and have more opportunities to see her. Now, in 1757, he planned his walks through the park to coincide with her riding excursions; he wrote notes to her, and he pined in solitude. But the horsewoman Sophie d'Houdetot—whom Jean-Jacques found irresistible in her broad-brimmed hat, riding trousers (a scandalous liberty at the time), and riding crop—already had a lover, the marquis de Saint-Lambert, an officer, poet, and frequent guest in Holbach's salon. She was not interested in his advances—proof to Rousseau that members of Holbach's coterie had already blackened his name.

If Rousseau's romantic ambitions remained unfulfilled, his domestic arrangements with Thérèse were quite satisfying, as he proudly related in his *Confessions*: "My third child was . . . carried to the Foundling Hospital as well as the two former, and the next two were disposed of in the same manner; for

I have had five children in all. This arrangement seemed to me to be so good, reasonable and lawful, that if I did not publicly boast of it, the motive by which I was withheld was merely my regard for their mother: but I mentioned it to all those to whom I had declared our connection, to Diderot, to Grimm."[6]

Rousseau's lack of concern for his mistress, five times pregnant and five times robbed of her baby, suggests that she felt very differently about the arrangement that pleased him so much. But his needs were paramount. He needed silence in the house. He was, after all, working on his novel *Émile*, which breathtakingly has as its subject the ideal education of a child. To Diderot, whose daughter Angélique was his pride and joy, his former friend's rejection of his own children must have been sheer, unadulterated selfishness and may well have played a part in alienating the two men.

In the relative quiet of a house free of squealing infants and surrounded by a park, Rousseau experienced a rush of creative energy and wrote his three works in quick succession: the novels *Julie ou la nouvelle Héloïse* and *Émile*, as well as his great philosophical work *Du contrat social* (*The Social Contract*).

As Rousseau's reputation quickly grew, his inner turmoil continued to rage on. His infatuation with Sophie d'Houdetot had reached fever pitch, and he would wait to meet her in the park as she came riding by and implore her to become his lover. The young woman continued to ignore Rousseau's advances. The Marquis de Saint-Lambert, her lover, was currently at the front, serving as an officer in France's ill-fated campaign during the Seven Years War (as, incidentally, was Friedrich Melchior Grimm).

Rousseau was unsure what to do. Despite his best efforts he had not become Sophie's lover, but the attention he had paid to her had not gone unnoticed in the literary circles of the capital. Rumors of a liaison between himself and the beautiful Sophie were bound to make the rounds and would hardly do any favors to his reputation as a virtuous philosopher. Finally, Diderot was able to persuade him to come to Paris after all and stay with him for a few days. Rousseau asked his friend for advice. True to his character, Diderot counseled him to be frank about his attachment and write to the Marquis de Saint-Lambert before he would hear of it from another source. Jean-Jacques promised to take his advice and returned to Montmorency. He did write to the marquis but not to confess his love; instead, he remonstrated with the officer that the countess was inexplicably cold to him and asked him to put in a good word for him.

What happened next is far from clear, as the fragmentary accounts by Diderot, Louise d'Epinay, and Rousseau vary widely. It appears that Denis, knowing that a letter had been written and believing things to be out in the open, made a remark that was more revealing than intended, and Jean-Jacques immediately went on the hunt for a traitor who had sullied his reputation and his holy love. His suspicions settled on his hostess, of all people. Separated from her lover, Grimm, who had always sought his downfall, Louise, Rousseau believed, could not stand seeing others around her happier than she was, and she had therefore spied on him and sabotaged his happiness. Enraged, he went up to her house and made a furious scene.

Louise was dumbfounded. She had extended her hospitality to this man, had welcomed him into her house and at her table, and had put up with his tirades, his self-righteousness, and his exaggerated sense of himself ("he is poor as Job but has vanity enough for four," an acquaintance had tartly commented on meeting him), only to be accused of the basest conduct and the lowest jealousy by a man she had trusted. When Jean-Jacques finally came to his senses, he was overwhelmed by guilt and threw himself at her knees begging forgiveness, but the bond of friendship between them was broken. Grimm took a dark view of the matter. "You know madmen are dangerous," he wrote to Louise from his camp, "especially if one panders to them as you have sometimes done to that poor devil through your ill-judged pity for his insanity."[7] Rousseau drew his own consequences from the affair. It was all Grimm's doing, he decided, and resolved to have no further dealings with him. In his *Confessions* he makes his longtime friend out to be a notorious liar, a fop, a manipulator, and, worst of all, a homosexual.

The whole drama left Jean-Jacques in an awkward position. He was still dependent for his entertainment and the roof over his head on the kindness of his worst enemy's lover, and he was morally indebted to her for her unfailing generosity to him. Of course, none of this prevented him from continuing to pursue the beautiful Sophie d'Houdetot with letters sweltering with passion. It did, however, prevent him from acceding to the one request Louise d'Epinay made to him in the course of their friendship. In October 1757, she had fallen ill with a serious chest complaint and believed that only one doctor, Théodore Troncin in Geneva, could help her. Grimm had only just returned from his army service and had his literary business to attend to. Who therefore could be better to accompany her on her trip there than Rousseau, the proud citizen of Geneva? The journey would not last long, and it would be a great comfort to her.

Jean-Jacques thought it beneath his dignity to be a mere companion and travel guide, and refused. His friends implored him to reconsider, but he remained unmoved. Diderot wrote him urgent letters recalling the debt of gratitude he owed to Louise. Rousseau responded furiously—indeed, he recalled that he trembled with anger when he read Diderot's letter, so much so that he found it almost impossible to read it to the end. It was clear, Rousseau thought, that his former friend was trying to damage him and had sided with his enemies. The extent of the conspiracy against him was proven by the fact that nobody seemed to reproach Grimm for not offering to accompany his mistress, and so Rousseau wrote a letter to him, in which he outlined his conception of his relationship with her. As far as he was concerned, there was nothing at all to be grateful for. "What has Mme d'Epinay done for me? . . . She had a little house built for me at the Hermitage, and persuaded me to live there. . . . What have I done, on my side, for Mme d'Epinay? At a time when I was thinking of returning to my native city, and wished very much to do so, and ought to have done so, she moved heaven and earth to keep me here. With her pleas, with intrigues even, she overcame my very proper and prolonged resistance."[8] In all this, he explained, he had violated his own preferences and felt a prisoner in her house. One moment of weakness and indulgence of a woman's will had caused him incalculable misery. His time as Louise's guest had been "two years of slavery."

Deeply disappointed, Louise d'Epinay set off for Geneva, writing to him: "You make me pity you. If you are sane, your conduct horrifies me on your behalf, because I do not think it straightforward. It is not natural to spend one's life suspecting and wounding one's friends."[9] Jean-Jacques answered with a missive soaked in hot tears and cold self-righteousness and once again decided that it had been she who had made his happiness impossible. To live virtuously, he decided, he would have to leave the hermitage. He would go to war with the entire band of hypocrites who had once been his companions and confidants. If they had chosen to intrigue behind his back, he would attack them in the open.

There is a second, deeper level at which Rousseau's endless, dreary litany of paranoia and suspicion actually expressed a real and growing distance between himself and his former friends, a philosophical chasm that was becoming too wide to be bridged with soothing words.

The nature of the split separating Rousseau from Diderot and Holbach is best described as a difference in how much philosophical courage and consistence they each showed in dealing with questions of faith. Holbach had accepted for himself that there was no possibility of being a philosopher and also believing in God, a decision that may have initially caused considerable internal turmoil, as the anecdote with Diderot at the print shop indicates. Diderot himself always remained nostalgic for the faith of his fathers but saw that it was rationally untenable. This conflict between head and heart, between conviction and instinct, became one of the mainsprings of his creative work, but as a philosopher he remained unequivocal about his atheist principles.

Rousseau, whose own relationship with religion was intense but fraught, could not possibly subscribe to this abolishment of divine presence, especially not one that acknowledged the emotional difficulty of this intellectually necessary step. As a young man he had somewhat opportunistically converted to Catholicism and had then become a Protestant again, but his real allegiance was not to an institution but to his own emotional needs and certainties. He passionately rejected the atheism of his friends, not on rational grounds, but because a godless universe would simply be too awful to confront. "No, I have suffered too much in this life not to expect another," he wrote to Voltaire in 1756. "All the subtleties of metaphysics will not make me doubt the immortality of the soul for a moment; I feel it, I believe it, I want it, I hope for it, I shall defend it to my last breath."[10] In the struggle between wanting to believe and seeing the impossibility of providing a rational basis for religion, Rousseau came down on the opposite side from Holbach and Diderot. He followed his psychological need, not his analytical head.

Rousseau's God was a God of reassurance, born out of the need to believe, to have an unchanging existential reference point—the impossible dream of philosophy since its inception. In his novel *Émile*, the author slipped into the coat of a Savoyard priest explaining his faith to the protagonists. He had tried philosophy, the priest said, but "I pondered . . . on the sad fate of mortals, adrift upon this sea of human opinions, without compass or rudder, and abandoned to their stormy passions with no guide but an inexperienced pilot who does not know whence he comes or whither he is going."[11]

To be a radical skeptic would be impossible, the priest argues, because this kind of doubt is "too violent for the human mind." The philosophers, in any case, had nothing to teach him: "I found them all alike proud, assertive, dogmatic. . . . Braggarts in attack, they are weaklings in defense. Weigh their arguments, they are all destructive; count their voices, every one speaks for himself; they are only agreed in arguing with each other. I could find no way out of my uncertainty by listening to them."[12] This distasteful scene of cowardly hypocrites squabbling over strange "systems of force, chance, fate, necessity, atoms, a living world, animated matter, and every variety of materialism" is Rousseau's revenge on Holbach's salon, a skewed, poisoned portrait of the discussions held there.

The Savoyard and his author found no way out of uncertainty through methodical investigation. Instead of concluding that there simply is no such way, Rousseau let his character conclude that Truth must lie elsewhere, that the world must be "governed by a wise and powerful will." He thus comes full circle to a conventionally Christian conception of a God who "hides himself alike from my senses and my understanding" but who exists "of himself alone" because the priest simply feels that he must.

This was the real chasm that had opened up between Rousseau and his former friends. As he himself candidly admitted, he felt that he simply could not bring himself to confront the materialist universe his friends were elaborating in their discussions and their writings. A life lived without transcendent meaning, without the hope of redemption, was simply too bleak a possibility for him. To Diderot and Holbach, Rousseau's refusal to follow reason must have seemed like cowardice. For Rousseau, a man in need of spiritual reassurance, their world without God presented a real threat. He resented them because they were attacking what was most important to him: his instinctive, unthinking belief.

Rousseau's need for faith had made him an enemy of the radical Enlightenment, and he was determined to fight his war in the open. His first volley could not have come at a worse time for Diderot. A lifelong lover of the theatre, Diderot had written a play, *Le Fils naturel*, which in 1757 was performed privately and with little success, at the theatre of the Duc d'Ayen in Saint-Germain-en-Laye, close to the capital. The piece had flopped not because its author had been sloppy, but because he had tried too hard. In his first attempt for the state, the theatre-mad Diderot had overloaded his lines with philosophical weight and formal ambition. He had failed because it was too important to him. Jean-Jacques decided that this was the obvious moment to attack Diderot. Himself the author of several plays and a forgettable but highly successful light opera, Jean-Jacques published a pamphlet in the form of an open letter to Jean d'Alembert, in which he portrayed all drama and comedy as vehicles for the corruption of innocent minds.

Amusements are not all bad in themselves, writes Rousseau, "in as far as they are necessary," but unnecessary amusement can do terrible harm to people, whose lives are too short to be spent with frivolous diversions. They have work to do, after all, civic duties to discharge. But the theatre is worse than other entertainments because it is morally rotten to the core. Without naming names, Rousseau then targets an idea often put forward by Diderot: that the emotional impact of a play can produce in its public an empathy strong enough to change minds and thus society. "How puerile and meaningless such pretensions are," sighs Rousseau, with a stinging swipe in Diderot's direction. Instead, the public makes a strict division between fact and fiction and identifies only with the virtuous characters, for "the ugly face does not seem ugly to him who is carrying it." Visits to the theatre do not produce moral betterment but self-satisfied emotional thrills.

It is hard not to think that Rousseau is playing the role of sanctimonious, reactionary prig just to annoy his friends. The only thing worse than the false emotions of tragedy are the true ones of comedy, he writes, singling out Molière as a particularly bad sinner: "Look how . . . this man upsets the social order; how scandalously he turns the most sacred rules on which it is founded on their head; how he derides the venerable rights of fathers over their children, men over their wives, and masters over their servants!"[13] He goes on in the same vein, singling out actors for particular abuse because of their immoral lives, which are apt to pollute the rest of society.

Even the fact that the letter was addressed to d'Alembert was a calculated insult to the Encyclopedists and to their friends, as the mathematician had just committed a mistake that had almost ruined the *Encyclopédie* and had endangered everyone connected to it. Vainglorious and self-satisfied as he was, he had made the pilgrimage to visit Voltaire in the golden exile of his country estate. There, the grand old man had talked his younger friend into writing a lengthy entry about the city of Geneva for the forthcoming volume of the *Encyclopédie*. Voltaire suggested that d'Alembert might take the opportunity of saying one or two truths about the city republic. Unsuspectingly, d'Alembert had done just that and penned a rambling piece in which he made some rather snobbish remarks about the fact that the choral music sung at church was bad and the verse worse, that the burghers were prigs not to allow theatre in their walls, and that the theological doctrines of the Calvinist clergy did not hold up to scrutiny.

There was an outcry from Geneva when the seventh volume of the *Encyclopédie* was published in 1757. Furious diplomatic notes were exchanged, and the allegations were treated as a matter of state—an official insult. The many enemies of Diderot and his encyclopedic enterprise had waited for just such an opportunity, and soon pressure mounted. Members of the Paris *parlement*, pious Jansenists for the most part, wanted to drum the heretics out of town, have them imprisoned, or at the very least stop the publication of further volumes. "Up to now hell has spat out its venom drop by drop," the powerful attorney general, Omer Joly de Feury, had thundered in the debating chamber, suggesting the *Encyclopédie* and its godless poison must be destroyed. The other main Catholic faction, the Jesuits, had different designs: They wanted the manuscripts impounded in order to continue the *Encyclopédie* themselves, as they had long been jealous of the project, which was in direct competition with their own encyclopedia, the *Dictionnaire de Trevoux*. Factions formed, long and furious debates were held at the *parlement*, and Diderot's arrest was demanded.

Throughout, Voltaire's Parisian correspondents kept him abreast of every turn of events. He was rubbing his hands almost audibly. Initially, he may have put the gullible d'Alembert up to this mischief for no better reason than that he resented the fact that his own plays were not performed in Geneva because of its strict Calvinist laws. Shaming the city into overturning the policy would have been very convenient indeed and possibly quite lucrative.

But now something much better had happened: Diderot, who had begun to challenge his position as chief representative of Enlightened opinion in Europe, was suddenly in trouble. He would have to be more cautious with grand pronouncements and daring books in future, and this enforced caution might be enough to neutralize him as a threat to Voltaire's throne.

Voltaire played the situation for all it was worth, pulling strings from his study in a steady stream of letters. He wrote to d'Alembert, telling him, "I think that the City Council [of Geneva] owes you solemn thanks," and strengthening his resolve not to apologize, and then he turned to Diderot, disingenuously asking, "Can it be true, monsieur, that while you are rendering a service to humankind," others could be allowed to blacken his name? Voltaire counseled Diderot to leave Paris and take the *Encyclopédie* with him. Immediately afterwards he wrote to Charles Pallisot, the implacable foe of the *philosophes* and one of the main powers behind the current crisis, informing him: "Everything from you, Monsieur, will always be precious to me. . . . I will welcome you in Lausanne, better still than I did in Geneva. . . . I have a charming house here."

For several days and weeks it seemed as if the church could be victorious and arrests were imminent. Even Voltaire grew nervous. After all, he, too, had contributed articles to the *Encyclopédie*, and if all manuscripts were to be impounded and used as evidence, he might be caught up in the vortex of events. He wrote to Diderot demanding his manuscripts back, and when he received no reply, he turned to d'Alembert with the same request. "I can no longer furnish a single word to the *Encyclopédie*," he announced. He was not the only one to withdraw his support. D'Alembert had been throwing tantrums, demanding apologies for being insulted as author of the offending article, and had finally resigned his post as coeditor altogether, leaving the responsibility entirely with Diderot during the most difficult of times.

Rousseau had watched the entire crisis from his spectator's seat at his hermitage. As soon as it began to die down, he twisted the knife once again by publishing his open letter to d'Alembert about the theatre, adopting a position that could not have been more antagonistic.

The attack and the insult of Rousseau's intervention were all the more grave, as they were likely to worsen a situation that was already at crisis point, especially as the Geneva incident happened on the back of another scandal involving an author close to Diderot and Holbach, Claude-Adrien Helvétius (1715–1771), who also had a salon, just around the corner from the baron's house. Holbach and Helvétius were frequent guests at each other's salons, as were Diderot, Marmontel, and others. Together they formed the progressive faction of Parisian intellectual life.

Believing himself protected by his court connections and his wealth, Helvétius had published a philosophical work, *De l'esprit* (*On the Mind*, 1758). When the book was granted a printing license by the royal censor's office, he himself presented the royal family with a copy. His name did not appear on the title page, but his authorship was beyond question, almost as if he had regarded the anonymous publication as an act of courtesy or convention, not of bitter necessity. Soon, the censor realized his mistake; the book was condemned, the license revoked, a political machine set in motion that would have crushed any less well-connected author. Protection at court meant that Helvétius could survive the ensuing storm, but for several weeks not only his career and public office but even his life appeared to be under threat. The frightened philosopher let himself be talked into publishing a retraction, as well as resigning his ceremonial post of court.

The work that had caused such an outcry consists of pure and humane, if at times unrealistic, pragmatism. Its motto is taken from the Latin poet Lucretius and proclaims that "we must see what life consists of, and the spirit . . . how they work and what forces drive them."[14] In carefully argued sections, Helvétius makes the case for a purely material understanding of the human mind, arguing that the mind consists of nothing but the flow of sensations, the perception of difference and similarity, and the stored "continuing images" of memory, also an exclusively physical phenomenon.

Phenomena, Helvétius contends, are ordered by perception and grouped together in classes: things that are hard; things that are hot; bodies that are beautiful or ugly, laugh or cry; and so forth. Grammar and vocabulary provide labels for these abstractions, and these labels can be handled as if they were no mere abstractions from experience but realities in themselves—as if there were "hardness," "heat," and "beauty" existing independently of the object world.

Many of the problems in philosophy, writes Helvétius, are caused by this simple misunderstanding of the nature of grammar. Lakes of ink have been spilled trying to define the true nature of "beauty," "space," or other generalizations, without ever arriving at a positive, indisputable result. The underlying error, the author argues, is a lack of understanding of grammar. Abstractions like "beauty" are grammatical constructs that do not necessarily refer to anything that exists outside of the web of language. Muddled thinkers confuse the world of our senses with the way in which it is depicted by language.

Instead of adding to this black deluge, it would be better to turn away from irresolvable, speculative arguments and toward questions that allow of a positive solution. Instead of dreaming up grand systems, "if we are to avail ourselves as much as possible from observation, we must walk only by its side, stop at the very instant when it leaves us, and nobly dare to be ignorant of what is not yet to be known."[15] In his clear rejection of metaphysics, Helvétius made the bulk of Western philosophy out to be nonsense. And as for theology, whose object was totally beyond the possibility of perception, it had lost all right to exist. Unsurprisingly, the theologians at the Sorbonne were outraged. But Helvétius went further—much further.

What made the philosophy of Helvétius so scandalous to theologians was that it dispensed altogether with the idea of metaphysical Truth (the truth about something that cannot be perceived), replacing it instead with a purely utilitarian ethic. This morality takes into account only whether an action is helpful or harmful to others, without acknowledging any authority other than human welfare. Ultimately, the author writes, our actions and ideas can only be judged insofar as they are useful, detrimental, or indifferent to society. Utility is the only yardstick human beings have, while education provides them with an ability to judge. We always ultimately and legitimately act out of self-interest, but to understand where our true self-interest lies, to prosper and avoid punishment, to be able to act morally, we need information.

Enlightened morality is nothing more than the application of useful ideas to society and to individual action. But if morality depends on holding useful ideas, then education is the key to all moral behavior, a political imperative: "Few have leisure sufficient for information. The poor man, for instance, can neither reflect nor examine; he receives truth or error only by prejudice: employed in daily labour, he cannot rise to a certain sphere of ideas."[16] Limited in their understanding of the world, people act wickedly because of their ignorance and the prevalence of superstition over scientific fact. Society fails to provide them with this useful guide for moral action, as its laws were formed before science had been able to instruct society about the real relationships between things, "before they had learnt, from observation, its true principles. The system being formed, no farther notice was taken of it; thus we have, in a manner, the morals of the world in its infancy."[17]

These childish morals, of course, are Christian morals, even if Helvétius never makes this link explicitly. But there is a way forward. Good laws consist in "practice of actions useful to the greater number," and the progress of science allows us to progress in the discovery of their principles. Universal education and rational laws will necessarily make a better society. A society in which one can be respected for doing what is useful to the greatest number, in which one is not punished for doing what is indifferent but strongly sanctioned for doing what is detrimental, is a just society.

The enemies of Enlightenment thought at court and in the church quickly recognized how dangerous an opponent Helvétius was: Educated, well-mannered, polished, and intelligent, he had excellent connections. The great and the good could be found hobnobbing in his salon and paying their compliments to his strikingly attractive wife. This was no wild-eyed backstreet anarchist but a man at the center of society. And from that center he politely explained that there could be no such thing as a true, revealed religion—indeed, no such thing as Truth itself. Instead, he posited that all actions and ideas should be judged solely according to how useful they were to the greatest number here and now—a criterion by which not only the church but also the monarchy failed spectacularly. This was treason striking at the very heart of France.

Seizing the moment, the authorities increased pressure on those who were seen to be associated with him. Rumors about imminent arrests were rife; Diderot, who had already been imprisoned once for writing a philosophical work, was terrified. Meanwhile, d'Alembert decided that the *Encyclopédie* had become too dangerous and washed his hands of it entirely. His judgment was correct: Together with *De l'esprit*, the *Encyclopédie* was also forbidden by official decree in 1757. The work of a decade seemed in ruins. The lightning that had been sparked by Helvétius had hit Diderot.

Two catastrophes, first the Geneva incident and then the affair surrounding *De l'esprit*, had come close to crushing the voice of the radical Enlightenment, which was just beginning to make itself heard in the world. Officially, the *Encyclopédie* remained forbidden, but work was allowed to continue with a view to lifting the ban at some unspecified future date. The savior of the encyclopedic enterprise worked in an unlikely position. Chrétien-Guillaume de Lamoignon de Malesherbes (1721–1794) was a member of an influential family. A man highly respected for his probity, he held the office of chief censor. He was also a relatively young man who had considerable sympathies for Diderot and his project, so much so that when police finally came to Diderot's house with the intention of impounding all manuscripts and papers pertaining to the *Encyclopédie* and handing them to the Jesuits, they found the office inexplicably clean and empty of all papers. Their search revealed nothing. The thousands of manuscripts, proofs, and notes were in a safe place: in Malesherbes' office, where he had had them brought after a tip-off about the raid. They stayed there, undetected, until the crisis was over.

The chief censor began to negotiate and convince important people at court of the importance of Diderot's enterprise, if not for the Church then for "*la gloire de la France*." Finally, a deal was reached under which no further volumes could be published until further notice, but the authorities agreed to close their eyes to Diderot's continuing work on the great project. This made it possible to prepare further volumes, but left the enterprise in an agonizingly uncertain position: The seventh had only brought the alphabet up to "Foang–Gythium." The bulk of the texts and all the illustrations were still unpublished, and there was no guarantee they ever would be.

For Diderot, work on the *Encyclopédie* had long since become a continuous drudgery. And now that d'Alembert had resigned, indignantly feeling insulted and misunderstood, all responsibility lay on one editor's shoulders. Voltaire had counseled him to take the great work abroad to a more tolerant place, such as Amsterdam, Berlin, or Geneva, but Diderot refused to give in to his siren calls. He had signed a contract, he replied somewhat stiffly by letter; he had a responsibility to the workers and their families in Paris.

Privately, however, Diderot felt somber and despondent, and his thoughts turned to futility and loss. Like Rousseau he felt a nostalgic longing for being able to believe what reason forbade, but unlike his former friend he knew that philosophy merely becomes wishful thinking if it is made to express what the author wishes to be true. But Diderot did not just miss the comfort of faith—he missed Jean-Jacques himself. Having arrived in middle age, he was haunted by the coldness of a universe made up of random particles. "O my Sophie," he wrote in a letter to his mistress in October 1759, "there is just one hope of touching you, feeling you, loving you, of seeking you and uniting with you when we are no more! If there were a kind of law of affinity among our organizing principles, if we could make up one shared being . . . if the molecules of your dissolved lover could become agitated, move and seek your molecules scattered through nature! Leave me this chimera; it is such a sweet thought, it assures me of eternity in you and with you."[18]

MARVELOUS MACHINES

The good man is a machine whose mechanism is regulated to create pleasure. No, I do not blush at being such a machine and my heart would jump with joy if I could assume that one day these thoughts might be useful and consoling for those who are like me.

THIRY D'HOLBACH

Upon the whole, we may conclude, that the Christian Religion not only was at first attended with miracles, but even at this day cannot be believed by any reasonable person without one.

DAVID HUME

CHAPTER 8

LE BON DAVID

> Sir.—I have received with the deepest sense of gratitude your very kind and obliging letter of the 8th inst.: favors of great men ought to give pride to those that have at least the merit of setting the value that is due upon them. This is my case with you, sir; the reading of your valuable works has not only inspired me with the strongest admiration for your genius and amiable parts, but gave me the highest idea of your person, and the strongest desire of getting acquainted with one of the greatest philosophers of any age, and of the best friends of mankind.[1]

As the Baron d'Holbach was writing this letter on August 22, 1763, he knew that he was about to make the acquaintance of a truly extraordinary man, David Hume (1711–1776), who was about to take up his position as embassy secretary in the French capital.

The meeting between Hume and the Holbach circle marks a second period in the life of the salon, the most productive and perhaps the most brilliant. After the hiatus in salon life following the death of his first wife, Basile-Geneviève, in 1754, the baron had remarried two years later and had reopened his salon. In 1759, perhaps to escape the shadow of his first marriage, the couple had moved to a handsome building on the rue Royale Saint-Roch. Once again his house had become a magnet for thinkers and intellectuals, but while the salon had previously attracted French guests, visitors to the capital still tended to attend other, grander salons. Now, however, aided by the fame of the *Encyclopédie* and publicized by Grimm's *Correspondance littéraire*, the baron's house had become a place of pilgrimage for traveling intellectuals throughout Europe. It was therefore almost a matter of course that David Hume would announce his imminent arrival to the philosopher baron, whom he had not yet met.

When Hume arrived in Paris on October 18, 1763, to take up his assignment as embassy secretary, he had reason to expect a warm welcome. Even before he had decided to accept the position, rumors about his fame in France had reached and greatly flattered him. His friend Lord Elibank had written to him in May: "I should only add that no author ever yet attained to that degree of reputation in his own lifetime that you are now in possession of at Paris."[2]

Elibank was right, at least as far as Hume the historian was concerned. He was the author of the six-volume *History of England* (published from 1754 to 1762), a runaway best seller, so his star was in the ascendant. His lucid style and the enlightened skepticism with which he described periods of absolute royal power and political violence had made him famous in French intellectual circles, where censorship would have made it impossible to write any such work on French history. Hume's work was regarded as an example of courageous, free expression. While the *History* was reserved for those with a sufficient grasp of English, two French translations of his *Essays Moral and Political* (1741–1742) were available.

Such was the admiration for Hume that the salon hostess Marie Charlotte Hyppolite de Campet de Saujon, Comtesse de Boufflers-Rouvel, or simply Madame Boufflers, had in 1762 traveled to London to meet the great man whose writings she had devoured. On arriving in the British capital, she was disappointed to find that Hume was staying in Edinburgh, but took the opportunity to visit other luminaries, including the art critic and antiquarian Horace Walpole and, through his introduction, another writer whose fame had obviously crossed the Channel, Samuel Johnson. (Madame Boufflers found herself somewhat surprised by the latter's shambolic appearance. Dr. Johnson, she reported, saw her out to her coach wearing "a rusty brown morning suit, a pair of old shoes by way of slippers, a little shrivelled wig on the top of his head, and the sleeves of his shirt and the knees of his breeches hanging loose."[3] Hardly the manner of dress the countess was accustomed to during her Paris social calls.)

When Hume learned that an admirer had come all the way to London to see him and that he had disappointed her, he wrote a gracious letter promising Madame Boufflers that he would make her acquaintance as soon as possible. His chance came more quickly than he had anticipated, when Lord Hertford, recently appointed the English ambassador to France, asked him to accompany him to Paris. Hume was torn between his wish to live a quiet life in Edinburgh, with his friends and his beloved books, and the undoubted honor and opportunity of a diplomatic mission, to say nothing of the flattering reception his works had received in France. "I hesitated much on the acceptance of this offer," he had written to his friend, the philosopher and economist Adam Smith. "I thought it ridiculous at my years, to be entering on a new scene, and to put myself in the lists as a candidate of fortune."[4]

Hume was a candidate of very good fortune, it soon transpired. Hardly arrived in the French capital, he became the object of intense adulation. Hume's friend William Mure of Caldwell described the "immense court" paid to him, as all of Paris society scrambled to meet the brilliant Scottish writer. What they found came as a considerable surprise. They had expected a wisp of a man, "a person very little encumbered with matter," as a friend wrote, but instead they saw that Hume's razor-sharp wit was very comfortably ensconced in an envelope of exceedingly generous proportions: He was fat. A portrait from 1766 by Allan Ramsay shows the philosopher wearing a red, richly embroidered coat, his waistcoat straining to contain his bulk, while his face blooms in ruddy, double-chinned health and only the steady, quietly assured gaze reveals something about the sitter's intellectual stature. Even Diderot, on their first meeting, had to be assured that the rotund foreigner in the room was the author of the *History* and the *Treatise* and not, as Denis put it, "*un gros Bernardin bien nourri*."[5]

Whether or not the philosopher looked like a fat Benedictine monk, his popularity was only enhanced by his jolly appearance. Even the court at Versailles seemed to be in his thrall, as Hume himself recounted, puzzled by so much ceaseless veneration. A duchess had been so eager to see him that her valet had demanded he come immediately, without changing into formal clothes. He appeared in front of her grace in his boots and was met not only by a grand lady reclining on a sofa and telling him what a great man he was but also by the Duke of Orléans, the king's brother. Hume airily reported home that this kind of attention was "very frequent and even daily."[6]

The *célèbre* Monsieur Hume quickly became a coveted guest in the salons of the capital. Madame Boufflers had been ecstatic to meet him at last, but she soon found that he was not hers alone. Other *salonières*—such as Madame Deffand, whose salon could boast to have hosted Voltaire before his days of exile; d'Alembert's companion, Julie de Lespinasse; and the famous and famously intellectual Madame Geoffrin—vied for his presence at their soirées. Hume thoroughly enjoyed the attention of so many spirited, beautiful, and jealous women, and noted that they moved in society with much greater freedom than their English counterparts. Hume was particularly fascinated by the apparently confident and easy way in which women moved in male company. One night he visited the famous Madame Geoffrin, who "immediately flung herself carelessly into an elbow chair, almost half reclined, with one leg thrown over the knee of another, and so she sat for two or three hours and . . . in the loose, easy and negligent dress of the Frenchwomen, she had more the appearance of a person just having got out of bed, with a night gown flung hastily over her, than a person dressed to make a visit in an evening."[7]

Hume—*le bon David*, as he was known to Paris friends—definitely had an eye for the ladies, as Diderot's friend Grimm remarked archly in his *Correspondance littéraire*: "All the pretty women had a great run on him, and . . . the fat Scottish philosopher was pleased with their society." An eternal snob as well as a man jealous of attention, Grimm commented, "This David Hume is an excellent man; he is naturally placid; he listens attentively, he sometimes speaks with wit, although he speaks little; but he is clumsy, he has neither warmth, nor grace, nor charm of humour."[8]

Perhaps Grimm could not forgive the Scottish guest for monopolizing his friends in a language he did not understand. Hume's French, such as it was, was hidden beneath a rumbling Scottish burr, but both Diderot, who had started his career as a translator, and Holbach spoke excellent English. At the rue Royale, Hume found not only the excitement of his new pop star status but people of like mind with whom he could discuss ideas at a level beyond that of social pleasantry, people who not only admired him as a historian but also understood his philosophical ideas. He enjoyed their company, much in contrast to sourly Walpole, who fired off one broadside after the other against the *philosophes*, jealously complaining they all seemed to love Hume and that nothing was sacred to them in their attack on the existing order: "Men and women, one and all, are devoutly employed in the demolition. They think me quite profane for having any belief left."[9]

Walpole obviously felt left out and he had no time at all for the ideas discussed by his Parisian host. The conversation at the salon was far too scientific and lofty for his liking: "I sometimes go to Baron d'Olbach's [*sic*]; but I have left off his dinners, as there was no bearing the authors, and philosophers, and *savants*, of which he has a pigeon-house full. The Baron is persuaded that Pall Mall is paved with lave or deluge stones. In short, nonsense for nonsense, I like the Jesuits better than the philosophers."[10] Walpole cultivated the very British stance of finding all things Gallic frivolous, including, and with an unmistakable tint of envy, their devotion to the embassy secretary Hume, who was in fashion with all the salons, despite the fact that "his French is as unintelligible as his English."[11]

While Walpole was sulking in his corner, Hume wrote full of enthusiasm to his Edinburgh friend Hugh Blair: "The men of letters here are really very agreeable: all of them men of the world, living in entire, or almost entire harmony among themselves, and quite irreproachable in their morals. It would give you . . . great satisfaction to find that there is not a single deist among them. Those whose persons and conversation I like best, are D'Alembert, Buffon, Marmontel, Diderot, Duclos, [and] Helvétius."[12]

Interestingly, Hume makes no mention here of Holbach and his table, quite possibly because he wished to mention names that were also known in Edinburgh—Holbach, after all, had published only specialist scientific works under his own name, and nothing of consequence. His authorship of *Christianisme dévoilé* was known to only his closest friends, and Hume was probably not aware of the fact that his host was also an author whose work had already once created a publishing scandal; later, in any case, Hume consistently expressed his admiration and affection for the baron.

At first, Hume was almost shocked by the openness of the discussions at Holbach's salon, as Diderot relates in a letter to Sophie Volland: "The first time Mr Hume found himself at the Baron's table, he was sitting next to the host. I don't know what made the English [*sic*] philosopher tell the Baron that he did not believe in the existence of atheists, and that he had never met any. The Baron said to him: 'Monsieur, count how many of us are here.' There were eighteen people present. The Baron added: 'It is a good start to be able to show you fifteen straight away. The other three haven't yet made up their minds.'"[13]

In public, Hume himself kept a carefully burnished facade of noncommittal skepticism, but to anyone who read his philosophical works (he was famous as a historian, after all) there could be no question that his own thinking was at least as radical as that of the Holbach circle. He had been existentially terrified by the philosophical implications of his own early works and had practically given up his epistemological research. He chose to concentrate instead on history and enlivening his bachelor life with vivacious dinners at which he himself decided to do the cooking; instead of hunting the firebird of reason he had settled for roasting chicken for his friends. His girth testified to the consequences of this philosophic turn.

Born in Edinburgh and raised in the Scottish Lowlands after his father's early death, young David had returned to the Scottish capital to read law at the tender age of twelve, which was not unusual at the time. The growing boy's environment was not yet the Athens of the North it would become, partly through his own later work and influence. It was in 1730 a town of 40,000 souls, affectionately dubbed "Auld Reekie" for the omnipresent smell of peat fires and human filth emptied from all windows into the high street every evening.

The grimly Protestant inhabitants were firmly in the grip of the elders of the all-powerful Kirk. On Sabbath, the churches were full, while the streets looked "as if some epidemic disorder had depopulated the whole City,"[14] as the historian James Buchan writes. Anybody brazen enough to be late or to stand on the streets engaged in idle talk was grabbed by the town's patrols of "seizers" and dragged to the nearest service, or punished by the magistrates. In 1696, just one generation before the young David Hume lived here, the eighteen-year-old Thomas Aikenhead had been tried and hanged for blasphemy after he had bragged in front of some student friends that he regarded Christianity as a "rapsodie of feigned and ill-invented nonsense."[15]

While the city folk regarded alcohol as the sole legitimate escape from such severity (in 1716 a prominent citizen and his brother were so sozzled that they forgot their mother's body on the way to her funeral), young David developed, in his own words, "an insurmountable aversion to everything but the pursuits of Philosophy and general Learning."[16] Like Denis Diderot at his Paris college, David preferred reading the authors of antiquity. Instead of training for the bar, the teenager preferred returning to his mother's country estate and immersing himself in books.

Hume had ideas of his own, ideas so radical that he realized they would make him an outcast, an intellectual leper. He was terrified that if he pursued his ideas he might be viewed as "some uncouth monster, who not being able to mingle and unite in society, has been expelled from all human commerce, and left utterly abandoned and disconsolate," he wrote.[17]

Young David's fears were much more than an ordinary adolescent crisis. The ideas preoccupying him were revolutionary in their clarity and compelling argumentation, but like Spinoza he did not expect to be treated with anything but derision and even hatred if he published them: "When I look abroad, I foresee on every side, dispute, contradiction, anger, calumny and detraction. When I turn my eye inward I find nothing but doubt and ignorance."[18]

The pressure of his internal conflict weighed on the young man. Age eighteen and suffering from severe physical symptoms that we would today interpret as stemming from a nervous breakdown, he was in deep despair and lay ill for weeks. He sought medical help, only to have the doctor tell him that he now belonged to the great brotherhood of thinkers who were stricken with "the Disease of the Learned."[19] There was a therapy for this disease—a pint of claret and a daily long ride in the fresh air—which finally showed positive results.

Upon his recovery, Hume was still undecided as to which career to choose. As the second son of a minor nobleman, he would have to earn his own living, and he decided to travel south. For a little while he worked as a merchant's secretary in Bristol—only to be sacked for correcting his master's prose style. The driven young scholar went on his way south again, this time buying a passage to Paris, the capital of new ideas. He arrived there to find the city in the grip of the miracle craze around the Church of Saint-Médard, which also left a lasting impression on the young Denis Diderot.

Hume was determined to use his time in France in order to overcome his intellectual and spiritual crisis, and to make his money last as long as necessary. When he found that the metropolis was simply too expensive, he traveled to Rheims and from there to the small town of La Flèche in Anjou. There he rented rooms, learned French, and began to work, read, and talk with members of the nearby Jesuit college, who gave the bright young man the run of their excellent library.

Far away from the world in which he had grown up, the young man finally dared to put his ideas to paper, to question them by reading the works of previous philosophers, and to think them through to the very end. Day and night, he worked on a large manuscript, which he finished at the age of twenty-six. In *A Treatise on Human Nature* he attempted nothing less than to start again where Descartes had failed: to rechart the mind and what it could know for certain. When the ink of the last words had dried on the page, he bundled up his possessions and returned to Britain to oversee the printing of his work, which, he thought, would make him famous and revolutionize Western philosophy. He published it, and what happened next was the one thing he was not prepared for: nothing. Apart from a few lukewarm reviews the world at large took no notice. Nobody, it seemed, understood his work or its implications.

Even if the treatise did not, as he would later claim, fall "deadborn from the press," the lack of response and acclamation was a serious blow to the young Hume, who had staked his hopes on it. He would have to look for alternative employment. He unsuccessfully applied for a professorship in logic; he became tutor to a lunatic nobleman who threw him out after a year; he even took to the seas as secretary to his cousin, the grandly named Lieutenant-General James St. Clair (and in so doing, witnessed a military campaign against France). Finally, he took the post of librarian at Edinburgh University, not for the meager pay but for the access it gave him to the 20,000 volumes in the library, the ideal research base for his great project: a history of England from the invasion to the present day.

When the history was finally published from 1754 to 1762, the success was such that Hume could retire from his librarianship and live off writing alone.

In his own day, Hume was most famous as a historian, a great man who had published an ill-advised, impenetrable book on philosophy early in his career. And indeed, the author's own relationship to his "firstborn" remained powerfully ambivalent. He redrafted the presentation of his fundamental thoughts several times and published other versions of it, but he had also chosen against the life of a philosopher, a life whose dangers he knew all too well, as it had once almost cost him his sanity. One is reminded of Rousseau's refusal of skepticism on the grounds that no constitution could stand radical doubt for long.

Hume sought refuge instead in gregariousness. He loved entertaining and did so regularly, and he must have been one of the first gentlemen in Europe to insist on cooking for his friends himself, treating his guests to such dinners as roast chicken and minced collops, a dish described by James Buchan as an eighteenth-century hamburger. Hume established a regular circle of friends, a round table, laden with food and wine, at which the guests talked with animation—a place not unlike the rue Royale in faraway Paris. Surrounded by like-minded people, Hume could forget philosophical work, only to be reminded once more when his friends had gone: "I dine, I play a game of backgammon, I converse, and am merry with my friends; and when after three or four hours' amusement, I wou'd return to these speculations, they appear so cold, and strain'd, and ridiculous, that I cannot find in my heart to enter into them any farther."[20]

So what exactly were the philosophical questions that so terrified Hume? The ideas that made Hume feel an outcast in society and that troubled him throughout his life are dizzying even today. Already Descartes had brought about a philosophical sea change by granting the mind absolute sovereignty (and then retreating from it), by making radical doubt, not certainty, the point of departure of all thought. The Scottish thinker went further, spearheading a Newtonian revolution of thought.

Isaac Newton's fundamental physical insight had been that natural phenomena must not be judged inductively, starting from a theoretical construction such as the account of the Creation or the Flood, to which individual data are then fitted ("if X does not accord with the history of Creation, it must be false"). Instead of this approach, factual knowledge can only be reached deductively, by infinitely patient, quantitative observation that might eventually allow predictable patterns to be extrapolated into laws, formulated in the language of mathematics.

Hume's basic and ultimately terrifying idea was to do exactly the same with the workings of the human mind and the sense data it receives. If Newton had understood that all matter was subject to gravity, Hume set out to determine the center of gravity of the mind. His ambition was to replace the metaphysical speculation of ages past with a philosophy of scientific deduction, "an Experimental Method of Reasoning." This meant that all forms of knowledge that could not be taken from observing nature had to be discarded as worthless, as Hume knew: "If we take in our hand any volume of divinity or school of metaphysics, for instance; let us ask, *Does it contain any abstract reasoning concerning quantity or number?* No. *Does it contain any experimental reasoning concerning matter of fact and existence?* No. Commit it to the flames: for it can contain nothing but sophistry and illusion."[21] This he writes in his *Enquiry Concerning Human Understanding*, in which he developed the ideas of the *Treatise*. Theology was complex and intellectually challenging, but it contained no knowledge that could be proved or disproved, and therefore it was simply worthless for anyone seeking to understand the world.

With the irrepressible optimism of his age, Hume believed that the workings of the human mind could ultimately be analyzed in the same way as the "celestial mechanics" of the physical universe. The "laws and forces" governing the human mind were nothing but impressions, ideas, and the connections between ideas. As simple as this thought seems, it has astounding implications. The human mind can know nothing, writes the philosopher, but what is presented to it through the sense organs. There is no innate knowledge, no necessity *prior* to perception. The impressions caused by the senses are transformed into ideas and memories, which can be freely regrouped: I can conceive of the mythical flying horse Pegasus not because I have ever seen a flying horse in nature, and not because I can conjure up such a creature out of some mythical depth of my own mind, but because I have seen (or read about) horses and winged creatures such as birds, and I can recombine these different memories to form the idea of a flying horse. Nothing in the human mind is new or original.

This notion of the combination of ideas suggests that every idea is itself the result of previous combinations, that everything has an origin, a previous state, a cause. Indeed, for Hume, cause and effect seem to be the most powerful and most important connection between ideas. Cause and effect are necessary for our survival. They allow us to predict what will happen or to deduce what has taken place. We would be lost without them. They also appear to be logical: The ground is wet; *therefore* it must have rained. Fire is hot; *therefore* I will burn my finger in a flame. This assumption, however, is based not on logic but simply on habit, argues Hume. The faculties of individual objects are discovered not through deduction, but through habit and observation: No child playing with water can know from its fluidity and transparency that one can drown in it. Only experience can teach us about the world.

Just when we thought we were being most logical (X is *because of* Y), we were, in fact, just being lazy. There is no logical connection between facts and impressions as there is between mathematical entities; we simply infer a connection because certain things always appear to be connected in a particular way. That, however, is no guarantee that they will remain so. How do I know that the sun will rise tomorrow? Because it did yesterday and for as long as anyone can remember. How can I prove logically that the sun will rise tomorrow? How can I logically prove the laws of gravity, of physics? I can't. I have to content myself with the fact that it has always risen and it is therefore likely to rise again.

At first, Hume's point appears to be little more than a thought experiment (very few actually *believe* that the sun might not rise tomorrow), but then its power begins to unfold. The intention is not to argue that we may one day all awake in total darkness, but to take the iron certainty of logic out of the ideas formed from experience. Once this point has been conceded, entire worlds come crashing down. If there is no logical force to the connection between ideas, if habit alone governs our conception of the world, then we will never be certain of anything; instead of knowing, we will simply have to *assume* that the sun will do what it always has done, in order to continue living our lives and planning for the future. Therefore, if there is no a priori knowledge (no certainty apart from what we can deduce from observation), and if the stream of impressions and memories is all we can know, then there is actually no such thing as a "self" at all—just a constant background noise of perception and interconnecting ideas that appears to be a coherent, constant being that exists over time.

On a pragmatic level, this assumption is as good as certain knowledge. On a philosophical level, however, it changes everything. How do I know my senses do not betray me about the outside world? I don't, but on a practical level it makes sense to assume that running into a wall is not good for me, simply because from experience and from other people's stories it consistently appears to be a bad idea. But if I cannot know anything to be true and logically necessary, then how can I know that God exists? How indeed? His existence cannot be inferred with certainty, nor is it a logical necessity.

Suddenly, the son of pious Edinburgh has lured his reader into a trap. I cannot know anything but what I can get through my senses (but I can have no sense data about God), and even my senses may not represent the truth, but merely allow me to make pragmatic assumptions helping me to navigate my environment. The notion of cause and effect, while impossible to prove, is a useful guideline for planning into the future, but if there is only a stream of sensations, how can there be such a thing as an immortal soul? If miracles are said to be caused by God, but cause and effect is nothing but a habit of thought, how can I attain certainty about the truth of religion? If God is neither immediately knowable nor necessarily the certain First Cause (which does not exist) of anything, then what exactly might he be? Why should I believe a particular book more than, say, Thomas Aikenhead, hanged for blasphemy in 1696?

Hume had an answer to this, and it reads like a description of the believer Jean-Jacques Rousseau. "We abandon ourselves to the natural undisciplined suggestions of our timid and anxious hearts,"[22] Hume wrote. Faith becomes a supposed cure for anxiety and fear, but at the same time it makes people more worried about enraging their God, more fearful of transgressing against his will. They will become "tame and submissive" if they are scared by the idea of a terrifying and unpredictable God. They will abandon their critical reason, accept the "ghostly guidance" of priests, and end up believing whatever is presented to them.

Through simple and forceful analysis, Hume had laid an explosive charge at the bedrock of Western philosophy. "What can I know?" Descartes had asked a century before him and had, through sleight of hand, reassured his readers that even the most uncompromising doubt leads to the possibility of absolute certainty and to a life of faith, guided by reason. Hume's answer was deeply unsettling and impossible to disprove. I cannot know anything, he concluded, not about the world and not about God—the very notion of personhood crumbles under his gaze, leaving nothing but stimuli, perception, and psychology. It was this the adolescent genius had been so afraid of: an argument leading him inexorably to the abolition of all certainties, all faith, all trust in a higher truth.

How can one live in such a void? One cannot, replied Rousseau and Voltaire, almost in unison—one needs absolute truth, even if one has to invent it. But Hume thought differently. To create his own kind of meaning, a possibility of shaping a life worth living, he turned to the philosophy of ancient Greece and Rome. He chose as his inspiration not the dominant tradition of Plato and Aristotle, but the Stoics, who had already then sought ways of facing life with dignity and without having to tell edifying lies. What was needed, Hume wrote, was "a manly, steady virtue, which either preserves us from disastrous, melancholy accidents, or teaches us to bear them. During such calm sunshine of the mind, these spectres of false divinity never make their appearance."[23] This virtue is difficult to sustain, because it is effectively an existential choice for clear-eyed courage and against the comfort of superstition, but it has its own rewards: the "calm sunshine of the mind," the true origin of goodness in the world, the reason why people can fill each other's existence with the light of human kindness.

Hume's atheism was robust but ultimately (and in line with his philosophical convictions) so pragmatic that he preferred to think of himself as an agnostic. If there is no ultimate proof that anything outside the sense impressions exists, it is also impossible to prove that something does not exist. It is therefore impossible to prove or disprove the existence of God. To call oneself an atheist therefore rests on no more certainty than that the sun will rise tomorrow—it is an intellectual shortcut, a habit of thought. For the true philosopher agnosticism is the only reasonable stance.

Hume's own conclusion was essentially pragmatic. For the purpose of day-to-day decision making, being agnostic about the existence of God is a little like being agnostic about the existence of real objects: theoretically valid but practically useless. While it is *possible* that there is no world, no matter, nothing that is actually depicted by the senses (we remember this being Descartes' problem once he had formulated his famous *cogito ergo sum*), it is, in fact, not pragmatically *sensible* to operate on this assumption in our daily lives. The pragmatic choice is to believe the senses and the sequence of cause and effect, just as it is the pragmatic choice to assume that there is no being that defies all perception and all natural laws.

Hume's investigation into the workings of the human mind had other, surprising results. If the concept of cause and effect is a mere product of habit and if our senses ultimately are an unreliable guide to the world, then any belief about the world is ultimately based on individual choice. Every judgment we make is therefore ultimately subjective, even if, like cause and effect, it apparently follows a law, a necessity. In the case of artists this seems immediately true: Their creative interpretations meld together their individuality and a wider set of cultural rules.

A work of art is a product of taste and style. But the same is true for rational argument, Hume believed: "When I am convinced of any principle, it is only an idea, which strikes more strongly upon me. When I give the preference to one set of arguments above another, I do nothing but decide from my feeling concerning the superiority of their influence."[24] Within a few sentences, Hume had made an astounding claim: Those who would be convinced of his argument would be convinced not because it is *simply true*, but because their feeling—their emotional makeup—makes them more susceptible to one idea than another. Philosophy is not the search for a great Truth that finally everyone may agree on, but a huge marketplace with different constituencies following one style of argument rather than another simply because it made them feel good. And there was nothing to be done about it.

Hume's conclusion about human psychology had an important effect on his ethical thinking. If there is no absolutely right principle (everything absolute is a priori and therefore illusory), just one that was relatively most effective most of the time, then the same must be true for moral questions. Ultimately every choice is based on personal preference and taste. Just as a musician interprets a musical score, we interpret the world around us. Like the musical interpretation, the result of such a choice is never absolutely right or wrong; it is simply more or less effective, convincing, and authoritative. Such interpretations might "work" or not, might be strong or weak, but they are not determined by any principle apart from memory and practicability, and they are likely to change with the tides of taste and cultural habit. Values, Hume suggested, are not God-given; they are not even universal—they are simply an abstract way of articulating what appears humane and useful at a particular point in time.

When Hume began his visits in the rue Royale, he found a circle of thinkers who not only had read and understood his ideas but were ready to face their implications. He had many things in common with them, starting with a thorough dislike of Christianity. While in Paris, he complained to his friend Hugh Blair that the English were "relapsing fast into the deepest Stupidity, Christianity & Ignorance."[25] But what made him such a compelling adversary in discussion was his unparalleled genius for systematic argument, a challenge for the salon regulars, who had perhaps become a little too used to one another's rhetorical strengths and weaknesses. Diderot's mercurial mind was ultimately uninterested in purely theoretical questions, while Holbach was always more scientist than philosopher. *Le bon David* forced them to defend their views not against believers but against his own total, all-pervasive skepticism leading straight into the void, an attitude even more radical than their own.

Le bon David, *as he was called in France, David Hume became a regular guest at Holbach's salon during his years in Paris. Oil portrait by Allan Ramsay, 1766.*

The anti-Christian stance taken by Holbach and to some degree also by his friends was radical and courageous in a political sense, but it essentially replaced a belief in religion with a belief in science. Like religious faith, the scientific atheism of the Holbach circle upheld the idea of a single, attainable Truth. Hume, on the other hand, had taken epistemological skepticism (skepticism about what it is possible to know) far beyond anything written since the most radical thinkers of ancient Greece, reducing the human self to a mere illusion born of sensation and habit.

Hume's agnosticism brought him into conflict with his atheist host. Atheism, for Hume, represented a kind of certainty for which his philosophy did not allow. While Holbach had written *Le Christianisme dévoilé*, the most sustained attack on Christianity published at that time, Hume had penned, but not yet published, a work of his own, *Dialogues Concerning Natural Religion*, in which three characters debate the merits of different degrees of faith and skepticism.

The author does not openly identify with any of them, but Philo, the most skeptical of the three, echoes most closely Hume's positions. There may be some sort of God, he states flatly, but "we have no *data* to establish any system of cosmogony." Demolishing one "proof" of God's existence after the other, while leaving open the possibility that there is a reality that is unproven and improvable, Philo is the supreme Humean skeptic—so much so that one of his codisputants attests, "The task which you have undertaken, of raising doubts and objections, suits you best, and seems, in a manner, natural and unavoidable to you."[26] Hume, it seems, thought that the task he had undertaken, that of destroying all rational foundations of religious belief, was infinitely more important than the question of whether or not there was a possible reality outside our senses, a reality about which no statement of fact is possible.

Holbach, whom his friends dubbed the "personal enemy of God," must have been impatient with this extremely cautious philosophical stance. After all, even if the natural laws are nothing but formal statements of what we have come to expect ("the sun will rise tomorrow"), to all intents and purposes we do well to live as if such empirical expectations *were* objective necessities. Hume's principled agnosticism seemed trivial in the face of the overwhelming power of the church—of censorship, imprisonment, forced labor, and executions. Attacked in Britain for not being sufficiently religious, the empiricist thinker was taken to task in Paris for refusing to renounce all faith. This was in part a misunderstanding of Hume's position. As a young man, he had, philosophically speaking, sailed out to the open seas in an attempt to net the ultimate Truth, the biggest fish in the pond of objective knowledge. He had returned with nothing but small fish, a haul of pragmatic assumptions beyond which there was nothing that could be known. Diderot and Holbach had no such epistemological ambition. As philosophers, they were content to sit on the shore and admire the view, willing to assume that what they saw was really there. Their quarrel was not with the nature of the sea or the creatures of the deep, but with people who claimed they could walk on water.

This difference in philosophical stance led to a certain amount of mutual teasing. Hume ridiculed, somewhat unfairly perhaps, the apparently inexhaustible optimism of the friends, who continued to believe "that human Society is capable of perpetual Progress towards Perfection,"[27] despite abundant indications that such progress was extremely limited. Hume the historian had learned to be a skeptic not only in metaphysics but also in politics. Meanwhile, Holbach and Diderot simply could not believe that Hume would not go along with their all-out attack on the church. When the great historian Edward Gibbon (he of *Decline and Fall*) attended the baron's dinners in 1763, he noted the "intolerant zeal" of the French philosophers, who "laughed at the scepticism of Hume, preached the tenets of Atheism with the bigotry of dogmatists, and damned all believers with ridicule and contempt."[28]

Gibbon was the most worldly of men, and his observation is significant for two reasons. On the one hand, it demonstrates that the tone of the salon could shock even the most Enlightened of sublimely skeptical minds. Gibbon's obvious irritation at the sermon he was subjected to also suggests that the Holbach-Diderot duo had a tendency to perform in tandem, flattening any objections with well-rehearsed arguments and practiced strategies, much like an old married couple or a comedy routine.

Both Hume and Gibbon were obviously treated to the famous *how-can-you-really-still-believe?* routine by Holbach and Diderot, and they found it a little too slick for their liking—Gibbon out of skeptical detachment, Hume because he was convinced that the real challenges of philosophy lay elsewhere. From his fundamental perspective, the greatest task was to understand the absolute impossibility of certainty, a certainty the *philosophes* appeared to cultivate for reasons Hume must have considered philosophically irresponsible. From their vantage point, Hume wasted his great energies on questions that could not serve their central purpose: to change a society and a morality—an entire culture—whose injustice and needless suffering they found unbearable. Hume's was, properly speaking, a philosophical project, theirs a political one.

Despite these differences, *le bon David* and his Parisian friends knew that they stood on the same side, squarely in opposition to the general way of thinking. Hume was too much of a skeptic to believe that this way of thinking could be changed, while Diderot and Holbach insisted that one must try, even in the face of overwhelming odds. Their mutual respect and support remained unbroken even after Hume's return to London in 1766. Both the baron and Diderot continued to correspond with him, the latter addressing his letters to the "well-beloved and greatly honored David," with promises that "Mme Diderot will kiss your two large Bernardine cheeks"[29]—a facetious pledge, as Diderot's wife hated her husband's irreverent and dangerous friends. Their friendship was a lasting one, even if it was about to be put to the test, not for philosophical reasons, but because of an explosive mixture of vanity and paranoia.

CHAPTER 9

A NATURAL PHILOSOPHY

The philosopher friends of the rue Royale had a strong, optimistic belief in science's capability to improve society and explain the universe. Scientific method was the obvious alternative to religious faith, and in their almost boundless optimism, the *philosophes* had a tendency to be swept along by a general enthusiasm for scientific discovery. They moved in scientific circles and were the first to hear about new discoveries and publications, the seemingly inexorable progress of knowledge.

This excitement about scientific certainty was very much in the air, so much so that it had left the academies and salons and descended into the streets. "Everywhere, science calls out to you and says 'Look!'"[1] wrote the roving reporter of eighteenth-century France, Sébastien Mercier. "Our boulevards have become schools of physics,"[2] exclaimed another writer, thinking, perhaps, of the *Affiches de Paris* promising courses in all the sciences, or of the shows of "amusing physics" on the Boulevard du Temple, designed to use natural phenomena as fairground attractions with the greatest possible spectacle.

The Paris of Holbach and Diderot was a place awash with ideas, abuzz with scientific discoveries and astonishing possibilities. The excitement of experimental thought seeped out of the laboratories and onto the boulevards. Showmen and charlatans gave demonstrations of the power of electricity, and everybody with a few sous to spare could witness the seemingly miraculous powers of nature—miracles that could be harnessed, predicted, and explained.

One experiment in particular had caught the public imagination. In April 1746, the famous Jean-Antoine Nollet, professor of experimental physics and member of the Académie Royale des Sciences, revealed the power of electricity at Versailles, transmitting electric shocks first to a row of 180 royal guardsmen holding hands and then to 200 "volunteer" Carthusian monks. A debate ensued as to whether it would be possible to similarly electrify eunuchs (who were obviously thought to be less easily "electrified" by emotional or other phenomena): Tests on three castrato singers from the king's musicians showed very satisfyingly that they jumped and twitched just like other men. A favorite scientific demonstration of Nollet's involved a small boy being suspended from the ceiling by silken cords and then being connected to an electric wire. The charged child could not only attract objects with his outstretched hand like a magnet; when he gave a kiss to a little girl, the breathless audience in the darkened demonstration room could actually see sparks fly between their lips—an instance of poetic metaphor made visible by science.

Electrical phenomena appeared to bear the secret of life itself, of emotions, of movement—perhaps even of the soul. Every demonstration made its audience slightly more disposed to entertain the idea of *l'homme machine*, as La Mettrie had put it. If some scientists were trying to explain the mysterious inner movements of body and mind by electrical means, others approached the question from the opposite direction by building automata designed to imitate life as perfectly as possible. In part this was, of course, the old alchemists' dream of creating life, but the mechanics of the day as well as the public taste for spectacle made possible increasingly perfect mechanical dolls with moving eyes and flexible limbs, capable of talking, drinking water, or even singing. The sensation surrounding the 1770 appearance of the "Chess Playing Turk" (a hoax containing a small human chess master moving the pieces of the board with a sophisticated mechanism) was only the culmination of a craze for mechanics, for imitating life.

The scientific model operated in a material world, observing a reality that could, in principle at least, be measured, counted, predicted, and explained. While chemists, physicists, and zoologists attempted, in a muscular metaphor popular at the time, to "tear secrets from the bosom of nature," the *philosophes* around the Baron d'Holbach were concerned with developing a new morality out of this world without enchantment and without "ghostly guidance" from beyond.

A key thinker in the search for moral principles, a man whose work profoundly influenced the radical Enlightenment, was a poet who had died almost two millennia earlier. Despite the fact that he remains a shadowy figure in the history of ancient Rome and almost nothing is known about his life, he helped open the eyes of generations of searching minds.

Titus Lucretius Carus lived in Italy sometime during the first half of the first century BCE. Most of what we do know about him is contained in his unfinished epic poem, *De rerum natura* (*Of the Nature of Things*), in which he interpreted and explained the world around him with singular lucidity. All thinkers of the Enlightenment had read him, Holbach had translated him into French, and Diderot had taken most of the conception of nature he laid out in *Le Rêve d'Alembert* from the ancient poet. For the main protagonists of the radical Enlightenment, with plenty of enemies and very few friends, Lucretius was a key ally and a constant presence, almost a member of the salon himself.

De rerum natura is a materialist manifesto, but it is also a great, ecstatic poem exalting the beauties of nature and the wonders of the world, an epic journey in rolling hexameters, showing the reader not only all of nature from the infinitely small to the grandness of the universe, but also through the cycle of human life and experience—the first line of the gigantic, 7,500-verse work contains the word "mother"; the last one abruptly ends on a vision of corpses.

Lucretius himself had taken his inspiration from the Greek philosopher Epicurus. It is a supreme irony (as well as a direct result of centuries of propaganda by the Church) that Epicurus is often seen as the philosopher of total, unbridled indulgence, a "philosopher for swine," as he was dubbed by his enemies. The very reverse is true. For him, the goal of human life is an intelligent moderation of the passions, freeing the human spirit, and the body, from all enslavement. While it is natural to seek pleasure and flee pain, untamed passions and unattainable objects of desire create the greatest pain, and any attachment bears within it the tragedy of loss. The mind will therefore only find its true, unshakable equilibrium, the state of *ataraxia*, by understanding the causalities of the material world, its unchanging mechanisms, and drawing the appropriate conclusions. For Epicurus, only the material world can be a source of dependable knowledge. As there is nothing knowable about the immaterial world, about gods or life after death, the goal must be to achieve the freest, most painless state in this life.

Lucretius venerated Epicurus as humankind's liberator from religion, a word deriving, after all, from the Latin *religio*, "binding down"—a shackle on the human mind. Lucretius sought to make the human mind soar by breaking the bonds of ignorance, which seeks a spirit behind every tree, a demon in every cave, and a god behind every bolt of lightning. Epicurus had put a stop to fearful groveling before the unknown, an achievement celebrated by Lucretius with an intensity worthy of the young Shelley:

> Once human life was cowering in the dust
> For all to see, gravely pressed by religion,
> Which raised its head up in the heavens
> Menacing mortals, glowering from on high.
> A Greek man was the first who dared to raise against it
> His mortal eyes, pitting himself against it.
> Neither the fables of the gods, nor lightning,
> Nor the roar of thunder bent his knee, but his keen mind
> quickened by virtue, burned to smash the bolt
> barring the gates of nature, and to throw them open.[3]

Reading *De rerum natura* is stepping into the open, into the bracing wind of intellectual freedom—a storm followed by David Hume's "calm sunshine of the mind."The key to the freedom found in perfect mental calm, Lucretius claims, lies in accepting the evidence of the senses and the finality of death. Once we have understood that we must die and be extinguished, we will not be in thrall to the unknown, will no longer live in fear of eternal punishment or in the vain hope of heavenly rewards, but will seek the greatest happiness and the most perfect justice in our own world, for the benefit of the living.

There is a truly Promethean courage to these verses, written before scientific experiments could confirm what the poet had deduced from observation. The stuff of the world, the cause of fruit growing on the tree, the constancy of matter, is not divine interference, writes Lucretius, but "primordial germs." These smallest particles make up all matter and are different in kind, so that no substance can suddenly turn into another. Matter must be made up of such imperceptible atomic particles, he argues. How else could moisture evaporate from laundry hanging in the sun? How could a ring be worn down by years of wear, or a votive stone from the touch of generations of pious fingers? How could a piece of transparent horn be penetrated by light but not by water, if not that light atoms must be much smaller than water atoms?

So far, Lucretius said nothing that had not been said by Democritus and Epicurus centuries before. What makes *De rerum natura* not only one of the most exhilarating poems in Latin literature but also a great work of philosophy is a language pulsating with vivid imagery, an astonishingly close observation of nature, and the moral courage with which Lucretius pushed the basic ideas of Epicurus to their ultimate conclusion. Somewhat like Hume would, Epicurus argued from an individualist, skeptical standpoint that we can know nothing about the gods and should therefore not waste our precious time trying to. Lucretius, however, took a more political position that would inspire Holbach and Diderot: Gods were tissues of poetry, ephemeral shadows. Life was here and now; unnecessary suffering is abundant and largely caused by religion. To enlighten people about the material nature of the universe and the irrelevance of the gods was to put a stop to this suffering.

The atomist theory of matter put forward by Lucretius had also originally been developed in ancient Greece, but the Roman developed it into a very personal theory that strikes modern readers as remarkable in its anticipation of central tenets of modern physics.

Atoms are not stationary, Lucretius holds, but are constantly hurtling through space with incredible speed, colliding and bouncing off one another, forming new matter in a process governed by chance—similar to dust particles performing their radiant, chaotic dance in a shaft of sunlight. Everything is made up of atoms, including the gods, who live in perfect happiness and do not interfere in the course of nature. In fact, in writing about the gods, Lucretius appears to consider them as more like psychological realities, like poetic archetypes, rather than as active beings—a vision from which Spinoza would take much in his own conception of God, for him just another name for the laws of nature.

Like his master Epicurus, Lucretius argued passionately against fear of death, and of the afterlife. The mind itself is made up of extremely fine atoms, and as every compound of atoms is destined to decay and recombine in other forms, the mind will die with the body and vanish with it, just as it was formed and gained maturity during a child's physical and mental development. Mind and body are one, are different manifestations of the same thing, and subject to the same laws, and after we die, there will be no mind to regret its shadow state, no one to be punished or rewarded. *Nil igitur mors est ad nos*—"Therefore death is nothing to us," Lucretius concludes.

Once we accept the mortality of body and soul, understanding death not as eternal suffering but simply as nonbeing, the greatest terror overshadowing life is lifted. The fear of hell can be cast out, and with it the "blackness of death" that sullies every aspect of mortal life with fear of the unknown and of the afterlife.

Liberated from fear, we can recognize in the gods mythical personifications of serenity. *De rerum natura* begins with an invocation of Venus, pictured here as the creative principle of all life, who is implored to keep the god of war distracted, a scene Lucretius pictures with great immediacy, as Mars, "vanquished by the eternal wound of love . . . leans upon your holy body."

While Lucretius granted the gods their share of earthly pleasures, his own attitude towards physical love was colored by a very Epicurean distrust of strong passions. Too often, he believed, transitory pleasure leads to lifelong suffering. It is particularly poignant that despite his almost puritanical insistence on moderation in all things, the Roman poet-philosopher was posthumously vilified as an immoral hedonist whose lewdness had been appropriately punished: Four hundred years after his death, the Christian writer Hieronymus claimed to know that Lucretius had died by his own hand after a love potion had driven him insane. Only a madman, after all, could have such ideas as his.

It would take a millennium before the humanist scholars of the Renaissance rehabilitated *De rerum natura*. Only the most daring could embrace the work's uncompromising materialism, but nobody could deny its qualities as a great work of poetry. If young Denis Diderot in Paris and David Hume in Edinburgh were allowed as students to read such a dangerous work, it was because of the ringing hexameter verse echoing with Homer's voice. No doubt the boys would also have been told about the poet's supposedly terrible end (crazed by love), and no doubt his pessimistic emphasis on extreme moderation of the senses—though in flat contradiction with his alleged suicide—was a useful message for the teachers to impart to adolescent boys. Condemned as a philosopher, Lucretius survived as a poet, and from the great French essayist Pierre de Montaigne to Spinoza and Holbach, everyone had read him and heard his message:

> for you shall see that nature
> Freed from the arrogance of haughty masters
> Will generate herself and freely everything,
> Rid of all gods.[4]

With his mixture of extreme intellectual clarity and moral pathos, Lucretius was perhaps the most direct intellectual ancestor of the radical Enlightenment. Had he been able to sit down at Holbach's table, he could have taken part in the discussion almost immediately, as all main ideas were familiar to him and could be traced back to his great poem.

"There is a book published in Holland, in two volumes octavo, called *De la Nature*," Hume wrote to his friend Hugh Blair in 1764. "It is prolix, and in many parts whimsical; but contains some of the boldest reasonings to be found in print."[5]

The exact title of the work that had so impressed the Scottish philosopher was *Système de la nature* (a respectful nod towards Lucretius, who also had "nature" in the title of his great work, as did Hume himself in his *Treatise on Human Nature*), published in Amsterdam and smuggled back into France. A recently deceased academician by the name of Mirabaud was listed as its author. Behind this prudent facade was once again Thiry d'Holbach, the genial host of the rue Royale.

In his previous work, *Le Christianisme dévoilé*, Holbach had specifically attacked Christianity and had attempted to prove in detail how absurd its beliefs are, in that they are grounded not in spiritual fact but in oriental myth and political interest. In collaboration with the scientist and writer Jacques-André Naigeon (1738–1810), another regular guest at his table, he had pressed home his point with *Théologie portative* (*Portable Theology*, 1767), a mock catechism, and *La Contagion sacrée, ou Histoire naturelle de la superstition* (*The Sacred Contamination, or Natural History of Superstition*, 1768), as well as a *Histoire critique de Jésus-Christ* and a *Tableau des saints* (both 1770). Not content with this workload, which he undertook in addition to his articles for the *Encyclopédie* and a good number of translations of antireligious books and tracts from English, he also translated *De rerum natura* into French.

In *The System of Nature*, Holbach emulated Lucretius in going beyond an attack on religion and setting out to construct a worldview based not on ancient myths and alleged revelation, but on the revelations of the senses. "The source of man's unhappiness is his ignorance of Nature,"[6] the baron claimed at the very beginning of the work, and his position is contained in this short statement, from which the author draws nothing less than the necessity of a total revolution of our way of being in the world and our way of being governed.

Reading *The System of Nature,* one can easily see why Hume was so impressed with the "boldest reasonings to be found in print." At the same time one cannot help thinking that his characterization of the work as "prolix" and "whimsical" is a polite understatement. Holbach's voice rings with dignified principle and sober fact, but the seven-hundred-odd pages in two large volumes are riddled with repetitions and redundancies, almost as if they were more of a protocol of the discussions at the rue Royale, faithful transcriptions of discussions over many evenings, during which the thread of a conversation is dropped and later taken up again, and new visitors have to be convinced by reiterating well-known arguments. Even their counterarguments have survived in the shape of anticipated objections: "some might say," "it has been remarked," "the objection may be raised"—interjections like these give the reader the impression of actually being in the room as an idea is presented and debated furiously.

Thiry d'Holbach was a man of great intellectual courage and moral fortitude, but he was not a great stylist. He certainly wrote in haste—his output was phenomenal—as well as in the greatest secrecy, but his repetitious, insistent prose can be heavy-handed, despite some beautiful examples (which may not have been his own) and the undeniable dignity of his tone (which certainly was). His friends recognized this deficiency, as even the author may have done, and edited his works, a task that fell particularly to Diderot, Naigeon, and Helvétius.

In all likelihood, the baron's great works were partly collaborative efforts, testimonies from the discussions in his salon. At times one almost hears individual guests speaking: Diderot with a beautiful image or a dazzling paradox; Jacques Naigeon with his cutting sarcasm; the irrepressible *abbé* Galiani facetiously putting in a word for the Lord; Buffon and later Augustin Roux with one of innumerable examples drawn from biology; the novelist Marmontel interjecting an ironic observation; Jean-Baptiste Suard, a particular friend of the baron's, burnishing a turn of phrase while the cautious deist *abbé* Morellet (who later protested that he had heard no impieties being uttered there) blocked his ears, no doubt.

As the resulting, lengthy works were often still indigestible for the reading public, some of the anonymous friends took it on themselves to condense them into shorter, more manageable, and more structured tomes, distilling from the behemoth that was *The System of Nature* a punchy volume with the title *Le Bon sens* (*Good Sense*, 1772), which made much the same argument more effectively on less than a third of the pages. "It is the *System of Nature* rid of its abstract and metaphysical ideas; it is atheism put into the reach of chambermaids and wigmakers,"[7] sighed Friedrich Melchior Grimm, famous for his love of formal wigs and apparently worried about future supplies.

Despite its lack of elegance and its unwieldy structure, the "damned *System of Nature*," as the outraged Voltaire called it, is a compendium of all arguments for materialism the eighteenth century could muster: a monumental appeal to reason, which promptly caused a huge scandal. The religious writers fumed and threw themselves into a flurry of activity, writing refutations and indictments, while the patriarch of the Enlightened once again did everything from the safety of exile to discredit a work that was doubly dangerous for the ideas it propagated and for taking attention away from him. "One would have to be completely mad not to admit the existence of a great intelligence, if one's own is so small," Voltaire needled against the anonymous author, adding that the work had done "irreparable damage."[8]

Holbach hammered his points home with relentless logical consistency. All problems afflicting humanity arise from an unfortunate tendency to ignore what is in front of our eyes in favor of vapid speculation, he argues: "Men will always deceive themselves by abandoning experience to follow imaginary systems. Man is the work of Nature: he exists in Nature: he is submitted to her laws: he cannot deliver himself from them; nor can he step beyond them even in thought."[9]

If we trust our senses, we will understand that the world consists of nothing but matter and motion, strictly governed by necessity, by cause and effect. This thought is fundamental for Holbach, and it becomes easier to understand why he could not follow Hume in his psychology of habits of perception. Holbach needed a rock on which to build his system, and he found this rock in Spinoza's pure necessity, in Cartesian doubt and Newton's physics, not in the kind of empiricist skepticism that allowed not even natural laws to stand.

Why do people believe in God? the baron asks himself, concluding that it could only be because of ignorance and fear. As nations and societies, people have long been entirely in the dark about the true causes of natural phenomena. Science will eventually simply replace the former superstition by explaining the powers at work in nature and showing the clear link of cause and effect, but it may be harder for us to accept the blind workings of necessity than the hidden purpose of divinely inspired creation, he writes. Baffled by the mechanical play of natural forces beyond our control and comprehension, we attach a hidden intention to natural events, a will like our own. We live in a social world, dominated by the intentions of others, by good and evil, which are nothing else but ways to describe whether a human action is helpful or harmful to us.

This idea clearly echoes Spinoza, whose proto-atheist argument was that creation is perfect and that any perceived imperfection was grounded in the limited perspective of humans, not in nature itself. Now this argument had been developed one step further, to become a precursor of Darwin: Nature is not a moral universe; it is a blind mechanism of which humans are an ever-changing part, just like other organisms are.

Self-centered and childish as we are, we expect nature to exist for us and want to think of our suffering as important, as meaningful: "Man believes that his welfare is a debt due to him from nature; that when he suffers evil she does him an injustice."[10] We project intentionality, good and evil, into nature, because we are with mysterious forces. We humanize nature by ascribing a will to its blind workings, a social reflex that at the same time reveals us to be deeply narcissistic; we simply cannot believe that anything around us could exist very well without us, that we are neither the purpose of creation nor the center of the universe.

God is born of our ignorance of nature, but also of our fear and our longing for meaning. We find ourselves weak and infirm, and so we create a vision of strength; we are mortal and long for immortality; we are surrounded by meaningless suffering and make up the idea of justice after death. Nothing seems to be more terrifying than the prospect of our physical and mental annihilation in death and of living in a world without meaning, without purpose, and so there takes shape the idea of a being that rights all perceived wrongs of our existence, the very antithesis of our imperfection. The radical members of Holbach's circle were not immune from this mental reflex: Diderot himself could never quite accept the absence of any link between virtue and happiness, and he relapsed into a religious way of thinking when he challenged Holbach during a discussion to show him a single wicked man who was truly happy or a virtuous person who was not, deep down, content with life, despite all trials and obstacles.

Holbach was more hardheaded, allowing no exceptions. "The first theology of man was grounded on fear, modeled by ignorance,"[11] he wrote. "Nature, you say, is totally inexplicable without a God: that means that to explain something you understand badly, you need a reason which you do not understand at all,"[12] as the author (in this case very possibly Diderot himself) succinctly puts it in *Le Bon sens*.

The tragedy of this self-centered and superstitious misconception is that it induces terrible suffering and causes the believer to commit, as Holbach powerfully writes, "a slow suicide." Cowed by the allegedly heavenly statutes, we are permanently afraid of a phantom's all-seeing eyes, reduced to a state of superstitious infancy, and forced to live fixated on the illusory existence after death, at the expense of our present life, filled with guilt and fear of supernatural punishment or vain hopes for heavenly rewards, and manipulated by priests who base their very earthly power on divine authority.

Instead of this diminished existence of spiritual bondage, Holbach proposes a life free of phantoms and demons, a society based on the understanding of human nature, and of natural laws. "Indeed," he wrote, "what is an atheist? He is a man, who destroys chimeras prejudicial to the human species, in order to lead men back to nature, to experience, and to reason."[13]

Having demonstrated the folly of faith in transcendental phantoms, Holbach argued for useful, constructive knowledge. The universe consists of matter and motion, motion being a state of matter under certain conditions. Different kinds of matter combine, decay, and recombine to form the material world according to the necessity expressed by the laws of physics. There is nothing else: no Cartesian second substance of which the immortal soul consists, no life after death, no Providence, no inherent meaning to existence, no God.

Driven by necessity, specific circumstances lead to the organization of matter in such a way that the motions of its internal parts appear to act unprompted, bringing it to life. Like many of his contemporaries, Holbach believed in the spontaneous creation of life: Wood and flour will, if left in a moist and warm place, eventually teem with small organisms, which were commonly taken for the beginnings of life out of dead matter. This, however, does not mean that the great chain of being has been interrupted. "Man is purely physical," the baron insisted.

The internal motions of matter, however, can be so subtle, so surprising, that primitive humans could only explain them by assuming that an entirely different substance was at work here—a soul, mysteriously interacting with the material body. Just as in the automatons that created such a sensation on the boulevards of Paris, the invisible hidden spring made the mechanism appear animated by a divine spark, and fearful humans assumed that this enigmatic wellspring of movement was outside their world and immortal, that their own death was not the annihilation of the individual, but just the soul's shedding of a temporary vessel. Instead, writes the baron, not only is life material, but we ourselves are parts of this material world: "Man occupies a place amidst that crowd, that multitude of beings, of which nature is the assemblage. . . . His life itself is nothing more than a long series, a succession of necessary and connected motion, which operates perpetual and continual changes in his machine; which has for its principle either causes contained within himself, such as blood, nerves, fibers, flesh, bones, in short, the matter, as well solid as fluid, of which his body is composed."[14]

As part of the physical world, all life is subjected to its laws, and it is therefore likely that it was not created suddenly, but over the course of the ages: "Although the matter of which the earth is composed has always existed, this earth may not always have had its present form and its actual properties—perhaps, it may be a mass detached in the course of time from some other celestial body."[15] Life from outer space? The baron thought it possible. In any case, life as it is now was not created six thousand years ago, as the biblical story would have it, but has changed with its external circumstances and will continue to change in response to them. All life-forms, after all, are adapted to their environment: "If by any accident our globe should become displaced, all its productions would of necessity be changed. . . . All productions, that they may be able to conserve themselves, or maintain their actual existence, have occasion to co-order themselves with the whole from which they have emanated: without this, they would no longer be in a capacity to subsist."[16]

Having made the case against the illusion of a universe inhabited by demons and a morality dictated by an unknown God, Holbach goes on to propose a new ethics based on the laws of nature and on reason. Every organism instinctively strives for self-preservation, flees pain and seeks pleasure, and in understanding this, he argues, we find the key to a healthy society: "Pleasure and pain, the hope of happiness or the fear of misery, are the only motives capable of having an influence on the will of sensible beings; to compel them, then, it is sufficient that these motives exist, and may be understood; to know them, it is sufficient to consider our constitution, according to which we can love or approve in ourselves only those actions from whence result our real and reciprocal utility, which constitutes virtue."[17]

As Epicurus had already taught, the greatest pleasure is not necessarily the most intense but the most sustainable one; it may even necessitate transitory pain—for instance, in a medical procedure. But if the greatest possible pleasure is the only true goal of all life, then morality is to be found in recognizing that no individual is completely autonomous and that I have to choose my pleasures wisely, to educate my desire, and that at some point my pleasure will be dependent on the cooperation of others. "Thus virtue is everything that is truly and constantly useful to the individuals of the human race living together in society; vice, everything that is injurious to them."[18] Human beings are social animals, pleasure can only be reached through society, and virtue is whatever is most useful to increase the pleasure of the greatest number.

This natural and beneficial social covenant, which allows people to live according to their nature and follow their best impulses, is countermanded by the nefarious influence of religion, which Holbach compares to the custom, practiced among Incas in Peru, of elongating skulls by forcing them into shape with bandages and wooden planks: "The institutions of man . . . commonly conspire to counteract nature—to constrain—to divert—to extinguish the impulse nature has given him."[19] Infantilized and deformed by a constant diet of falsehood, human beings are "amused with marvelous chimeras" and prevented from developing according to their essentially healthy, innermost nature.

Religion, writes Holbach, forces people to disregard and even damage their only chance of happiness in the vain hope of a better life after death. It makes people guilty from birth and advocates pain and suffering as positive values to be sought rather than avoided in the name of salvation, depraving and perverting humanity in the process. Violence in the name of a higher truth, the hopeless struggle against healthy natural impulses, and the enslavement of entire peoples are the consequence, as priests and princes use the perversions of religion to keep the masses ignorant and powerless.

Here Holbach speaks in remarkably frank tones. "Authority," writes he, "commonly believes itself interested in maintaining the received opinions; those prejudices and those errors which it considers requisite to the maintenance of its power, are sustained by force, which is never rational."[20] Princely power is "the true source of moral evil," he argues. Human beings have been "wickedly governed," and it is time to see the truth and seek freedom from servitude, if necessary by violent means. Revolution was in the air, even in the writings of the otherwise gentle baron.

Just about every established power and every authority of the eighteenth century had reason to be scandalized by these opinions. Sheltered behind the pseudonymous Mirabaud, Holbach might have been a repetitious writer and a clumsy stylist, but his voice had real nobility, and the clarity of his vision was exhilarating to some and utterly infuriating to others. With characteristic intellectual lucidity and courage, the baron and his friends (whose opinions and arguments resonate throughout the book) had also envisioned ideas that were far beyond the scientific reach of their own time, from the theory of evolution to the outlines of a systematic cultural anthropology and psychology. This strictly materialist interpretation of the world advocated rationality, observation, and a morality based on enlightened self-interest and solidarity, an idea whose time had not yet come.

CHAPTER 10

SHEIKHS OF THE RUE ROYALE

Holbach and Diderot had anchored morality not in revealed truth or the doctrine of free will, but in human nature. Their belief that philosophers should live by their principles had been tested in the quarrel with Rousseau. But in 1762 their ideas about morality and human nature became the center of a distinctly unphilosophical comedy of manners.

While Louise d'Epinay's estate, La Chevrette, and its inhabitants encouraged experiments in living—moral experiments that dragged after them the usual round of suspicions and rumors—the circle's main center of gravity, Holbach's house in the rue Royale, was more conventional. The baron was a devoted husband, so high-minded and possibly disapproving of adultery that Diderot, who was invited to his country house at Grandval, initially did not dare to tell his host about his affair with Sophie Volland.

Holbach's marriage was a happy one, but he was also jealous, and his very attractive younger wife appears to have given him reason for jealousy. Several times rows shook the entire small community assembled at the baron's salon, as a guest was seen to be rather too intimately interested in Madame. Madame was all too often flattered by the attention and seems to have encouraged these advances up to a point.

It has often been observed that the passionate lives of intellectuals and moral thinkers are at least as convoluted and comical as those of people who do not make it their business to tell others how to behave. And indeed, the one time

Appearances can be deceptive. While depicted as a solid citizen, Baron Paul Thiry d'Holbach funded and ran a clandestine publishing operation from his own house, a center of intellectual resistance. Watercolor by Louis Carmontelle, 1766.

the salon's existence was threatened, it was not because of political pressure, censorship, or other external threats, but because of a stage-worthy imbroglio around *Madame la baronne.*

Diderot in particular was richly amused by the dramatic scenes that followed and that appeared to have been taken directly from the stage of the nearby Comédie Française. "You must know," he wrote to Sophie Volland in July 1762, "that our friend [the journalist Jean-Baptiste-Antoine] Suard has been flirting with the baroness, and has developed a strong taste for her." In the beginning the baroness did not mind a little flattering extra attention, but soon her would-be lover became insistent, making his feelings for her clear for everyone to see. "The baroness was amused by this at the beginning," comments Diderot, "but when there were scenes involving pathetic sadness, sighs, and tears, she decided to sober up."[1]

Despite being told to pull himself together, the lovelorn Suard would not listen and continued to make his advances. His antics did not go unnoticed in the tight group of regulars around the baron's table. The rest is comedy. Suard received an anonymous letter accusing him of behaving ridiculously and immorally in his pursuit of a married woman, a letter (written, apparently, in the hand of two different people) he took straightaway to Madame Holbach, who was beginning to doubt the wisdom of having allowed her admirer to get his hopes up.

The baroness managed to contain the problem and to keep the letter from her husband, even if that meant continuing to see the lovesick Suard sulking around, as his sudden absence would have aroused suspicions. But the stress of duplicity and desire was becoming too much for Madame Holbach. She fell into a depression and was prescribed a diet of milk and regular exercise, ideally long rides in the countryside. Her companion on these rambles among nature was Charles-Georges Le Roy, the royal lieutenant of the hunt. He was the perfect escort, for in his company she would have access to the royal estates and woods in all their landscaped charm.

Unfortunately, Le Roy himself ("a satyr," as Diderot called him), also had a secret passion for the convalescing baroness. Soon the innocent excursions on horseback turned into amorous obstacle courses for the baroness, who nonetheless found it impossible to deny that she was flattered by the attractions of two attractive men.

Baron d'Holbach, a moderate by nature as he himself had written, was a great advocate of passion in theory, but his wife had long felt that he was really more faithful than passionate. In fact, Holbach seemed to be genially unaware of his wife's increasingly impossible situation—which suggests one reason why she had been flattered by Suard in the first place. With all the writing, translating, hosting, debating, and generally being an important man in intellectual Paris, Holbach did not always show his wife the attention to which she felt entitled. At times, she was simply bored in her marriage to a great and virtuous and very busy man, and she consoled herself with the steady supply of youthful and intellectual hangers-on.

Madame's flirtations were no doubt a source of great pleasure for her, so long as things did not get out of hand. But things did get out of hand. Even as Madame d'Holbach desperately sought her next move, caught as she was between the lovelorn Suard and Le Roy, the priapic equestrian, the furious Madame d'Epinay appeared. She herself had been the object of the attentions of another member of the circle, the historian and novelist Charles Pinot Duclos. Duclos had tried to clear the thorny way to her heart by informing her (erroneously as it turned out) that her lover, Friedrich Grimm, had been carrying on a secret affair with the baroness, right under the nose of her husband and his host.

Louise d'Epinay swallowed the bait and reacted angrily. She informed the baron of the alleged state of affairs, and now it was his turn to be enraged. As Diderot reported to Sophie Volland in July 1762, the scandal erupted into "sadness feigned or real, recriminations, anger, complaints, absences, returns, reproaches, sulking, words that were now sweet and now sour—in a word, an infinity of other things which are the marks of strong passion."[2] The whole, blustering cluster of flirtations and guilty consciences was a reminder that, while lust can be the force swelling the sails of morality with the steady trade wind called pleasure, it is just as likely to be roused beyond control and to shipwreck morality in a violent storm. Many times, they had discussed moral questions into the small hours of the morning. They had high standards, but once passion intervened they behaved just like the comic characters in the lewd plays performed on public squares in the popular parts of the city.

The glut of betrayals of confidence, arguments, and secret heart-to-hearts shook the entire group. It was not easy to discuss philosophy, entertain foreign guests, and run a clandestine translating and publishing operation when members of the core group no longer trusted one another. Eventually the baron intervened, ending the farce with a solution that appeared to be straight out of a Mozart opera. Duclos was asked not to come back; Suard groveled and apologized until he was allowed to return on condition that he cool off, which he did by marrying the first eligible woman who crossed his path; Grimm convinced his lover, Louise d'Epinay, that the accusations against him had been false; and the baron resolved to pay a little more attention to his wife. They were united in their indignation about Louise d'Epinay's accusations, which Holbach did not immediately forgive. Diderot attempted to play go-between, but without success. Of all concerned, only Le Roy, the satyr, managed to escape, despite his advances, without inconveniencing himself too much.

Diderot, who was used to dividing his life between his intellectual mistress and his bitter wife, was not directly involved in the episode around the baroness. He attempted to mediate, but with little success. The habitual atmosphere at the salon was depressing: "Today, everybody is serious. People keep out of one another's way. When they enter, pass by, or leave, they inundate one another with compliments. They listen, but hardly speak, because nobody knows what to say, and nobody dares to say what he knows. Everything seems important because nothing is innocent. And I see all this, and I die of boredom."[3]

For Diderot, the whole affair raised a question about principles and practice. Could morality really amount to more than polite conversation if any adolescent infatuation and any petty jealousy appeared to invalidate the beautiful ideas they had discussed? The *philosophes* liked to portray themselves as virtuous, but where was that virtue now? Where they more than a philosophical equivalent of the emperor's new clothes?

As so often, Diderot chose literature to consider and dramatize this question, this time in an autobiographical character study, an essay entitled fittingly enough, "Regrets About My Dressing Gown" (1769). Once again, the philosopher appears as a writer, an amused essayist, whose easy prose hides a formidable alertness to the ambiguities of life, to the often subtle but always persistent gap between high principle and irrational desire. This time, however, he is a philosopher in borrowed—or rather, donated—robes.

The immediate inspiration for the essay was a generous if curious gift. Diderot had directed the fortunes of the *Encyclopédie* from his home office, a plain and workaday room crammed with papers, furnished functionally with a simple pine chair and desk, and sparingly adorned with a few engravings after great paintings, which the owner had pinned to the wall without frames. The wealthy Madame Geoffrin, herself hostess of another famous philosophical salon, had taken it upon herself to end this undignified mess by renovating and refurnishing the great man's room, sparing no expense on fine furniture, silk wall coverings, and finely carved chairs.

Swept up in charitable enthusiasm, Madame Geoffrin also had a new dressing gown in scarlet satin fitted for Diderot himself. Usually, he chose to dress in an extremely simple manner, but now, there he was, surrounded by unfamiliar splendor and feeling, as he wrote, unfamiliar to himself. He was sorry to have thrown away his old, more modest housecoat, which had enveloped Denis the man, not Diderot the *philosophe*:

> Why did I not keep it? It was made for me, I for it. It moulded itself around the folds of my body without encumbering me. I was picturesque and beautiful. The other, stiff, heavy, transforms me into a fashion doll. The other gown lent itself to every possible use, for indigence is almost always eager to help. A book was covered by dust? One of its panels offered itself to wipe it off. Thickened ink refused to flow from my plume? It volunteered its side. From the long, black lines one could see how frequent service it had provided. These long lines announced the author, the

> writer, the working man. Now I look like a rich idler. Nobody knows who I am.[4]

Holbach's moralizing friends and their very private lies and relationships and the private face of Diderot, unhappy about having to wear the coat of the Great Philosopher, had an essential element in common: the danger of falling hostage to their growing reputations, and the difficulties of living up to them.

They were becoming famous now even outside of France, even if they were no fixed group, no circle, no club, and their opinions diverged widely. Not all of Holbach's guests were atheists or published books, not all Encyclopedists visited the rue Royale, and not all regulars wrote for the *Encyclopédie*. Even the names given to the dinners and discussions varied widely, indicating the continuing openness of the salon.

Rousseau had branded the friends "Holbach's *coterie*," and had accused them of plotting against him. The baron himself simply invited people *chez moi*, and Diderot speaks in his letters about dining *chez le baron*. On other occasions, he calls the rue Royale the Synagogue of the Enlightenment. Diderot used the original sense of the word "synagogue" as a place of assembly, but his choice of word was also with an ironic acknowledgment of the at-times-almost-religious fervor of their atheist sermons. Another aspect of the group's activities was accentuated in Diderot's affectionately designating the group the *Boulangerie*. This obviously referred to the scientist Nicolas-Antoine Boulanger, who had attended the dinners before his early death in 1759 and had posthumously lent his name to Holbach's *Christianity Unveiled*, which was published with the intentionally misleading addition "by the late M. Boulanger" under the title. But the word *boulangerie* also conjured up another image: a busy workshop, constantly mixing and kneading, and pulling dangerous books out of the oven as if they were so many hot baguettes.

David Hume had his own, ironically affectionate name for the friends and their salon: the Sheikhs of the rue Royale,[5] and while they were no oriental potentates, the comparison was just insofar as, during the 1760s, more and more foreigners would knock at the baron's gates. These ambassadors from other Enlightened countries and groups (some of them actually were diplomats) came armed with a letter of recommendation, or just with a winning smile. They were always admitted.

The most important among these recent arrivals, a diplomat himself, was the *abbé* Ferdinando Galiani (1728–1787), a man who became one of the fixtures at the salon for some years. Galiani worked as secretary of the Neapolitan embassy in Paris, but he was not well suited to life as a diplomat, partly because he was so tiny that he constantly had to fight for attention, which he often did by being more witty than his opponents. In 1759, during his presentation to the king, he had greeted the sniggering of the courtiers with the words "Your Majesty, what you see before you is merely a sample of the secretary. The real secretary will come later."

Born in the Italian town of Chieti in the Abruzzi region, Galiani had shown his brilliance early, and when he took the lower orders to become an *abbé* at the age of twenty-two, he had already published books that made him famous in the two areas that would establish his reputation: an economical treatise, *Della moneta* (*On Money*), and a satirical one, *Raccolta in morte del boia* (*Eulogies on the Death of a Hangman*). In 1759, at age thirty-one, the *abbé* took up his diplomatic appointment, and soon he was found regularly at some of the leading salons, including Holbach's, whose intellectual range and frankness attracted him.

Galiani was a scholar and a scientist as well as a wit, and he was used to winning every debate he engaged in. Soon Holbach and his friends discovered that the *abbé* was a man who could stand up even to Diderot's provocative views and rhetorical volleys. Diderot himself noticed it and was delighted; Galiani was "all gaiety, imagination, esprit, folly, and jokes, who makes you forget the drudgery of life,"[6] he wrote to Sophie.

If Galiani's impish humor made the circle laugh, his enjoyment of controversy made him adopt the position of Christian in residence at the baron's godless table. One evening, when Diderot and his friend Roux had argued the atheist case with particular abandon, "saying things that should have attracted a hundred bolts of lightning to the house," the diplomat could bear it no longer. "The abbé Galiani . . . had been listening patiently, but finally he said '*Messieurs, messieurs philosophes*, you are going very fast,'" recounted

Madame Geoffrin. "'Let me start by saying that if I were Pope I would deliver you to the inquisition and if I were King of France, to the Bastille, but, as I have the happiness of being neither one nor the other, I will come back to dine next Thursday.'"[7]

Galiani took up with great alacrity his role as the exact opposite of a devil's advocate. Every atheist argument earnestly expounded by the radicals would be countered with a facetious defense of faith that could drive even Diderot to despair. Once, the *abbé* challenged him to a game of dice. After Denis had lost a fair amount of money, he furiously turned on Galiani, saying that the dice were loaded. "What, *monsieur le philosophe*," the Italian replied delightedly, "you lose a few Francs and immediately you believe that the dice are loaded, but in this universe of ours, where the odds are so much worse, you are content to believe that all is chance?" Galiani's friends called the small but shrewd and sarcastic priest "Machiavellino," and he became a key member of the salon, as well as a close personal friend of Mme d'Epinay, with whom he would maintain a wonderfully lively and humane correspondence for years after his return to Naples, where he was recalled in 1769. There, separated from his companions at the rue Royale, he wilted. "I no longer have the time or the taste for reading," he wrote to Louise. "Reading alone, without being able to talk about it, to have a dispute and to shine, or listen, or make oneself listened to, is impossible. Europe is dead for me. They've put me in the Bastille. I now belong to the vegetable kingdom."[8]

While Galiani was moping in Naples, his place was taken by other foreign guests, especially from London, who attended so frequently that Holbach's salon almost became a place of literary England in exile, a place where a good part of the country's intellectual elite met.

Before Edward Gibbon began his oceanic and wickedly perceptive *Decline and Fall of the Roman Empire* (1776–1788), a multivolume investigation of the collapse of the greatest power in the world, he embarked on a grand tour to Europe. During his stays in Paris he repeatedly visited Holbach's house and was enthusiastic about the company he found there: "We may say what we please of the frivolity of the French, but I do assure you that in a fortnight passed in Paris I have heard more conversation worth remembering and seen more men of letters amongst the people of fashion, than I had done in two or three winters in London,"[9] he reported home.

In his own great work he even put Holbach's salon on a level with the great symposia of ancient Rome and Greece, remarking in a footnote that the emperor Julius would find that in Paris he could converse "with men of science and genius, capable of understanding and of instructing a disciple of the Greeks."[10]

Not all British visitors, however, were so impressed by what they found. Used to the sober empiricism of London debates, many disapproved of the theatrical cut and thrust at the salon and faulted the circle for too much Gallic flamboyance. Horace Walpole famously detested it, and the Scot Sir James Macdonald reported home to the impeccably bluestocking novelist and salon hostess Elizabeth Montagu in London that Diderot was "noisy and talkative, and somewhat fond of a Dispute; he is certainly very learned, and very conscious of his own knowledge—he would be a better philosopher and a more agreeable companion if he did not make philosophy a matter of Party, and treat subjects of the gravest nature and which require a cool examination too much like the head of an opposition."[11]

Macdonald obviously preferred a cooler tone as well as, one may suspect, an openness to deist views, but he and others failed to understand the political aspect of Holbach's salon. The circle was dedicated to overturning conventional modes of thought, to liberating humanity from the leaden hand of theology. They were, in fact, heads of an opposition. Living in a less repressive regime, in which political ideas could be freely articulated, many British intellectuals were wont to misunderstand this covert political interest in the rue Royale.

Even Edward Gibbon was irritated with the salon's more preachy moments and the vehemence with which the friends argued their atheist case, but in the end he also saw the imposition of faith as a cynical imposition of power, commenting that "the various models of worship which prevailed in the Roman world were all considered by the people as equally true, by the philosopher as equally false, and by the magistrate as equally useful."[12] This was the difference between the enlightened spirits of ancient Rome and eighteenth-century Paris: The former were willing to accept an imperial imposition of religion in their own interest, a position closer, perhaps, to the British pragmatic tradition. The French radicals, meanwhile, thought that religion always had an oppressive character and needed to be opposed.

Sir James Macdonald might have preferred more quiet, decorous tones during a debate, but political radicals like John Wilkes, Holbach's friend from university days in Leiden, loved the heady atmosphere. By the time of his visit to Holbach's house in 1762, Wilkes had become a member of Parliament in London and a notorious advocate of political freedom and American independence, as well as a sharp critic of the government. The dinners also allowed him to meet other British figures he would not have met easily in London, particularly David Hume, with whom he drank and "laughed much."[13]

Another friend of Hume's, the Scottish moral philosopher and economist Adam Smith, repeatedly dined at the rue Royale in 1765, and remembered it fondly. Having continued to correspond with André Morellet for more than a decade, he asked his French friend in 1786: "I have not heard of Baron d'Holbach these two or three years past. I hope he is happy and in good health. Be so good as to assure him of my most affectionate and respectful remembrance, and that I shall never forget the very great kindness he did me the honour to show me during my residence at Paris."[14]

Known today mainly as an economist and the inventor of the infamous "invisible hand" of the market, he was much better known during his lifetime as a moral philosopher. Like his friend Hume, he had rejected the Christian faith of his childhood and preferred keeping close counsel about his actual belief. Like Holbach, he argued that human lack of understanding of nature's workings was at the root of religion. In his main philosophical work, *The Theory of Moral Sentiments*, he asked almost the same question as Holbach had: How can people, who are driven by self-interest, act morally, even altruistically? The answer was, Smith wrote, compassion: "The greatest ruffian, the most hardened violator of the laws of society, is not altogether without it."

At the salon, Smith particularly enjoyed meeting Jacques Turgot, one of the leading economic heads of France, but his conversations with Diderot, Holbach, and the *abbé* Galiani, too, would have been carried by similar interests, which had led them to very similar conclusions.

Men such as Wilkes and Gibbon brought a different tradition of political thinking into the salon. Others contributed less to the debates but were enthusiastically welcomed. Much admired for his satirical masterpiece *Tristram Shandy* ("so mad, so wise, and so gay"[15] in the words of Diderot, who used it as an inspiration for his own novel *Jacques the Fatalist*) the novelist Laurence Sterne thoroughly enjoyed being entertained there during his visit in May 1764. "The Baron d'Holbach . . . is one of the most learned noblemen here," he reported home, "the great protector of wits, and the savants who are no wits. . . . [He] keeps open house. . . . His house is now, as yours was to me, my own." Obviously satisfied, he added that he admired the *philosophes* for their ability to live together "without biting or scratching." Instead, "an infinitude of gaiety & civility reigns among them-& wh. is no small art, Every man leaves the room with a better Opinion of his own Talents than when he entered."[16]

Officially the "Rabelais of the English," as Diderot called him, Sterne was in the capital on a highly official and respectable mission as preacher at the chapel of the British embassy, for he was a chaplain as well as a writer, but privately he enjoyed the flattering attentions and the freedom of the "joyous sett." He was obviously sorry to leave, asking a friend in Paris after his departure to pay "my best respects to the worthy Baron d'Holbach and all that society."[17]

Among all British visitors, only David Hume became as close a friend of Holbach and Diderot as the great London actor-manager David Garrick. A famed interpreter of tragic as well as comic roles, Garrick had reintroduced Shakespeare's plays to the London stage—at age twenty-four he made his name as Richard III. He starred in many roles and staged, wrote, and arranged plays of his own. He also worked as both a theatre director and a wine dealer—all of which equally endeared him to his mentor and later friend, Dr. Samuel Johnson.

Garrick was Holbach's guest during two long visits to Paris in 1763 and 1765. "We had a fine laugh at Baron d'Holbach's (where you din'd once) about the *wicked company* I keep: I am always with that set,"[18] Garrick wrote to a friend in 1765. Cast in a Roman mold, though very much a modern Englishman, the theatrical genius was dubbed "Roscius" by Diderot, in deference to the most famous actor the classical world had known.

During his stays in the French capital, Garrick stayed at the house of Claude Helvétius, whose salon rivaled that of the rue Royale, attracting often the same people, though on different days of the week. The actor, an imposing presence, gave several impromptu performances for his hosts, and Diderot, who also attended the salon of Helvétius at times, was particularly struck by these displays of artistry. He himself wrote for the stage and had loved the theatre ever since reciting plays during solitary walks in the Jardin du Luxembourg and hanging around stage doors as a teenager to catch a glimpse of his favorite actresses. Now he saw a great artist in full flight, a tragic actor trained not in the declamatory French tradition of Racine but in a much more naturalistic, fluid style. Garrick fascinated his select Parisian public, giving improvised performances during which his face would pass through a whole gamut of emotions, from surprise to astonishment and sadness to horror and despair.

Diderot noted that the actor could not possibly feel all these emotions, impersonating a comic Little Pastry Boy in one moment and Hamlet in the next. The secret of Garrick's art, he concluded, must lie in his control over expressions, in a certain professionalism that did not require him to experience everything he put his public through.

Diderot was captivated by the actor's apparent ability to divorce expression from feeling, to represent emotion to perfection without actually feeling it. This raised a number of intriguing philosophical questions. If true acting demands of the actor to be indifferent to his or her material, then what about the emotional truth of the piece? How could art express truth by lying? And how is communication possible at all if it is so vulnerable to deceit? The *philosophes* had set out to reveal the truth about the human condition behind the facade of religion and conventional morality, to establish a new morality based on natural values, rationality, and honesty. But what if this truth should be essentially unknowable, if human communication is indistinguishable from effective manipulation?

In Diderot's musings, expressed in his correspondence and in works such as *Jacques le fataliste*, we see the beginnings of a skeptical philosophy of language. Up to this point, the bulk of philosophers had taken language for granted. Our senses might deceive us, as Descartes had worried so memorably, but once we have gained certainty that our impressions correspond with a physical reality (or are at least coherent in themselves, irrespective of the possibility of such a correspondence), we can communicate about the world and about our emotions using words that clearly denote facts. Communication is direct and, depending on the speaker, unequivocal.

Much of Diderot's writing on this theme is standard Enlightenment fare. To escape ignorance and barbarism, philosophy must purify language, he wrote in a letter to the sculptor Falconet. It must purge words of accrued falsities, of accepted, conventional meanings and philosophical errors—a huge project in itself, requiring a kind of ideal Académie Française to define the vocabulary clearly and down to the smallest details. Only a purified language, in which every word denoted a clear, empirical reality, could become "the rich and varied language of a civilized people."[19]

Diderot the *philosophe* looking for a clean-cut solution may have been content with this, but Diderot the psychologist and artist could not be. We do not use pure language as we might use pure water—our words are always burdened with experiences and associations; they have a life of their own, beyond our intentions. Philosophers, wrote Diderot, use common language "without noticing that it is no longer appropriate for our opinions. You have become a philosopher in your system, but you remain a child of the people in your words."[20]

Questioning how he himself used language, he came to the conclusion that the particular structures of grammar must influence the structures of knowledge and thought, an argument which Helvétius had also made in his *De l'esprit*. Diderot singled out abstractions as particular dangerous to philosophical ideas. Just because words such as "ugliness" and "beauty" exist does not mean that these qualities exist in an abstract way. They are attributes of real objects and have no existence outside of the context in which they are experienced. An abstraction, Diderot concluded, "is a sign empty of content."[21]

But how could a philosopher hope to find a kind of truth if there only exist the language of the people, which is pregnant with superstition, and the language of abstraction, which is empty of content? Was it possible to mix the filth of everyday experience with airless abstraction and gain understanding about the world? And what if it was impossible to clean words of their accretions in the pursuit of pristine meaning? What if communication was not a method for reaching the truth but simply an inescapable web of manipulation—what if all the world really *is* a stage?

Once again, the question of public and private, of communication and intention, exercised the *philosophe*. During the imbroglio around Madame d'Holbach, the Boulangerie had demonstrated that the friends were philosophers in their philosophical systems, but children of the people not only in the words they used, but also in their feelings. Real people with anarchic desires were dressed up as philosophers, regarded as such, but Diderot was no longer sure whether all this was more than a game, a high-minded deceit in a world in which one has to lie to tell the truth and it is impossible to speak directly and unequivocally.

Garrick maintained his contact with the rue Royale even after his return to London. When Holbach traveled to Britain in 1765 to stay in the capital for a total of six weeks, he visited the actor and reported back enthusiastically, noting that Garrick had a mausoleum, or rather a memorial, to Shakespeare in his garden.

Other aspects of Holbach's trip left a less positive impression. The liberal British Isles were much closer to the Enlightened ideals of individual freedom and universal rights, but, as always, the reality lagged far behind. Having come to see the Promised Land of liberals and empirical philosophers, he was dismayed to find that the English were very different from what he had expected, as Diderot related to Sophie Volland after his friend's return:

> Perhaps it is the effect of the climate, perhaps the common use of beer and spirits, fat meats, the continuous fog, or the smoke of coal which ceaselessly envelops them, but this is a sad and melancholy people. The gardens are cut into tortuous and narrow alleys. . . . But what best characterizes the national melancholy is their manner of living in these immense and sumptuous edifices which they erect for pleasure. One could hear the footfall of a mouse in there. A hundred women promenading, upright and serious, around an orchestra set up in the centre. It plays the most delicious music. The baron compares these circular walks to the seven processions the Egyptians used to make around the mausoleum of Osiris.[22]

London, seen through the baron's eyes, was a frightening and joyless place. Despair and boredom drove scores of its inhabitants into the Thames (one place was even considerately "reserved for women" alone), and when they were not drinking, gambling, or drowning themselves, Diderot reported, they turned into missionaries, trying to convert the most far-flung people to Christendom. The thought that people who had so far escaped the perverse yoke of Christianity would now be infected with it aroused the particular ire of the baron and also of Diderot, who noted with satisfaction: "There was one of these chiefs who told one of the missionaries 'My brother, look at my head: my hair is entirely grey. In good faith, do you believe you can make a man of my age believe all these imbecile stories? But I have three children. Don't talk to the oldest, you will make him laugh: but take the little one, whom you can persuade of whatever you like.'"[23]

Holbach felt miserable in the coal-sodden London fogs and could not even be cheered by the thought that despite the missionary zeal of some, religion appeared to be "almost extinct" in Britain; the islanders had become deists, after all, and to be called an atheist was treated as the worst of insults. His overriding impression, though, was disappointment. He found the British unwelcoming, and he missed his friends.

Diderot was highly amused by the entire affair and poked fun at Holbach's general sniffiness in a letter to Sophie. The baron had been forewarned, he noted, but still he had returned dissatisfied with just about everything: the countryside, the towns, the "bizarre and gothic" architecture, the famous English gardens, the public taste and the entertainments, the people, "on whose faces one never sees trust, friendship, gayety, sociability. . . . Dissatisfied with the great, who seem sad, cold, highhanded, disdainful and vain; and with the little people, who are tough, insolent, and barbaric."[24]

Despite his German birth, Holbach had become more French than the Parisians. The sullen atmosphere made the otherwise placid baron highly agitated. One day, he told Diderot, he caught himself walking down a London street thinking, "'Ah! Paris, when will I see you again? Ah! My dear friends, where are you? Oh! Frenchmen, you are flighty and mad, but you are worth these stingy and sad pedants a hundred times over!'"[25] London might not be for everybody, David Garrick told his guest, with acid if unappreciated irony.

But Holbach was dissatisfied not only with all things British. He appears to have suffered a general crisis, quite likely through overwork. During a few months in 1765 he appears to have been gripped by a general distaste for the circus of society life. Even the fame of his salon became a burden, as aspiring writers and liberal aristocrats on their grand tours beat their path to his doorstep in droves. Diderot wrote to Sophie in December of the same year: "I forget if I have told you already that our dinners in the rue Royale have been less regular of late. The baron has finally become bored with twenty-seven or twenty-eight guests, when he was prepared for no more than twenty. The baroness is delighted."[26] Holbach, however, soon missed the conviviality of his dinners, and before his wife could put up much resistance, the regular feasts and nightly discussions were reinstated—if with a more restricted list of guests.

CHAPTER 11

GRANDVAL

During the summer months, when those who could fled the swampy heat of Paris and its regular fevers, the great, noisy gang of radicals temporarily disbanded. The baron retreated to his country house in Grandval, close to the city, a gracious house set among rambling parklands. Every year he invited houseguests to spend some days or weeks with his family, and every year one of the guests was Diderot. In a letter to Sophie Volland, Diderot wrote of his activities at Holbach's country seat:

> I have been installed in a small, separate apartment, very quiet, very friendly and warm. There, between Horace and Homer and the portrait of my friend, I spend hours reading, meditating, writing and sighing. It is my occupation between six o'clock in the morning and noon. At half past one I am dressed and go down into the salon, where I find everyone assembled. Sometimes the baron visits me; he is wonderfully discreet. If he sees me busy, he greets me with a wave of the hand and vanishes. If he finds me not working, he sits down and we chat. The mistress of the house pays no visits and requires none. We are at home, and not in her house. . . . We dine at great length. The table is laid like last night, only perhaps even more sumptuous. It is impossible to remain sober, and it is impossible not to be sober and to behave well. After dinner, the ladies chat; the baron sinks into a sofa, and I become whatever I want.[1]

During the 1760s and 1770s, Diderot spent at least part of his summers as the baron's houseguest, enjoying the easy conviviality far away from the politics of Paris. Away from the monotonous grind of the *Encyclopédie*, Diderot loved the fresh air and delicious food. At Grandval, he had a steady supply of friends for conversation when he felt like talking, but also the opportunity to go for long walks, play silly games, and have endless, blissful hours for reading, writing, and daydreaming—in short, every author's dream.

This dream was all the more delicious, as it provided him with a respectable excuse to get away from his pious and disapproving wife. Anne-Toinette had married her handsome and clever tenant not suspecting that he would turn into a propagator of wickedness and atheism, and she remained stubbornly loyal to her Catholic faith. She remained intensely superstitious—after the death of the first three of her children, she had "dedicated" her daughter to the Holy Virgin and to Saint Francis and always dressed the child in white to protect her from the fate of her older siblings. As for her husband's professional activities, she did her very best to ignore them completely: She never even learned how to pronounce the word *Encyclopédie* correctly.

Much as he missed the company of his little daughter during his stays at Grandval, the *philosophe* nevertheless relished his personal freedom there, even if his letters occasionally strike a very different note. In many of his letters to Sophie Volland, he dwells on the terrible weather, the trivial conversation, and his longing to get back to Paris. Grandval, he complained in a letter dated October 15, 1760, was anything but exciting. It was raining. Mme d'Holbach was absorbed in her embroidery, her mother mainly with digesting food, and the baron in his reading, "enveloped in a dressing gown, his nightcap pulled over his ears."[2] Denis himself was pacing up and down despondently and vainly looking out the window for a change in the weather.

Of course, Diderot would not have been well advised to enthuse about his own good fortune in his letters to Sophie, who was stuck at home with her overbearing mother and her sister. Sophie almost went mad with boredom during the quiet summer months when her lover was away, and she wished nothing more than his speedy return. And yet despite his best attempts at concealing the many pleasures of Grandval from Sophie, Denis the storyteller could not completely deny what a good time he was having: "It is impossible to remain sober here. I can't even think about it. I am becoming round like a ball. If I go on like this, you will no longer be able to embrace me; your sister will no longer dare look at me, and . . . I was about to add something quite mad here, which I will let you guess instead."[3]

Sophie stayed away, as if banished from her lover's life. While other members of his circle had a remarkably relaxed approach to public opinion in moral matters, Diderot was careful to keep up appearances, and the two lovers were never seen together in public, not even in the relative privacy of Grandval. His friends had no such qualms. Friedrich Melchior Grimm lived openly together with the married Madame d'Epinay, Rousseau was in a long, common-law marriage with Thérèse Levasseur, and d'Alembert shared salon and bed with the witty and beautiful Julie de Lespinasse.

Initially, not even the baron himself knew about Diderot's relationship with another woman, and the houseguest had misgivings about telling him. At least, that is how he explained to Sophie his inability to visit her in Paris even for a day. Instead of rushing to her, he spent his time pining for her, as he wrote in letter after long letter, once adding that Holbach's mother-in-law had warned him that she would have him drowned out of pity rather than continue to watch the sad spectacle the lovelorn philosopher made of himself. Obviously, the old lady had guessed what her son-in-law was too preoccupied to notice.

An almost bucolic feeling of simple pleasures and eternal sunshine imbues the letters Diderot wrote from Grandval, undercut by darker currents of passion. Indeed, the passionate life—the life of passion lived well—became the friends' main philosophical preoccupation, the center of many a debate at the rue Royale and during long nights in front of the fireplace at Grandval. The radical philosophers had demolished the great church that centuries of Christian tradition had erected in the human soul—indeed, they had destroyed the very conception of a soul, leaving nothing but pure matter conscious of itself. There was no revelation, no divine law, no life after death, and, most important of all, no guilt induced by the age-old curse of original sin. Life was to be lived *now.*

For Diderot and Holbach, the most determined of the determinist friends, there was a question they simply could not avoid—one answer they had to give or see their entire philosophy turn into absurdity. They had set out to abolish a morality they considered poisonous in order to replace it with a new, constructive one, but they had to face up to one very obvious objection: If the world is material and governed by necessity, if there is no free will, if all actions are predetermined, if consciousness is nothing but a stream of sensation and conscience a mere social construct, and if there is no transcendental being to reward and punish, why bother being good?

The traditional, Christian idea of morality is built on the guilt of original sin, on the negation of desire, which is seen as the central evil of humanity. Lust is the gate to all of the vices and to hell itself: It must be dominated, crushed, punished, or at the very least denied or hidden. This notion was a powerful tool of coercion, a Machiavellian stroke of genius, as Holbach had argued. No one is free of lust and hence of vices; a single lapse can cause one to die in a state of mortal sin and be damned for all eternity, and therefore everyone needs the forgiveness of the Creator, dispensed solely through his catholic and apostolic church.

More often than not, Western philosophers had simply stripped the ecclesiastical trappings of this idea without attacking its integrity. Lust—the "search for pleasure"—was treated like an embarrassing relative, periodically impossible to ignore, but otherwise best not talked about. Lust was too impure to find a place within any metaphysical concept of the world. Its compulsions were infinitely inferior to duty, philosophers claimed, when they did not merely treat it as the antithesis to a separate, abstract law imposed by God or by his secular substitute, natural law. From Plato to the German idealists of the nineteenth century, this was the main tenor of philosophical opinion in the West.

Only a handful of thinkers stood against this overwhelmingly dominant way of seeing things. Epicurus and Lucretius were part of this opposition, as were later thinkers, such as Michel de Montaigne and Francis Bacon. In this phalanx of intellectual courage, the friends of the rue Royale occupied a key position, reviving and focusing this line of thought and projecting it into the future. It was one of the great achievements of the radical Enlightenment to advocate a different conception of the human body. For centuries, the Christian tradition had conceptualized it mainly as a receptacle of ailments, pain, and sinful lusts, something to be shed at the earliest opportunity in preparation for celestial bliss or eternal damnation.

The first step towards grounding morality not on the negation of pleasure, but in its enlightened pursuit, is to acknowledge that the impulse for pleasure is central to human life and to make clear that pleasure exists *before* morality, that there is nothing inherently immoral in desire or its fulfillment. In good Spinozist vein, Holbach argues that nature exists independently of any moral judgments, that what we experience as pleasurable or painful, as good or bad, is nothing but the blind play of natural forces. Desire and passion are equally natural mechanisms inherent in the workings of *la machine humaine*; only moral ideas, the aspirations and dreams of a community, attach values to them.

An acceptance of the laws of nature, Holbach argued in his *Système de la nature*, is what distinguishes a good society in which people can thrive and prosper through virtue from one that twists minds and emotions into the corset of vice. The laws of nature are the only authority we have to submit to; the answers to all our ills lie in understanding and following the laws of the physical universe, not in creating "chimaeras of our imagination."

The baron was insistent on this point—so insistent that when he took up the pen again to explain his system at even greater length in his most voluminous work, *La Morale universelle* (1776), his ponderousness began to exasperate even his friends. "It is well written," reported a cool Mme d'Epinay to Ferdinando Galiani in sweltering Naples. "Everything is stated very clearly, but there isn't a single new idea, and everything in it that is true is already so strongly established that it really wasn't worth the trouble to write a whole book about it."[4] Perhaps Louise d'Epinay, a writer herself, was a little more acerbic than necessary, but it is hard to deny that Holbach had made most of his points already in his previous works, and already at considerable length. Not even Diderot could always bear his ethical disquisitions: "The baron . . . turns everything into a moral issue,"[5] he sighed in a letter to Sophie.

The virtuous baron was at pains to acknowledge the role of the passions, but at the same time he extolled intellectual pleasure over physical enjoyment: "I do not pretend that happiness consists of voluptuousness (*volupté*), because, even if I have once made flow from my quill all the drunkenness which it had spread through my senses . . . I subscribe (perhaps by temperament) to more moderation & I want that only need, that father of pleasure, will call me from now on, & shall toll . . . the hour of my highest pleasure."[6] The pleasure of the senses, he wrote, was simply too short-lived, too unreliable.

Holbach's very Stoic, skeptical attitude towards desire was reinforced by an almost simplistic rationalism. At times he comes close to arguing that if only people were to understand that it was in their interest to be moral, all crime and all selfishness must surely cease. To Holbach, the ultimate root of all wickedness is ignorance, and evil can be remedied simply by giving all children a good education. This theory showed honorable intentions, but it was not exciting, nor did it have the taste of human truth.

For Diderot, who was not named after the god Dionysus for nothing, the human psyche was more contradictory, more richly complex, and largely under the sway of individual character and irrational impulses. Despite the fact that he was liable to get carried away by his enthusiasm when speaking about the sweetness of virtue and the grandeur of morality, Diderot had none of his friends' scruples when it came to discussing human passions. On the contrary, he relished his attacks on conventional decency. Readers are hypocrites, says the narrator of Diderot's posthumously published novel, *Jacques le fataliste* (*Jacques the Fatalist*), which was written for the drawer from 1771 to 1778. They want to be supplied with love stories but accuse authors of licentiousness; they demand that a writer be true to life but they refuse to recognize themselves in his stories. The narrator proposes a simple contract to his audience: "Carry on fucking like rabbits, but you've got to let me say fuck: I grant you the action and you let me have the word."[7] Physical love, he informs his readers, is "natural, necessary and right," but for most people it seems easier to pronounce terrible words such as "kill" and "betray" than "*that* word." What hypocrisy, he scoffs. After all, "*futuo* (Latin: 'I fuck') is no less common than the word 'bread.' It is known to every age and idiom."

In passages such as this one, Diderot's instinct was as far from Holbach's as possible. Holbach could be a bit of a moralist, but Diderot was a flesh-and-blood moral thinker whose writings were always provocative and often a liberating shock. The baron's works give the impression that he regards desire as undeniably real and fundamentally unobjectionable but a bit much to deal with. Diderot, on the other hand, saw it as the very stuff of life—aesthetically its highest pleasure, existentially its fundamental reality, and ethically its greatest challenge. Desire is not something we *have* to live with but the motor of life itself and its fulfillment.

On occasions, Diderot's language soars as he writes about the pleasures of the flesh. His article "*Jouissance*" (enjoyment, orgasm) in the *Encyclopédie* is a small, defiantly lyrical masterpiece of sensualist thought and human insight.

Enjoyment and desire go hand in hand, he wrote, and among all possible pleasures, "is there one more worth our efforts, whose possession & the enjoyment can make us as happy as that of a being who thinks & feels like you, who has the same ideas, who feels the same heat, their same transports, and who extends her tender & delicate arms towards yours, who intertwines herself with you, & who was precarious this will be followed by the existence of a new being who will resemble you?"[8]

The name of this supreme transport still made honest men and women blush with shame, despite the fact that it is the highest of all pleasures, so strong that all mothers risked their very lives in order to attain it. Only pleasure, Diderot concluded, "has brought you forth from nothingness." *Jouissance* not only is at the origin of life but also makes us stronger and more successful, as women choose among their potential mates according to the merit they possess—the process of natural selection in action. "Trust, time, nature & the freedom of the caresses cause us to be oblivious of ourselves," the *philosophe* concluded. "We swear, after having tasted the last intoxication, that there is no other comparable to it; & this has proved true every time that young & sensitive organs have come together, a tender heart & innocent soul knowing neither distrust nor remorse."

It is striking how far into the future this short analysis of human passions carries. The happiness of sensual fulfillment is nature's way of ensuring the survival of the species, according to Diderot. Erotic love is not only a fundamental instinct but also part of a process of selection, in which partners choose each other for certain qualities, allowing species to prosper and humans to leave the cave. Real and imagined merits conspire to bring about sensual gratification. For those happily freed from prejudice, this fusion of two bodies and two souls is the most natural of things. Its "unspeakable pleasure" can be enjoyed without the guilt imposed by religion—and with, in his beautiful phrase, "a tender heart & innocent soul knowing neither distrust nor remorse."

This was the Diderot who was also the author of two erotic novels. It was also the Diderot whose marriage with Madame Diderot was nothing but a facade, allowing him to have affairs with several women, most lastingly and memorably Sophie Volland. In his writings, if not in life, he was disarmingly frank about sexual matters, certainly in the context of the morals of his time. It is easy to understand why during the considerably more prudish nineteenth century, his daughter, whom he had so adored, could not bring herself to publish most of her father's manuscripts, among them *D'Alembert's Dream*, in which he takes great, mischievous pleasure in provoking and questioning the moral ideas of his contemporaries.

A satire as well as an investigation of the nature of life, *D'Alembert's Dream* also offers a gleefully provocative look at sexual instincts and mores. Before the doctor's arrival, Julie de Lespinasse reports, the feverish arch-rationalist d'Alembert had been contemplating the continual procreation of the world and the creative desire driving all organisms. He became agitated, as she remembers perhaps a little more innocently than plausible: "Then his face became flushed. I wanted to feel his pulse, but he had hidden his hand somewhere. He seemed to be going through some kind of convulsion. His mouth was gaping, and his breath gasping. He fetched a deep sigh, and then a gentler sigh, and still gentler, turned his head over on the pillow and fell asleep."[9]

Intellectual exertion, imagination, and physical response were here fused into a single, delicious moment. For the scientist Bordeu, who also appears in the story, this is nothing very shocking, as he makes d'Alembert's mistress, Julie de Lespinasse, understand. Everything agreeable and useful without harming anyone is by definition good, the doctor holds, and the young woman agrees with him. The most useless of all the virtues is chastity, because it gives pleasure neither to the individual nor to society.

When Julie agrees with Bordeu about the uselessness of chastity, having concluded that nothing can very well be immoral if it harms nobody, he springs the question of what she thinks about "solitary acts." The otherwise liberal actress puts on a face of shocked morality, but the scientist holds that his is also a moral vantage point: "Yes, Mademoiselle. . . . It is a need, and even if the need were not to demand it, it is always sweet. . . . He is a poor devil who does not know to address himself, to despatch himself in the manner of the Cynic," an allusion to the notorious practice of the Greek philosopher Diogenes, who used to pleasure himself in public. The doctor continues, arguing that not everyone can be with the person he loves: "What, must I forgo a necessary and delicious moment just because circumstances deprive me of the greatest happiness one could imagine?"[10]

Not only is desire a positive force in life, but it clearly demonstrates that the mind is just an extension of the body. Thinking and feeling are physical phenomena. Desire forms a connection between body and mind: "You see a beautiful woman, her beauty impresses you; you are young, and immediately the organ of pleasure assumes its full form, you are sleeping, and this incorrigible organ becomes agitated, and immediately you once again see the beautiful woman and perhaps you feel the most voluptuous pleasure."[11]

What interests Diderot about this "voluptuous pleasure" is that the causality appears to be inverted. An adolescent boy may experience an erection at merely seeing a beautiful woman; in his sleep it is the stimulation of his "incorrigible organ" that brings back the image of the beauty seen on the street. Even while the body is asleep, image and action fuse into orgasm. Just as in the case of the fictional, hallucinating d'Alembert, the mind and the body are one, divided only by grammar, by being called by different names.

To Diderot, erotic desire, the nonrational impulse to live and to seek pleasure, was fundamental to all consciousness, to all culture: "There is a bit of testicle at the bottom of our most sublime sentiments and most refined tenderness,"[12] he wrote to his philosopher mistress, Sophie Volland (Diderot used the word "testicle" also for the ovaries and thus for both sexes). Reason takes second place in this conception: It is merely there to organize the space created by desire, to regulate what would otherwise become overwhelming, and to create a consciousness in which rationality and desire are bound together. Thus morality and the creative urge can coexist.

"Whatever passion inspires, I forgive," he announced to Sophie Volland, who had herself inspired considerable passion in him. "After all, you know, I have always been the apologist of strong passions."[13] In this respect at least, Diderot's attitude was truly liberal: No consensual sexual practice should be prohibited at all, he believed, as long as it did not involve children.

Diderot was careful to distinguish lust from its social consequences. The selfish pursuit of pleasure was reprehensible insofar as it was selfish and therefore likely to hurt others, not insofar as it involved or sought sensual pleasure. This idea was in stark opposition to the reigning Catholic doctrine, which regarded sensual pleasure as a terrible danger at all times and a necessary evil at best and which threatened the faithful with eternal damnation for a single, unrepented, "impure thought."

Diderot was not the only author whose outspoken views and explicit works shocked even liberal readers of his time, even if his own two excursions into this genre, *Les Bijoux indiscrets* and *La Religieuse,* are not particularly scandalous by our contemporary standards. During the mid-eighteenth century, a wave of pornographic novels, prints, and pamphlets was swelling the pockets of the colporteurs and delighting gentlemen (as well as the occasional lady) in private moments. They were racy and outrageous and often left very little to the imagination.

At the respectable end of the scale, suitable for public consumption, were teasing painters such as Boucher and Greuze (whom Diderot idolized). Their works depicted voluptuously nubile, half-clad maids and cunning little vixens, and they used every trick in the book to evoke sexual pleasure without actually showing it. Painting was not the only medium testing and transgressing what was accepted. Literature also explored intense emotions, be it implicitly or explicitly. Suggestion and metaphorical evocation were cultivated into a new art form: Novels such as Rousseau's *Julie* were crammed with hearts palpitating, eyes fluttering, and hands shivering, all sensations that could arouse their readers, without ever going into too much unseemly detail.

But detail, of course, was much valued by readers, especially male ones, and in the market of desire, everything could be had. During the 1740s, when Holbach, Diderot, and friends were rebellious young men just out of their teens, a glut of libertine novels appeared: Jean-Charles Gervais de Latouche's *Le Portier des Chartreux* (1741), *Thérèse philosophe* (1748) by Jean-Baptiste Boyer d'Argens, and Fougeret de Monbron's *Margot la ravaudeuse* (1750) were only the best known of them—not forgetting, of course, John Cleland's *Fanny Hill: Memoirs of a Woman of Pleasure* (1749), which was published in English in London, but quickly found its way across the Channel.

But while there were obvious similarities in subject matter between Fanny Hill and her continental sisters, there were also important differences: Fanny was a jolly prostitute who pleasured gentlemen (and the odd lucky man of a more modest background), a reflection of Britain's lasting preoccupation with class. Not only were the French libertines interested in elegantly raunchy descriptions of close encounters; they were of a distinctly political and philosophical bent. Morality—particularly sexual morality—was the exclusive fiefdom of the church. Access to the kingdom of heaven could only be gained by depriving oneself of pleasure and fighting against lust and licentiousness in all its forms. To show, in this context, a cast of sympathetic characters simply having fun and not being damned for it was, in effect, an act of subversion, a political act.

In his *Thérèse philosophe* (1748), Jean-Baptiste Boyer d'Argens, a scandalous aristocratic French philosopher who had spent most of his career at the court of Frederick the Great in Potsdam, makes the same point Diderot and company would later emphasize. His young protagonist tells the reader that it would be madness to suppress the delicious instincts leading her to the encounters. "Imbecile mortals! Do you really believe you could extinguish the passion which nature has put in you: they are God's work. You want to destroy these passions, to restrain them in narrow limits. Madmen!"[14] After this tirade, the heroine of the novel moves on to describe in lusty detail her first erotic experiences in a convent.

Convents, monks, priests, and nuns featured heavily in libertine literature, and this, too, was a form of opposition. Every time a libidinous confessor abused a young girl's confidence by teaching her one lesson too many about original sin, every time two nuns found mystical ecstasy in each other's arms, every time a monk quite literally revealed himself to be a man underneath his habit, the moral authority of the church was eroded a little more, as the entire institution was portrayed as a monument of hypocrisy, a whorehouse disguised as the house of the Lord.

While much of the erotic literature of the ancien régime was anti-Christian in impetus, it also provided a moral alternative—always in the most appealing way, of course. Their characters left no pleasure untried, no opportunity wasted, but they were also personally attractive, intelligent, and often very decent incarnations of the Enlightenment ideal of marrying moral principle and sensual ecstasy. The authors of some of these works were anonymous hacks churning out salacious stories, but often they were highly literate and capable, endowed with good brains and a fine turn of phrase. They were cultured men, intent on more than just bragging about the good times they'd had or had imagined others having. These decades were, after all, the apex of Casanova's hectic career throughout Europe, and the story of the most enduring literary hero, Don Giovanni, existed in several versions for the stage, most famously, of course, Mozart's opera, composed in 1787.

French authors, in particular, wrote explicit literature with great abandon and remarkably loaded their works with moral and philosophical disquisitions. The journalist Rétif de la Bretonne, whose fine descriptions of Paris by night are still a pleasure to read, dabbled in pornography, as did the capable if languid aristocratic Claude Prosper Jolyot de Crébillon. The worldly gentleman

Choderlos de Laclos published *Les Liaisons dangereuses* in 1782. The finest erotic stylist of them all, Gabriel Riqueti, comte de Mirabeau, a great wit, statesman, and orator, would play an important role as a moderate in the early years of the Revolution; his work *Le Rideau levé ou l'education de Laure* (*The Lifted Curtain, or Laura's Education*, 1786) combines audaciously graphic metaphor with lively characterization and philosophical ideas.

There is a great deal of sighing and panting in *Le Rideau levé*, and snow-white breasts, alabaster thighs, and pink flesh are in rich supply, along with charming jewels and mighty members, as the young protagonist discovers just how delicious life can be. But titillation was not the author's only goal. Pleasures were enjoyed freely but not indiscriminately. Apart from the sensuous passages, *Le Rideau levé* also contains long educational dialogues about, of all things, responsible enjoyment and avoiding pitfalls like unwanted pregnancies and venereal disease. Paternal advice is dispensed to the young girl by her mentor, who then takes it upon himself to induct his charge into the world of carnal delights in a joyous ritual, once he has judged her mature enough for this enjoyment.

The purpose of works like this was neither the simple thrill nor the fact of transgression alone: This life-affirming sensuality offered a philosophical, ethical alternative to the dominant morality of the church. The narrative naughtiness was backed up by philosophical analysis—first and foremost, of course, by Julien Offray de la Mettrie, the prophet of sensuality in exile. La Mettrie's *L'Art de jouir* (*The Art of Pleasure*, 1751) was a sensualist hymn to enjoyment: "Pleasure, the sovereign master of men and gods, in front of whom everything vanishes, even reason itself, you know how much my heart adores you, and all the sacrifices it has made to you."[15]

In *The Art of Pleasure*, the infamous philosophical libertine counsels an imaginary young woman not to renounce her beauty and all chance of a life of happiness for the sake of a misconceived notion of virtue; an adolescent boy who witnesses two birds mating in a tree is advised that, "to you, everything is a living lesson in love." What follows is a pretty little exercise in rhetorical rococo, for the boy is becoming fascinated by a gift of Love, a "vermillion rose, whose button is only just covered over and wants to be harvested; a charming rose, every leaf of which appears covered and surrounded by a fine down the better to hide the loves, which are hidden inside."[16] Among all these amazing anatomical details and poetic metaphors, the author suggests, lie not only physical satisfaction but also moral fulfillment.

Like other materialist moralists, La Mettrie believed that the secret to a good life was finding and honing pleasures that would not be exhausted in an instant: "Pain is a century, and pleasure a moment." The pleasure lover (*le voluptueux*) loves life because he has a healthy body and a free spirit without prejudice. A follower of Epicurus, he fears neither the bolts of lightning hurled by an angry god nor death itself. He (always "he," the ideal philosopher is hardly ever female) is the master of his own fortune.

Diderot, of course, detested La Mettrie, whose apparently irresponsible hedonism for its own sake made Denis deeply uneasy, even if this was a misreading of the older man's works. Having chosen the freedom of exile over a life in France, Frederick's court philosopher, La Mettrie, had simply taken the morality of materialism to the extreme: There was only pleasure; everything else was distraction, illusion, or hypocrisy. If the pleasure of one person coincided with that of another, so much the better, but no morality apart from self-love (and, by implication, self-preservation through social behavior) could stand before the bench of nature.

Diderot and Holbach were convinced that their attack on Christianity must serve to replace one, sick morality with another, healthy one. Holbach himself had shrewdly observed that the determination of religious thinkers to defend God against his detractors stemmed ultimately from narcissism: They could simply not accept that there might be no God, precisely because that would mean that life was not inherently meaningful. In their heart of hearts they were unwilling to confront the possibility that they themselves, the vast universe of every individual consciousness, could be as meaningless and as random as a leaf whirled into the air by a gust of wind.

The friends of the rue Royale resolved to stare into this ultimate moral void, but not for long. They were atheists, not moral nihilists—but theirs was a narrow path to negotiate. Morality must be based on solid ground, on some basic truth. Having rejected religious revelation, they were left with the laws of nature—laws about which, as they freely admitted, they could hypothesize and attempt to gain experimental knowledge but could never posit beyond reasonable doubt. Once one takes God out of the game, one has thrown open the doors of a room for a moral debate wide enough to contain the nihilism defined by La Mettrie, a flat negation of the project the Paris *philosophes* had set themselves—their nightmare.

The solution to this dilemma was to define morality according to what was good not for the gods but for humans, to construct meaning out of culture, as Holbach saw, quoting his great predecessor Michel de Montaigne: "In and of itself, life is neither good nor bad; it is the place of good & bad, according to what you do. In my opinion, it is living happily, & not dying happily, which creates human happiness."[17] Living happily, living well, was nothing less than living passionately, realizing every kind of pleasure in the context of a community—by making other lives richer while doing as little harm as possible.

Passion is crucial to the radical Enlightenment. Passion is primordial, an incontrovertible fact of human life, and as such it offers itself as a cornerstone for an analysis of human behavior, and hence for ethics. "We speak not strictly and philosophically when we talk of the combat of passion and of reason. Reason is, and ought only to be the slave of the passions, and can never pretend to any other office than to serve and obey them,"[18] wrote David Hume, whose insistence on clear analysis has often been misunderstood as cold rationalism.

If the passions are at the base of all culture, they do not turn us into impulsive monsters: They drive our actions and our thoughts, but they also make us into social beings. By drawing us out of ourselves, passion turns us not into automata isolated in our selfishness but into individuals needing protection and approval of their peers. It leads us to fear pain, to empathize, to feel pity and sadness as well as joy. Passion, the natural impulse of the human animal, could serve as the basis of a new morality, as Holbach observed. We all love pleasure and flee pain; we are all surrounded by people like us, who are following the same goals. If our pleasure coincides with the good of society, we will be virtuous while living happily at the same time. No other foundation of morality is necessary.

At first glance, the search for pleasure seems egotistical and incompatible with communal goals. Our strongest natural impulse is self-love, self-interest. Demonized by the church as the sin of Pride (or of Lust, Greed, Sloth, or Gluttony), it was reinstated by thinkers of the Epicurean tradition not as a burden to be carried but as the central motivation of all ethical behavior: "Instead of extinguishing in the heart of men the essential and natural love for themselves, morality should use it to show them the interest in being good, human, sociable, and trustworthy: far from wanting to destroy the passions inherent in his nature, morality will lead him to virtue, without which no man on earth can ever enjoy true happiness."[19]

In order to appreciate the interest in being good, we need a conscience, which is born out of compassion and out of a need to belong, to be well regarded, as Holbach argues in his *Morale universelle*: "The laws of conscience, which we believe to be born from nature, are born from custom: every one of us has an internal veneration of the opinions and the manners approved and received around him and cannot rid himself of them without remorse, nor apply them without applause."[20] Applause may seem a vain motive for feeling good, but if it occurs for the right reasons, it can be an important driving force for building a just society.

We need this applause. The approval and disapproval of those we love will keep us from straying into the wilds of reckless indulgence and rampant selfishness. "I have erected in her heart a statue which I never want to break," Diderot wrote to Sophie, addressing her as the ideal beloved. "What pain it would cause her if I were ever guilty of an action which made me small in her eyes! Is it not true that you would rather have me dead than wicked? Therefore, love me always, so that I will always fear vice."[21]

Evoking a graceful, Greek temple with marble figures of gods and goddesses, the image of the statue was chosen advisedly, for Epicurus and the Latin authors such as Lucretius and Cicero remained the main inspiration of the radicals. Hume thought that in contrast to the "Antients," modern philosophers had allowed themselves to become overly rationalist, which "carry'd them away from Sentiment."[22] Diderot likewise contrasted the Christian ideal of evangelical perfection ("nothing but the deadly art of stifling nature"[23]) with the place desire had occupied not in the shade, but in the heart of the religion of the ancient world: "There is no comparing our saints, our apostles, and our sadly ecstatic virgins," he wrote in 1769, "with those feasts on Olympus where virile Hercules, leaning on his club, amorously beholds fragile Hebe, where the master of the gods, intoxicating himself with the nectar poured brimful by the hand of a young boy with ivory shoulders and alabaster thighs, makes the heart of his jealous wife swell with spite."[24]

The boundless sensuality of this vision, in which the thighs of a young boy are as much objects of desire as the features of "fragile Hebe," bespeaks Diderot's own roving imagination. Jealousy and spite were sentiments the enthusiast for the human passions knew only too well from his own wife, as the long-suffering Madame Diderot had to put up not only with her husband's terrible reputation ("he ought to be burnt at the stake" was a common opinion held by contemporaries) but also with a string of mistresses, both before and during his marriage. Before Sophie, there had been Mme de Puisieux, a lady from the minor aristocracy (who apparently got her young lover to write *The Indiscreet Jewels* within a fortnight as a literary dare); after her there was at least one other woman he courted assiduously and very probably successfully.

So much passion and *volupté*, on the page as well as in real life, beg the question whether the great, sensualist philosophy that particularly Diderot professed so enthusiastically and others like Grimm and Holbach supported was anything but a justification for their own, rather unorthodox love lives. But their private arrangements were not all that unusual. Holbach was a devoted and faithful husband; Diderot always kept his affairs as quiet as possible and was careful not to embarrass his wife in front of outsiders; Grimm and Louise d'Epinay lived in what we might call a common-law marriage, as did others associated with the circle, such as d'Alembert, the Comtesse d'Houdetot, and also her hapless admirer Rousseau. Even Voltaire preferred a simple living arrangement with a woman to a union forged by the church. Arrangements such as these were common far beyond the circle of friends at Holbach's salon.

This, after all, was a time in which it was paramount to pay lip service to religion and propriety, but social life and gossip would have withered within a week if Parisians of all social classes were not having more or less discreet affairs and shady living arrangements, including positions expressly and at times exclusively created for the purpose, from simple chambermaids to tutors, private chaplains, and the householder living with many a priest.

Even marriages were not for life. The average marriage lasted for eight years, after which one of the partners usually died, often the woman in childbirth, like Holbach's first wife. Divorce was impossible, but convenient arrangements could usually be found—Mme d'Epinay spent most of her adult life living in legal separation from her profligate husband. It was customary to marry someone considered a promising life partner and a good catch, rather than the love of one's life. Marriage was a contract, and extramarital affairs simply a fact of life, far less frowned on than in our own, differently moralistic age. The children of these unions were either educated in the family or given away, as had been the case for Jean d'Alembert.

What set this group of friends apart was not so much what they practiced but how they talked about it. They believed the system as it was to be perverse, to bend people's morals, make them habitual liars, force some of them to live with guilt and fear for having done nothing else than follow their healthy instincts. Not believing in an afterlife or a revealed Truth graven in stone, the radicals simply did not believe these instincts to be sinful—indeed, Buffon's proto-evolutionist approach to nature had shown them that passion was not just an agreeable goal for hedonists but the very stuff of life. Passion was not an obstacle on the way to happiness; it *was* happiness—or could be, if society could be arranged in such a way as to allow healthy passions to flourish instead of being suppressed and forced underground. The emotional agenda of the radical Enlightenment was ultimately a moral one.

It is remarkable how many intellectual radicals and philosophical revolutionaries appear to have lived remarkably ordinary lives themselves, and for Diderot and friends, everyday life was anything but a constant succession of casual conquests, amorous trysts, and ardent affairs. They had their families to think of, they were happy with the lives they lived, they were jealous as people always are, and if the sensualist ethics of the rue Royale were no excuse for debauchery, they may have partly served as an escape from a more prosaic reality. This does not detract from their validity, but it may serve to explain some of the emotional intensity poured into these arguments.

Grandval, Holbach's country seat, became the scene of a number of these arguments, as well as a summer retreat for many of the baron's friends. For several years, it was Diderot's primary escape from his life as dutiful editor of a multivolume behemoth that, he felt, was swallowing up his life. It was here, in the countryside, that he could breathe and think freely and entertain his Sophie with long, leisurely letters about his life, his thoughts, and the foibles of his hosts and fellow guests. It is easy to imagine how much Sophie and her sisters looked forward to these long, effusive letters, brimming over with anecdotes, conversations, and warm feeling, bored rigid as they were in their own countryside retreat, where they had to stay at the insistence of their mother to keep them away from Paris and its wicked ways—in a country seat they sold immediately after her death.

Even if an invaluable part of this long and passionate epistolary exchange was sacrificed to propriety, the remaining hundreds of letters still give an extraordinarily vivid portrait of a meeting of bodies and minds that extended over two decades. For in addition to his feelings, Diderot wrote about books they were both reading, and he carried on conversations begun during their encounters. But what Sophie and her sisters were really looking forward to was Diderot's return to the city, and every year as autumn drew near, the Holbach household prepared to move back to the rue Royale, reopen the salon, and take up the normal train of life. The summer holidays were over.

CHAPTER 12

THE BEAR

While Diderot, Holbach, and their circle were formulating an ethics of desire that perceived itself as a true alternative to any religiously inspired morality and the very opposite of the body-hating moral teachings of Christianity, Jean-Jacques Rousseau—"The Bear" as his former friends had nicknamed him—had further developed his own ideas on the matter.

The 1760s were a very fruitful period of his life. After the turmoil of the previous decade, during which he had tried his luck as a composer and a diplomat, he had moved back to Geneva, converted back to Protestantism, returned to Paris—and quarreled with all his former friends. Finally, he had openly come out as their enemy. In the aftermath of the Geneva affair and the subsequent publication ban of the *Encyclopédie*, the group had been at its weakest and most exposed, an ideal moment for Rousseau to attack with his *Letter to d'Alembert About the Theatre*, in which he poured bile on their ideas and on the theatre, beloved particularly by Diderot.

Having also high-handedly refused to accompany his dangerously ill patroness and last friend, Louise d'Epinay, on a convalescence journey to his hometown of Geneva, he had had to leave her cottage. He had found a different house lent to him by a new protector, but his temper and his paranoia had not improved, and eventually Jean-Jacques moved back to Switzerland. For a while he was living in a country village that, he must have hoped, would remind him of the happy childhood days spent in the hamlet of Bossey.

His itinerant and often difficult life, however, belied the success he had enjoyed. He had finally become a famous author. In a rush of creativity, he had penned two hugely successful novels, *Julie ou la nouvelle Héloïse* (1761) and *Émile* (1764), and an important philosophical work on social justice and ethics, *Du contrat social* (1762), as well as other, smaller works. With its vivid invocation of strong sentiments and moral conflict, his fiction particularly had made the author into a literary star. Success suited him:

> I was truly transformed; my friends and acquaintances no longer recognized me. I had ceased to be that shy creature, who was shamefaced rather than modest and who had not the courage to show himself or even to speak. I had ceased to be a man who was put out by a joking word and blushed at a woman's glance. Bold, proud, and fearless, I now carried with me wherever I went a self-assurance which owed its firmness to its simplicity and which dwelt in my soul rather than in my outward bearing.[1]

But Rousseau had not suddenly shaken off his shyness to become a bold and conquering literary hero. His self-perception as a giant was never without its relentless shadow: the paranoia of a man who felt persecuted by everyone. As his sketched self-portrait continues, it veers off in the direction of megalomania: "The contempt which my deep reflections had inspired in me for the customs, the principles, and the prejudices of my age made me insensible to the mockery of those who followed them; and I crushed their little witticisms with my observations, as I might crush an insect between my fingers."[2] To emphasize the simple grandeur that set him apart from other mortals, Rousseau now commonly wore an Armenian-style tunic and fur cap. He had turned his back on the big cities, which he regarded as breeding grounds for decadence and corruption, veritable wrecking yards of morality. Instead, he had found a simpler life in the countryside, where he could meditate, go for long, solitary walks, and be inspired by the beauty of creation.

Rousseau's shift of existential orientation away from metropolitan intensity and towards the enchantment of rural simplicity was mirrored by his thought. At the beginning of his career, he had been an integral part of the Enlightenment, that most urban of intellectual currents, which thrived in salons and academies, in learned journals, books, and personal encounters. Nowhere was the Enlightenment battle cry "*Sapere aude!*" (Dare to know!) taken more seriously and acted upon more decisively than by Diderot, Holbach, and their friends, who published, translated, wrote, and transcribed a library of intellectually audacious books while at the same time pushing forward the *Encyclopédie*, the most distinguished and most significant encyclopedia project in history.

Rousseau, however, no longer wanted to know, or rather he was convinced that he already knew all that really mattered. He had understood the nature of humankind, plumbed the depths of the human soul. He needed no more lecturing from those unable to understand his vision, which set him apart from the spirit of the age.

Rousseau's contrarian philosophical attitude would be little more than a historical footnote had it not become hugely influential—much more so, in fact, than Diderot and Holbach, whose moral ideas were only resurrected, a century after their formulation, during the second half of the nineteenth century.

The morality of desire as argued by Diderot, Holbach, and other members of the salon accords to everyone the same right to seek pleasure and flee pain, and it demands of everyone to show empathy towards others and responsibility towards oneself. This notion, however, was too frighteningly radical for later generations because it presupposed a material universe populated by evolving animals, "marvelous machines" animated by instinct. It offered no metaphysical solace, no life after death, no soul, no God, no eternal law.

Rousseau's moral ideas offered all this, and more, and the difference between his own moral ideas and those emanating from Holbach's salon describes a lasting rift between Enlightenment thinking and its most determined adversaries. The works that made Rousseau into one of Europe's most idolized and most widely read and translated authors combined sentiment with a philosophical defense of religion and of noble sentiment against the anarchic force of Eros and the cold glare of rational inquiry.

For Rousseau as for Voltaire, healthy sentiment and religion were essentially the same. A universal watchmaker—Voltaire's metaphor—had created the mechanism of the world and of humankind according to his divine reason. If only people could learn to listen to their inner voice, to trust the voice of nature speaking through them, then they would automatically be in unison with God's intentions, with his reason. This, of course, was a very Christian approach to psychology as well as philosophy. It reversed what the Enlightenment had fought for long and hard: to emancipate reason from theology. For if all true reason was divine, then any idea questioning this primitive, "natural" religion was by definition perverse and harmful. If God and reason were by definition one and the same, intellectual opposition was directed against the order of creation.

But Rousseau was certainly no medieval writer. On the contrary, his work contains the seedlings of a movement that would grip younger generations: romanticism, which venerates the drama of individuality; inner turmoil and transformation; and the importance of nature as a repository of the great, ineffable Truth that is beyond language and analysis. He effectively transposed theological ideas into a secular vocabulary.

Rousseau's opposition to the Enlightenment, and to its exponents, was not of the old-fashioned kind; it was anticipating a culture seeking to reenchant what the cult of reason had stripped bare. For a younger, post-Enlightenment generation grown up with an internal conflict forcing them to take a position in the struggle among reactionary church hierarchies, the insipid religious twitches of Voltaire and other deists, and the apparently pitiless perspective of materialism, Jean-Jacques appeared to offer a way out. Admiring Rousseau, one could be modern and a believer, at home in contemporary culture and at ease with one's inner need for faith.

Reading Rousseau against the radical Enlightenment reveals both of them more clearly. They fed from the same sources, they share a vocabulary and a horizon of knowledge, they were written by people who knew one another intimately—and yet they could not be more different in intention or result.

Always fascinated by childhood development (unless, it must be added, it occurred in his own house), Rousseau based much of his moral thought on observing children and extrapolating from their growth to arrive at principles he believed to be true for all humankind. We have all been children, he appears to argue, and this shared experience is the truest teacher of who we are. In early life, Rousseau writes, a child is neither good nor wicked. Like an animal it is simply amoral, acting on impulses and needs, loving those who are good to it, and possessed by a healthy, life-preserving self-love. Then puberty strikes. An adolescent notices changes in his body, new strength, new desires. He is confused (the development is described from the male perspective), he looks around himself to compare his development with that of his peers, and he seeks to gain advantage and distinction to impress girls.

Comparison engenders value judgments and competitiveness; it twists a child's healthy self-love (*amour de soi*) into a narcissistic, egotistical love, or *amour propre*. The latter spawns inequality, personal property, and hatred—the moral ruin of society. If people seek the society of others, it is because they are doubly weak: physically because their survival makes it necessary to co-operate in the struggle for survival and morally because they are unable to bear their loneliness. "Every attachment is a sign of insufficiency," Rousseau writes in his great novel about education, *Émile*, which became a bible to engaged parents and teachers alike. "If no one among us had any need of others, he would never think of joining up with them. Thus our frail pleasure is born from our infirmity. A truly happy being is a solitary being; God alone enjoys absolute happiness."[3]

If the human is corrupted by carnal competitiveness and social tyranny, the evident goal of a good life, and therefore of education, must be to restore human beings to a state of harmony with nature. Only through creation can we hear the soft but majestic voice of the Creator, "engraved at the bottom of his heart," a very Calvinist thought of direct communion with God. One can imagine how the devout deist Rousseau must have felt at the baron's table, where only rational exposition could carry the day. "You know, Madame," he wrote to a correspondent, "that I have never thought highly of philosophy, and that I have detached myself absolutely from the party of the *philosophes*. I do not like them to preach impiety: that is, in their eyes, a crime for which they will not forgive me."[4] This telling rejection of the kind of discussion that would have taken place at the rue Royale, in which everyone had to subject his ideas to scrutiny and possibly ridicule, becomes a badge of honor in this account: a principled opposition to impiety, atheism, and blasphemous talk. Rousseau was, he implies, too decent to play along with their little game and was ostracized for it. Here, as so often, he casts himself as the virtuous victim of his own, high principles—the most comfortable moral position one can possibly be in.

For Rousseau, fulfillment of our human destiny was to be found not in Enlightenment, the arts, or simply humane laws and customs, but in a return to

God's nature, the closest we can get to his ultimately unknowable primary intentions. While a return to childhood itself is impossible, reason alone can purify morals and create a just society according to the laws of nature and ultimately to those of the Creator. But Rousseau's idea of reason is not that of Diderot and Holbach, whose position is easily misrepresented by the term "Enlightenment."

So much of the Enlightenment was or was represented as a cult of "pure reason" (in Immanuel Kant's key phrase) that it is still common in our day to think of this great philosophical paradigm shift as being concerned merely with making life more rational, more efficient, and less superstitiously medieval. This may be partly true for moderate, often deist thinkers such as Leibniz, Montesquieu, Voltaire, and Kant, and even for Diderot's friend Helvétius, but it was never true of the radical Enlightenment around Diderot and Holbach.

To the Enlightenment radicals, reason is merely a technical faculty of analysis, part of our material constitution. But while moderate thinkers wanted to create a life governed less by the passions and more by rational behavior, a life purified of physical desire and instinctive acts, Holbach and particularly Diderot wanted to create a society in which individuals could live as far as possible in harmony with their desires and fulfill them. Reason was simply a tool for a life that was essentially passionate and governed by vital drives, by pleasure and pain.

Rousseau, by contrast, accepted neither of these positions. He agreed with moderate thinkers against the radical wing that passion, and especially sexual passion, was to be mistrusted; it was liable to cloud judgment or control it altogether. But unlike Voltaire and the Enlightenment radicals, Rousseau also thought that purely analytical reason was at least as much of a problem as passion was, because its fruits—civilization, technology, the arts—inexorably led to decadence and immorality: "All is good as it leaves the hands of the Author of things, all degenerates in the hands of men,"[5] as he wrote at the very beginning of *Émile*.

Anxious about the grip of passion and distrustful of the empire of reason, it would appear that Rousseau was in an impossible position, but he had a surprising answer: education, or rather, teaching. Despite the fact that he himself had been only a distracted music teacher and an indifferent house tutor,

Jean-Jacques loved teachers, figures of benevolent authority. The whole of *Émile* revolves around the relationship between a teacher and an inquisitive boy throughout childhood and adolescence.

Eventually, a girl, Sophie, also receives an education in time to be united with Émile. The teacher thinks it best not to overload her pretty little head with mathematics and geography and teaches her piano playing, sewing, and cooking. Indeed, the narrator has firm views about the moral relations of the two sexes: "One ought to be active and strong, the other passive and weak. One must necessarily will and be able; it suffices that the other put up little resistance. Once this principle is established, it follows that woman is made specially to please man."[6]

It is significant that at the end of the novel, Émile and his faithful Sophie decide not to leave their tutor but to continue to thrive under his kind guidance. This was very close to Rousseau's social ideal, in which the role of a great father figure and wise lawmaker is a central feature. This almost authoritarian aspect seems more than a little unusual in a philosopher who valued freedom over everything else and whose greatest passages devoted to the topic are still genuinely moving and have the ring of universal truth: "Man is born free; and everywhere he is in chains. One thinks himself the master of others, and still remains a greater slave than they."[7]

The apparent contradiction between Rousseau's nostalgic longing for a return of the father and his hymns to freedom is resolved by his uniquely influential understanding of the two great cornerstones of Enlightenment thought: reason and the passions. While some Enlightenment philosophers celebrated pure reason as the highest expression of humanity, Holbach and Diderot regarded it as a weak flame dimly illuminating the heaving ocean of the passions, humanity's real element. To Holbach this was cause for some regret; Diderot greeted this fact with joyous odes to *volupté*. Rousseau's suspicion of both Enlightened rationality and sensual pleasure made him recast them in a different mold: There was nothing wrong with pleasure, after all, as long as it was innocent, just as reason could be a useful tool as long as it was used in accord with nature.

Using reason the better to release our deepest nature? Diderot himself might have said that! Indeed he might, for once again we find the same terms used for different things by Rousseau and the rue Royale. *Their* nature is a purely material universe of immutable laws and evolving organisms, while Rousseau's nature is God's creation, his infinite mind. Using reason in harmony with nature therefore means submitting it to God's Truth. The voice of nature could only speak to hearts unspoiled by modern decadence, and adults as well as children need to be protected from its corrupting charms. How this is to be accomplished and what life in harmony with divine creation might look like are the subjects of *The Social Contract*, written in 1762.

Human beings are born free, Rousseau had written, and his great political essay was conceived as an exposition of this idea. Following his breathtaking arc of argumentation is also an excellent introduction to his thinking: always beginning with Enlightenment ideas and then wildly veering off in the opposite direction. To many of the guests at Holbach's table, freedom was a matter of special concern. It even pushed the baron to condone the idea of revolutionary violence to end oppression.

Rousseau also begins his *Social Contract* with an urgent defense of freedom. To guarantee this most basic of human rights, a social contract is necessary, he argued. The seventeenth-century philosopher Thomas Hobbes had already proposed the necessity of a social contract, arguing in his great work *Leviathan* that the natural state of society was a "war of all against all," resulting in lives that were, in his immortal words, "solitary, poor, nasty, brutish, and short." Only mutual help, a social contract, could raise people above this state of murderous anarchy and allow individuals to flourish, protected by the security of laws. Rousseau had taken this idea and expanded on it.

Initially there is broad agreement between his ideas and those of Diderot, Holbach, and Helvétius, testimony to their firm friendship, shared reading, and frequent debates.

At the beginning of human history, Rousseau writes, relative freedom and mutual protection were destroyed by exclusion, control, and violence:

> The first man who, having enclosed a piece of land, thought of saying, *This is mine*, and found people simple enough to believe him, was the true founder of civil society. How many crimes, wars, murders, miseries and horrors might mankind not have been spared, if someone had pulled up the stakes or filled in the ditch, and shouted to his fellow men: beware

> of listening to this imposter; you are ruined if you forget that the fruits of the earth are everyone's, and that the soil itself is no one's.[8]

Personal property, Rousseau felt, was the basis of modern civilization—and therefore of exclusion, serfdom, violence, and oppression. His conclusion was that the only way of getting rid of these evils would be to live in a more communal way, unthreatened by possessiveness and brutality. In his philosophy of education, he had laid out that these dangers are the consequence of puberty, a race for the most attractive girl, in which young men compared themselves with others in their attempt to distinguish themselves and to defeat their rivals.

Again, Rousseau's analysis of this competition for survival is not far from the proto-evolutionary views of Buffon, Holbach, and Diderot, to whom "the survival of the species" was nature's highest aim, and again, Rousseau's conclusion is radically different. While the radicals regard what we have come to call "evolution" as a necessary, immutable part of nature that can be harnessed in the service of a just and moral life, Rousseau sees this urge to compare and compete as the moral root of evil in society and believes the only cure lies in abandoning it.

Returning to a life before the fall, a life before puberty, might not be possible, but a healthy education and the right kind of social rules can at least take us as close as possible to utopian bliss. Rousseau lived in an age of stark social differences and obvious decadence on the part of nobles whose great wealth rested on the labor and misery of others. It is not difficult to understand the appeal of an egalitarian society, a community of equals. In fact, Rousseau's ideal is the next best thing to a return to childlike simplicity: a community of contented, rural freeholders, living in harmony with nature and without competition, without property, oppression, or duplicity—a perfect kibbutz, in fact, long before the first socialist Zionist set foot in Palestine.

This radiant vision of personal fulfillment and social harmony suffers from the problem afflicting all such utopias: how to guarantee its survival and its purity beyond the moment of initial enthusiasm. Every community needs a minimum of enforceable rules, but the nature of authority is deeply ambiguous, even sinister at times: "The human species is divided into so many herds of cattle, each with its ruler, who keeps guard over them for the purpose of devouring them."[9] These rulers are not legitimate; might is not right. Even the argument that a strong hand will end all strife between competing powers does not hold water. "Tranquility is found also in dungeons," Rousseau writes brilliantly, "but is that enough to make them desirable places to live in?"[10]

The only alternative to this rule by iron fist is a voluntary association in which each member submits entirely, relinquishing "all his rights"[11] to the community, so that the conditions are the same for all and everyone has the same need of solidarity. Now the governing principle is no longer the will of a tyrant, but the general will (*volonté générale*) of the community, an aggregate of the healthy, natural instinct expressed by uncorrupted individuals, fusing together into an ideal republic. As the will of every human being tends towards survival, health, justice, and prosperity, the general will is by definition healthy and good. This voluntary subjection to the general will transforms the selfish animal that is a human being into a nobler, moral being.

It is clear why so many left-leaning utopians have been attracted to Rousseau's idea of the voluntary association, particularly when it is read in conjunction with his critique of the corrupt morality of advanced societies and his wish to return to a simpler, truer, more natural way of life. This, however, is where Rousseau's vision takes on a darker hue and eventually plunges into the blackness of totalitarian dictatorship in the name of freedom. His genius, like Nietzsche's, leaps off the page in flashes of insight but becomes increasingly deeply compromised by personal fears, grudges, and paranoia undercutting the verity, and the humanity, of the remainder.

The first problem with Rousseau's concept of the social contract is that the "general will" he posits has, like God, no voice to make itself heard directly. For its expression and interpretation, it must rely on particular, wise individuals to lend it theirs. Rousseau argues that its voice can be heard clearly in every person because it represents nothing else than our healthy instincts, but he adds a significant rider: "It is therefore essential, if the general will is to be able to express itself, that there should be no partial society within the State, and that each citizen should think only his own thoughts." The "partial society" expresses itself in a divergence of wills and opinions, in debates questioning the decisions of the general will, a great danger to the cohesion of this utopia. The only sensible consequence is to neutralize all party interests, if necessary by force. The use of force against any free expression of opinion occurs in the name of general freedom, of course, as he explains: "These precautions are the only ones that can guarantee that the general will shall be always enlightened, and that the people shall in no way deceive itself."[12]

A republic without partial societies, without parties and interest groups (which would, after all, only mislead the healthy instincts of the individual), is effectively a one-party state, a dictatorship. It needs to be controlled and policed, and Rousseau is aware of this. To ensure the morality of society, censorship is needed to guarantee that books and newspapers are constructive for public morality and do not run counter to it. "The censorship upholds morality by preventing opinion from growing corrupt, by preserving its rectitude by means of wise applications, and sometimes even by fixing it when it is still uncertain."[13] Truth is not a matter of debate, not subject to learned agreement, but it relies on the insight of individuals who are beyond being corrupted by low motives such as lust, pride, and envy.

Wisdom is reason in harmony with nature, and those who make just laws know that there can be only one fountain from which to draw their counsel: "All justice comes from God, who is its sole source."[14] God's mind must ultimately remain mysterious and beyond understanding, and for practical purposes it is therefore necessary to represent this sublime mystery in the form of simple stories they can believe and take solace in. Wise legislators have always put laws "into the mouth of the immortals." A good society needs a strong official religion.

But how are the great legislators chosen from the people? Ultimately, Rousseau believes, they will reveal themselves, for "the great soul of the legislator is the only miracle that can prove his mission."[15] Such great men are rare, and mere analytical reason cannot appreciate their stature, as Rousseau writes with a clear side sweep at his former friends, whose "pride of philosophy" and "blind spirit of faction" will not admit to the existence of such great souls but see in them no more than impostors. The true political mind, Rousseau believes, is "the great and powerful genius which presides over things made to endure."[16]

The great legislator is an embodiment of the general will, its purest receptacle. It is the legislator's natural place to exercise his wisdom and his power. The republic, it emerges, is merely the *res publica*, the common cause, not a matter of democratic participation, for humans are simply too ignorant to choose wisely. "Were there a people of gods, their government would be democratic. So perfect a government is not for men."[17] Instead of unstable democracy, the ideal society needs a stable religion to bind together the disparate wills of people unable to hear the voice of nature: a divine cult instilling love of the Creator, the nation, and the state, along with a wise prince whose will is sacred law.

With the long and voluble discussions of the rue Royale still reverberating in his head, Rousseau knew that this idea could not remain unopposed, and in his ideal society there would be ways and means of dealing with intellectual troublemakers. Those who do not believe in the wisdom of the general will and its executors—people very much like his former Paris friends—are to be banished as "anti-social being[s], incapable of truly loving the laws and justice." In persistent cases, the just sanction is more severe: "If anyone, after publicly recognising these dogmas, behaves as if he does not believe them, let him be punished by death: he has committed the worst of all crimes, that of lying before the law."[18]

Not only had Jean-Jacques effectively condemned his former friend Diderot to death, but with a few short argumentative steps, he had moved from a celebration of liberty and universal brotherhood to the murderous tyranny of virtue, a blueprint for every brutal dictator who ever soiled the face of the earth. In the name of the general will, which only he claims to understand, he is licensed to control, to censor, to lie, to punish, even to kill.

Starting from a celebration of freedom, Rousseau created a dystopia of Stalinist severity, a state with censorship, sweeping police powers, and official propaganda, in which all dissidents are shipped off into "exile" or simply killed while happy crowds of healthy peasants salute the great leader.

With his reenchantment of nature, Rousseau inverts the *volonté générale* that can serve as a basis for common moral rules. While social philosophers such as Hobbes, Holbach, and Helvétius perceived it as an aggregate of preferences in any group, Jean-Jacques elevated it into a theological principle beyond the reach of logical deduction or debate. Rational argument is valid only when it is "healthy," when it accords with the general will as represented by the lawgiver. The most strikingly brutal consequences of Rousseau's social theory directly target Diderot, Holbach, and their friends. Civilization and abstract reason, he believes, are in and of themselves corrupt; science serves mainly to alienate the human from his healthy feelings; argument is morally inferior to collective feeling; the soul is immortal; and atheism is a crime punishable by death.

Perhaps it is possible to draw the line between Rousseau and the rue Royale even more sharply. No author intertwined biography and philosophy more than Jean-Jacques, and it is therefore tempting to identify motivations connecting the man and the thinker.

Rousseau puts forward a philosophy with clearly biographical traits, an arc spanning childhood, puberty as the moment of the fall, adulthood as struggle and strife, and eventually, hopefully, a return to a simpler life under the guidance of a wise teacher. The main problem identified by the philosopher was also the greatest anxiety of the man Rousseau, who filled page after page with revelations and ruminations about it: sex. Jean-Jacques the motherless boy, the mature man who lived with an illiterate washerwoman and believed that all women existed "to please man," the masochist who dreamed of being whipped, had his desires only rarely satisfied, and by his own admission he felt guilty when he did. He desired what he himself thought inadmissible. Desire, to him, was the great force pulling him away from inner peace, from being at one with nature. The only possible solution was a return to a state before, or beyond, sex: a return to the father and to faith.

Rousseau's self-loathing clearly expresses itself in his moral ideas, most clearly and most shockingly in the advice the author gives in *Émile* to parents facing that perennial classic question "Where do babies come from?" For the best and most poetic possible answer, the author quotes a simple woman of the people, adding that he challenges the greatest sages to find a more appropriate rejoinder to the child's innocent question. The woman told her son: "The women piss them out under great pain which sometimes costs them their life."

Rarely have the most depressing aspects of Christianity been put more succinctly: Marked by dirt, agony, and death, earthly existence is nothing but a vale of sorrows, made infinitely worse by the sins of the flesh. To Rousseau, however, this answer is simply ideal, precisely because "the ideas associated with pain and death cover [the idea of the birth] whether a veil of the sadness which discourages the imagination and represses curiosity; everything directs the mind towards the consequences of the birth, not to its causes." Everything, that is, draws the mind towards pain and possible death, and away from sensual joy, as he remarks approvingly: "The infirmity of human nature, disgusting objects, images of suffering, these are the explanations to which this response leads."[19]

Could it be that the basic difference between what we have come to think of as the radical Enlightenment and Rousseau's counter-Enlightenment is little more than an inflated difference concerning *les histoires de cul*? Perhaps. There are other genuine differences, but none greater than the fact that Diderot made *volupté* the true driving force and only meaning of life, while his former friend was secretly terrified of it, of his own guilt-ridden, masochistic cravings.

"I cost my mother her life, and my birth was the first of my misfortunes,"[20] Rousseau had written in his *Confessions*, indicating where his feelings of guilt and his ambivalence about sexuality might have had their origin. But he could no more escape desire than he could cease to breathe; he was condemned to sin. His response was to take refuge in the hope of a just and forgiving Creator and a childlike life before the Fall, and it was exactly this hope that Holbach, Diderot, and their friends attacked most bitterly.

A founding member of the *Encyclopédie* as well as a friend of the first hour for Diderot and Holbach, Rousseau had drifted away from his friends, beyond a point of no return, steadily towards their philosophical antipodes. He had become the opposite pole to their thinking, differing in every fundamental aspect and every crucial aspiration; indeed, in his own work he had condemned people very like his former friends to death for their stubborn apostasy.

Their difference in personal disposition and philosophical temperament tore apart their formerly close friendship and effectively bundled two intellectual traditions that were to play a powerful part in history: one, a materialist, evolutionary understanding of the universe and our place in it; the other, an attempt to reenchant the world exposed so harshly by this approach and to bathe it in the soft light of religion, even if this light was threatening to cast harsh shadows over those who disagreed.

For Holbach's salon, Jean-Jacques was at the same time very present and far away—the traitor in their midst, their greatest personal disappointment, and their most dogged opponent. The rift affected Diderot dramatically. He had put his faith in friendship, only to see it abused and finally shattered. But the momentum of events swept him along, too. Work on the *Encyclopédie* left little time for solitary ruminations, and after all, there were other friendships to build, people to encounter, discussions to be had, ideas to be elaborated. The salon was reaching its high point of fame and recognition. This was no time for looking back.

THE ISLAND OF LOVE

CHAPTER 13

CRIME AND PUNISHMENT

During the mid-1760s, as Holbach's salon reached the peak of its fame and influence, the baron, Diderot, and the *abbé* Raynal turned to a field of philosophy they had only touched on before. Having attacked religion and put in its place a materialist worldview and an ethical approach based on desire and empathy—animal instincts, both of them—they now attempted to elaborate a theory of social justice, a society built not on age-old ignorance but on an understanding of human nature.

Several works written by regulars at the rue Royale show how intensively social and political questions were discussed in the salon were. Some of these books were devoted to fundamental considerations, such as Holbach's weighty *Politique naturelle* (1773) and the even larger *Morale universelle* (1776); others discussed slavery, human rights, and international relations (Diderot and Raynal in the *Histoire des deux Indes*, 1770–1774); and still others were devoted to education and human development in *De l'homme* by Helvétius (published posthumously in 1773).

One aspect not covered in any detail by Holbach's guests was legal theory, an evident gap in their otherwise wide-ranging philosophy. When in 1766 a visitor from Italy announced his imminent arrival, there was a definite buzz at the baron's table.

The visitor, Cesare Beccaria, hailed from Milan, where he had written a short book, *Dei delitti e delle pene* (*Of Crimes and Punishments*, 1764), that had made him into a prodigy of the European Enlightenment almost overnight. He was twenty-six years old.

An aristocrat from a conservative family, Beccaria had set himself no lesser goal than to reform penal law according to rational principles. Justice, he argued, should be neither divine nor poetic, but transparent and proportional to the crime, and always based on necessity, on the defense of society.

Like Diderot, whom he had read voraciously and whom he called a "sublime soul," Beccaria believed that ideas of what constitutes a crime were not fixed, but rather change over time: "Hence the uncertainty of our notions of honour and virtue; an uncertainty which will ever remain, because they change with the revolutions of time, and names survive the things they originally signified; they change with the boundaries of states, which are often the same both in physical and moral geography."[1]

Crimes are thus whatever a society decides to criminalize at a particular historical moment, hopefully in accordance with the laws of reason. A rational application of penalties for such acts must serve the community; efficiency and utility are paramount. From this perspective, eighteenth-century justice, according to Beccaria, is an abomination. Torture is neither efficient nor useful, and it is also unnecessarily cruel: The accused will say anything to make the torment stop, and both truth and justice are abandoned. Torture, in fact, recreated in a very brutal, physical way the religious detestation of the physical world: "The law by which torture is authorised, says, *Men, be insensible to pain. Nature has indeed given you an irresistible self-love, and an unalienable right of self-preservation; but I create in you a contrary sentiment, an heroic hatred of yourselves. I command you to accuse yourselves, and to declare the truth, amidst the tearing of your flesh, and the dislocation of your bones.*"[2]

A more just society is created not by more barbaric punishments, but by more rational organization and access to education. A good education forms minds with enlightened principles, rather than superstition, oppression, and all-pervasive vice: "There are no spontaneous or superfluous sentiments in the heart of man; they are all the result of impressions on the senses."[3] The young Italian had absorbed the lessons of the Paris radicals.

All too often, Beccaria wrote, punishments had been used not to dispense justice, but to exercise and preserve the power of the ruler by crushing all opposition while satisfying the bloodlust of the plebes. The most useless and most revolting of all punishments, however, is the death penalty. In natural law, no person has the right to take another's life, and if legislation serves to civilize anarchic and selfish instincts, executing criminals has the opposite effect: "The punishment of death is pernicious to society, from the example of barbarity it affords."[4] Killing a person who has broken society's injunction against killing makes no sense, because society itself not only breaks its most sacred law but also communicates to its citizens that homicide is a legitimate way of solving problems. "Is it not absurd," Beccaria asks, "that the laws, which detest and punish homicide, should, in order to prevent murder, publicly commit murder themselves?"[5]

The only reason why the death penalty has been so pervasive throughout history, the author writes, is that it is rooted in human sacrifices of pagan times, when the ire of the gods had to be assuaged with blood: "Human sacrifices have also been common in almost all nations. That some societies only either few in number, or for a very short time, abstained from the punishment of death, is rather favourable to my argument; for such is the fate of great truths, that their duration is only as a flash of lightning in the long and dark night of error. The happy time is not yet arrived, when truth, as falsehood has been hitherto, shall be the portion of the greatest number."[6]

Such impassioned rhetoric was bound to impress the friends of the rue Royale—and, indeed, intellectuals throughout Europe. Almost immediately, one of the circle, the writer André Morellet, began to prepare a French translation of the work. He also corresponded with the author, who asked him to "above all, tell M. le Baron d'Holbach that I am filled with veneration for him, and that I desire above all that he find me worthy of his friendship."[7] Holbach and Morellet invited the brilliant young man to come to Paris and be received with all honors. Beccaria was beside himself with happiness; those who invited him had been his heroes, his greatest inspiration: "D'Alembert, Diderot, Helvétius, Buffon, Hume . . . your immortal works . . . are the subject of my occupations during the day and my meditations in the silence of the night,"[8] he wrote.

Beccaria arrived in Paris on October 18, 1766, and was celebrated by the *philosophes*. The reception at Holbach's house was more than he had dared hope: "You would not believe the welcome, the courtesy, the praise, the expressions of friendship and esteem with which we have been overwhelmed," he gushed in a letter to his wife. "Diderot, Baron d'Holbach, and D'Alembert especially showed themselves enchanted with us."[9] Alessandro Verri, Beccaria's travel companion and fellow reformer, wrote of Diderot: "He declaims constantly, vehemently; he is in transports. He is ardent, ardent in everything, in conversation as in his books."[10]

Verri also described the topics covered during one of the evenings he attended at the rue Royale, the only detailed account of such an evening in existence. The first subject of discussion was Voltaire, whom the baron described, not without justification, as "jealous and nasty." Soon, attention turned to the furious quarrel between Rousseau and Hume, which had just erupted and was commented on by John Wilkes, who also offered some trenchant observations on the political situation in Britain. The tone became notably less agitated when André Morellet recited a poem about Venus that he had recently written, and from the contemplation of the goddess of love, the conversation floated to Newton's comments on the Apocalypse, an apparent paradox coming from such a great scientific mind. Holbach was insistent that religion had to be viewed as the principal source of all human suffering, an opinion that disturbed Verri, who had to admit, however, that Holbach was an admirable man who served wonderful food.

Despite the generous reception, Beccaria's enchantment with the *philosophes* soon wore off. He was unhappy far away from home, he missed his beautiful wife, and he was uncomfortable speaking in French, ill at ease among men twice his age, frightened by their atheism, and tongue-tied during their boisterous meetings, where his ideas were by no means taken for granted. On one occasion he witnessed Holbach reading from his "catechism," a brief summary of his most important arguments against religion cast in question-and-answer mode, much like the catechism of the church, intended "to prove with, at once, great passion and precision, that Religion is the source of all human evils."[11] Beccaria was progressive, but he was also Catholic, and such brazen ideas seem to have been too much for him. Hardly six weeks after making his "philosophical pilgrimage," he packed his trunks and set off for Milan. He would never leave Italy again.

There was, in fact, ambivalence on both sides. Diderot had received his Italian admirer with great kindness and spoken warmly about his book, but ultimately he was unconvinced by it. Both he and Holbach thought that the death penalty—and even cruel, public punishments—might be valuable even in a just society precisely because they were so repulsive and would send a clear message. In a society without religion, in which people could not be dissuaded from becoming criminals by threats of punishment in the afterlife, there had to be measures showing that virtue was rewarded and vice punished severely, they believed. A public execution, both men argued, could be an effective deterrent.

Diderot's cavalier treatment of such an important topic—particularly for a philosopher—reveals a curious lack of interest in the question. There is an offhand quality about his responses to Beccaria, and from Diderot's own handwritten annotations to the Italian's book, it becomes clear that he thought the young man naïve: "I am neither hard-hearted nor perverse," the *philosophe* wrote in the margins of his copy. "Nevertheless I am far from thinking that the work *Des délits et des peines* is as important, or its basic ideas as true, as is claimed for it."[12]

It is difficult to fathom why Diderot would not have welcomed Beccaria with the generosity and enthusiasm for which the *philosophe* was justly famous, instead of belittling his ideas. Was he jealous of a youth celebrated at an age at which he himself, no doubt the more brilliant mind, had still been laboring in the literary underworld? But there is no sign of rancor in his reaction. Rather it seems that he simply did not think the death penalty important enough to merit so much attention—fewer than three hundred executions per year in France were quite an acceptable number, he felt. His interests lay elsewhere.

There were other, even more critical voices about *Of Crimes and Punishments* in Holbach's salon. Friedrich Melchior Grimm, the official voice of the radical Enlightenment in Europe, dismissed both the book and its author as facile and immature. The social contract, on which Beccaria's ideas were based, was a mere illusion born out of a life of wealth, Grimm wrote in his *Correspondance littéraire*, a pious dream by a young man who had no idea how harsh the world could be and how quickly a social contract could cede to total, murderous anarchy. There could be no such thing as a social contract, argued the journalist. The only stable society was the iron rule of the Enlightened few over the great mass of the uneducated and unwashed: "Let us not be infants, let us not be frightened of words," he urged his readers. "The fact is that there is no other right in the world except the right of the strongest, and that, since it must be said, this is the only legitimacy."[13]

These were fitting words for a man who made his living off the pay of princes who fancied themselves to be just those Enlightened rulers. But Grimm's poor opinion of human nature and justice was quite genuine. To him, humanity was a lost cause not capable of salvation. In the real world, the world he moved in as a diplomat and journalist, selfishness and brute force always carried the day. Some individuals could afford to live their lives according to Enlightened principles, and some Enlightened ideas might even be temporarily realized—but in the end, humankind would always lurch back into barbarism. "The human race in general has always remained the same," Grimm argued, adding that it had become "neither better nor more perverse," despite the "chimera of progress" that so many, including his friend Denis, adhered to in his own century.[14]

Both Diderot and Grimm had an ultimately pessimistic view of the progress of the Enlightenment, which, as Diderot had famously claimed, ended in the suburbs. Beccaria, they thought, had enjoyed a sheltered upbringing and seen no more of the world than the wealthier streets of Milan. The ambitious young man was simply too young, too unrealistic, to understand human nature. But while it was easy for a pride of literary lions to patronize a mere youngster for his inexperience, the underlying difference of opinion preoccupied many Enlightened thinkers. Once again, the balance between passion and reason reared its head.

Is humanity essentially rational or essentially instinctive? Which—reason or instinct—takes precedence over the other, or can they be evened out? The partisans of reason were in no doubt that irrational acts come from irrational motives and can be eliminated by a completely rational system of education and justice. This view was expounded in the famous 1759 treatise *De l'esprit* by Holbach's kind and cerebral neighbor Claude Helvétius, which had not only influenced Beccaria's thinking but made such waves that it had almost caused the *Encyclopédie* to founder in its wake.

Helvétius took the position that the character and abilities of human beings are simply the result of their education, and that a perfect education would necessarily create a perfect society. Even if this might be an unattainable goal, public morals would improve with society, and ultimately crime would simply cease. Public executions, he believed, did not serve the public good, since they merely punished criminals for being morally ignorant and not having received a rational education.

The first French translation of Beccaria's book was published with an anonymous reflection praising the author. Voltaire had written these lines. He thought it prudent to support the young man's noble ideas, though not quite publicly. For once, however, it seems certain that he acted out of quite sincere admiration and agreement. A rationalist himself, he had always opposed the death penalty and had courageously and publicly defended three victims of famous miscarriages of justice in France, the would-be royal assassin Robert Damiens (1757); the Protestant Jean Calas, who was falsely accused of having murdered his son (1762); and finally the young Chevalier de la Barre, accused of blasphemy in 1766. His advocacy did not help them—all three were executed publicly and cruelly despite the fact that Damiens was clearly insane, while the other two were patently innocent—but it was an honorable cause, taken up out of genuine conviction.

Beccaria's impassioned plea for a more humane and scientific justice system crystallized philosophical opinion. Propelled to international fame by the debate that soon sprang up around it and quickly translated into German and English, *Of Crimes and Punishments* became hugely influential and was instrumental in judicial reform throughout Europe and in the United States. Catherine of Russia mentioned Beccaria in her new and decidedly Enlightened legal code, the *Nakaz*, in 1767: a grand legal project in which she had also invited Diderot to participate. (The *philosophe* duly supplied a draft for a constitution, which she subsequently ignored almost entirely in her own exercise of power.) When Sweden abolished the death penalty and the use of torture in 1772, the first country in the world to do so, it was Beccaria who had inspired the new penal code. His own home country, the Grand Duchy of Tuscany, followed suit in 1786. By then the former philosophical firebrand was an administrator working on the economics council of the Habsburg government.

It is easy to imagine why the Italian visitor would have been so overwhelmed by the intensity of debate about his theses: For the friends of the rue Royale, Beccaria's ideas addressed a question crucial to their own philosophy. Having declared metaphysics sterile speculation and the sciences the only purveyor of verifiable truth, materialist thinkers—and particularly Diderot, Holbach, and Helvétius—were constantly appealing to science. "It is very difficult to be a good metaphysician or a good moralist without being an anatomist, naturalist, physiologist, and doctor,"[15] wrote Diderot.

Knowledge derived from natural laws and from experimentally verified hypotheses would eventually supplant philosophical debate in most areas, and this meant that philosophy must apply itself not to what we are, but to what we want to be or fear to become. It had to formulate moral principles and social visions. The goal of philosophy lay in politics. Beccaria had supplied such a vision, which the *philosophes* thought ultimately unrealistic, though honorable in its intention. Still, it touched a nerve of their debate: the nature of human rights, the legitimacy of power, and its proper exercise in society.

While several members of Holbach's salon were not swayed by Beccaria's opposition to the death penalty, they did, in fact, have social ideas that were revolutionary in their own right. Diderot particularly stands out in this respect. Never fond of systematic exposition and at home in dialogue and conversation, Diderot did not leave a single, grand vision of society and statecraft. Numerous miscellaneous reflections on questions of ethics and politics, however, show that he was less interested in the legitimacy of power than in the right to revolt, less in the concept of an ideal legislator than in the political reality of power exercised by people. Convinced, like many of his contemporaries, that democracy was probably impossible in large societies, Diderot was extremely skeptical of power. This set him apart not only from Beccaria and Helvétius and their unquestioning faith in rational administration, but also from Rousseau's dream of a wise lawgiver as dictatorial embodiment of the general will. Power corrupts, Diderot was convinced, and absolute power corrupts absolutely.

While Rousseau's *Social Contract* advocated a civil religion complete with inquisition and censorship, Diderot reflected on power from the perspective of those living under such a regime. Intellectuals would be "reduced to silence or strangled," the entire nation held back "in the barbarity of its religion," and ignorance would be endemic, he wrote, adding more optimistically that "one cannot stop the progress of Enlightenment, one can only slow it down, to one's own disadvantage."[16]

Under such authoritarian rule, Diderot thought, the oppressed had every right to reclaim their sovereignty from their oppressors and from a society that sees people—be they subjects, wives, children, servants, or slaves—as property of other people. Slaves are right to revolt against their ferocious masters, and medieval peasants had good reason to kill their feudal lords. Wherever people are reduced to servitude by a lord, a magistrate, or a priest, tyrannicide becomes a morally acceptable means of reclaiming freedom from the powerful.

Political influence in the hands of priests was a recipe for disaster, Diderot wrote, arguing that the distance between throne and altar could never be great enough. Priests were instinctive reactionaries whose allegiance to a supposedly higher law meant that they would never be simple citizens. Their influence on the people was to uphold superstition and dependency: "The priest, whose system is a tissue of absurdities, secretly wants to uphold ignorance; reason is the enemy of faith, and faith is the base of the power, the fortune, and the social standing of the priest."[17] There was no place for a state religion in Diderot's ideal society.

Utopias are dangerous precisely because they embody ideals. The distance between our own, messy reality and an abstract ideal of individual and collective bliss is usually measured out in the blood of those who are unwilling to be fellow travelers or who are simply in the way. In his *Social Contract*, Jean-Jacques Rousseau had argued that moral degeneration was a direct consequence of civilization and only a return to a state of innocence could save the moral health of humankind. Against this view, Helvétius had claimed that a thorough and thoroughly rational education was all that would be necessary to make all people equally good, since only ignorance and fear perverted their character. The Baron d'Holbach also tended to believe rather optimistically that the end of superstition would be the advent of a new, just society. Diderot was not so certain. These visions simply ignored human nature, he felt, and human nature was impulsive, driven, and often contradictory. While obviously believing, or making himself believe, that the progress of the Enlightenment would be unstoppable, he was far less certain that societies could indeed become entirely Enlightened.

Unlike his friends David Hume and Friedrich Melchior Grimm, Diderot did not feel the pull of conservatism on account of his skeptical views of human nature. His immediate goals were simply more concrete and closer to hand than those of Beccaria. Among his more striking views were his thoughts on women's rights and education, a case of applied social justice.

Just like Rousseau, Diderot was fascinated by the possibilities of education, but, unlike him, the *philosophe* thought that the education of girls was morally much more perverse than that of boys and that the ambition of girls' education should not be to produce singing, knitting, and charming helpmates for man the conqueror, but informed and intelligent partners.

If there was such a thing as feminism in the 1760s, the friends from the rue Royale were among its main exponents. True, the salon itself handled gender roles very conventionally. Women had no role to play in Holbach's salon—Madame Holbach was there in the conventional feminine role of charming hostess, much admired by her guests but not participating in their debates. Diderot and Grimm, however, sought out intelligent, independent women as their friends and soul mates. Louise d'Epinay and Sophie Volland were treated as intellectual equals by their lovers, although they did not attend the dinners, possibly to protect their reputations. It was one thing to meet and discuss ideas during dinner parties at Mme d'Epinay's country seat in La Chevrette or in Grandval, but unmarried women attending largely male gatherings notorious for their impiety in the heart of Paris would have left their public standing in tatters.

Of course, Holbach would not have had a great many women to invite to his dinners even if he had wanted to. There simply were very few women who had the formal education and the depth of knowledge in philosophy and the sciences the other diners had. This was no mere misogynist stereotype: Girls did not attend the great schools and universities; they were taught no Latin and Greek, no philosophy and mathematics, but instead learned to sew, embroider, play the harp, and sing edifying songs. The bright ones were allowed to poke their pretty little noses in the pages of sentimental novels, but reading works of scholarship was frowned upon. Medical authorities even believed that intellectual overstimulation would render women excitable and perhaps even infertile.

While many of their contemporaries believed this situation was acceptable because of the inherent intellectual inferiority of girls, Diderot, Holbach, and Grimm thought that the divergences in achievement between men and women were the result of a defective and even repressive education, of a vast system put in place to oppress women. Grimm made the case for women in his magazine, the *Correspondance littéraire*, pointing out that all the character flaws seen as typically female were in fact the result of a misconceived education, which is bound to make those who go through it artificial, hypocritical, and deceitful. Traditional ideas of duty were keeping women down, Grimm argued, and the lies of their convent education compelled them to marry virtual strangers who were deemed suitable. Women were therefore necessarily victims of men's desires.

But not only women's social position was more difficult than that of men. Diderot, for whom the highest pleasure was also the highest good, was perfectly aware of the fact that for many women marriage was not a path to legitimate sensual indulgence but a revolting ordeal. "I have seen honest women shudder with horror at the approach of their husband; I have seen them plunge into a bath, never believing themselves sufficiently cleansed from the filth of their [marital] duty," he chronicled in an essay on women's roles. Women were doubly unfortunate in this respect, because men could find pleasure more easily: "This sort of repulsion is almost unknown to us: our organ is more indulgent. Many women will die without having felt the extremes of *volupté*. . . . The highest happiness flees them even in the arms of the man they adore; but we can find it lying next to a compliant woman whom we do not even like."[18]

Written by a lover of spirited and intelligent women, Diderot's essay *Sur les femmes* (*On Women*, 1772) speaks about *la femme soumise* (woman oppressed). The author was convinced that though women were equal to men, they had to fight against great disadvantages from childhood onwards: "more constrained and more neglected in their education, abandoned to the same capricious fate, with a soul that is more mobile, more delicate organs, none of that firmness, natural or acquired, which prepares us for life, reduced to silence in their adulthood."[19] His own remedy for this sorry state was his devotion to the education of his only daughter, Angélique, whose intellectual and artistic development was the delight of his middle age.

As with every issue he regarded as important, Diderot's answer as a thinker was to dramatize the situation in a work of art. In his novel *La Religieuse* (*The Nun*, 1761), he describes the prison-like confinement of a young woman who is forced to enter a convent, where the rigid structures imposed by the male church hierarchy not only plunge her into despair but also work to pervert her morally. The healthy desire and passion that are part of the human condition are stifled by the vows of celibacy and the isolation of the women, and the young heroine ultimately falls prey to the advances of the lecherous abbess. For the barracked protagonists, there is no other outlet in this prisonlike situation than in the love for other women, an element Diderot painted in lurid colors and imagined with obvious delight.

Unsurprisingly, *La Religieuse* is usually read mainly as an erotic novel. It may not be as generously, voluptuously explicit as some readers make it out to be, but it was scandalous enough to be banned not only immediately after publication but also, in France, in a filmed version close to the original, as recently as 1966. Still, behind the sensuous scenes Diderot had enjoyed describing is a political dimension: an indictment of the lives wasted behind convent walls, of the unnatural and "useless virtue" of celibacy, of passions repressed and perverted by church dogma, a grand metaphor of the hopelessness of a woman's lot in a repressive, patriarchal society—as hopeless, indeed, as that of his own younger sister Angélique, who had become an Ursuline nun and had died insane in her convent at the age of only twenty-eight. Denis had named his daughter after her and did his utmost to give the girl every intellectual opportunity, hoping at some level, perhaps, to make up for his sister's tragically wasted life.

Beccaria's visit to Paris was no more than an episode for the advocates of the radical Enlightenment. Diderot had shown himself to be friendly but also unconcerned to the point of callousness when the discussion turned to the death penalty, and ultimately both he and Grimm had dismissed the young Italian. But despite this seeming lack of concern, the debates stoked by his courageous *Of Crimes and Punishments* continued. The main question was justice—both as enshrined in law and as social principle.

But how to bring about social justice? What would a society look like if it was organized to allow its citizens to flourish rather than to be kept in a permanent state of ignorance and fear? What was the key to human nature? The friends of the rue Royale never stopped debating these questions, refining their ideas, hardening them in the furnace of debate, and finally publishing them.

This social vision was an exhilarating creative and intellectual undertaking: to rethink human nature, human relations, and societies in the light of a materialist morality. In the long term, it was to be one of the main and perhaps most neglected legacies of the radical Enlightenment. In the short term, however, all thoughts were on the present. They had to be: Several years after his very public falling-out with Holbach and his salon, Rousseau reappeared from Switzerland in the full bloom of paranoia, feted and admired and ready to haunt the friends again.

CHAPTER 14

THE MOST UNGRATEFUL DOGG IN THE WORLD

After 1759, when Diderot had visited Rousseau in a final and unsuccessful attempt to salvage their friendship, the rift between Jean-Jacques and Holbach's "coterie," as Rousseau had taken to calling the salon, became permanent. The two friends had met in Montmorency several times during 1757, the last time in December. Then, after the bitter letters over Diderot's remarks in his play and Rousseau's refusal to accompany Louise d'Epinay to Geneva, they had stopped seeing each other and, eventually, writing to each other. All contact between the two men was broken—and with it all contact with Holbach's salon.

Diderot was baffled and embittered by what he saw (as was Rousseau) as the worst personal betrayal of his life. In 1759 he had even written *Tablettes*, an uncharacteristically spiteful and angry essay, in which he listed the "seven sins" his former friend had committed against him and against decency. He had not published his virulent diatribe, but he made it clear that he regarded Jean-Jacques as "false, vain as Satan, ungrateful, cruel, hypocritical and malicious." "In truth," Denis had concluded, "this man is a monster."[1]

The disappointed *philosophe* was quick to forgive, however, and he obviously missed the old Jean-Jacques. When in 1762 the publication of the novel *Émile* made Rousseau a target of attacks from the church and eventually forced him to flee France, it was Diderot who sprang to his defense. The offending passage was the "Confession of Faith of a Savoyard Vicar," effectively Rousseau's personal creed put into the mouth of one of the characters almost as a separate essay. Diderot thought the vague, deistic sentiment of the "Confession" that so enraged the church authorities amounted to little more than nonsense, but he still argued in his friend's favor, prompting the Genevan banker Toussaint-Pierre Lenieps, who was living in Paris, to report to Rousseau in 1763 that "M. Diderot takes the side of your writings in every respect and wherever he is."[2]

His championship did Diderot honor, but it also showed his emotional vulnerability and his naïve assumption that he could deal rationally with his friend. In 1764, the *philosophe* even embarked through a common acquaintance on an entirely unrealistic attempt at reconciliation, on the condition that Rousseau admit that he had been in the wrong—only to be informed via the same intermediary that Jean-Jacques was determined that friendships, once extinguished, must never be rekindled.

Rousseau was now living in the Swiss village of Môtiers, close to the town of Neuchâtel, which was under the protection of the Prussian king Frederick II, the friend of Enlightenment figures such as La Mettrie and Voltaire. Here, the writer hoped, he would finally be free from persecution and able to follow his inspiration undisturbed.

But even in his Swiss exile, Rousseau could not resist his contrarian impulses. He wrote a series of typically opinionated essays, the *Lettres écrites de la montagne* (*Letters Written from the Mountain*, 1764), against the burghers of Geneva and went so far as to renounce his citizenship in protest once again. The villagers of the otherwise quiet mountain hamlet did not take kindly to the temper tantrums of their resident philosopher, and in 1765 they drove him out, allegedly by stoning his house or booby-trapping its entrance with rocks. The local official called to investigate the incident at Rousseau's house allegedly exclaimed, "But this is a quarry!"

When one of the peasant women threatened to slit the throat of the famous but unwelcome intruder, Jean-Jacques fled, together with his mistress, Thérèse. Once again, they were homeless, victims of what Rousseau saw as his principled life and the corruption of others. He needed help, and it came—from unexpected quarters. The Countess de Boufflers was a woman whose literary and intellectual interests were so strong that in 1762 she had traveled to Britain in order to meet the great David Hume. Now she took it upon herself to find a solution for the embattled Rousseau and approached Hume for help.

It was his last year in Paris as embassy secretary, and he decided that it might be best to remove Rousseau to the more tolerant climate of Britain, where Hume could use his influence to see that the writer lived comfortably. There Jean-Jacques would be safe from the ire of the Catholic Church—and of Swiss villagers. The two men had never met.

David Hume, of course, had been told all about Rousseau's paranoia and backstabbing, but he believed that it had all happened because nobody had handled the prickly genius delicately enough. He knew only one side of the story, after all, and since he was a reasonable man with a philosophical mind, it was his duty to consider the argument from all angles.

When they learned of his plans, Hume's Paris friends uttered the most dire warnings. He would surely burn his fingers, Holbach and Diderot said. They knew Rousseau: He was a snake in the grass, a serial breaker of trusts and destroyer of friendships. "You don't know your man. I will tell you plainly, you're warming a viper in your bosom,"[3] Grimm exclaimed in despair. But Hume would hear none of it. He was proud of being a moral man and a good friend who would go to the greatest trouble to fulfill his obligations towards others. He invited the hunted philosopher, and his invitation was accepted. Their departure was set for January 1766.

Rousseau had been careful to flatter the famous Scot, writing to him: "Your great views, your astonishing impartiality, your genius, would lift you far above the rest of mankind, if you were less attached to them by the goodness of your heart."[4] His honeyed words had their desired effect; on finally meeting him in Paris in December 1765, Hume was charmed by his new friend: "I find him mild, and gentle and modest and good humoured. . . . M. Rousseau is of small stature; and would rather be ugly, had he not the finest physiognomy in the world, I mean, the most expressive countenance. His modesty seems not to be good manners but ignorance of his own excellence."[5]

Rousseau came to Paris to meet up with Hume, but instead of behaving as discreetly as possible—the Paris *parlement* had issued a warrant of arrest against him—he openly walked the streets and attended several salons, quite brazenly courting martyrdom. For once, the authorities were wise enough not to take his bait and left him his few days of glory, prancing around the streets and being treated as a celebrity, making a famous writer into a much more famous prisoner of conscience.

Isolation: Having broken with all of his old friends, Rousseau lived like a fugitive and ruined his chance of living peacefully in Britain by provoking a sensational row with David Hume. Marble and terra-cotta bust by Jean-Antoine Houdon, 1779.

RÉUNION DES MUSÉES NATIONAUX / ART RESOURCE, NY

Still hoping that some sort of reconciliation could be effected, Diderot did not leave his house for three days in case Jean-Jacques called. But instead of embracing his friend, Denis could do nothing but listen with growing concern to stories of the other man's exploits—Rousseau was risking arrest and harsh punishment with every minute he paraded through the streets. Eventually his old philosophical family decided that they could not let him go on courting arrest; they arranged for a quick passage across the Channel, together with Hume. When he was gone, those who had helped to protect Rousseau from himself let out a collective sigh of relief.

During the passage to London in January 1766, *le bon David* was pleased with himself—pleased at helping a fellow philosopher in need, pleased to have made the acquaintance of this extraordinary man, and pleased at his own moral stance. He was traveling alone with Rousseau—Thérèse Levasseur was making the passage in the company of James Boswell, who had also been visiting Paris. During the passage across the Channel, Hume began to suspect to his puzzlement that his new friend was less reasonable than he liked to assume: "With regard to his health . . . he is very fanciful. He imagines himself very infirm. He is one of the most robust men I have ever known. He passed ten hours in the night-time above deck in the most severe weather, when all the seamen were almost frozen to death."[6] Still, Hume thought, such little foibles could be accommodated. Rousseau's name had preceded him in London, after all, and the great welcome in the capital would surely dispel all imaginary ailments.

When the two men arrived in London, Rousseau was promptly invited to every social event of any note. He was famous as a novelist (more than as a philosopher), a Continental, and a man persecuted for his ideas—an irresistible asset at every fashionable party. Rousseau skillfully played his role as resident eccentric, appearing at elegant events wearing his fur cap and Armenian tunic.

Soon, however, the fickle attentions of society hostesses moved on. Jean-Jacques, who spoke only very little broken English and was brusque to the point of rudeness even in French, began to feel the cold hand of loneliness within a few weeks of his London debut. Not only the fashionable set turned away from yesterday's star guest. While Hume was still in thrall to Rousseau's apparent uncompromising honesty, the sharp-eyed Dr. Johnson had formed a very unflattering opinion of him only one month after his arrival. "I think he is the worst of men," he sad to his friend and biographer, Boswell, who had accompanied Thérèse across the Channel. "I would sooner sign a sentence for his transportation than that of any felon who had gone from the Old Bailey in these many years."[7] Indeed, the dyed-in-the-wool conservative Johnson added, Rousseau was as bad as the notorious deist Voltaire.

Oblivious to such criticisms or simply unaffected by them, David Hume, however, adored his guest, continued to lavish attention on him, and set about getting him a royal pension. While Hume was reveling in the early phases of what he hoped would become a lifelong friendship, Holbach wrote to him with caution: "I am very glad to hear that you have not occasion to repent of the kindness you have shown to M. Rousseau. I in particular never had any reason to complain of his conduct. . . . I wish some friends, whom I value very much, had not more reasons to complain of his unfair proceedings, printed imputations, ungratefulness &c."[8] Hume would have none of it and insisted that there was no one he would rather spend the remainder of his life with than his friend Jean-Jacques.

Even so, the London months were not without their complications and temper tantrums. The friends of the rue Royale followed every twist and turn of the affair. As André Morellet recalls, signs of trouble flared soon after Hume and Rousseau's departure: "Some three weeks or a month later, when we were all assembled at the baron's," he recalled, "he pulled from his pocket a letter from Hume and read it to us. In the letter, Hume told about the terrible fuss about nothing which Jean-Jacques had kicked up. Who was the one to feel stupid? I was, because I remembered the warmth with which I had defended him against the baron's warnings. The others in the round,

Grimm, Diderot, Saint-Lambert, Helvétius, etc., who knew Rousseau's character better than I did, were not in the least surprised."[9]

David Garrick also supplied the circle with news of increasingly difficult circumstances and grand scenes. Holbach wrote back gloomily: "I was not much surpris'd at the particulars you are pleas'd to mention about Rousseau. According to the thorough knowledge I have had of him I look on that man as a mere philosophical quack, full of affectation, of pride, of oddities, and even villainies."[10]

The baron was not surprised at Rousseau's antics, but he was truly disgusted with them. Not only had he publicly attacked Diderot, but he had abused Mme d'Epinay's hospitality, tarnished Grimm's reputation (as well as Holbach's own), and even left behind his mistress's mother, whose only support was due to Grimm's generosity. "Is his memory so short as to forget that Mr Grimm, for those 9 years past, has taken care of the mother to his wench of gouvernante, whom he left to starve here after having debauch'd her daughter and having got her 3 or 4 times with child?" the baron thundered. "That great philosopher should remember that Mr Grimm has in his hands letters under his own hand-writing that prove him the most ungrateful dogg in the world. . . . But enough of that rascal who deserves not to be with Mr Hume's company but rather among the bears, if there are any in the mountains of Wales."[11]

Eventually, and perhaps with a sigh of relief, Hume managed to find the famous exile both a place to live—not in the mountains of Wales, but at Wootton Hall, a Staffordshire manor house—and a court stipend that would pay for his living expenses in perpetuity. Here the famous exile could work far from the detested stench and noise of the city. "I would rather live in the hollow trunk of a tree than in the most splendid apartment in London," he had remarked.

Rousseau was actually grateful for Hume's efforts on his behalf. On March 19, 1766, before setting out to the countryside to start his new life of freedom, security, and tranquility, he visited Hume in London. It was to be the last time the two men met, and it was a memorable occasion. Rousseau appeared to be happy, but he soon found a cause to take offense. One of Hume's friends was patronizing towards him, he complained—and promptly fell into sullen silence. As Hume tried to smooth over the situation, the sulking philosopher flew into a tearful rage, as he himself recorded in his *Confessions*. Hume seemed threatening, he claimed—he darted piercing looks at him, frightened him. The honest face of *le bon David* appeared to hide a demon whose gaze made Rousseau all but faint in front of him, until he finally jumped up and "almost choked with sobbing, and bathed in tears." "No, no," he cried out. "David Hume cannot be treacherous; if he be not the best of men, he must be the basest."[12]

The next morning, the tantrum seemed forgotten. Rousseau set out for the countryside. Hume remained behind, beaming with bonhomie and proud of having extended himself to the great philosopher. He can hardly be blamed—even a more astute judge of character could hardly have imagined what came next. It took Rousseau just two months to transform Hume's act of kindness into a terrible personal betrayal through a series of increasingly insinuating and accusatory letters sent to his correspondents in Europe, as well as to Hume himself. Had his sponsor not profited from bringing a famous writer to Britain? Had it not enhanced his reputation? Had it not in reality been Hume who had been lionized in the elegant drawing rooms? Had he not now sidelined a greater mind by sending him into the country?

Rousseau was utterly convinced that Hume had been plotting against him all the time, along with the members of Holbach's salon. His conviction had a tenuous basis in fact. Before his departure from Paris, there had been some laughter at his expense on account of a prank played against him. An anonymous satirical letter had been circulating among the literary set, a hugely flattering eulogy of Rousseau purporting to be an invitation to Prussia from King Frederick the Great. There was no such invitation, of course, but the letter had made the rounds and was commonly seen as a parody of Jean-Jacques' inflated self-image.

But neither Hume nor Holbach's friends were behind this unkind mockery. The letter was penned by Horace Walpole, who was disdainfully impatient with Rousseau's behavior, envious of his fame, and brutally dismissive of all *philosophes*. It was not terribly witty, certainly not by the standards of the Paris salons, but Walpole nevertheless proudly recited it at several dinner parties, his chest inflated with the attention he was finally receiving from the people he otherwise affected to look down upon. "*Me voici à la mode*," he purred delightedly, showing just how much he resented the urbane *philosophes* for their lively conversations and literary games.

Hume had been present at one of these dinners but was unimpressed with Walpole's smug childishness. It is likely that he thought it best to ignore the feeble prank, which quickly made the rounds (the inveterate gossip Grimm even published it in his *Correspondance littéraire*). In any case, *tout Paris* smirked about the letter, or rather at the Swiss philosopher's delusions of grandeur it alluded to.

Walpole's practical joke had, however, caught up with Hume and Rousseau soon after they had arrived in London. It was printed in full in the *Saint James Chronicle*, a fashionable magazine, and caused a good deal of ill-concealed giggling whenever the bearish philosopher entered the room. Rousseau felt deeply humiliated and initially blamed Holbach's "coterie."

Once Rousseau moved into the countryside, Hume became worried about his guest. In Staffordshire, he wrote with a sudden dose of skepticism, the touchy writer would soon become bored of solitude and might be gripped entirely by his emotional outlook on the world: "he has only felt, during the whole course of his life; and in this respect, his sensibility rises to a pitch beyond what I have seen any example of."[13] It was as if the Genevan was a man without skin, vulnerable against even the slightest touch.

Hume was right. Once left to stew in solitude, Rousseau grew convinced that one huge plot had been orchestrated against him. On June 23, he sent a letter full of cold, barely contained fury to *le bon David*: "I threw myself into your arms," he railed. "You brought me to England, ostensibly to procure me an asylum, but in fact to bring me to dishonor. . . . Adieu sir, I wish you the truest happiness; but as we ought not to have anything to say to each other for the future, this is the last letter you will receive from me."[14]

Hume had anticipated some sort of trouble, but he was thunderstruck by the extremity of Rousseau's attack. He demanded an explanation; Rousseau replied with a hugely long letter in which he ranted against the imaginary plot against him—one which had been hatched, he was convinced, by his former Paris friends who had used Hume to ruin his reputation once and for all. He presented the conflict between his natural virtue and the baseness of Hume's supposed motives as a tormented interior monologue. Seeing what he describes as Hume's piercing gaze turned on him, the writer is gripped by terror, only to remind himself that the man sitting opposite is his friend: "*No, no, David Hume is no traitor, if he were not the best of men he would be the worst!*"

he says to himself, his face "inundated with tears." The scene goes on, for page after page, with the sole result of making Rousseau look like a saint struggling to believe in goodness, but in reality betrayed and persecuted by his last remaining friend.

Hume now began to fear for his most precious asset: his good name. Rousseau was working on his autobiography, after all, and with his skill as a writer and his public image as a virtuous martyr to the truth, he could blacken a reputation in a few sentences. Hume had little doubt that that was exactly what the outraged author planned: "I receiv'd today a Letter from Rousseau, which is as long as wou'd make a two Shilling Pamphlet; and I fancy he intends to publish it," he confided to his friend Richard Davenport.[15]

Now it was the Scotsman's turn to be outraged, and in a fit of righteous fury he fired off a stream of letters to Mme de Boufflers, d'Alembert, Holbach, and other Paris friends, anticipating Rousseau's strike.

In the small literary world of the eighteenth century, the quarrel between the two philosophers soon involved some of the greatest names in history. Frederick the Great of Prussia and George III of England had been implicated by the mock invitation and by Rousseau's touchy reaction to being offered a royal pension in Britain; Horace Walpole was also associated with it, as were Hume's friends Adam Smith, James Boswell, Samuel Johnson, David Garrick, and, across the Channel, Diderot, Holbach, d'Alembert, Grimm—and of course Voltaire, who could never resist meddling.

The very public falling-out between two famous men and implicating many others quickly became one of the hottest press topics of the day. The press immediately took sides, variously depicting Rousseau as an abused innocent and as a manipulative demon. One cartoon, which represented Rousseau as a wild man from the woods, a savage beast dragged into civilization, particularly delighted Hume, who described it in a letter to his friend Hugh Blair: "I am represented as a farmer, who caresses him and offers him some oats to eat, which he refuses in a rage; Voltaire and D'Alembert are whipping him up behind; and Horace Walpole making him horns of paper maché. The idea is not altogether absurd."[16]

"Mr Hume . . . will have difficulty persuading his readers that the author of the *Héloïse* [Rousseau] has become an infamous impostor and a monster of ingratitude," wrote one pamphleteer. "Those who have admired Mr

Rousseau for years know that his heart is too true and his morals are too pure to give away to such actions which always reveal a black character and an evil soul."[17] Another anonymous author went even further: "The majority of the public has rendered in the same judgment as I have and that our compatriot, David Hume, has been declared in France tried and convicted of having conducted himself towards Jean-Jacques Rousseau as a badly brought up and uncivil man . . . a man who is dangerous in polite society and who was the scourge of all agreeable circles."[18]

The whole sad and ridiculous affair took on all the hallmarks of a nasty divorce, a squabble between two famous minds. "He is plainly mad, after having been long maddish," Hume opined, angry at "the monstrous ingratitude, ferocity, and frenzy of the man." He confided to his Scottish friend Blair that Rousseau was "surely the blackest and most atrocious villain, beyond comparison, that now exists in the world, and I am heartily ashamed of any thing I ever wrote in his favour."[19]

Rousseau, meanwhile, fled to the moral high ground: "They say that Mr. Hume has called me the lowest of the low and a villain. If I knew how to reply to such language, I would deserve his description."[20] At the same time, he paid a lawyer to draw up a formal indictment against his new enemy, accusing him in several neatly enumerated atrocities, such as having stared at him in an unsettling way, having attempted to seduce his mistress, and even "having sent, or caused to be sent . . . in the most wicked and unnatural manner," a dish of beefsteaks to his lodgings, in order to insinuate that his guest was dependent on his charity.

Hume was aware that literary reputations were made and destroyed not in London but in Paris, and he continued to write letters protesting his innocence. He had adored his three-year stay in Paris, with the flattering attentions he received there as a famous man of letters as well as a sage, and he valued the respect his friends of the rue Royale had shown him. Holbach and Diderot, of course, believed him only too readily. They had warned him of Rousseau's rages and had had their own bitter experiences with the philosopher's paranoid conspiracy theories and his tendency to attack his enemies, real or perceived, in the most vicious and public manner.

The sad affair appeared to be uncontainable, as one insult after another was published in London, Paris, and beyond. Eventually Rousseau clandestinely fled back to France, considering the brief episode in Britain yet another station of the cross en route to his personal martyrdom.

Holbach and his friends were not surprised about the initial falling-out between Hume and Rousseau, but now even they were reeling from the consequences of the affair, which dredged up bitter memories of their own difficulties with the one member of their circle who had publicly turned against them. They rallied to Hume's defense. Holbach willingly made himself the mouthpiece of his friend's reputation in Paris, carrying with him the letters and showing them around whenever the opportunity arose. Never one to pass up a good story, Grimm, the rue Royale's propaganda minister, chipped in with stories spread throughout Europe in the *Correspondance littéraire*. This time, it seemed, Rousseau had bitten off more than he could chew. He had publicly directed his fury against a group of men whose reflexes and tactics had been honed by decade-long persecution and adversity, a formidable publicity machine ready to spring into action.

For once, their efficiency would work to their disadvantage. A private quarrel had become a public affair, with major reputations at stake. As they used their considerable influence to swing public opinion on their way, supporters of the other side skillfully played off their professionalism, arguing for pity on behalf of the poor and idealistic philosopher who had fallen prey to those more powerful and envious of his literary talents and popularity.

The case for the defense was made by Grimm, an old hand at literary controversy—not one easily impressed with a pamphlet or two. In his *Correspondance littéraire* he wrote scathingly about the "majority of the public," which already appeared to have made up its mind. Groupies were not to be relied on: "Celebrated writers normally have in their train a certain number of curs who, at the first sign of the dispute, deafen the world with their yelping. . . . Four pamphlets have already appeared in favor of Mr Rousseau, all detestably written by rascals who are entirely unknown, and who are driven to take up the pen by idleness and, most likely, wretchedness."[21]

Voltaire had initially been watching on the sidelines. He could not stand Rousseau's cult of sentiment and had taken Hume's side in the dispute. He was an old hand at public controversies, and he wisely advised Hume against any publication of messy details. Voltaire had called Rousseau "a madman, snared by his own delusions of grandeur [*orgeuil*]."[22] Jean-Jacques' greatest punishment would be to be forgotten, he wrote, but even Voltaire's influence was insufficient to calm down the opposing parties.

If this messy orgy of epistolary mudslinging did have a winner, it was Rousseau. His novels had found a substantial audience of readers who reveled in the celebration of strong feelings and regarded Rousseau as the prophet of a new, more natural, and more honest way of living. They were certainly not going to forgive a group of sophisticated French philosophers for attempting to defile his reputation. They were atheists, after all, people without morals, who could not bear to be confronted with a great and good man, whose virtue and abiding faith elevated him to another plane.

To those who did not know the man, it seemed plausible that Rousseau, the artless thinker and nature lover, had been snared by a plotting sect of atheists and publicly humiliated by Hume, a philosopher synonymous with emotional coldness and intellectual detachment. Rousseau had become a target for the hatred and vengeance of a philosophical cabal—Holbach and his friends.

As the affair died down towards the summer of 1766, the public exposition of personal differences between Rousseau and his former friends had also revealed a deeper, philosophical rift between them. Rousseau was indeed the father of Romanticism insofar as he regarded sentiment as far more important than any amount of argument, proofs, and refutations. He simply *knew* something was true, because he felt it had to be. His conviction was led by an emotional imperative.

Neither Holbach nor Diderot nor their friends could accept that. Indeed, their entire philosophical project was built on the notion of empirical certainty, of accepting facts and deducing principles, whether or not one's personal feeling accorded with the idea. Diderot in particular spent a lifetime struggling with his nostalgia for religion while at the same time adhering to his atheist and materialist principles—precisely because he knew that evidence and observation must supersede emotion. He refused to follow Rousseau by letting his emotional needs dictate his conviction.

Rousseau's intellectual differences with Hume were structured in a similar way. Hume's ruthless pursuit of what is certain had made him come to the conclusion that we can know almost nothing about the world surrounding us and that most of our convictions and decisions are based on habit and personal preference, rather than objective truth or logical necessity.

To Hume, much of philosophy was psychology, and what individuals believe is determined not by what is true but by what enables them to navigate in the world successfully. In other words, it makes no difference whether one believes in God. As there is no way of proving or disproving the object of this belief, it remains a personal choice, much like a preference for a particular dish or for strong coffee. You may believe what you want, as long as it helps you live.

This view, of course, was unacceptable for Holbach and Diderot, whose conception of truth was more immediate than Hume's, but it left plenty of space for them to discuss and enjoy one another's arguments. To Rousseau, however, Hume's thought was anathema. Rousseau quite explicitly wrote that he needed to believe in God and in a meaningful creation. The void at the center of Hume's thinking threatened to swallow the believer.

Hume came to think of Jean-Jacques as an untutored sentimentalist with a nice turn of phrase. Philosophically, they were divided by the question of ultimate truth, which split Rousseau off from the thinkers of the radical Enlightenment. To Holbach truth was knowable: right there, in front of his eyes. For Diderot, it was material but irrational and mysterious. Hume argued that it was unknowable but that pragmatic choices can work just as well. Only Rousseau was passionately certain that there was a Truth and an afterlife, a God and an immortal soul, and that mere mortals need religion to give them hope and keep them from sinning.

It was an unbridgeable divide.

CHAPTER 15

FAME AND FATE

In 1765, as David Hume was suffering his greatest defeat, after the hand he had extended in friendship was savagely bitten by his guest and protégé Rousseau, Diderot celebrated his greatest professional triumph: After some twenty years and against great resistance, he finally published the remaining ten volumes of text of the *Encyclopédie* (the last volume of the plates was published in 1772).

A political sea change had made the publication possible. The hostile Jesuit faction in France had suddenly collapsed following a scandal involving South Sea speculations, which had left the once powerful order impoverished and discredited. The most determined enemies of the *Encyclopédie* had vanished, and six years of intense but clandestine work after the formal condemnation by the Paris *parlement* in 1759 came to fruition. So many people had pushed Diderot to give up on the project: Voltaire had insisted he take it abroad; d'Alembert had abandoned it altogether, leaving his coeditor to do all the work and face all the critics on his own; others, among them the former contributor Rousseau, had even turned against it. It had been an almost impossible task, but now it was accomplished, and heavy volumes in rich brown leather bindings and with crisp, golden letters embossed on the spines were being shipped to subscribers. Officially the work remained forbidden but was distributed in France with tacit permission by Malesherbes, the chief censor, under condition that no volume was to be imported into or sold in Paris or Versailles. When André-François Lebreton, one of the booksellers publishing and financing the work, smuggled a few copies into the Royal Palace nevertheless, he was incarcerated in the Bastille for one week. The sanction, however, was an impotent gesture. The work was out. A motley group of writers, scientists, and philosophers had carried the day against the opposition of church and state.

Diderot, however, no longer relished his victory. In 1764, he had found out when checking some page proofs that the bookseller Lebreton had taken it upon himself to preempt any further problems and censor the articles himself, behind Diderot's back. Diderot was crushed by the discovery and by the deception. He wept with rage when he finally understood what had happened. The best articles, Grimm testified, were in "a fragmented and mutilated state, robbed of everything that made them precious, without even the connections between these scraps and these skeletons that had been hacked to pieces."[1]

Diderot was disgusted at the censorship and the political wrangling over the project. Having devoted the best years of his life to the gigantic enterprise, he now declared the whole work worthless and all but washed his hands of it. He had wanted to become a great stage author, a famous philosopher, or both, and he had squandered thousands of hours on a work that was rendered useless at the very last moment by a man he had thought was his ally.

In fact, the impact of Lebreton's alterations was not quite as dramatic as Diderot in his disappointment and anger had made it out to be. The twentieth-century discovery of page proofs of the original articles shows that the bookseller Lebreton had mutilated certain articles, but his changes were relatively few, and the *Encyclopédie* nonetheless still presents an imposing achievement, a summit of literary history. The sheer numbers are impressive: The seventeen volumes of text contained 71,818 articles on 18,000 pages, a total of more than 20 million words, supplemented by eleven volumes containing 2,900 engravings showing eighteenth-century arts and crafts, natural phenomena, and engineering feats in minute detail. It was a huge publishing success: 4,000 complete sets were sold despite the fact that they cost the equivalent of the annual wage of a master craftsman. Together with several pirated editions, the *Encyclopédie* was printed some 25,000 times before the century was out.

Today, the work is still known as the "*Encyclopédie* by Diderot and d'Alembert" despite the fact that the mathematician had abandoned it in 1757 and

Diderot himself had contributed fewer articles with every passing year. His sign appears underneath 1,984 articles of the first volume and almost as many for the second. But in the last three volumes, his original contributions had dwindled to 7, 8, and 6 respectively, indicating how quickly his disillusionment had set in. This was no longer *his* work, but a huge behemoth bearing down on him, exacting its daily tribute of hard work. He did what was necessary but increasingly left the writing itself to others.

But it was not its sheer bulk that made the *Encyclopédie* such an important event in the history of the Enlightenment. It was first of all the simple fact that the publication had succeeded despite the massive opposition by important figures at court, the leaders of the Paris *parlement*, and most church dignitaries. A new spirit had asserted itself and had prevailed against threats and intimidation. Even if censorship prevented the articles from being absolutely candid, taken in its entirety the knowledge contained in the *Encyclopédie* revealed a new world to its readership—a new world of science, human ingenuity and industry, artistic genius and objective fact. While it paid lip service to the importance of aristocracy and religion, the *Encyclopédie* made it perfectly plain that this new world could get along very well without them. *Think for yourself!* every article exhorted the reader, citing alternative versions and different sources for ancient myths, and replacing conventional wisdom with recent research and scientific theory. Hearsay and myths were useless for science, as a boisterous Diderot himself had insisted in an early article:

> * AGUAXIMA (Hist. nat. bot.) a plant growing in Brazil and the islands of middle America. This is all we are told; & I would like to ask for whom descriptions like this are made at all. It cannot be for the natives of the country, who obviously know more characteristics of the aguaxima than this description contains & who have no need of being informed that it grows in their own country; it would be like saying that the pear tree grows in France & in Germany. It is also not made for us; for what does it matter if there is in Brazil a tree that is called aguaxima of which we know nothing but the name? To whom is this name useful? It leaves ignorant those who were ignorant in the first place; it teaches nothing to anyone; & if I mention this plant, & several others equally badly described, it is to oblige those readers who prefer finding nothing in an ar-

> ticle of the Dictionnaire, or even finding a stupidity, than not finding an article at all.[2]

Dotted with literary flourishes, laden with facts, and spiced with subversive thought, the *Encyclopédie* was much more than a simple reference work. At its very best, it afforded the reader a seat at Holbach's table, allowing him to listen to the flow of argument and the sheer exhilaration of ideas out of the mouths of some of the great intellects of the age.

Reason was the stated program of the *Encyclopédie*. It was also one of Diderot's constant philosophical preoccupations, but in the context of his own private study it assumed darker, less optimistic connotations. Intellectually convinced of the necessity of atheism and strict materialism, and politically engaged in a campaign to carry these ideas into the world and change the general way of thinking with his *Encyclopédie*, the son of a pious provincial family who had once himself wanted to become a Jesuit was still nostalgic for the enchantments and the certainties of faith. "My heart wants one thing, but my reason wants another," he sighed in 1772.[3] He was, and remained, at war with himself.

Diderot's greatness as a philosopher lies partly in the constant, pulsating tension between rationality and instinct. In contrast to Enlightenment thinkers such as Voltaire and Kant, who suggested a totally rational world order that would free individuals from the troubling influence of irrational forces within themselves, Diderot wrote about a complex, contradictory, and essentially dark human nature illuminated only rarely by the sunlight of reason. Holbach believed that life must be liberated from superstition and oppression, but he was essentially serene in his belief in reason; for Diderot, life was always marred by error and destruction because human beings can never be purely rational. As he pessimistically wrote to Sophie Volland, life could be seen as a journey from imbecility to error, need, and sickness, and then back to imbecility: "From the moment one babbles to the moment one gibbers, living between crooks and charlatans of all kinds; to extinguish one's mind between a man who feels your pulse and another [a priest] who troubles your head; not to know where one has come from, where one is going: *voilà*, that's what they call the present of our parents and of nature, life."[4]

What sets Diderot and other radical thinkers apart from moderate Enlightenment philosophers is the fact that he never saw an entirely rational life as a possible or even desirable goal. Instead, his view of humanity was both tragic and hedonistic. To the Church, in which he had grown up and which he had initially wanted to serve, the human body was a kind of temporary ailment of the eternal soul, a lecherous and greedy bag of dirt to which it was shackled during a period of trial. To the thinkers of the moderate Enlightenment, it was the epitome of stubborn ignorance, awaiting its quasi-religious redemption through reason.

For Diderot, the body was everything there was, and reason was a bodily function with a tendency to transcendental megalomania. True insight lay not in fighting, ignoring, or sublimating physical desire, but in building a life in which it had its place. The tension between reason and instinct appeared at precisely this moment. As a philosopher who wanted to change the general way of thinking, he had to believe in the power of persuasion and of virtue, but at the same time his materialist conviction made him uncertain of both. What if, as David Hume maintained, rational discourse was nothing but personal taste dressed up in state robes? And what if virtue was ultimately a useful fiction of society, disguising the only real motivation behind our act—desire and the natural urge to survive?

In his writings, Diderot never resolved this potential contradiction, and as a result, he had an essentially tragicomic relationship to his own unruly, unphilosophical body. While the philosopher Diderot found the existential tension between rational convictions and emotional urges troublesome, the letter writer and novelist Diderot made it a rich mine of material. "They wanted to purge me today against my wish," he complained in a letter to Sophie, "and they did. Oh! How much refuse even the healthiest man contains! As long as that is the case only physically, I can live with it. Since seven in the morning and up to seven in the evening, which it is now, I evacuate, I evacuate, and even while writing to you I can hear my innards protesting that all's not finished yet."[5] Behind the joyful earthiness of this and other passages stands the awareness that the irreducible, irrational refuse contained in all humans is not only physical—it constitutes a fundamental aspect of their being.

An observer of the world, Diderot was always poet first, philosopher second. Captured in this portrait bust, his humane perspective animates all his writings. Terra-cotta bust by Jean-Antoine Houdon.

ERICH LESSING / ART RESOURCE, NY

In the end, Diderot was too much artist, too much in love with the stage, with company, voices, and characters, to pour his thought into objective prose. His temperament—his ambivalence, his sense of the absurd—lent itself more readily to animation, whether in the form of characters in a novel or in his prolific acquaintanceship. He enjoyed the inconsequential, illogical aspect of humanity, be it in the discussions at Holbach's salon, in literary characters such as his own feverish d'Alembert or his Jacques the fatalist, or in Laurence Sterne's Tristram Shandy, whom he adored.

At times his ambivalence created a measure of distance between him and the serenely rationalist Holbach, who sought complete and unyielding logical coherence. Holbach was inherently baffled by his friend, who once deliciously declared, "Our true opinion is not that from which we have never wavered, but that to which we have most habitually returned."[6] Loving the creativity of doubt much more than the stern demands of certainty, Denis most enjoyed being with people who made him laugh. "He goes to mass without believing too much," he reported to Sophie about an acquaintance, a churchgoing chemist. "In general he is a large heap of contradictory ideas which make his conversation a complete pleasure."[7]

But Diderot's bursts of liberating laughter masked a deep philosophical concern about free will. Is "man a machine," as La Mettrie had claimed, no more responsible for his actions than a chess automaton? Diderot reacted vehemently to this suggestion, which would mean the death of virtue, of social meaning, despite his own conviction that nature "is not concerned about good and evil. She has two ends: the conservation of the individual, the propagation of the species."[8] As an evolutionist and a materialist, his insights anticipate Darwin, but he could never quite reconcile himself entirely to this view. He needed the possibility of personal choice and goodness beyond the confines of natural pressures.

In view of this unresolved conflict it is not surprising that the philosopher Diderot most detested was a fellow materialist, Julien Offray de La Mettrie, who symbolized to him the feckless, selfish face of materialism. Predictably, he attacked the courageously Epicurean author for having choked himself to death on a game pie: "La M***, dissolute, impudent, a buffoon, a flatterer, chose for the life at court and the favor of the great. He died as he had to die, victim of his intemperance and his folly; he has killed himself through his ignorance about what he was preaching," Diderot thundered, angrily but not entirely convincingly.[9]

For Diderot, the problem was that, if one follows La Mettrie, there is no morality, but only the mechanism of a machine playing itself out. But the idea that we can lead a good life without having to believe in God was Diderot's most—and possibly only truly—unshakeable conviction. So if nature itself is blind, how can humans, who are part of nature, be good? How can they see beyond sheer impulse and act accordingly?

These questions are still being hotly debated by scientists, and Diderot was never quite unequivocal on the matter, but he held elements of a solution. Reason, he argued with Lucretius, is not independent of our body but caused by its material organization. Its analytical capacity combines with the drive of our passions, steering them towards pleasure and away from pain, and with empathy, which is a constant in human nature and may cause us to behave altruistically, against our own immediate interest.

Other thinkers in Diderot's immediate circle had different, much simpler ideas about rationality and freedom. To Holbach and Helvétius the answer was quite clear. We are natural machines, we do not have free will, and therefore our actions depend on the society we live in and its values. In an ignorant and superstitious society we will act ignorantly and superstitiously and, impelled by our belief in phantoms, against our own nature. In an Enlightened society, in which morality is in harmony with our nature, we will act accordingly and will by necessity become virtuous.

Diderot would have dearly loved to believe this, but he could not. There were two difficulties with this argument, and they were both insurmountable. First of all, how is it that within a deeply ignorant society some individuals emerge who can see further than others and recognize superstition as such? If we are only the product of our surroundings, how could a boy from the countryside, the son of a pious craftsman, be transformed into an atheist?

Several key thinkers among Diderot's friends simply underestimated the importance of the body and its cravings for the human condition, he believed. Hume claimed, for instance, that our individuality and our self-awareness are simply a result of the continuous stream of experiences flooding into our senses. Take them away, and there is only the memory of past experiences. Take memory away, and nothing remains. But to Diderot this simply did not explain the differences he observed. Would two children educated in the same, ideal way become the same kind of ideal person, as Helvétius had claimed? Of course they would not.

"Can education or chance make passionate people out of those born cold?" the philosopher asks. "You can preach all you like to someone who does not feel; you will blow on extinct coals. If there is a spark, your breath can bring it to life, but the spark must be there first."[10]

To Diderot, the reductionist approach to human nature taken by many thinkers throughout history was profoundly naïve. People simply are born different: different in their intelligence, in their sensitivity to pain and pleasure, in the intensity of the passions, and in their entire makeup, their "organization," depending on what they have inherited from the "filaments" of their parents. As a result, no ideal society was possible, no ideal education conceivable. Ultimately, human beings would always be at the mercy of their own character, ability, and impulses, which can be steered by reason but will always be the first and most important factor in our lives. Reason may distinguish us from other animals, but only desire makes us human. The philosopher of *volupté* was nailing his colors to the mast.

This is how morality comes in the world, according to Diderot: Our passions impel us to seek pleasure, but inborn empathy makes us extend our own aversion to suffering to include the suffering of others. Good and bad reside in our self-awareness as individuals. The conflict between the egotistical love of pleasure (the survival instinct) and our emotional identification with others (empathy) allows our faculty of reason to assess each situation, understand our desire as part of a larger whole, and tip the scale of our behavior this way or that, making us behave morally or wickedly.

We need the light of reason, Diderot says, and we must defend it against those seeking to extinguish it. Only reason can allow us to find a path through the thickets of choices we have to make. In a little fable, Diderot tells of a man wandering through a dark forest by the light of a single torch that guides his step. A stranger approaches him and advises him that he will see much better once he has put out his torch. "The stranger," the *philosophe* remarks drily, "was a theologian."

But how can reason assume this position outside the immediate pull of the passions? How can it decide objectively? How and why are we self-reflecting beings? How is it that we understand the feelings of others, that we have a theory of mind? And if our reason is not Cartesian and objective but part of our "organization," and different people can come to different conclusions, how is it possible for us to arrive at any kind of truth at all? Diderot does not clearly answer these questions—and they still have not been answered conclusively by either philosophy or science.

As a public figure, the thinker Diderot was subject to strong intellectual constraints. In works destined for publication, Diderot had to be both less atheist (to avoid being locked up again) and arguably more optimistically moralist than in private. He stood for a cause, there was work to be done, and arguably the last, darkest doubts of the philosopher were of no help in the struggle for a more just society. In his private correspondence and in his unpublished works he shows a more skeptical, even existentialist face.

While Diderot struggled to rescue some element of freedom for moral choice, Holbach was quite content to say that freedom of will was a total illusion, a position that is also more political than it seems: Christianity—Christian morality—relies on free will. Without it, there can be no choice; without choice, no sin, no guilt, no salvation. If Adam had been fated to eat the apple, no part of the story that followed would have made any sense. The entire edifice of the church rested on the existence of free will. Fatalism simply abolished free will, and with it the stranglehold the church had on human nature. Following your impulses, its proponents argued, does not make you wicked; it means that you are human, the kind of animal humans are.

Diderot remained caught between his fatalist conviction, which he rationally subscribed to but remained emotionally ambivalent about, and his passion for the truth, a conflict he could never fully resolve, torn as he was between different identities: "You are a fatalist, and at every moment you think, speak and write as if you were clinging on to the prejudice of liberty, a prejudice in which one has been cradled, the base of the vulgar language you babbled as an infant, which you are still using, without noticing that it is no longer appropriate for our opinions. You have become a philosopher in your system, but you remain a child of the people in your words."[11]

For the outside world, Diderot's identity and the identity of his friends were clear. After fifteen years of meeting at Holbach's house, a period of intense debate, of furious writing and courageous work, they had become famous to some and infamous to many others. The *Encyclopédie* was the official monument to their achievements, recognized and celebrated as such. Some of the baron's regular guests had achieved their highest ambition: They were now regarded as great men, spoken about by *tout Paris*, flattered—and insulted—in the fashionable papers, visited from abroad, painted in oils, and cast in bronze. They were approaching the pinnacle of their power.

But while the public image was as brilliant and as definite as a bronze bust, their private thoughts were both more diverse and often darker than the ideas they were being associated with. The public image had set in the minds of both admirers and adversaries. The private journeys, however, were far from finished. Baron d'Holbach continued producing books, mapping out his vision of a new and just order and a new society, with his house, as ever, a meeting place as well as an unofficial translation agency and publishing house of subversive ideas.

The year 1769 brought sudden and unwelcome news. The *abbé* Galiani, still secretary of the Neapolitan ambassador in Paris, had allowed his fondness for chatting to get the better of his diplomatic discretion. At Holbach's salon he had passed on information to the Danish ambassador which, though not damaging, was enough to annoy his employer and have him recalled immediately. After ten wonderful years in the capital, the *abbé* had to leave. He lost his appetite and became nauseous, even feverish, but the decision was irrevocable. With his wit, his quick counterarguments, and his provocatively religious stance among the atheists, Galiani had been one of the most important members of the salon. He could not bear the thought of leaving the city he had grown to love, as well as his pregnant mistress; he was beside himself. Louise d'Epinay promised to write to him regularly and quietly tried to ensure that the young woman and her child were well.

The wonderfully lively and informative correspondence of Galiani and Mme d'Epinay was to last until her death thirteen years later. Initially, the *abbé* was miserable in his native city. "My mother is dead, my sisters are nuns, my nieces are stupid," he complained in 1771. "The only company I have is a cat."[12] Obviously bored by his new duties as commercial councilor, he began to live almost entirely vicariously, peeking through the window on Paris that was kept open through his letters to Madame d'Epinay as well as to Diderot, Holbach, and others.

Other changes marked the lives of the group of friends. Ruined by having to pay the debts of her only son, a chronic gambler, Madame d'Epinay had to sell her pretty country estate in Montmorency, where she had lived with Grimm and had given Rousseau a home for a while—only to be publicly insulted for her kindness. Now she had to take a smaller house in town, a constraint that revealed itself as a blessing. Living in Paris, she became more involved with the writing and publishing business of her friends. When Grimm had to travel on diplomatic duty in 1769, she "minded the shop" of his *Correspondance littéraire* together with Denis Diderot, writing and editing the entire journal.

To a man with Diderot's capacity for work, the often laborious task of writing up literary news, penning reviews, and preparing essays for publication was not enough to fill his day. Like someone emerging from a prison sentence, Diderot wrote essays, stories, and endless entertaining letters about his daily life, his reading habits, and his budding ideas to his mistress, Sophie, and about posterity and fame to the sculptor Falconet. But it was not just sheer exuberance that pushed the *philosophe* to work. He was fighting disillusionment. The scandal surrounding the falling-out of Rousseau and Hume had dredged up the most bitter personal disappointment of his life: His own estimation of the *Encyclopédie* as hopelessly compromised threatened to invalidate the work of his entire adult life. There were personal changes afoot, too. His relationship to Sophie was changing, growing less warm; the lovers were slowly becoming estranged.

Diderot was restless, driven from one intellectual distraction to another. Soon he would be traveling not just emotionally and intellectually. He would board a coach to begin the greatest voyage of his life—to Russia.

CHAPTER 16

THE EMPRESS AND THE BEAN KING

On January 6, 1770, at Holbach's salon, Diderot was recipient of a very French honor. During the Epiphany dinner, he found the bean baked into the *galette du roi*, the traditional Epiphany cake, and by ancient custom he was declared king for the night. The impromptu monarch took his duties seriously, and before the dessert was cleared from the table he had composed his own poetic law book, the *Code Denis*. Every sovereign wants to legislate, the verse ran, but Denis wanted his subjects to rule over him, to unite them instead of ruling by division, leaving all to do as they pleased in his bucolic empire.

> The frontispiece of my code
> Reads: Be happy in your own way.
> For this is our pleasure.
> Written in the year one thousand seven hundred and seventy . . .
> Sitting next to an appealing woman,
> My heart bare on my hand, the elbows on the table.
> Signed: Denis, without lands or *château*,
> King by grace of the *gâteau*.[1]

It was one thing to be king for a night. To become acquainted with one of the world's mightiest rulers was quite another, but that was exactly what was about to happen to the *philosophe*, whose principles and convictions would be put to the test by an extraordinary journey into the real world of politics and power.

By the mid-1760s, Diderot had become increasingly preoccupied with his future, which was precarious at the best of times. In 1766, the dangers of the life he had chosen were brutally brought home to him by the trial for blasphemy and subsequent execution of the Chevalier de la Barre, a nineteen-year-old nobleman from the devout town of Abbeville, in northern France. The young chevalier had, in fact, not committed any crime, but in the wake of the publication of the *Encyclopédie* the church obviously felt that it was time to crack down on religious heterodoxy.

The whole affair had begun in August 1765 with an act of drunken vandalism: A roadside crucifix in Abbeville had been willfully damaged one night. As the search for the culprits led nowhere, witnesses began to come forward claiming to have witnessed how a local youth, Jean-François de la Barre, had once refused to take off his hat before a passing religious procession. He had also been heard singing blasphemous songs.

A search at the suspect's premises brought to light no evidence whatsoever linking him to the damaged roadside cross but yielded instead a copy of Voltaire's *Philosophical Dictionary*, which the pope had placed on the Index (the church's official list of banned publications), as well as two erotic novels. De la Barre was arrested, interrogated, and condemned to make a public penance, which consisted of his kneeling in front of the cathedral in a penitent's shirt and with a large wax candle in his hand, before having his tongue cut out and his hand removed and then being burned alive at the stake, together with Voltaire's book. Before any of this was to take place, however, the irreverent teenager was to submit to the "ordinary and extraordinary question": severe physical torture intended to make condemned criminals give up all their accomplices. The ordeal included crushing the subject's legs between wooden planks and waterboarding.

A judgment of such severity against a youth whose only crime was possessing a forbidden book had to be confirmed by the Paris *parlement*, which also functioned as a high court. In May 1766, the case was retried, and it soon became apparent that hard-liners among the magistrates were determined to make an example of de la Barre and issue a stern warning against impiety and godless talk in general. One of the judges stated during the sessions that blasphemy could not be vanquished as long as only books were being burned publicly by the hangman.

De la Barre certainly did not aid his own case. He might have thought that his family connections could save him, and he struck a defiant attitude. During the trial he even succeeded in evading his guards and running to the entrance of the courtroom. Throwing open the door to the courtroom, he showed his naked bottom to the gaping crowd outside.

As sentencing approached, observers were uncertain whether or not the young man might be set free by a lenient court, intent on overriding the excessively zealous provincial judges. But the optimists, de la Barre's lawyer among them, were disappointed. On June 4, 1766, Omer Joly de Fleury, the judge who had been the main force behind the suppression of the *Encyclopédie* in 1759 and who had then also campaigned for Diderot's arrest, sentenced the teenage prisoner to public execution, including the ordinary and extraordinary question, but commuted the manner of death to the slightly more clement version of having his tongue pierced and being beheaded, with the corpse burned at the stake.

Having been sentenced, the shocked prisoner was transferred back to Abbeville for his public execution. The first hangman of Paris, Charles-Henri Sanson, followed, together with four assistants. One month after his trial, at five o'clock on the morning of July 1, the executioners dragged the prisoner from his cell.

Holbach and his circle were both disgusted and deeply disturbed by the barbaric execution and the trial that had preceded it. The church, it seemed, was preparing to strike back. As editor of the notoriously impious *Encyclopédie* and as an author who had already once been imprisoned for blasphemy, Diderot was particularly vulnerable. If a previously blameless minor nobleman with connections in the local power elite could be cruelly put to death, what could happen to a notorious atheist? He was aware of the dangers facing him, but he decided not to yield. "I know very well that a ferocious beast which has licked blood can no longer be without it," he wrote to Voltaire, who was urgently advising him to leave before it was too late. "My soul is full of alarms; I hear a voice at the bottom of my heart, joining itself to yours and telling me,

Flee, flee."[2] But he would not go. There were his family, his wife's age, his daughter's education, his friends—too much to keep him where he had always lived.

Already highly exposed and compromised in the eyes of the authorities, Diderot could not himself write in defense of the Chevalier de la Barre. He was right that the "ferocious beast" was already eyeing him, that he might be the first one to be arrested if he gave the authorities any excuse. But there were other, less direct means of opposition. Despite his protestations of admiration, he had always kept his distance from Voltaire. Now he supplied the famous exile with information about the case, and Voltaire wrote about the trial and the horrific execution in an open letter to Cesare Beccaria, the young Milanese reformer who had only recently been a guest at Holbach's table. Indignantly, he lamented that such barbaric executions were taking place in Enlightened times. His Enlightened readers nodded their approval, but his eloquence did not save the unlucky condemned man from being put to the sword.

A justified fear of being targeted by hard-liners in the *parlement* amplified Diderot's own anxieties about his future and the future of his family. For two decades, he had lived mainly on the payments by the publishers of the *Encyclopédie*, a de facto salary, especially as he himself had no claim to royalties. Now that the great work was complete, his sole reliable source of income was the rent he received from his portion of his father's estate. It was hardly enough to live comfortably, however, and certainly far too little to guarantee his daughter, Angélique, a decent dowry and thus the start in life he wanted for her.

Diderot decided to sell his only financial asset: the library he had accumulated over twenty years of reading, writing, and editing. He had been thinking about doing so for some time already. He suggested as much in an admiring essay on the English novelist Samuel Richardson: "If a friend falls into poverty, if the mediocrity of my fortune does not allow myself to give to my children all the care necessary for their education, I will sell my books, but you will stay with me; you will stay on the same shelf as Moses, Homer, Euripides, and Sophocles, and I will read you one after the other."[3]

It proved difficult, however, to find a buyer for the library of the infamous atheist—until Grimm came up with the idea of writing to General Betski, the great chamberlain of Empress Catherine of Russia. The reply was swift and enthusiastic. The tsarina offered to buy the entire library, including all manuscripts, on condition that Diderot become caretaker librarian in his own house, and that all books and papers be transferred to St. Petersburg only after his death. In the meantime, a regular salary would be paid to him for his troubles, in addition to the purchase price. Overwhelmed by this truly princely gesture, Diderot accepted.

Catherine's generosity freed Diderot of all financial worries, but it created troubles of a different kind. He had always been wary of associating with power. Despite frequent invitations he had never visited Voltaire, had not appeared at the French court or cultivated aristocratic contacts, and had not traveled to meet the patron of many Enlightenment thinkers, King Frederick the Great of Prussia. Now he owed a debt of gratitude to the greatest of all absolutist rulers. Although undoubtedly highly intelligent and generally interested in reforming her empire in accordance with Enlightened ideas, Catherine had come to the throne by having her own husband murdered, and she was at the head of a ruthlessly authoritarian state. Diderot was now on her payroll.

The moral implications of this personal entanglement with absolutism preoccupied Diderot a good deal, but soon another, more practical question loomed. Catherine had repeatedly invited him to St. Petersburg, and he knew that he could not refuse to come or postpone the visit indefinitely. Initially he had been able to placate his patroness by rendering services to her, such as buying artworks for her palaces (he had become a highly respected art critic through his long essays on the annual salon exhibitions of paintings) and recommending the gifted sculptor Étienne-Maurice Falconet to execute a grand commission for St. Petersburg, a bronze statue—known now as *The Bronze Horseman*—commemorating Tsar Peter the Great.

Finally, in 1772, Diderot ran out of excuses for not visiting St. Petersburg. The remaining work on the *Encyclopédie* had kept him in Paris, but now even the illustrations were published. His family obligations were also reduced—his daughter had finally been married with a dowry made possible by the tsarina's largess (Mme Diderot had strictly prohibited any of her husband's friends to be present at the ceremony).

Diderot began preparations for the long journey east. Perhaps he was also glad for the change of scenery. The work of a quarter of a century had suddenly ceased, and despite his still-phenomenal workload, he had another reason to seek distraction: After Angélique's departure from home, the house seemed empty to him, empty but for the constantly disapproving voice of his wife. "I no longer have a child," he lamented to his trusted sister, Denise, in Langres. "I am alone and my solitude is unbearable."

On June 11, 1773, Diderot said good-bye to his cantankerous wife, Toinette, and to his daughter, who was now Mrs. Vandeul. Since his arrival in Paris more than thirty years earlier, he had made only four short journeys, all to his hometown and on family business. Now he would travel an enormous distance, passing through countries and cities he knew only from books. Mme d'Epinay was among many visitors who had come to bid him farewell, and she reported on his desolate state: "He is a kind of peculiar child, this philosopher. He was so astounded the day of his departure to be obliged to start out, so frightened at having to go further than Grandval, so woebegone to be having to pack his bags."[4]

Apprehensively, Diderot set off for The Hague, where he would spend some weeks at the residence of Prince Dimitri Alexeyevich Galitzin, who as Russia's ambassador to France had been a frequent guest in Holbach's salon and had now, as ambassador to the Netherlands, offered to let his friend stay with him for a while. The stopover was supposed to last not much longer than a fortnight, but weeks turned into months. Diderot was reluctant to travel on, especially since he had begun to enjoy the city: "The very day of my arrival, I saluted Neptune and his vast empire, which is only half a *lieue* from here," Diderot reported to Sophie Volland after an impromptu visit to the sandy North Sea shore. "Yesterday, I visited the schools [of the university] of Leiden. I have seen paintings, prints, princes and scholars. We have projects of all kinds."[5] He also reported that he liked the cheerful people with their large hats, and the omnipresent herring. Surrounded by unfamiliar sights and impressions, his mind responded, and new ideas began to form.

Diderot's journey to Russia continued on August 20. In Duisburg, in western Germany, the *philosophe* and his fellow traveler, Alexis Vasilievich Narishkin, were held up when Denis had an attack of colic. From there they went on to Russia via Leipzig and Dresden, a swifter alternative to the otherwise mandatory visit to Frederick the Great in Berlin.

Wherever he went, the curious tourist took the opportunity of seeing sights and meeting people, even if the pleasure of the encounter was one-sided at times: "His vivacity is extraordinarily great," reported a Leipzig resident. "He speaks with a warmth and vehemence that almost benumbs us colder-blooded souls. Anyone who wants to make an objection or contribute something to the conversation must seize the moment quickly and at the same time speak with confidence. . . . He seizes all occasions to preach atheism, and sometimes he preaches it really with the passion of a fanatic."[6] Karl Lessing, another of his new acquaintances, could hardly close his mouth for wonder when he wrote to his famous brother, the playwright and philosopher Gotthold Ephraim Lessing: "Guess what he did there! Publicly in front of the door [to his room], surrounded by a lot of professors and merchants, he preached atheism."[7]

Having caused a sensation along the way with his forthright manner, Diderot arrived in St. Petersburg on October 8, "more dead than alive" because of another attack of colic, followed by diarrhea. While he was disappointed with the cool reception he received from his own protégé Falconet, he was deeply relieved to embrace his old comrade Friedrich Melchior Grimm, who was in the city on diplomatic business. Within a week Denis had sufficiently recovered to be presented to Catherine. Soon he was received by her every day, as the philosopher reported in a long letter to his wife.

Diderot did not have an easy time. The courtiers regarded him with suspicion or outright hostility. Many of them had not time for French frills and new ideas—so little, indeed, that the empress had had to impose fees for nonattendance at her new, European-style theatre.

The effusive Frenchman was not used to court life. Grimm had been so concerned about his friend's simple manners that even before the journey, he had implored a Russian friend to look after him and make him aware of the rules of etiquette. Now, in St. Petersburg, Diderot had to make acquaintance with the intricacies of protocol, with ceremonial bows and endless waiting around in antechambers. He was not good at this game. He was frequently late for his imperial appointments, while at other times he stayed far past his allotted time, excitedly discussing ideas with Catherine, while her secretaries and chamberlains shot icy glances at the unwelcome foreigner with his unruly ideas, a man who appeared to wear the same, simple black suit day in and day out and who had even forgotten his wig somewhere along the route to St. Petersburg.

Despite or because of his unconventional manner, the *philosophe* was a great success with the empress, as Friedrich Melchior Grimm wrote to their friends in France: "And with her he is just as odd, just as original, just as much Diderot, as when with you. He takes her hand as he takes yours, he shakes her arm as he shakes yours, he sits down by her side as he sits down by yours."[8] Catherine herself, used to being surrounded by bowed heads, bent backs, and murmured reverences, was equally enchanted. In a letter to Mme Geoffrin in Paris, she described him as an extraordinary man whose enthusiastic gesturing left her thighs so black and blue with bruises that she had to interpose a table between herself and her guest in order to protect herself.

Diderot backed up his irrepressible stream of ideas with a series of memoranda on different aspects of modernizing the Russian empire according to Enlightened principles, including the importance of tolerance, the promotion of manufacturing, a complete overhaul of the administration, a draft constitution, and a plan for a new university system. Despotic rule and total authority would inevitably lead to a society marked by servility, superstition, and lack of initiative, he told his hostess, the most absolute of absolute monarchs.

Gripped by reformist zeal, Diderot appears actually to have believed that he could make Catherine a convert to the cause of the radical Enlightenment. He was setting himself up for terrible disappointment. Politics was encroaching on his presence at court. The French ambassador made it clear to him that he expected Diderot to behave like a Frenchman and to advance the interests of the king. Russian courtiers resented the influence this intruder had upon their sovereign and worked behind the scenes to discredit him.

Despite this resistance the philosopher persisted, clutching the hand of the empress and earnestly imploring her to modernize the state. Finally the monarch, who was engaged in fighting off a serious challenge to her rule posed by a rebellion of the Don Cossacks, replied:

> Monsieur Diderot, I have listened with the greatest pleasure to all that your brilliant genius has inspired you with; but all your grand principles, which I understand very well, though they will make fine books, would make sad work in actual practice. You forget, in all your plans for the ref-

> ormation, the difference between our two positions: you will work only upon paper, which submits to everything; it is altogether obedient and supple, and poses no obstacles, either to your imagination or to your pen; whereas I, a poor Empress, work up on human nature, which is, on the contrary, irritable and easily offended.[9]

Diderot was thunderstruck and finally brought to his senses. "He looked on me as one possessed only of a narrow and ordinary mind," the poor empress commented. "From that moment he spoke to me only on literary subjects, and politics disappeared from our conversations."[10]

During the last few weeks of his stay in St. Petersburg, the philosopher and the empress appear to have hardly met, each disenchanted with the other. Catherine was engaged in a war, while Diderot was kicking his heels in his accommodations, waiting for the winter to end. He was so demoralized that he was unable even to write letters, which usually poured forth from his pen in a steady stream: "I am too far off from my friends to talk with them. I have tried twenty times. After I have said 'my relatives, my friends, I want to get away, I want to get away,' nothing else occurs to me."[11]

When Diderot finally left St. Petersburg on March 5, 1774, he was so unwell that he had to be transported in a carriage especially designed to allow him to lie down in it. Having traveled through the middle of Germany on his way to Russia, he chose this time to go via Hamburg, on the coast. During both journeys, he avoided Potsdam, the residence of King Frederick the Great, the Enlightened prince and friend of Voltaire, who had cordially invited him. More than ever before, the *philosophe* was uneasy about aristocratic patronage. When he arrived back in The Hague after four chilly and exhausting weeks on the road and three broken carriages later, he was so ill that he looked far older than his years and spent a good deal of time asleep. When he recovered his strength, he began to write about his experiences, partly reflectively, partly in the voice of bitter satire. The sovereign of Russia was an autocrat, he concluded; he had smelled in St. Petersburg "an odor of despotism."[12] He had thought—naïvely—that verbal persuasion alone could succeed in transforming the tsarina. And, much worse, he was also now indebted to a monarch who, though intelligent and charismatic, otherwise stood for everything he himself rejected. Even more unhappily, Catherine, a consummate politician, had used her association with him to present herself as more Enlightened than she actually was.

It took Diderot six months to find the courage for the last leg of the journey—he was tired. In a letter to Sophie he confessed that he believed he had only ten years left "at the bottom of my bag." But there was another reason for his reluctance to return home: He liked the Netherlands and the wind of freedom blowing through the narrow streets and canals, straight from the endless seas. France was as despotic as Russia, but in The Hague, a philosophical mind could express itself without having to fear for life and limb.

Eventually the pull of Paris, of his friends and family, was stronger than all temptations of pursuing his intellectual ambitions in peace. On October 21, 1774, after almost 3,000 miles in the cabin of a coach in bad weather and on atrocious streets, Diderot finally returned to his apartment in the rue Taranne, feeling more wary and much older than when he had set out on his journey.

The Bean King who wanted his subjects to rule over him and be happy in their own way had encountered the world of real power. In this world, monarchs ruled with an iron fist and chose to gild the iron by inviting philosophers to their palaces. Diderot had been lavishly patronized and flattered by the empress herself, who had given him license to speak with all the freedom of a true philosopher—or a court jester. Eventually he had been dismissed with the condescending remark that he, after all, only worked on paper.

To Diderot, who never thought or wrote about anything *but* human nature, this was a double insult. Any illusion he might have cherished that he could be the philosopher to carry the bright sun of the Enlightenment into the largest empire in the world was well and truly crushed. The experience in St. Petersburg hardened his attitude to power and made him into an even more determined advocate of personal freedom, a declared enemy of autocratic rule.

But the *philosophe* was not only humiliated by his experience at Catherine's court and embarrassed by his association with a tyrant but also troubled by a moral question. His self-esteem as a philosopher, an artist, and a person depended on the answer he could give to it. The question is familiar: Why bother being good? That is, why be outraged at a tyrant if she and her subjects and the philosopher himself were merely results of the inexorable course of nature, of evolution? "In the last analysis, all our thoughts, all our work, all our views are resolved into kinds of sensual pleasure,"[13] Diderot had written en route to St. Petersburg. But that would mean that only instinct is real, that moral values are only illusions.

Diderot was disturbed by this argument. Are we or can we be moral agents even if our minds are nothing but a succession of strictly causal physical processes? Are we all La Mettrie's amorally hedonistic human machines? Or is there another way, a truly enlightened hedonism that admits of free choice, of morality? Is *everything* merely predetermined and instinctual, or is there a point at which choice can intervene in the course of nature?

Diderot attempted and failed to resolve these issues as a philosopher, but he succeeded all the more brilliantly in exposing, dramatizing, and playing with them as a novelist. He was a great admirer of the English novelist Laurence Sterne, whom he had met at Holbach's salon in 1762, and whose comic masterpiece *Tristram Shandy* he had started reading in October of that year. "For a few days now," he had written to Sophie, "I have been holed up with reading the maddest, wisest and funniest of all books."[14]

Three years after his encounter with Sterne, in 1765, Denis had begun work on a novel, *Jacques the Fatalist and His Master*. On his return from Russia, he took the manuscript up once again, changing, revising constantly, right up to the year of his death. While the novel consists largely of exuberant dialogues between Jacques and his unnamed master, it constantly circles around the lurking contest between goodness and causality.

The strict materialist ultimately has to admit that since all is written in the great book of nature, moral choice becomes impossible to defend. This is the position taken by the servant Jacques, who tells about his life, insisting that he had no say in anything at all, since everything was "written up there" already. A fatalist of the first water, he was not unlike Don Giovanni's faithful Leporello. Both are religiously resigned to a life controlled from beyond, and both accompany a master whose cynicism makes them quake in their rough boots. "It is written up there!" Jacques assures us time and again, and his resignation is such that even when pursued by a furious mob he walks slowly, much to his master's anxiety, because if it is written up there that they will be caught, it is useless to work up a sweat.

Even philosophy, for Jacques, is a useless endeavor, as its much vaunted, detached rationality is no more than an illusion: "Not knowing what's written up there, one does not know what one wants or what one does, and one follows one's fancy which one calls reason, or one's reason, which often is nothing but a dangerous fancy which sometimes turns out well, sometimes badly."[15] For the author of these lines, who had devoted his life to pursuing Enlightenment, such an argument was more than an intellectual game; it was a hard self-reproach. The possibility that all his endeavors were nothing but a dangerous fancy perturbed him deeply.

Diderot's philosophical redemption lay in his irony. In *Jacques the Fatalist*, the narrator mocks the reader's fear of being a mere plaything of fate. The reader, whose questions and demands are also in the text, wants to be told a straight story, but the narrator keeps on intervening, veering off onto tangents and making the tale lurch back and forth between the servant and his master, and their stories. Time and again the reader protests against this willful treatment. The reader wants to know where the two heroes are headed, but the narrator insists that this is none of his business—after all, none of us can know where we are headed. The reader would prefer to hear more of the promised story of Jacques' love life, but the narrator refuses to satisfy his pedestrian curiosity. He can do as he pleases, he purrs: marry them off, let them be cheated on or have accidents, send them to the colonies and back again. Making up stories, he concludes, is terribly easy.

Diderot's conceit of holding his reader to ransom is more than just a game or an act of homage to Sterne. The real reader experiences firsthand what it means if everything is "written up there," and reading a novel becomes a philosophical exercise, an experience not unlike life itself: a series of absurd but often entertaining digressions in which the suffering individual believes he recognizes the invisible hand of a smirking demiurge, as malicious god or as faceless necessity.

There are several ends to the novel, several implied outcomes. Will Jacques finally get lucky in his quest for a pretty girl? Will he be thrown into prison or realize his dream—the perfect happiness of an aging veteran and manservant—as concierge in a castle somewhere in the provinces, married to a younger woman? It is "written up there," but it is not revealed to us, not quite yet, either to Jacques himself or to the reader.

This, perhaps, is the closest Diderot ever came to a philosophical answer to the question of morality. The strict, faceless necessity that La Mettrie had posited and that Diderot's own friends Holbach and Helvétius so willingly embraced dissatisfied him, precisely because life seemed so chaotic and absurd. Should not a truly causal world be more rationally ordered, somehow more clipped and symmetrical? And were not the riotous disorder and waste of reality proof that life was ultimately inexplicable, deeply absurd, and bearable only with an ironic smile?

Diderot not only accepted life's deeply anarchical energy but relished it. Despite insisting on a society ordered according to rational principles, he was too much of a born storyteller not to be delighted by the sudden twists and paradoxical turns that life could take. In St. Petersburg, he had propagated reason, but he had come away more than ever convinced that its feeble power must fail against instinct and that generally speaking, principle is no match for pleasure. Perhaps it was still possible for reason to outwit the passions, but he was less confident of that now. Too often, life seemed to be nothing but a series of absurd coincidences.

For a few months, Diderot had been caught up in the retinue of an intelligent but harsh and autocratic ruler, and he had been shocked by what he had seen both in her and in himself. How could he know that he was right to fight for a reasoned morality if perhaps everything was "written up there," if might was right, after all? He had naïvely wandered into the halls of power, trying to convert the rule of the sword into reasonable and compassionate leadership. Observing the empress at close quarters, he had finally understood that this transformation was every bit as impossible as the alchemists' dream of turning lead into gold.

CHAPTER 17

SEX IN PARADISE

> I have to admit that it was nigh impossible to keep 400 young Frenchmen at work, sailors who had not seen a woman for six months, in view of what followed. In spite of all our precautions, a young Tahitian girl slipped aboard and placed herself on the quarterdeck immediately above one of the big hatchways, which was fully open to allow air in to the sailors sweating at the capstan below. The young girl casually let slip the only piece of cloth which covered her, and appeared to the eyes of all the crew exactly as naked Venus appeared to the Phrygian shepherd. Truly, she had the celestial form of the goddess of Love. More and more sailors and soldiers crowded to the foot of the hatchway, and no capstan was ever wound with such alacrity as on this occasion. Only naval discipline succeeded in keeping these bewitched young fellows from rioting; and indeed we officers had some little difficulty in restraining ourselves.[1]

The European who wrote these lines was Captain Louis-Antoine de Bougainville, whose ship *La Boudeuse* had returned to France in March 1769 from a circumnavigation of the world. His storerooms were richly laden with plants (one of which, blossoming with particular luxuriance, was named after him) and artifacts. But more precious still were the stories he had to tell of the island of Tahiti, abundant with flowers and inhabited by a people who apparently had little sense of personal property or of social restraint.

Bougainville had set off on his famous journey in November 1766 and sailed for almost three years on a journey that took him as far afield as New Zealand. Despite the fact that Captain James Cook had already covered most of the same route, Bougainville's voyage caused a sensation in France, particularly because of his experiences in Tahiti, which had caused him to name the island La Nouvelle Cythère, after the mythical Greek island of love.

The islanders had been welcoming—very welcoming indeed. Whatever they had to offer they freely shared. The stunned Europeans were treated to fruit and festivities—vegetables, fish, and pigs were delivered, unasked, to the ship. Most amazingly, the young women simply approached the men who pleased them, inviting them to follow them into their huts or to some shady spot and engage in an exchange of favors that would have carried a heavy moral burden in the travelers' country of origin but here was treated as nothing but affectionate fun. The sailors, who had lived under strict naval discipline on an all-male ship for months, thought that they had arrived in paradise.

The utopian vision of peace and universal goodwill was not to last, of course. Soon it became apparent that while the islanders set little store by their own property, they treated the belongings of their new guests (who saw themselves, of course, as conquerors) equally casually. Items went missing from the ship and were recovered forcefully, backed by weapons; a native was shot dead, to the deep shock of the community, who were left scarred and bewildered by this brief visit of fire-toting foreigners.

Despite these discordant notes, Bougainville's journey was a triumph in his home country. News of the expedition spread rapidly, and for a short time a Tahitian native who had braved the long voyage into the unknown created a sensation in Paris—despite the fact that it proved impossible to teach him French. But while the South Sea islander in his European clothes drew some attention, it was the idea of an Island of Love that really set imaginations alight, particularly when Bougainville published an account of his journey in 1771. It seemed to fit in perfectly with Rousseau's ideal of the noble savage whose simple life and natural manners have not yet been poisoned by the perversity of advanced civilization.

Even before his Russian voyage, Diderot had become increasingly critical of authority, in the form of both aristocratic rule at home and colonialist ambitions abroad. In 1772, he had joined the *abbé* Raynal in writing a commentary on Bougainville's journey and the implications of European colonialism for other cultures. After his return from Russia, his interest in questions of absolutist power were rekindled. Tahiti, he felt, might be a symbol for the injustices of power and of history.

Diderot was struck by the explorer's accounts, not because they showed people uncorrupted by competition and city life, but because they showed a civilization living free from the idea of original sin, free of the demonization of the human body and of physical pleasure. He had written about the possibility of such an existence, and now it seemed there were societies that were indeed living in harmony with nature, without being oppressed by the twin evils of church and aristocracy, which had long been conspiring to monopolize power and property and keep the common people ignorant, ashamed, frightened, and compliant. Freedom, it seemed, was actually possible.

Diderot was fascinated by this discovery, but at the same time he immediately understood that this paradise was threatened, even doomed. The Europeans had arrived, and with them ideas such as shame and jealousy, property and theft—all of which would be forced on the islanders by colonial oppression and missionary zeal. Even if Bougainville and Cook had stayed for only a short while, there would be others. It was only a question of time.

In 1772, Diderot had dramatized this conflict and the differences between the two moral codes in a philosophical story, a literary by-product of his work on the *Voyage aux deux Indes*, a long essay whose full title was also its agenda: *Supplement to Bougainville's Journey, or Dialogue Between A and B About the Disadvantages of Attaching Moral Ideas to Certain Physical Acts Which Do Not Call for Them.*

Part of this fictional account of the French visit to the island kingdom consists of a speech given by an old Tahitian man, who warns his countrymen of the impending destruction of their community at the hands of foreigners: "One day they will come back, the piece of wood which you see in the belt of the one over there in one hand, and the iron that hangs on the side in the other; they will put you in chains and cut your throats, or subjugate you to their extravagances and to their vices; one day you will serve them, as corrupt, as vile, as unhappy as they are."[2]

The old man sees that he is powerless to avert his people's fate. He can do nothing more than implore the foreign captain to board his ship and never come back—a futile wish. "We follow the pure instinct of nature, and you have tried to efface the character of our souls. Here, everything belongs to everybody, and you have preached some kind of distinction between *yours* and *mine*. Our girls and our women are shared, and you have partaken of this privilege with us; and you have come to light unknown fury in them."

The urge to possess and control is the root evil in the character of the voyagers, the old man believes. They have even claimed that the island itself now belongs to them:

> This land is yours! And why? Because you have set foot on it? If a Tahitian came one day to your coast, and if he engraved on one of your stones or on a tree trunk: *This land belongs to the inhabitants of Tahiti*, what would you think? You are stronger! . . . You are no slave, and you would rather suffer death than become one, but to want to make us slaves! . . . He whom you want to use like a brute [animal], the Tahitian is your brother. You are both children of nature; what right do you have over him that he does not have over you?[3]

Diderot was adamant about this principle: The human family must live in solidarity, and no person and no culture has special rights over any others. Moving from the general to the particular, he devotes another chapter to the meeting between the expedition chaplain and Orou, the chieftain of the village, host to the churchman during his stay on the island. On the first evening, the chaplain is stunned to find just how Tahitians understand hospitality when Orou presents his wife and three daughters, all naked. "You have eaten, you are young, you carry yourself well," Orou says to the chaplain. "If you sleep alone you will sleep badly; a man needs company by his side during the night. Here is my wife, here are my daughters: choose the one you like best; but if you want to oblige me, you will prefer the youngest of my daughters, who has no children yet."[4] The mother adds that the daughter is a good girl, and her childlessness is not her fault.

Torn between his holy orders and his desire as a man, the priest declines, arguing that his religion does not allow for such indulgence. Orou is baffled. "I don't know what you call religion, but I have to think badly of it," he replies, "because it hinders you from tasting an innocent pleasure, to which nature, our sovereign mistress, invites us all; to give life to someone like us, to do a service which the father, mother, and children are asking for; to oblige a host who has welcomed you freely, and to enrich a nation by giving it one person more."[5]

Protesting, "but my religion, but my holy orders," the priest nonetheless eventually feels obliged to humor his host, and after four nights, four contented women in the house can testify that he had made his contribution to the island's future with growing enthusiasm. For him, though, the work with the natives is only beginning. Having sacrificed his own body, he must now save their souls, but it proves strangely difficult to convince them of even the most basic tenets of the Christian faith. Creation surely means that there must be a Creator, he says, a master craftsman who has made everything. The practical natives, however, remain skeptical. If the priest is right, the world was created a long time ago, and the Creator must be old and feeble by now, they think. They are also troubled by the fact that he no longer intervenes in the world, almost as if he had no limbs to use. An old workman without hands or feet, who cannot help or harm his creatures, is not worth praying to, they believe. If he were truly powerful, there would surely be less suffering. Therefore, either he is too old and frail or he is indifferent to their suffering.

Other aspects of Christian morality also trouble Diderot's fictional natives. On hearing that in his guest's home country a young woman is dishonored if she is no longer a virgin, Orou is shocked by such a perversity, proclaiming that "your society . . . will never be anything but a mass of hypocrites, who are themselves the instruments of their torture by submitting to it; or imbeciles, in whom prejudice has quite extinguished the voice of nature."[6]

Diderot's own voice rings loud and clear from this attack on conventional morality, as do his convictions about sexual mores. Marriage for life? How absurd. Incest? Why not, provided both parties are old enough and consenting? Children born out of wedlock? A boon to everyone, to be cared for by all. Homosexuality? Not for him—despite his enthusiastic affection for Grimm—but of no harm to anyone.

The sensuousness of Diderot's vision combines provocation and high moral purpose. Religious superstition, not civilization itself, creates an obsession with human misery. It has buried the joy of living and erected artificial barriers to humanity's natural capacity for happiness. This idea had accompanied Diderot throughout his career; his very first sentence as a philosopher, in his *Pensées philosophiques*, is a defense of the passions and pleasure. Now it had very specifically taken the form of impugning Christianity's hostility to sensual pleasure and its cultural consequences.

Written in 1775, the same year as the *Supplement*, Diderot's *Unconnected Thoughts on Painting* develops this theme in one of the most brilliant and startlingly provocative passages he ever wrote. The essay itself was a result of his continuing fascination with art criticism and collects his own opinions and observations about painting, its techniques, and its subjects. While talking about the scenes most commonly depicted in art, Diderot also considers the paradox that a building filled with images of people undergoing grotesque and cruel suffering—"one man skinned, one hanged, one baked, one grilled, a disgusting butchery"—should be considered a temple of divine love. This, the *philosophe* writes, is one of the core problems of religious art and, by implication, of the Christian faith itself.

Instead of glorifying the mortification of the flesh, art should be able to celebrate the joy of life and the beauty of the world. Painting especially should be able to depict the virgin Mary as the mother of pleasure, who attracted the Holy Spirit with "her beautiful eyes, her beautiful breasts, her beautiful buttocks":

> If the angel Gabriel had been praised . . . for his beautiful shoulders; if Magdalene had had a gallant adventure with Christ; if, at the Wedding at Cana, Christ had, between two wines, a little unconventionally, let his hand stray over the neck of one of the maids of honor, or the buttocks of Saint John, unsure whether or not he would remain faithful to the apostle whose chin was already shadowed by a light, feathery beard: you would see what would be the matter with our painters, our poets and our sculptors, in which tone we would speak of these charms, which would play such a great and marvelous role in the history of religion and of our God; how we would look at the beauty to which we owe our birth, the incarnation of the Savior, and the grace of our redemption.[7]

This was Diderot in full flight: teasing and ambivalent, but never without serious intent. The text was written for publication in Grimm's *Correspondance* and could not be overtly antireligious. Even so, the Christian metaphor becomes a philosophical message: Grace and redemption lie in the enjoyment of love, and it is the role of art to create and unite communities of experience.

Earlier in his writing life, Diderot had asked how it could be possible to affect the actions of individuals, to override or at least shape the determining influence of heredity. Now he had given the answer. If only experience (as opposed to rational persuasion) can change a personality, then it was the purpose of art to create such experiences. According to the *philosophe*, art can in fact improve you. The creativity of art is nothing else than the erotic life of the mind, a common ritual allowing us to accept nature, pleasure, and pain. The greatest, the deepest pleasure of all, erotic love, is the best incentive for creating a society more in tune with our nature and ultimately with nature's drive towards the survival of the species.

If all this is beginning to sound like an early Woodstock in a poet's heated imagination, Diderot soon poured cold water on the idea. Lust is not lawlessness, and in the *Supplément* the chieftain of Orou quickly makes clear that his village is no community of proto-hippies. To the Tahitians at least, sex is a lustful act that should also result in offspring. If old, infertile women should get it into their heads to go on the prowl for young men, they are banished to the other side of the island or even enslaved.

Suddenly, the tropical idyll looks less idyllic, for this society has its own laws, based not on any individual moral standard but on the only universal principle Orou can identify: "You cannot judge the morals of Europe by comparing them to those of Tahiti, and consequently not those of Tahiti with the morals of your country: we need a more certain rule; and what could be that rule? Do you know one apart from the general good, and the utility for the individual?"[8] If the general good on a sparsely populated island required that more children be born, then even pleasure had to be put to its service. Elsewhere, other conditions might apply, and the general good might require other measures. No idea of virtue can claim to be universal, and only compassion could serve as a global yardstick of morality.

The extravagant punishment of sex that cannot result in pregnancy is uncharacteristic of Diderot's broad and tolerant approval of erotic love. It is possible that Diderot put these opinions in Orou's mouth to emphasize that his Acadian society was not a moral void, but that every society must have rules, perhaps even illogical laws. Nonetheless, the attitude remains puzzling—and puzzlingly conventional. Here, too, lies the great divide between him and Julian Offray de la Mettrie, who advocated pleasure for its own sake. For Diderot, pleasure is the only goal worth pursuing, but only in the context of utility to society.

There is also a whiff of paternalism about some of the passages of the *Supplément*, and at times Diderot's attitude is contradictory: Orou offers his wife and daughter to the chaplain; they do not make the first step themselves. The father Diderot showed similar attitudes in deciding for his own daughter, Angélique. He had insisted on choosing a suitable husband for her and even tried to arrange a marriage between Angélique and Grimm—who was exactly thirty years older than she. Eventually he did arrange another match with a promising young man from a good family. Angélique apparently had little say in the matter.

And yet while behaving like a thoroughly conventional *pater familias*, Diderot was also a determinedly progressive father who lavished much more care on a female child than was thought necessary at the time. He taught her not only the keyboard but arithmetic, oversaw her extensive reading, and engaged the popular scientist *abbé* Nollet, the one who had made whole chains of monks and soldiers jump with the jolt of an electric discharge, to give her private lessons in physics. He also took a keen interest in her emotional development: When Angélique approached puberty, he had a midwife come to the house to demonstrate to her the secrets and mechanics of human reproduction by using anatomical wax models.

Such an education and such devotion to a daughter's personal independence and intellectual emancipation were exceptional in his day (it was certainly more daringly modern than anything proposed by Rousseau). Diderot's pious wife fought it every inch of the way, for her great wish was to see her daughter enter a convent.

Living without religious prejudice, Diderot's Tahitians had mastered the only true rationality and the only true moral code there was: to understand and follow the laws of nature. They had learned to do this far more perfectly than their more sophisticated European visitors. The whole idea was little more than a fanciful conceit (Diderot was perfectly aware that all cultures had their superstitions), but it allowed the philosopher to investigate ideas of morality and to propose an alternative society, an Island of Love in an ocean of human cruelty.

In *Jacques the Fatalist*, Diderot had taken the helplessness of the rationalist to its comical extreme, creating a character who is also the perfect excuse for intellectual resignation. It is "written up there"; the future is predetermined. In his writings about the South Sea islanders, he created a vision of a better life, a society uncorrupted by the lies of Christianity.

Beautiful as it was, Diderot's Tahiti was no utopia. On the one hand, its inhabitants obeyed laws that were appropriate only to their island and could not necessarily be applied elsewhere. On the other hand, the encounter between islanders and Europeans carried the seeds of destruction into the peaceful island's life. Diderot had learned his lesson on political power and its moral dangers. It was this power, he wrote, that would ultimately destroy the only paradise on earth.

Diderot's dignified chieftain Orou is the typical "noble savage," a popular trope in eighteenth-century literature particularly beloved by the *philosophe*'s one-time friend Jean-Jacques Rousseau, whose social thought was built on a very religious idea of Edenic innocence corrupted. Despite their apparent similarities, however, both authors mean very different things when they write about noble savages, corruption, and the might of civilization. Their differences exemplify both the striving of the radical Enlightenment and the growing resistance to it. They are based on two diametrically opposed conceptions of human nature.

Both Rousseau and Diderot saw the morality of their own time as perverse: Rousseau because it was "civilized" and not religious enough, Diderot because it had been twisted by religion and was not yet civilized enough. Both therefore saw the "savages" as morally superior to their own society, and both advocated a kind of return to the values of apparently more primitive communities.

For Jean-Jacques Rousseau, the savage man was an amoral creature, akin to an animal that simply satisfied its immediate needs without reflection or moral judgment: "The only goods he recognizes in the universe are food, a female, and sleep: the only evils he fears are pain and hunger. I say pain, and not death: for no animal can know what it is to die; the knowledge of death and its terrors being one of the first acquisitions made by man in departing from an animal state."[9] This blessed state of innocence was the childhood of humanity, its earthly paradise. But the snake was already lurking at its heart.

The destruction was wrought by sex: by competition (especially for women), self-awareness, and self-consciousness, and hence personal property, laws, morality, and guilt. Individuals began to compare themselves with others, looking for those who were most handsome or strongest, who would surely get the girl. This inequality was "the first step towards vice," creating vanity, contempt, shame, and envy—the end of Arcadian happiness.

In a climate of competition, tasks are delegated, and the old cohesion dissolves. Stronger, cleverer, more skillful people control others, accumulating wealth and power; exploitation begins as the rich discover refined pleasures and idleness. Social unrest must follow: The passions are inflamed and fanned by envy, greed, brutality. Humankind is ruined and will only be able to find happiness again by abandoning the civilization that so twists the emotions in favor of a simple life or rustic, self-dependent virtue or, better still, a return to the woods, to a state of innocence before language, society, and ritual.

In the current, artificial climate, sexual love is, as Rousseau writes, "the enemy within." Love is either taking, as in a sexual act or an affair conducted to seek pleasure, or giving, as the love of a faithful spouse and parent. The two are irreconcilably opposed, as Rousseau illustrated in his immensely successful novel *Julie ou la nouvelle Héloïse* (1761), in which the heroine sacrifices herself on the altar of love. Married to the philosopher Wolmar (a scarcely disguised portrait of Holbach) and living in a "fraternal familiarity and in the pace of innocence," she secretly loves another man.

Wolmar's relentless virtuousness begins to bore the younger woman, as Holbach bored his pretty baroness; happiness itself bores her. Julie seeks satisfaction in her role as wife and mother, in prayer and duty, but when her former lover returns after years of absence, she must admit that her passion still burns, now more destructively than ever. Torn between the two men, the unfortunate woman suffers moral torment until she contracts a fatal fever while saving one of her children from drowning. On her deathbed, she has an apotheosis and finally finds redemption and happiness in her faith.

It is easy to see why it was Rousseau rather than Diderot who became the spiritual father of the Romantic movement. The human mind as battleground on which opposing forces are wrestling for supremacy, its soil churned and whipped up by explosions of passion and storms of desire, desperately in need of redemption through God's grace—this dark vision spoke powerfully to a generation seeking to reenchant the world.

Rousseau's hope of personal redemption is also, surprisingly perhaps, a very Calvinist idea. Calvinism not only preaches the sinfulness of passion but puts particular emphasis on the fact that no one can be redeemed through good works or repentance—only the gift of divine grace can save the soul from the jaws of damnation.

For Rousseau, too, human beings are in desperate need of redemption, but few are chosen ever to attain it. Our sinful amour propre, our egotistical self-love, will almost always claim our soul for earthly misery. The Christian abhorrence of physical desire and its suspicion of reason run like rivers through his writings, driving and suffusing everything.

For Jean-Jacques Rousseau, the noble savage is a memory of a distant, happy life. Diderot's *homme sauvage*, on the other hand, does not live in a remotely innocent, primitive state; other cultures are simply more intelligent in the moral decisions they make. Where Rousseau postulates a state of nature, an idyllic moment before humans ate the forbidden fruit, Diderot gathers the best ethnographic knowledge he can find—even if it is not always very good. He describes cultures with horizons entirely different from his own but possessing complex beliefs and customs—not primitive but merely different and in some ways even superior to his.

Whereas Jean-Jacques yearns for a state of childlike "innocence" (a much-loved word), a return to a time before sex and sophistication, his former friend looks to non-Christian cultures as examples of how life can be lived passionately and free of the fear of sin, free of the disgust with physical desire that marks Christianity. In philosophical parlance Diderot is de-Christianizing the human body by resurrecting a pagan attitude towards sensuality, an Epicurean stance celebrating pleasure while opposing selfishness. He warns against mindless indulgence, proposing instead to develop and refine pleasure by cultivating the senses and the mind through art.

Attitudes towards faith and passion mark out the unbridgeable chasm between the mature philosophies of Diderot and Rousseau. Having blinked in the light of reason, Rousseau wants nothing more than to creep back into the womb of faith, away from "the slavery of sense, the tyranny of the passions."[10]

To Diderot, the passions are not tyrants but the inexorable forces of life itself, which he tries to illuminate, to use Hume's beautiful phrase, with the calm sunshine of the mind.

Diderot's ethics of the passions had important political implications. If good is only what allows us to live life passionately and without harming others, then it is not the good in the eye of God, the good of revealed Truth. Between two passionate lives, there is no higher vantage point, no moral claim to the high ground. Cultures are great if they are respectful of human nature, not if they accumulate wealth or power or even sophistication. Unlike Rousseau, Diderot did not see sophistication as an impediment to happiness. On the contrary, it was good and necessary to refine one's passions, as long as they were natural passions. The sophistication of perverse values, however, remained perverse. The church had refined the values of suffering, and the result was a terrible perversion of human nature that made countless European Christians less happy than the most primitive natives. If only its respect for human life and happiness distinguished one society from another in moral terms, then Europe's moral claim to ownership of the entire globe must collapse. What right did Europeans have over Tahitians? Diderot had made the proud old man ask in the *Supplément du voyage de Bougainville*. In stark contrast to most of his contemporaries, his answer was that there could be no such right at all. This moral relativism—or, more precisely, this relativism of customs—was, if not exactly new, a revolutionary position at a time when wars were fought for the One True Faith, whatever that faith might be.

Nevertheless, despite his insistence that Europeans had no reason at all to feel superior to other civilizations, Diderot's portrayal of foreign peoples was rarely flattering and often wildly inaccurate. "All ugly peoples are crude, superstitious, and stupid," he opined in the *Encyclopédie*. "The Lapps and Danes venerate a fat, black cat. The Swedes call the devil with a drum. . . . They have almost no idea of God or religion." He also confidently announced that the Chinese were "indolent, superstitious, submissive, slavish & ceremonious;" in the provinces they were "fat, brutal, without morals & without arts"; while Egyptian women were short and male Hottentots had only one testicle.[11] Rather predictably, the Europeans were the "most beautiful & best proportioned" of all peoples on earth. Not content even with these generalizations cobbled together from travel accounts and learned monographs, he often simply wrote about *l'homme sauvage* (savage man).

What is interesting here is not that Diderot shared many of the ethnic prejudices of his day (which was partly due to a lack of reliable information) but the fact he transcended them by drawing conclusions that flew in the face of received opinion. Even peoples who were neither beautiful nor well proportioned, nor indeed European and baptized, had in his eyes a perfect right to live their lives and practice their customs without outside interference.

The question Diderot poses in his writings on "savage man" is fundamental: What makes a good society? The "Hottentots" (we shall retain his ethnographically incorrect designation for simplicity's sake) had by all accounts a primitive culture as close to a state of nature as any. Were they happy? They might have been, because they had many things Europeans could only dream of. They were free, they knew of no sickness other than old age, they satisfied their desires, and they had no vices. True, they might have been dirty and dressed in animal hides, but at least this dirt was on the surface only, while European hypocrisy and corruption penetrated the darkest corners of the soul.

Even the obvious hallmarks of primitive life may not be as remote from civilization as they appear. Hottentots may believe in irrational myths, Diderot argues, but Christians also cut one another's throats in the name of "incomprehensible questions." Hottentots may not have enlightened philosophers, but at least they don't talk about virtue without practicing it. The European colonizers, however, have committed countless sins in the name of virtue; they abandon all morality and all humanity once they cross the equator. Instead of greeting the Hottentots as brothers and offering them the means of attaining "a more regulated life," they have robbed, murdered, and pillaged, making entire indigenous populations into little more than beasts of burden, a fate worse than death.

In 1770, Guillaume Raynal published his *Histoire des deux Indes*, a strong critique of France's foreign policy and colonialist ambitions in which Diderot had collaborated anonymously. Four years later, after Diderot's return from St. Petersburg, the two men revised the *Histoire*, and now Diderot became much more passionate in his condemnation of tyrannical violence. "Flee, unhappy Hottentots, flee!" he wrote, thinking about the colonization of their lands: "Entrench yourselves in your forests. The ferocious beasts living there are less threatening than the monsters of the empire under which you will fall. The tiger may devour you, but he will only take your life. The others will rape your innocence and your freedom. Or, if you feel you have the courage, take up your axes, take your bows, and make poisoned darts rain upon the strangers. May not one of them survive to carry back to his fellow citizens the news of the disaster."[12]

Diderot knew that this wish was little more than an exercise in rhetoric; in his moral indignation he cared little that Hottentots did not live close to forests, and there are no tigers in Africa. His point was clear and forceful: Power alone did not give the Europeans the right to enslave others and to poison their cultures with one that was morally corrupt to the core. "To conquer and to destroy with violence—these two amount to the same. The destroyer and the violent man is always despicable."[13] Invasion, expropriation, slavery, forced conversion, and mass murder were forms of cruelty that could not be justified on any grounds—certainly not with reference to a religion Diderot considered to be superstition on the part of the faithful and conspiracy on the part of those in power. Instead, Europeans must accept that their common humanity makes all humans members of the same family: "You are brothers. How long will you refuse to accept this?"[14]

But refuse to accept it they did, and none more blatantly than those trading in human cargo, a trade that moved Diderot to write a magnificent indictment against slavery. In the *Encyclopédie* he had published the article "*Traité des nègres*" ("Trade in Negroes"), a moving plea by his indefatigable collaborator, the Chevalier de Jaucourt, who had written that the practice "violates religion, morality, natural law, and all rights of human nature. . . . If such a commerce can be justified by a moral principle, then there is no crime, however atrocious, that cannot be legitimated. . . . Europe's colonies must sooner be destroyed than to cause misery to so many people!"[15]

Slavery was a cardinal evil of his time, Diderot believed, a conviction that partly stemmed from his belief that no individual and no society had the right to rule over others and that no advantage in sophistication and technology conferred such a right. Far from home, Europeans behaved worse than barbarians. In the *Histoire des deux Indes*, Diderot described how merchants in France made money out of misery abroad. To them, the terrible deaths of slaves were simply an accounting factor in their profit calculations. But the moral debt remained, and the only remedy might lie in a revolt against this evil. "The thief attacks and takes money; the merchant takes the person itself. One violates the social institutions, the other violates nature. Yes, without a doubt, if there were a religion which authorized, which tolerated such horrors, if only by its silence . . . its ministers should be suffocated underneath the debris of its altars."[16]

Slavery, however, was only the worst form of despotism. Countless people were suffering under the rule of absolute monarchy, prevented by force from making decisions about their lives, their beliefs, and themselves.

Diderot's relation with power had always been ambivalent and antagonistic. First, he had fought against his father; then he had tried to outwit the authorities and had been imprisoned for it. Unlike others in his situation, he had kept his distance from potential patrons at court and other people in influential positions such as Voltaire. His attitude had always been marked by a strong love of independence from his elders, who were in a position to influence his life.

Now, however, around the time of his sixtieth birthday in 1773, Diderot himself was in a position of influence, and he realized that the problem with power was not that it was held by the wrong people but that it was inherently corrupting. In his 1769 essay "Regrets About My Dressing Gown," he had written humorously about the effects the generosity of a wealthy patroness had on his daily life. In his writings for and with Raynal, he attacked the root cause of despotism: the arrogance of believing that one society could be entitled to pass judgment on others, to conquer, and to enslave foreigners—all in the name of religion and in the service of profit. Despotism, Diderot argued, must never be countenanced.

Social rules were there to facilitate the greatest common good. If they failed to ensure it, both their moral rules and their rulers were redundant. No great principle, no ancient tradition, and no proud faith was above this simple test. At the same time, however, Diderot recognized that there was no simple fix for all the world's ills. He was unconvinced that a republic could work in a large country peopled largely by ignorant peasants; the Enlightenment, after all, stopped in the suburbs, as he had written. But while he had no recipe for universal happiness, he was convinced that absolutism was the wrong path and that there must be other, more democratic, freer ways of living.

An Enlightenment thinker who despised despotism and admired republican experiments and new ways of ordering societies, Diderot was also an intense admirer of the United States, which was in the process of gaining its independence from Great Britain. He wrote admiringly about the American Revolution, hoping that the new United States could offer "all inhabitants of Europe a place of asylum against fanaticism and tyranny, [and] instruct those who govern men about the legitimate usage of their authority."[17]

For the inveterate Parisian Diderot, all thoughts of a place of asylum outside of his city and surroundings remained a purely abstract concept. He had found the journey to St. Petersburg an ordeal, and only The Hague had pleased him so well that he felt almost as much at ease there as in Paris. Some of his close friends, however, discussed the possibility of emigrating to the United States, even if they appear to have treated it more as a running joke than a serious project. Still stuck in Naples, the *abbé* Ferdinando Galiani was bored with Italy and with the old world: "Everything is rotten here: religion, laws, arts, sciences; all will be rebuilt in America," he declared in 1776, advising Louise d'Epinay to buy a house not in Paris, but in Philadelphia. In her reply, Louise generally approved of the idea and promised to mention it to her grandchildren. "But as for me, I could never bear to be so distant from the bit of earth that contains the precious remains of my dear dog Ragot."[18] At only age fifty the fragile Madame d'Epinay, who had always been dogged by health problems, was beginning to feel old—and nostalgic for the affections of the past.

Apart from distant admiration, there were also direct personal and intellectual links between the rebellious colony and the Enlightenment radicals. Benjamin Franklin and later Thomas Jefferson lived in Paris while working for their young home country and against British intervention. Jefferson's stay (1785–1789) was too late for him to meet Diderot or witness Holbach's salon in its prime, but the third president's personal library shows how far the influence of Holbach and his friends extended across the Atlantic. The salon members' writings became an integral part of how the founding fathers thought about the nascent United States. Jefferson's handwritten catalogue of books lists not only works by British empiricists such as Hume but also titles by Voltaire and a whole list of crucial books of the radical Enlightenment: the famous *De l'esprit* by Helvétius (the cause of the 1757 crisis of the *Encyclopédie*), Holbach's *Système de la nature* his *Théologie portative* (here interestingly attributed to Diderot), a set of *Oeuvres philosophiques* by Diderot, several anonymous or pseudonymous works such as Holbach's *Christianity*

Unveiled ("by Boulanger," in Italian) as well as Raynal's *Histoire des deux Indes* and Beccaria's *Of Crimes and Punishments*, and a wide selection of precursors, such as Montaigne, Francis Bacon, Baruch Spinoza, and Pierre Bayle. Holbach's Paris library had the same books on its shelves—as philosophers he and Jefferson were speaking the same language.

While Jefferson came too late to become involved with Holbach's circle, Benjamin Franklin, who was the congressional ambassador to the French king from 1776 to 1785, was there at exactly the right time. This raises a teasing biographical question: Did Franklin, Holbach, and Diderot know one another? Franklin was seventy when he arrived in Paris and was already well-known in French intellectual circles as a hero of the fight for American freedom. The king's weary secret police recorded: "Doctor Franklin, who lately arrived in this country from the English Colonies, is very much run after, and feted, not only by the savants his confrères, but by all people who can get hold of him."[19]

But did Holbach and Diderot actually get hold of Franklin? He would have been a prized and admired guest at the rue Royale, and it is highly probable that he was there. His biographer Max Cushing calls the founding father and the baron "intimate friends," but neither Cushing nor other historians can adduce any direct evidence such as a mention in a diary, a letter, or published works. Even in the absence of documentation, however, it would have been almost unthinkable for Franklin not to attend Holbach's salon at least a few times during the nine years of his residence in the French capital.

During the late 1770s, the fame of the rue Royale was at its apex. Franklin was a "natural philosopher" who had made a name for himself with his experiments with electricity and invention of the lightning rod, as a courageous campaigner for individual freedom and national emancipation, and as a foreign man of letters. The doors of the fashionable salons stood open to him, and Holbach's would have been a natural port of call. Franklin himself appears to have thought so. On his arrival in Paris, "I was asked whether I would like to see anyone in particular," wrote Franklin in a letter to Mme Helvétius. "Take me to the *philosophes*,"[20] he replied, indicating that he knew about the Holbach circle and was eager to shake their hands.

But if Franklin did visit Holbach, he did not come often, and the men may not have liked one another. The American ambassador lived in the suburb of

Passy, and his gout at times made traveling by coach an ordeal. Still, he did visit several salons with great enthusiasm, especially those with a decidedly feminine touch, such as the house of Madame Helvétius, the widow of the philosopher, who had died in 1771. The reason for Franklin's frequent visits was sentimental: The spry and energetic ambassador had fallen in love with the famously graceful lady of the house, and eventually he even proposed marriage to her, an offer she refused.

Franklin generally sought the company of pretty women such as Anne-Louise Brillon, at whose table he was invited for tea and games of chess twice a week. Another favorite was the dashing Countess d'Houdetot, who had been so hotly pursued by the lovelorn Jean-Jacques Rousseau a little over a decade earlier and who also corresponded with the older man. Perhaps it was she who brought together Franklin, Diderot, and possibly Holbach at an outdoor party she celebrated on her country estate in honor of the American guest on April 12, 1781. Like a legendary hero, the corpulent ambassador was welcomed in a park decked out with garlands and by a posse of Paris friends and acquaintances singing hymns to freedom and reciting verse in praise of liberty. A whole orchestra was there for his return to the capital. At least Diderot and Raynal were reputedly present at this occasion.

In view of his persistent and energetic flirtations with several educated and significantly younger women (the three aforementioned ladies were not the only ones to receive Franklin's attentions), it is possible that the atmosphere and conversation at Holbach's coterie were simply too masculine to interest the diplomat, who found that the French air revived not only his spirit but also his flesh.

Another reason for Franklin's lacking enthusiasm for afternoons of vigorous discussion may also have been that his French was up to a teasing conversation but not to the fast cut and thrust of philosophical debate, with arguments being exchanged simultaneously across the table. There are few things more frustrating than having something to say without being able to say it in another language, and even if Holbach and Diderot spoke excellent English, it is likely that after a first, stately visit of introduction, the group would have lapsed into their native tongue during the course of the discussion, as almost all groups do.

It is almost impossible to imagine that Franklin never met Holbach and his friends, or indeed Diderot—a visit would have been a very pointed gesture towards people he knew to be on his side. In his correspondence, Franklin does not mention any direct acquaintance with Holbach or Diderot, but it may be that his discretion had political reasons. At a time when letters were routinely opened by censors and other government agents, the American envoy would have been very naïve and possibly reckless to record and advertise any association with some of the most subversive and suspicious characters in the kingdom.

While Franklin might have had good reasons to keep any association with a group of philosophical rabble-rousers out of his correspondence, one might suppose that at least Diderot or Holbach would have mentioned so famous an acquaintance in their letters, but unfortunately Diderot's correspondence with Sophie, the most intimate and most informative by far, had already ceased, and there are only fifty-five surviving letters from the period between 1776 (Franklin's arrival) and 1784 (Diderot's death), many of them of an official nature. Holbach left only a handful of letters over his lifetime, and they do not mention Franklin. The paper trail falls short.

There are other indications, however, that Franklin knew Holbach and Diderot personally. Both Diderot and Holbach were themselves frequent guests chez the captivating Madame Helvétius, and if Franklin did not come to the rue Royale, they may have met him there. Franklin was also regularly visited by two other members of Holbach's closest circle, the writers André Morellet and Jean-François Marmontel. When Benjamin Rush, who was later to sign his name on the American Declaration of Independence, came to Paris in 1769, he carried with him letters of recommendation from Benjamin Franklin, who was then in Pennsylvania on diplomatic business. One of these letters was addressed to Diderot, who welcomed the American visitor with great kindness, offering to write a letter of introduction to David Hume in London. It is unlikely and would have certainly been unusual for Franklin to have written such a letter to Diderot had he not met the *philosophe* in person. Ultimately, though, the relationship between Franklin and the Enlightenment radicals remains mysterious and uncertain.

Faced with tyranny in many forms, the Island of Love had become a philosophical counterweight to Diderot and his friends, a society living according to human nature, free of Christian self-disgust. This radiant vision was a literary fiction, as Diderot well knew, but several friends at Holbach's table had become increasingly troubled about the nature and justification of authority and of coercion. It was impossible and almost suicidal to speak openly about the way things were in France, but violent, brute power was everywhere. It was the grim reality behind the splendid stage sets at Catherine's court; it was imposed on slaves in the ports of western Africa and the plantations of the American South; it was bitterly resisted by the defiant United States when it came from London. In all of these cases, the friends of the rue Royale took the side of the weak. Guillaume Raynal and Denis Diderot were particularly adamant in condemning slavery and colonial rule, while Holbach wrote about power and religion, concluding that sometimes only a revolution could rid oppressed peoples of the violence from above.

Right was on the side not of those who lived in chateaux and merchants' mansions but of those whose lifeblood had paid for these luxuries, the baron and his friends believed. No society can be judged by its customs, wrote Diderot, but only by the contentment of its inhabitants, who must all have a share in that central idea of the American Declaration of Independence, a notion straight from Holbach's table and the sum of the philosophical ideas defended there: the pursuit of happiness.

CHAPTER 18

FIFTY HIRED PRIESTS

By the late 1770s, Holbach's salon and its lively evenings were slowly winding down. The host and his longtime friend Denis Diderot were past middle age, and neither was in good health. Diderot's heart was troubling him, and he suffered from pain in his joints and from various stomach ailments, as well as swollen legs, a symptom of cardiac weakness. Baron d'Holbach was in an even worse condition. For some years he had been burdened with health problems. In 1766 he had written to Garrick that he was "very sorry to hear that you are enlisted in the numerous troupe of gouty people. I have myself the honour of being of that tribe. I don't desire my friends should enter into the same corporation."[1] A decade later, his health had deteriorated considerably. "We are falling to ruins, one next to the other," Diderot commented in 1777 to Grimm, who was on an extended second visit to St. Petersburg. "The baron has become subject to bouts of kidney colic accompanied by the most frightening symptoms. Sometimes he is between life and death for seventeen hours. Add to this peril that of a half-knowledge of chemistry, medicine and pharmacy and a natural impatience which makes him try out ten medicines in a single morning."[2]

With its two fixed stars almost eclipsed, the salon had all but ceased to be. The dinners, it appears, grew less frequent, and the guests were no longer the band of young philosophical troublemakers hungry to change the world and to gorge themselves on sumptuous dinners, but an assembly of still-spirited but gouty philosopher friends. Having been a place of subversion, the salon had by now transformed into a place of worship, the "philosophers' synagogue," as Diderot ironically referred to it.

The courageous friends had made it in the world. Now they came together less to test out new ideas among themselves but more to welcome the foreign guests who knocked at Holbach's door nearly every other day. His salon had become an attraction on the European grand tour, like Voltaire's graceful little castle at Ferney or like the imperial ruins of Rome and the remains of Pompeii.

Many of these curious visitors were aristocrats—the ambassadors of Denmark, England, Naples, Saxe-Gotha, Württemberg, and Sweden, as well as assorted German counts and Russian grand dukes, Lord Shelburne, the prince of Brunswick, and the prince elector of Mainz. Unlike most of their contemporaries, Holbach and Diderot had not built their careers on aristocratic patronage. (Diderot's acceptance of Catherine's generous offer was an exception that proved hugely troubling to its recipient.) Now, while French nobles continued to avoid all contact with the rue Royale, aristocrats from other countries came to seek the philosophers' blessing.

Both Holbach and Diderot felt ambivalent about being honored in this way. The baron was deeply pessimistic about a future built on aristocratic power, and Diderot had set out to become the voice of Enlightenment in the ear of one of the world's great monarchs and had returned, more than a year later, feeling ill, deeply disappointed, and secretly tainted by his association with a tyrant.

To his deep sadness, Diderot had also gradually grown estranged from Grimm, his friend of so many years. Grimm had never made a secret of his social ambitions and of his fascination with aristocracy, but what once had been a mannerism had become a life's obsession. Now an ambassador of several German princes to the court of Catherine the Great, he had become completely enthralled by the life of the nobility, by titles and ceremony. More woundingly for Diderot, Grimm's view of human nature, which had always been bleakly skeptical, had taken a decisively reactionary turn. The former sharp-tongued advocate of the radical friends and editor of the *Correspondance littéraire* had in 1769 abandoned his magazine, leaving it to be written by Diderot and Mme d'Epinay. By 1775 he had finally turned his back on their opinions and dreams entirely, taking on his bread givers' views with their livery.

Baron von Grimm, as he was called since being ennobled by the Habsburg emperor Josef II, was an ambassador and advisor to several German princes as well as to the tsarina Catherine the Great, at whose St. Petersburg court he spent an entire year, from 1776 to 1777. By 1786 the former journalist of intellectual subversion had become Baron Grimm of Grimhof, Knight of the Polar Star of Sweden, holder of the Order of Saint Vladimir of Russia, baron of the Holy Roman Empire and holder of the Russian Grand Cross, member of the Imperial Academy of Sciences of Russia, counselor of state to Her Imperial Majesty, and minister plenipotentiary of Saxe-Gotha.

Almost exactly twenty years earlier, Diderot had felt deeply betrayed as he had lost his most trusted fellow philosopher, Jean-Jacques Rousseau, not only to increasing paranoia but also to their growing philosophical differences. Now the same was happening with Grimm, who had only scorn for the arguments of the *philosophes* and who increasingly took the side of the powerful. In 1760 Louise d'Epinay had already concluded that her lover was changing: "He becomes vain. He loves appearances. . . . The strictness of his principles is vanishing. He distinguishes two kinds of justice: one for ordinary people, another one for sovereigns."[3]

To Diderot, a man who could neither live nor think without close personal relationships and mutual loyalty, this second treachery was hard to bear. "Ah, my friend," he wrote in 1781 in a desperately angry letter to Grimm, "I see clearly, your soul has been whittled down at Petersburg, at Potsdam. . . . In the antechambers of the great . . . I no longer recognize you. You have become, perhaps without your knowing it, one of the most concealed but one of the most dangerous anti-*philosophes*. You live with us but you hate us."[4]

Diderot never mailed this bitter indictment to Grimm, but still it was clear that their friendship was at an end. Grimm had chosen sides precisely at a moment when reflection about his own experience had made the aging Denis more republican than he had ever been—even revolutionary. While in earlier days he had been willing to concede that monarchy might be the best form of state, he had now fully embraced Jean Meslier's maxim that the world would only be happy "once the last king has been strangled with the guts of the last priest."

Not only had Grimm opened up a political abyss between himself and his former comrades, but his example also vividly demonstrated to Diderot the moral dangers of associating with the powerful. Denis had already confronted this danger in his own life, of course. As with all the great conflicts in his life, he recast his ambivalence about his own role vis-à-vis Catherine the Great by telling a story about it. Like many of his finest works, the resulting essay was an occasional work, inspired by a request to write an afterword to a new edition of the works of Seneca.

In preparation for his essay, Diderot began to reread Seneca's philosophical works and letters. He came to recognize an alter ego in the Roman philosopher. Slowly the text outgrew its original intention and became a substantial work, entitled *Essay on the Lives of Claudius and Nero*, in which Diderot explored the Roman court as a world of intrigue, friendship, high principles, and low cunning.

At the heart of the story was not Nero but Seneca himself, who had become a personal advisor to his brilliant former pupil, a mad and pathologically cruel emperor. Seneca had thought that he could mold the boy and make him a wise ruler, but eventually he had to acknowledge that he had played an important part in the creation of a monster. Appalled and fascinated in equal measure by this development, and ambitious for himself, Seneca chose to remain close to the young autocrat, acting as his advisor and hoping, certainly at first, to exercise a positive influence on him.

Seneca's philosophy celebrated pleasure but was at the same time marked by profound skepticism. As pleasures are brief and because a strong attachment to the world will inevitably result in loss, disappointment, and suffering, it is best to practice self-restraint, to renounce the pursuit of worldly pleasures, and to be happy with the bare minimum to satisfy basic needs. Most importantly, one must give up one's attachment to life itself and one's fear of death. Death is annihilation, and there is no afterlife; therefore it is foolish to fear one's end.

It is almost impossible to read Seneca today without feeling an attendant hypocrisy sapping his argument. He was, after all, a stern moralist eating frugally and advocating a life of what he termed "voluntary poverty" on the back of a personal fortune of 300 million sesterces, amassed as advisor to a notoriously immoral Roman emperor while earnestly writing to his friends about the importance of disinterested virtue and freedom from material attachment. He was the Warren Buffett of the ancient world, telling us that money really isn't everything.

Compromised in life, Seneca at last proved equal to his teachings in the hour of his own death. Nero, now in the full bloom of paranoiac madness, sent an order for the philosopher to commit suicide because he suspected him of treason. On receiving the instruction from the hand of an officer terrified by his duty, the octogenarian philosopher comforted both him and the members of his family, gave a few last orders to slaves and family, and then slit his wrists. When the blood would not flow from his geriatric veins, he sat down in a hot bath, where he bled to death, calm to the end.

Despite his truly philosophical death, Seneca's reputation was permanently damaged by his closeness to one of antiquity's worst tyrants. Apparently succumbing to luxury and corruption had robbed the philosopher of the simple life of all credibility and made him a byword for hypocrisy. Now Diderot took it upon himself to defend Seneca against his detractors. In doing so, he was also defending himself: "Which man has enough reassuring mediocrity to enjoy the intimacy of a prince without being troubled by it?"[5] he asked rhetorically, implying that he himself was certainly not so mediocre.

Ironically, the attack ringing loudest in Diderot's ears was his own. In 1743, at the very beginning of his career, he had published his *Pensées philosophiques*, in which he had taken Seneca to task for having been "too busy with accumulating wealth" to concentrate on his duty, guilty "through shameful silence"[6] of the murder of good citizens he should have defended, and a philosophical hypocrite to boot. His was the sanctimony of uncomplicated youth—before he had been forced to make compromises himself, before he could have had a guilty conscience with regard to anyone but his family in Langres. Forty years later, he showed condescending indignation towards these views: "You are wrong, young man!" he shouted across the decades at his younger self in the pages of his essay.

Seneca, the conflicted philosopher, had become a mirror of Diderot's own internal struggles. While he was moved by Seneca's life and regarded Roman decadence as an anticipation of the mendacity and corruption of his own day, Seneca's stoic philosophy affected him no less deeply. Having labored for a quarter of a century over the great *Encyclopédie*, and having grown to hate this daily grind, which he saw as having stolen his best years, he undoubtedly recognized himself in the Roman's aphorisms: "One part of life is spent doing things badly, the largest part in doing nothing at all, and almost all of it doing something else than one ought to."[7]

Diderot had reason to feel that posterity's harsh judgment on the moralistic Seneca might also taint him, the great *philosophe* whose calls for human equality and freedom were underwritten by the notoriously tyrannical though intelligent tsarina. In taking the Roman's side, he defended his own future reputation.

Concern about his reputation was also the reason for a change of tone in Diderot's sympathetic and learned exploration of Roman imperial history and the interweaving of power and philosophy. Quite suddenly, the text erupts into a series of furious and sarcastic tirades against Jean-Jacques Rousseau, which punctuate the story of Seneca time and again, bubbling up in the most unexpected places—Rousseau ex machina—yanking the reader away from reflection on the lives of ancient Romans. Time and again, Diderot turns directly to his readers, demanding at one point that they "detest the ungrateful man who talks ill of his benefactors; detest that terrible man who does not hesitate to blacken his former friends."[8]

The reason for this sudden outburst lay in Diderot's fear about the impending publication of Rousseau's *Confessions*, his autobiography, extracts from which he had already read in public during his last stay in Paris, in 1770. He had arranged for the manuscript to be published after his death, and the passages he had chosen during his readings as well as his paranoid disposition had made it clear that the *philosophes* could expect nothing good from the autobiography of a man who was convinced that they were all hypocrites and liars who had done their utmost to destroy him. Rousseau's novels had gained him an extraordinary following across Europe, precisely because of the cult they made of utmost honesty and emotional truth. If Jean-Jacques condemned the *philosophes*, it was to be feared that their good names would never recover from it.

Diderot was right to fear the impact of the *Confessions*, which Rousseau had decided to have published after his death, precisely to deny his opponents any opportunity of attacking the truthfulness of his claims during his lifetime. Diderot dreaded its publication. Banned from publishing philosophical works, forced to provide for a family, and shackled to the great *Encyclopédie*, he felt in old age that only his good reputation could redeem him after his death. This idea had become something of an obsession with him. He had corresponded at length with the sculptor Falconet about his posterity and a literary afterlife, the only good he still had left, or so he felt. "Posterity is the same thing for the philosopher as the next world for the religious man,"[9] he wrote.

When Diderot published his *Essay* after the sudden death of his former friend on July 2, 1778, he was promptly criticized for attacking the memory of Rousseau. The *philosophe* was unrepentant and added further paragraphs to the revised edition of the book, arguing that Jean-Jacques had shown "the blackest ingratitude towards his benefactors. . . . I would write on his gravestone: *This Jean-Jacques You Can See Here Was Perverse.*"[10] Almost twenty years later, the betrayal still hurt.

What followed was an uncharacteristically bitter, grim demolition job, a great, graceless summing up of the case against Jean-Jacques. Rousseau, Diderot claims, attacked everything he loved, crossed everyone who trusted him, turned against everything his friends stood for; his work was nothing but a colorful rehash of others' ideas. Answering the hypothetical question of why he was so obsessed by this affair of the past, Diderot responds with great candor: "Ask a disappointed lover for the reason of his stubborn attachment to an unfaithful woman, and you will learn the motive of the stubborn attachment of one man of letters to another man of letters of distinguished talent."[11]

Diderot—a disappointed lover? While there is no evidence for this in the literal sense, the description was certainly apt on a platonic level. Diderot really had loved his friend and had later been attacked by him with the greatest bitterness. They had debated and worked together, only for Denis to find later that Jean-Jacques not only rejected his friends but also declared their ideas publicly and with great emphasis to be wicked, immoral, cynical, and dangerous.

Rousseau had turned against his friends, but also against friendship itself, just as he had turned against civilization, progress, reason, and social hope. His compulsive and paranoid rejection of Holbach, Diderot, Hume, and others had become a negation of their thinking, of their cause. Worse still, he had managed to get public opinion on his side and make himself out to be a martyr to the envy of the *philosophes*, thus damaging their most precious possession, the opinion of posterity.

Rousseau and Diderot, and later Rousseau and Hume, had grown into philosophical antitheses, the negation of each other. Rousseau owed much to Diderot (perhaps it was this he could not abide)—by his own admission the central idea for his famous "Discourse on the Arts and Sciences," the founding work of his career, had been Diderot's. Then in prison at Vincennes, Diderot had advised him in a spirit of Gallic contradiction to take the opposite position to everyone else, in order to make some waves and be noticed.

How could Diderot have known that his friend would make this principle into the driving force of a great career? And how could he have known that Rousseau would fight his war not against the powers that be, but against his friends? Over the years, Rousseau had constructed himself as a one-man negation of everything the thinkers of the radical Enlightenment stood for. They argued for atheism, and he became a deist; they sought truth in science, and he listened to the voice of natural goodness; they freed sensuality from sin, and he condemned lust and preached chaste love; they wanted to advance society, and he advocated for the primitive community.

"By other men's labours we are led to the sight of things most beautiful that have been wrested from darkness and brought into light,"[12] Seneca had reflected, and Diderot believed that he himself had contributed to this march of progress while Rousseau had ultimately betrayed it. Seeing himself as similarly compromised by an unwise association with power, as Seneca had been, the *philosophe* saw a kindred soul, even a personal friend, in a man who had died seventeen centuries before his birth.

When the doors of Holbach's salon had opened around 1750, its host was a young man barely out of university, a wealthy amateur whose passion for science, coupled with the generosity he displayed in his choice of sumptuous menus and fine wines, had attracted some of the brightest and most promising minds in Paris to his table. Intellectually uncompromising and politically daring, they had rethought the world, published what they could, braved the powers of the day, weathered storms together. Some of them had been sent to prison for their pains; others had narrowly and repeatedly avoided arrest or permanent exile.

They had survived through a combination of nerve and protection from sympathizers at court, and they had even risen to international fame. Their names became bywords for Enlightenment and intellectual courage, for freedom of conscience, and for thinking the unthinkable. More than any other physical place in the world, Holbach's salon had been transformed over the years into the living room of the world's intellectual elite. There had been hardly a progressive thinker, hardly a daring voice, during the later eighteenth century whose hands had not rested on his table, whose mood had not been raised by his wines, whose voice had not been heard answering a question or challenge from a guest or launching one. Slightly patronizingly, the *abbé* Galiani had dubbed Holbach the *maître d'hôtel de la philosophie*, and the baron, himself a distinguished and courageous author of many books, wore this title with pride.

An old man? At sixty-two, Paul Thiry d'Holbach was prematurely aged by gout and kidney stones. Oil portrait by Alexander Roslin, 1782.

But by 1780, Diderot was sixty-seven years old and running out of energy—and out of friends. Rousseau was dead, and Grimm had changed sides; Sophie Volland had grown estranged from him, and he had not written a letter to her since 1776. Helvétius had died in 1771, Hume and Garrick five years later; Louise d'Epinay was in ill health (she would die in 1783); and Galiani had long since been recalled to Naples, from where he was still corresponding with his former friends; while Raynal had been banned from Paris and was living far away, in Marseilles.

Only Holbach was still alive, but relations between him and Diderot also appear to have become more distant. Even if there is no evidence of a falling-out between the two, Diderot was increasingly irritated by the baron's tendency to moralize, which had become more pronounced as he reached his sixties. This may also be why Denis did not spent his last summers at Grandval but had instead accepted the invitation of different hosts. He and the baron no longer published books together, and Diderot ruefully wrote to his daughter that his old friend had recently even left town without saying good-bye to him.

The wicked company had grown old. Several early deaths had ripped holes in the fabric of their friendships and alliances, their own powers seemed all but spent, and the salon had become an attraction for foreign visitors and had lost the fizz and excitement of the early years. In fact, the group had simply said what it had to say; it had outlived its need to exist. Famous throughout Europe, wealthy for the most part, and regarded as legends in their lifetime, Holbach's "coterie" had done its work. Among them its members had published dozens of works, discussed the most contentious and important issues, and caused the greatest literary scandals of the day—from the great *Encyclopédie* to Holbach's *Christianity Unveiled,* his *System of Nature, De l'esprit* by Helvétius, the *Supplement to Bougainville's Voyage* by Diderot, and the *History of the Two Indies* by Raynal and Diderot—all of them works that had been condemned, forbidden, impounded, burned in public. No group of people had done so much to change society's general way of thinking.

In February 1779, the eighty-four-year-old Voltaire returned to Paris after a lifetime's exile. The wily, wizened philosopher who had been styled patron saint of the Enlightenment was celebrated with almost hysterical fervor throughout the capital and handed from one reception to another.

There is some evidence to suggest that Diderot and Voltaire met, though nothing to suggest that Voltaire honored Holbach's salon with a visit, if indeed it was still held. After almost three decades of mutual rivalry and admiration, Voltaire and Diderot were finally standing face to old face: "He resembles one of those ancient fairy castles that is falling to ruin on all sides; but you can easily see that it is inhabited by an old sorcerer,"[13] Diderot commented.

It was all too much for Voltaire, who died "of apotheosis and over-excitement."[14] The priest of the local parish refused to give him a Christian burial, and the corpse had to be dressed up, propped up in a carriage, and sneaked out of Paris, where a more tolerant curate could be found.

Despite the fact that he was nineteen years younger than Voltaire, Diderot himself, the philosopher of the passions, had to find that his heart was failing him. On his return from Russia in 1774, he had written to Sophie that he might have another ten years "at the bottom of the sack," and his feeling proved prophetic. More and more, he was suffering from painful swelling in his legs and dangerous shortness of breath. In early 1783 he was already in a grave state and was bled three times, which further weakened him, and on February 19, 1784, he suffered a crisis, most likely partial heart failure. He was so weak that his family kept from him the news that Sophie Volland died three days later. He may never have learned of her passing, and he certainly was not informed of the sudden death in 1784 of his eleven-year-old granddaughter Marie-Anne, his particular favorite.

In the spring of the same year, the Diderots moved out of the house in the rue Taranne on the Left Bank (the headquarters of the *Encyclopédie*) to the other side of the river. Their new home was just around the corner from the rue Royale, in the rue Richelieu, a stone's throw from Denis' beloved Palais-Royal with its colonnaded gardens, the scene of his great novel *Rameau's Nephew*. The elegant apartment was situated on the first floor and saved Diderot the exertion of climbing the four flights of stairs leading to his previous apartment. It had been rented for him by Catherine the Great, eager to be seen as a generous patroness to the last. Apart from fewer stairs and the closeness to Holbach and the Jardin Royal, the location of the new apartment had another advantage. It was situated in the parish of Saint-Roch, a church that specialized in burials of actors, writers, and artists, whose unconventional lifestyles could prove a serious impediment to a Christian burial. Perhaps Voltaire's posthumous indignity had struck home.

Whatever its advantages, the move could not halt Diderot's decline, and the loss of his familiar surroundings may actually have hastened it. In 1784 it was obvious that his days were numbered. He was a public figure now, and his slow demise was followed in the press: "At present the death of M. Diderot, who is under censure by the faculty [of theology at the Sorbonne] is being awaited with impatience," recorded one journalist maliciously and with obvious relish for the real meat of the story. "As this atheist, for such at least is the title given to him by the priests and the devout, belongs to no academy, is not related to any great family, has no imposing public standing in his own person, and does not possess powerful associates and friends, the clergy intend to avenge themselves upon him and make his dead body suffer every religious insult unless he satisfies the externals."[15] In ancien régime France, death was not the great leveler, after all.

To obtain this satisfaction—nothing less than a retraction of his books—a priest came to visit the ailing philosopher on several occasions, but he could not get anything more out of the *philosophe* than a general agreement that it was laudable to do good works and that some priests were to be applauded for helping the poor. In a last effort the churchman asked the philosopher to publish these maxims, adding a retraction of his most blasphemous comments, which would have a wonderful effect not only on the minds he may have confused but also on his own chances of salvation. "I am sure it would, *Monsieur le curé*, but you will agree that it would be telling an impudent lie,"[16] the sick man replied.

Diderot died, over lunch, on July 31, 1784. His pious wife and Monsieur de Vandeul, the son-in-law the philosopher had himself chosen and a social climber of the purest water, saw to it that he would not suffer the same indignity as Voltaire. The parish priest was discreetly assured a substantial donation, 1,500 to 1,800 livres, in return for burial in the church of Saint-Roch. No expense was spared for the funeral itself, and as if to expunge a life's work of freethinking and opposition to the church, fifty priests were hired to be present and lend the occasion an appropriate atmosphere.

Thiry d'Holbach, Diderot's faithful ally and friend whose house had been the focal point of genius in Europe, was buried in the same parish church of Saint-Roch four and a half years later, on January 21, 1789. His death was exquisitely timed: It avoided his being swept up in the storms to come. Both Diderot and the baron were interred in the ossuarium, a cryptlike room underneath the same altar, together with other famous Frenchmen, such as their friend Claude-Adrien Helvétius, the grand salon hostess Marie-Thérèse de Geoffrin, the great landscape artist André le Nôtre, and the dramatist Pierre Corneille.

During the Revolution, the burial place was ransacked, and the remains were torn from their resting places and scattered across the room. The rebels of the 1871 Paris Commune repeated this blasphemous ritual, and while the bones are still lying in the ossuarium, it was judged impossible to determine the parts of the individual skeletons.

Diderot, Holbach, and their circle had made history, redefining the terms of the debate between religion and science, of politics and morality. Their only judge, they thought, would be posterity. They had no idea just how right they were, no means of knowing how posterity would treat them, and they would have been appalled to think that, having weathered and triumphed over the storms of their own time, their legacy would be all but obliterated by what was to come. They would be practically forgotten for over a century.

"The first step towards philosophy is incredulity," Diderot had remarked to a visitor on the eve of his death. But in the end, even the materialist free spirit yearned for a kind of immortality: "The certainty that future centuries would be speaking also of me, that they would count me among the illustrious men of my nation, and that I should honour my century in the eyes of posterity, would be to me, I confess, infinitely sweeter than all present consideration, all present encomia," he had written years earlier. "But I am a long way from having such certainty. If the history of letters accords me a line, it will not be because of the merit of my works but because of the fury of my enemies."[17]

EPILOGUE

A STOLEN REVOLUTION

> It is that kind of life that we acquire in the memory of men. . . . We hear in ourselves the eulogy which they will make of us some day, and we sacrifice ourselves. We sacrifice our lives; we really cease to exist in order to live in their memory. If immortality considered from this aspect is a chimera, it is the chimera of great souls.
>
> DIDEROT, "IMMORTALITY," IN THE *Encyclopédie*

When Denis Diderot wrote these words, twenty years or so before his death, he could not know how prophetic they were. For even though it has never quite died, the memory of the radical Enlightenment has long remained a chimera of great souls.

From its inception the bold moral vision articulated by the friends of the rue Royale met with fierce resistance from critics who argued that godlessness would lead to immorality and debauchery, that the pleasure calculus would automatically turn the world into a Hobbesian war of all against all. Not so, Diderot and Holbach argued, demonstrating how desire itself is a natural spring of cooperation, that shared needs bind people together, and that empathy makes them help one another.

The battle between the ideas of the Enlightenment radicals and their critics was still raging when history intervened. On July 14, 1789, an enraged mob stormed the Bastille (finding and freeing only six prisoners, among them the notorious Marquis de Sade) and declared a new, revolutionary age, based on anticlericalism and opposition to aristocratic power. The hour had come for the ideas of Holbach and Diderot, it seemed. But as the general unrest gave way to a new government, it quickly became apparent that this was far from the truth. Instead of being celebrated in a grand apotheosis, they were subjected to an almost total eclipse.

The reason for this surprising turn of events was that the arguments of the "synagogue" of the rue Royale were simply too revolutionary for the Revolutionaries themselves, who were not interested in ushering in a philosophical society of equals in which all citizens were encouraged to live happily and peacefully in harmony with nature. Instead, the Revolutionaries wanted power, and like all proponents of violent ideological egalitarianism, they were firm believers in a strict chain of command. Men like Raynal, Holbach, and Diderot, who had questioned every kind of political authority and coercion, simply had no place in the plans of the new republic.

But there was more at stake than simply the philosophical justification of violence. Every dictatorship needs transcendence, the promise of a better tomorrow—a perfect beyond, a heaven, a paradise, an ideal dictatorship of workers and peasants, an end of history. After all, only the quasi-religious adherence to a great ideal hovering just out of reach and demanding great sacrifices can justify the cruelties and injustices of today.

Every revolution needs its religion. Among all Revolutionaries, the implacably zealous and all-powerful Maximilien Robespierre, a byword for murderous terror in the name of high ideals, had understood this best. During the violent second phase of the Revolution, from 1792 onwards, the iconoclastic vandalism of the mob and the anticlerical intent of the leaders attacked the spiritual and material power of Catholicism. They murdered or expelled priests, monks, and nuns; they banned all Catholic rituals, sold off great churches such as the abbey of Cluny for use as building material, devastated thousands of churches and their crypts (among them that of the *église* Saint-Roch in which Diderot, Holbach, and Helvétius lay buried), hacked the faces off the saints on portals and statues, and turned thousands of churches into pigsties, workshops, or prisons.

But the fanatical enemies of Christianity among the Revolutionaries were by no means atheists. One of the most notorious "de-Christianizers" was

Joseph Fouché, who in 1793 oversaw the campaign in Burgundy, where he forced priests to marry, prosecuted Catholic worship, and secularized burials and cemeteries. He also had a plaque with the inscription "*La mort est un éternel sommeil*" (death is an eternal slumber) installed above all graveyard gates, a clear reference to the immortality of the soul. One year later he was to distinguish himself by crushing the anti-Revolutionary rebellion of Lyon and having hundreds of prisoners executed with cannon loaded with grapeshot.

Pierre-Gaspard Chaumette was another anti-Christian Revolutionary, a great proponent of terror as a political weapon and one of the most fervent proponents of the guillotine. He was also a social conservative who supported the execution of the female Revolutionaries Manon Roland and Olympe de Gouges because they had, as he said, forgotten the duties of women. When he himself began to deny the existence of a Supreme Being and adopted the name Anaxagoras in homage to a Greek philosopher executed for godlessness, he was indicted and guillotined on April 13, 1793, by order of Robespierre. One of the crimes of which Chaumette had been accused was "seeking to destroy all morality, efface any idea of the divine and founding the government of France on the principles of atheism."[1]

The Supreme Being was the Revolutionaries' replacement for the Catholic God they had turned against, and they did not hesitate to put existing forms and places of worship into the service of the new. On the Cathedral of Clermont-Ferrand in the Auvergne region, the new masters daubed "The French people recognizes the Supreme Being and the immortality of the soul" above the main gate, while in Paris, the Cathedral of Notre Dame in Paris was declared a Temple of Reason. The great new church close to the Jardins de Luxembourg, which was to be consecrated to Sainte Geneviève, was dedicated as the burial place of France's national heroes and called the Panthéon, after the ancient Greek dwelling place of the gods.

The spiritual void left by the anticlerical zealots was thus quickly filled by a new national religion, the cult of Reason, of the Highest Being, which was propagated most energetically by Robespierre himself. Always systematic, the "incorruptible" dictator cast around for a philosophical template, a great and noble mind to serve as shining example.

The evolutionist, hedonist morality of the rue Royale was worse than useless for his purpose—it was a threat. How could he project the goals of the

Revolution and faith in its central tenets if the baron condemned all religion and Diderot skewered all belief in the immortality of the soul on the sharp blade of his wit? For the founder of a new cult of a Supreme Being, a group of philosophers whose life's work it had been to argue against all cults had to be combatted as intensely as the church itself.

Instead of being treated as heroic founding fathers of the Revolution, the friends of the rue Royale were quickly recognized as its enemies. A different philosophical inspiration was necessary, and the First Citizen found everything he had been looking for in the writings of Jean-Jacques Rousseau: unwavering religious faith that tied individual lives to a transcendental purpose; an ambiguous rhetoric mixing freedom, paternalism, and great hope with a justified use of even greater brutality; and a cult of healthy sentiment that emancipated faith in the values and goals of the Revolution from philosophical analysis.

If Reason was the goddess of the Revolutionaries, Rousseau was her prophet. Robespierre even embarked on a systematic deification of Jean-Jacques Rousseau. "Oh, divine Rousseau," he wrote, "you taught me to know myself. . . . I wish to follow your venerated path. . . . Happy will I be if, in the dangerous course that an unprecedented revolution now lays out before us, I remain constantly faithful to the inspirations that I have drawn from your writings!"[2]

Robespierre did remain faithful to his idol, ruthlessly putting his political vision into practice. Regarding himself as the only legitimate embodiment of the general will, he sent his enemies to their deaths without any qualms, exercising the repression, the control, the censorship, and the terror Rousseau had believed necessary to keep society virtuous and pure.

Nothing inspired Robespierre with greater enthusiasm than devising the rituals for a new, civil religion worshipping the Supreme Being, the Goddess of Reason. Huge public celebrations modeled on the Catholic Mass were held on newly devised public holidays, during which a bust of Rousseau, cut from a stone out of the walls of the Bastille, was honored as the embodiment of virtue and the spiritual father of the new republic.

With an immense flair for classicist bombast and ideological kitsch, the painter Jacques-Louis David, the chief decorator of the Revolution, designed huge, papier-mâché statues of Virtue, Liberty, and Nature—the latter endowed with multiple breasts that dispersed refreshing water, which was drunk out of a common chalice by eighty-six old men symbolizing the departments of France. On 20 Prairial Year II of the new calendar (June 8, 1794, to the uninitiated), Robespierre held a public ceremony for the Supreme Being in the Tuileries gardens. Attended by a crowd of thousands, it included not only a lengthy sermon by Robespierre but also the ritual burning of a statue of Atheism, the charred debris of which revealed an effigy of Truth—unfortunately blackened by smoke.

Implementing his new religion, Robespierre brooked no opposition, even from the dead. On December 5, 1792, the very day on which he was to give his famous speech demanding the execution of King Louis XVI, he had ordered the removal and smashing of a bust of Helvétius, which had been standing in the Jacobin Club next to an effigy of Rousseau. Helvétius had been celebrated by some Revolutionaries as a proponent of reasonable, republican government.

For Robespierre, the philosopher was an enemy who had argued that religion was nothing but a weakness of the human spirit, a superstition that even threatened the stability of society. Religion, Helvétius had written, bred a caste of priests living in idleness and intent on acquiring wealth and power, a class that would ultimately become the target of violent uprisings. Robespierre, who had led just such an uprising and was now himself becoming a member of a privileged class at the top of a social order supported by religion, could no longer have the man's head cut off, but he could at least see that his likeness was shattered.

Another of Holbach's humanist friends, the *abbé* Raynal, who was still living in Marseilles during the Revolution, had a lucky escape. He had collaborated with Diderot on the *Histoire des deux Indes*, a flaming indictment of colonialist exploitation. Raynal had written a letter to the National Assembly, pleading with the Revolutionaries to steer a moderate and less murderous course. Vilified as a bourgeois, only his great age (he was eighty-eight) saved him from the guillotine, but a bust of him standing in the Jacobin Club of Marseilles was transferred to the local lunatic asylum. Raynal died of natural causes in 1796.

After Robespierre's fall and execution in 1794, the fortunes of Holbach, Helvétius, and Diderot were revived very briefly by the left-leaning Gracchus Babeuf, whose political thinking would today be described as egalitarianism, perhaps even Socialism. But Babeuf's attempt to gain control of the reeling ship of state, the "Conspiracy of Equals," was betrayed, and so was he. During his trial in 1797, he frequently cited Diderot as an inspiration, to no other effect than that Denis was regarded posthumously as a dangerous enemy of the people.

While Rousseau was publicly venerated, Holbach and Diderot fell victim to the politics of national memory. After the Revolution, Diderot was remembered as little more than the editor of an outdated encyclopedia, as well as the author of a few raunchy and experimental novels and a play, *Le Père de famille*. (Even during the Revolution, the play continued its long run at the Comédie Française, no doubt because it showed how a family and by extension a nation might be reconciled with its father figure.) Still, Diderot was known and written about as a man with no respect for what was sacred, a typical product of the immoral ancien régime.

Diderot's reputation was cemented in the mind of the public by Jean-François de la Harpe, a minor publicist who had done everything to get into the *philosophe*'s good graces during his lifetime. Diderot had never trusted him. In 1771 he had written to Louise d'Epinay: "He is a cold head; he has thoughts, he has a good ear, but no guts, no soul."[3] This judgment was borne out when de la Harpe gave a highly popular series of lectures on literature from 1799 to his death in 1803, denouncing his former mentor for his alleged immorality and his lack of true artistry, and condemning the *philosophes* collectively. "Diderot, Helvétius and other sophists have argued against reason—without excuse or measure,"[4] he scoffed during his systematic misrepresentation of their ideas, during which he incidentally attributed two of Holbach's works to Diderot. Almost obsessively, the critic poured out his bile over his former friends, chastising them for their supposed intellectual sins and moral malignancy. The series proved so lucrative that he repeated it for several years running.

While Diderot's reputation as a philosopher was under systematic fire, the public was unable to make up their own minds about him as a writer. Several pirated editions of his works were published after his death—all of them incomplete and most of them heavily edited, cut, and rewritten. Original texts were almost impossible to come by, especially as the writer's daughter, the onetime apple of his eye, was so preoccupied with being respectable that she suppressed her father's manuscripts. The first French edition of the great novel

Rameau's Nephew appeared in 1821 and was in fact a retranslation from the German version by Johann Wolfgang von Goethe. The first time the French public was allowed to read the full, unadulterated text was in the edition by Georges Monval, published in 1891. Diderot's second great novel, *Jacques the Fatalist*, was first published in 1875, while other original manuscripts appeared for the first time well into the twentieth century. Important passages by him (for instance, his contribution to Raynal's work) were identified as such only after World War II. The reputation of Diderot the writer and the philosopher never recovered from this fragmentation, which had its roots in the suppression of his works during the Revolution.

But would Diderot have otherwise become famous as a philosopher? During his imprisonment at Vincennes, he had been forced to sign a statement in which he pledged never again to write philosophical books, and the threat of being incarcerated once again, this time for good, hung over him all his life. His work remained eclectic, partly because he was as much an author of fiction and a talker as he was a systematic writer. Both of these factors conspired against Diderot's recognition as an important thinker. The nineteenth century was the period of great systematic works, of Kant's *Critiques*, Hegel's grand expositions, Marx and his *Capital*. Diderot simply did not fit the mold: His best thoughts are to be found in his letters, his fiction, his writings on art, and his essays on other works.

Diderot published no great work of systematic philosophy that could have established his reputation in a climate obsessed with all-embracing answers. In addition to the heterogeneity of his writings, his constant, teasing ambivalence makes it impossible to read the *philosophe* as a dogmatic author. His work sparkles and often provokes—ultimately leaving the reader alone to make up her own mind. As a result, even historians and philosophers who should be his natural allies have too often overlooked him. The French writer Michel Onfray, for instance, has created a publishing sensation with his *Contre-histoire de la philosophie*, which concentrates on materialist and atheist authors. In his book *Les ultras de lumières* (*The "Ultras" of the Enlightenment*) he devotes entire chapters to personal heroes such as La Mettrie, Meslier, Helvétius, and Holbach—but not Diderot.

While Diderot may have been too eclectic for the systematic nineteenth century, Holbach had built a well-rounded philosophical edifice. His philosophical works had appeared under strict secrecy and used various pseudonyms, so that it took decades and in some cases centuries to establish their authorship. But even after major works such as *Système de la nature* had been attributed to him, his uncompromising atheism and materialism similarly prevented his entering the philosophical canon.

Hidden behind pseudonyms during his lifetime, Holbach remained obscure after his death, despite the fact that works such as the *Système* and his antireligious polemics were reprinted frequently and often in secrecy, and read with admiration by people as different as the Marquis de Sade and Karl Marx. The philosophical establishment, however, in thrall to Immanuel Kant and Friedrich Wilhelm Hegel, remained resolutely uninterested, and nineteenth-century historians of philosophy tended to see him as a minor Encyclopedist and a peddler of blasphemy.

The first renaissance of Holbach's thinking came from a society whose ruthless suppression of free thought would have horrified him. The party thinkers of the Soviet Union gave the baron (along with Helvétius and Diderot) considerable attention because their materialism fitted the ideological line. They sought to co-opt the *philosophes* for their purposes, despite the fact that the totalitarian idea of the general will they imposed on society was ideologically far closer to Rousseau's *Social Contract* than anything the baron had written.

Holbach's short-lived fame as a precursor of Marxism-Leninism, as Soviet history would have it, may have contributed to his obscurity after 1989. In an academic world in the thrall of postmodern and poststructuralist literary theory, there was no room for the works of a plainspoken philosopher whose greatest goal had been to make himself absolutely clear. Diderot could at least be interpreted as a subversive artist, but in Holbach's case there was nothing but the bare bones of his argument to contend with.

As a result of this academic neglect, Holbach has remained all but forgotten. There is no major biography of him (an endeavor that would admittedly be very difficult because documentation of his life is scarce and most of his letters have been lost), and most of his works are no longer in print or published by small presses and are often edited poorly, if at all. His name appears in histories of philosophy, but often only as a patron of the *Encyclopédie* and a host to other philosophers whose own works are rarely read. One of the most courageous and intellectually lucid and farsighted men of the eighteenth century is little more than a name appearing in footnotes of books on the Enlightenment.

During the nineteenth century, very few people could see and understand the achievement of the radical Enlightenment. The Romantics found resonances with their own thought in Diderot's praise of the passions, but they had no time for his insistence on rationality or for the dismissive attitude towards metaphysical mystifications taken by Diderot, Holbach, Helvétius, and Hume. The Romantics wanted mystery, sought truth in the darkest corners of the mind, and could not abide too much light being shone into the enthralling twilight of wonder. They found what they were looking for in the tortured soul searching and self-stylization of Rousseau, whose defrocked Calvinism informed their own thinking about fate and emotion, guilt and redemption.

In philosophy, the nineteenth century was the age of German Idealism, of Kant and Hegel, taught and venerated in universities the world over as the only valid and important tradition. Their works were canonized by historians of philosophy such as the Germans Heinrich Ritter and Karl Vorländer, whose hugely influential multivolume textbooks became common currency throughout Europe and who effectively relegated the radical Enlightenment to the status of a historical oddity, a gaggle of also-rans. In his standard work on the history of philosophy (*Geschichte der Philosophie*, 1903), Vorländer describes Diderot as "a versatile head" who failed to grasp the big picture and who "neither articulated original philosophical thoughts, nor had a lasting effect on his time." "Modest and warm-hearted" Holbach, meanwhile, is described as a dry writer (which he was, as well as an important one) unable to grasp both metaphysical philosophy and "the innermost nature of Christianity."[5] The next, long chapter is devoted to the genius of Rousseau.

The Enlightenment applauded and required by the capitalist and imperialist nineteenth century was a moderate version represented by Voltaire, who had always known on which side his bread was buttered, and by the exponents of Idealism, particularly Immanuel Kant. The question at issue here was skepticism. The Enlightenment radicals had argued that there is no grand, metaphysical Truth and that consequently the only valuable knowledge is based on evidence: Do what is useful; avoid what is harmful to yourself or others.

While this moral teaching had the advantage of being simple and easily understood, it was a thorn in the side of Europe's and America's burgeoning capitalist societies and their colonial empires. Implacably opposed to the "conspiracy of the priests and magistrates," to national claims of superiority, to the exploitation of the poor and the oppression of peoples on foreign shores, the radicals stood against the intellectual tide of the century.

The nineteenth century needed a philosophical tradition that justified the colonial enterprise as well as the industrial exploitation of cheap labor, and it turned to the moderate, rationalist Enlightenment to provide it by giving a philosophical justification of religious faith. Meslier, Diderot, and Holbach had pointed out how organized religion leads to an unholy union of priests and magistrates, and the great bourgeois societies of the nineteenth century drew their authority and their social hierarchy out of precisely this union. Historians of philosophy on both sides of the Atlantic therefore emphasized an ultimately deist, religious eighteenth century, with Kant and Voltaire as its greatest exponents.

In this model of history, Immanuel Kant fulfilled a similar function for the eighteenth century as René Descartes had for the seventeenth: His grand metaphysical investigation left open a door through which God could be introduced back into philosophy. Kant argued that our senses determine how the world *appears* to us and that we may never be able to perceive things as they really are, the "things in themselves." But instead of accepting that we cannot know anything beyond our perception and that it makes no sense to talk about what we cannot know, he conjectured a purely essential, spiritual reality that is inaccessible to human understanding, a reality in which we might imagine a deity beyond the grasp of the senses. One can read Kant safely without compromising one's religious beliefs, which can always be safely tucked away among the "things in themselves." Voltaire, the wit and critical commentator opposed to religious excess, fitted equally well into the designs of a civilization that saw itself as scientific and rationalist, without being antireligious or unpatriotic.

It is worth understanding this idea of rationalism, of scientific reason in harmony with the possibility of religious faith, which still dominates our understanding of the Enlightenment. Kant's idea of pure reason not only was a field of philosophical research but also represented a cultural ideal: If only we could rationalize the world in its entirety, if only we could rid ourselves of animal instinct and unreasoning impulse, the world would be a better place.

The nineteenth-century rewriting of the history of eighteenth-century Enlightenment thought removed or at least marginalized radicals such as Diderot, Holbach, and Helvétius, whose concept of reason was tinged with skepticism and who claimed the primacy of the passions. To them, the irrational driving forces of human nature can be perhaps understood and steered, but they cannot be abolished, nor should they be. *Volupté* is at once the primal drive and the goal it seeks.

At base, we are natural organisms whose only aim is to survive and procreate. We may be able to improve our lives by using our reasoning faculties, but they themselves depend on our bodily constitution. Diderot's idea that there was "a little bit of testicle," an erotic aspect, in even the most sublime feelings was ultimately much closer to Freud than to Idealist dreams of pure reason.

To the Enlightenment radicals, all belief in the ultimate rationality of human beings or of the world was implicitly theological. According to deist arguments, there must be a reason, a meaning to life, because creation itself is informed by a supreme reason, a divine purpose expressed in the universal order. To say that there must be a reason is another way of saying that there must be a God. From this perspective it is clear why Voltaire and Kant could not entirely abandon the conviction that humankind was ultimately rational and that by inference a perfectly rational society would result in a world without vice.

The soft Enlightenment of Voltaire and Kant was highly commensurate with bourgeois values. Reason was celebrated but confined to science, where it did not threaten to violate the sacred grove of religion. Ideally, the human mind was seen as abstract and pure. Merged with faith, it formed the heavy trap door under which the continual guilt of desire and passion was shut away once again in a distasteful *souterrain* of human nature.

With the aid of Kant and Voltaire, this murky region of dark instincts could be locked away. This solution required a great deal of emotional denial, but help was at hand: Rousseau offered his followers the opportunity to examine their own dark instincts and to find the way towards God's forgiveness through repentance and purified emotion.

It comes as little surprise that the robustly capitalist nineteenth century chimed in with Kant's worship of reason. After all, the goal of industrialization was to rationalize society as far as possible; to optimize manufacturing processes, such as division of labor and the assembly line; and to achieve the increasingly efficient planning and control of everything from transport and leisure to sex, punishment, and entertainment. The era that built the greatest railway stations and factories also erected the largest prisons, all according to the same organizing principles of tightly managed production and supply. When the twentieth-century Marxist scholars Max Horkheimer and Theodor W. Adorno published their *Dialectic of Enlightenment* in 1947, they had witnessed (and escaped) the most monstrous travesty of this logic: the fully industrialized murder of human beings in Nazi extermination camps.

Even if the logic of the rationalist, deist, moderate Enlightenment does not necessarily lead to the selection ramps of Auschwitz, it has a tendency to dehumanize, to subjugate human desires and impulses to the all-powerful needs of a system, which is itself a creature of human reason. As Adorno and Horkheimer remarked, and as Marx had pointed out before them, it leads to a feeling of alienation among those who live in it, to a world dominated by the inexorable progress of the clock and the needs of machines and factories, stock markets and corporations—the nightmare factory world of Charlie Chaplin's *Modern Times.*

While the moderate, deist Enlightenment became both a justification and a means of molding society into a machine geared towards productivity and control, the vision of the radicals among those who assembled at Holbach's salon was very different. Because they lived in a time yoked under the often cruel authority of the church, strident, combative polemics dominate parts of their writings, but beyond the immediate political battle was another, kinder voice, encouraging all people to delight in life and demanding the right to live in dignity and freedom.

The friends around Holbach's table had not invented these ideas. They had collected the lean tradition of Western freethinking, from Epicurus and Lucretius to Spinoza and Bayle, and had developed them. Arguments grew and intensified during their debates and found new ammunition in scientific discoveries, making them stronger and better supported by observation than they had ever been before. The radical humanism emanating from their works was read and understood by a small band of exceptional minds, among them not only the poets Johann Wolfgang von Goethe (who loved Diderot but detested Holbach), Heinrich Heine, and Percy Bysshe Shelley, but also Karl Marx, Friedrich Nietzsche, and Sigmund Freud.

With characteristic insight, Nietzsche intuited Diderot's modernity when he wrote that Voltaire was "the last mind of the old France, Diderot the first of the new."[6] Holbach's implacable opposition to Christian values was an inspiration for Nietzsche's writings against the "slave morality" of Christianity. His ideal for humanity, the sage Zarathustra, is also deeply influenced by the broadly Epicurean emphasis on cultivating the self, embracing desire and living through, but not against, the passions by transforming them from a merely physical instinct into a spiritual quest.

Sigmund Freud, whom the critic Peter Gay calls "the *philosophes'* most distinguished disciple,"[7] regarded it as his personal mission to destroy illusions. He found the groundwork already laid by the critiques of Holbach and Hume. But it was Diderot whose exploration of the passions and of the irrational founts of personality had the deepest influence on him. A century before Freud even began his work, Diderot had written about young children in *Rameau's Nephew*, which Freud knew and loved: "If your little savage were left to himself, keeping all his childish foolishness—*imbécilité*—and joining the bit of rationality of the infant in the cradle to the violent passions of the man of thirty, he would strangle his father and sleep with his mother."[8]

A little over two centuries after Holbach's salon closed its doors for the last time, we still face the choice among Rousseau's cult of sentiment and secularized self-hatred, Voltaire's worldly cynicism, and the ethics of Enlightened hedonism advocated at the rue Royale. Long banished to the margins of history by a society unwilling to listen, its message was drowned out by other voices; works written by its proponents were first burned in public and then read only by a select few. The triumphal transfer of the bodies of Voltaire and Rousseau to the Panthéon set a symbolic seal on their victory over their philosophical adversaries in the public imagination.

Diderot is buried anonymously, his bones scattered, while the very presence of Holbach's remains is being denied by the guardians of his grave. The ideas of the radical Enlightenment, however, are still with us, as vibrant as they ever were. They are still strong, still beautiful, and still a challenge to the unquestioned and often damaging assumptions on which so much in our lives is based. There are no graves to be visited, no photographs taken in front of a sarcophagus, but still they live on.

"We really cease to exist in order to live in their memory," Diderot had written about those who would live after him. Immortality, he thought, was nothing but "the chimera of great souls," and yet it is real, existing in the minds of all readers who have felt and still feel drawn into their discussions, sharing their fears, their enthusiasms, and their hope.

A GLOSSARY OF PROTAGONISTS

Faced with an embarrassment of riches in material and personalities, of books, letters, articles, novels, and so forth, I have had to make choices and leave out much I would have liked to include but that would have exploded the dimensions of this book. The list below is therefore far from exhaustive, and not all visitors at Holbach's salon, or even all of the regulars, have found places here. Instead, this glossary features the main characters in this book. For a more complete list, see Alan Charles Kors, *D'Holbach's Coterie: An Enlightenment in Paris* (Princeton, NJ: Princeton University Press, 1976).

D'ALEMBERT, JEAN LE ROND (1717–1783) was a brilliant mathematician and coeditor of the *Encyclopédie*. After the great crisis of the encyclopedic project in 1759, he withdrew from his role as editor. He maintained a cordial though distant relationship with Diderot and may have visited the rue Royale, without ever becoming a regular.

BOULANGER, NICOLAS-ANTOINE (1722–1759) was a civil engineer and historian and one of the early members of the Holbach circle. After his early death Holbach used his name as a pseudonym for some of his most important works.

BUFFON, GEORGES-LOUIS LECLERC, COMTE DE (1707–1788) was the greatest zoologist of his time and a consummate politician and power broker. Initially an occasional guest chez Holbach, he stopped his visits probably because he was annoyed at being outtalked and outshone by Diderot.

D'EPINAY, LOUISE-FLORENCE-PÉTRONILLE TARDIEU D'ESCAVELLES (1726–1783) was a novelist, patroness of Rousseau, hostess of her own salon, and lover of Friedrich Melchior Grimm. Her novel *Histoire de madame de Montbrillant* gives an extraordinary picture of her time and of her friends.

DIDEROT, DENIS (1713–1784) was a philosopher, novelist, playwright, editor in chief of the *Encyclopédie*, and essayist. One of Holbach's closest friends and the central force of the radical Enlightenment, he is simply one of the most extraordinary thinkers of modern Europe, as well as a man one would have loved to have dinner with.

Falconet, Étienne-Maurice (1716–1791) was a sculptor with whom Diderot corresponded about posterity.

Franklin, Benjamin (1706–1790) was ambassador of the United States to France. During his stay in Paris from 1776 to 1785, he knew most of the prominent figures of the Paris literary scene. There is no evidence for his having been present at Holbach's salon, but it is probable that he visited it.

Galiani, Ferdinando, abbé (1728–1787), also known as "Machiavellino," was a regular at the rue Royale during his tenure at the embassy of the Kingdom of Naples from 1759 to 1769. He was one of the most witty guests and one of the few to hold his own against Diderot, whom he loved to provoke with well-judged doses of deism.

Garrick, David (1716–1779) was a great actor and theatrical entrepreneur in London. He visited Paris several times during the 1760s and became a lifelong friend and correspondent of Diderot and Holbach, who greatly admired his talents.

Grimm, Friedrich Melchior (1723–1807) was German by birth, but he came to Paris as a young man and made an extraordinary career as a freelance diplomat for German and Russian aristocratic houses and as editor of the *Correspondance littéraire*, a literary magazine not subject to the censorship imposed on printed matter because it was handwritten and sent by diplomatic post. The most important publicist of the radical Enlightenment, he was an intimate friend of Diderot (it is uncertain how intimate), the lover of Louise d'Epinay, and a regular at the rue Royale.

Helvétius, Claude-Adrien (1715–1771) was a wealthy civil servant who held his own philosophical salon and increasingly turned to philosophy. The publication of his *De l'Esprit*, in which he argued for a utilitarian morality, caused a scandal and forced him to retreat from public life. He was a close friend of Diderot and Holbach.

Holbach, Paul Henri Thiry, baron (1723–1789) was born Paul Heinrich Dietrich Holbach in Germany. He was taken to Paris as a boy and educated there and at Leiden University. Having inherited his uncle's fortune, he devoted himself to science, to translating scientific works from German and Latin, and to writing a series of very stringently atheist works that he published under various pseudonyms. In his house in the rue Royale Saint-Roch, today rue des Moulins, he opened his salon to like-minded men of letters every Sunday and Thursday. It became the most important room in intellectual Europe.

Hume, David (1711–1776) was born in Edinburgh. He wrote his groundbreaking works of philosophy while he was still in his early twenties. In later life, he became a tutor, historian, and civil servant, partly because he feared he would go mad if he continued with his radical philosophy. In consequence, he was known mainly as the author of the monumental *History of England* during his own lifetime. Secretary at the British embassy from 1763 to 1765, he was a regular member of the

Holbach circle and remained in contact with Holbach and Diderot after his return to Britain. His attempt to help Rousseau ended in an éclat.

Lespinasse, Julie-Jeanne-Éléonore (1732–1776) was the longtime partner of d'Alembert and hostess of a salon. She appears as one of the characters in Diderot's *D'Alembert's Dream*.

Marmontel, Jean-François (1723–1799) was a journalist and writer, regular at Holbach's, and later perpetual secretary of the Académie Française. His testimony about the goings-on at the rue Royale is tainted by his later striving for respectability as immortal and royal historian.

Morellet, André, abbé (1727–1819) was an economist and a combative pamphleteer, dubbed "*abbé mords-les*" ("*abbé* bite them") by Voltaire for his incisive style. He was a regular at Holbach's table.

Raynal, Guillaume-Thomas-François, abbé (1713–1796) was an economist and a journalist as well as a former Jesuit. Together with Diderot, he wrote the *Histoire des deux Indes*, a searing indictment of colonialism and slavery. Threatened with arrest for his authorship in France, he fled to Prussia and then to Russia, but eventually returned to France.

Rousseau, Jean-Jacques (1712–1778) was born in Geneva. He led an unsteady, searching life but eventually, around 1742, arrived in Paris, where he befriended Diderot. The two were inseparable, and Rousseau was initially one of the most important collaborators on the *Encyclopédie*. In 1758, angry and increasingly paranoid, he broke with Diderot and Holbach, whom he believed to be plotting to destroy his reputation, and with Louise d'Epinay, his patroness and friend. When Hume took him to England in 1765, he was initially grateful but quickly accused Hume of treachery in an affair publicized around Europe, his final break with the Enlightenment and its protagonists.

Smith, Adam (1723–1790) was a Scottish economist and moral philosopher, as well as a close friend of David Hume. In 1764 and 1765 he visited Paris, where Hume introduced him to Holbach's salon.

Sterne, Laurence (1713–1768) was an English writer and Protestant curate whose novel *Tristram Shandy* was hugely admired by Diderot. He visited Paris, including Holbach's salon, in 1762.

Volland, "Sophie" Louise-Henriette (1716–1784) was Diderot's longtime mistress and soul mate, to whom he addressed 553 letters. Having met in 1755, the two remained close but grew progressively estranged during the last decade of her life. It is likely that Diderot did not know about her death, which occurred four months before his own.

Voltaire, formerly François-Marie Arouet (1694–1778) was the patron saint of the Enlightenment. He lived in exile in Switzerland, from where he corresponded with (and lent large sums of money to) princes and with men of letters across

Europe. The greatest entrepreneur of the Enlightenment, he played a very ambivalent role with regard to Holbach's salon and was distrustful of others likely to eclipse his fame. He was not above spreading rumors and ridiculing potential rivals in an effort to slow down their progress and secure his own position.

WALPOLE, HORACE (1717–1797) was a wealthy and aristocratic English man of letters who came to know Holbach's salon during a visit to Paris in 1765. Not used to the frank tone of the discussions at the rue Royale, he did not enjoy the experience and grew to detest Holbach and his friends.

WILKES, JOHN (1725–1797) was a radical English publicist and politician who had met Holbach during their university days at Leiden, in the Netherlands. Fleeing political persecution in London, Wilkes came to Paris in 1765 and renewed his friendship with the baron and his circle.

A VERY SELECTIVE BIBLIOGRAPHY

A comprehensive bibliography documenting the persons and subjects of this book would be of little help to readers curious enough to pursue these ideas further. The documentation is hugely imbalanced and needs clarification. Mountains of work have been published, for instance, about every last detail in the work of Rousseau and Voltaire, but there is hardly anything useful on Holbach or even a coherent exposition of Diderot as a philosopher. Hoping to assist readers in the search for further reading, especially original works in translation and good historical accounts, I have done a little gardening and weeded out everything but the essential, largely in good English translations.

ENLIGHTENMENT

For general works on the Enlightenment, which has fallen a little from scientific favor in recent years, I would recommend as the best, most penetrating, and most elegant Peter Gay's *The Enlightenment: An Interpretation*, volume 1: *The Rise of Modern Paganism*, and volume 2: *The Science of Freedom* (New York: Knopf, 1966–1969). A classic is Ernst Cassirer's *Die Philosophie der Aufklärung* (1932)—in English translation, *The Philosophy of the Enlightenment* (Princeton, NJ: Princeton University Press, 1968).

Among recent books, I would particularly recommend Jonathan Israel's standard work *Radical Enlightenment, Philosophy and the Making of Modernity 1650–1750* (Oxford: Oxford University Press, 2001), which also contains an excellent bibliography, and Michel Onfray's very readable and engaging but somewhat tendentious and inaccurate *Les ultras des lumières* (Paris: Grasset, 2008), which is still awaiting translation. For additional reading, Robert Darnton's elegant and insightful *The Great Cat Massacre and Other Episodes from French Cultural History* (New York: Basic Books, 1999) is a true pleasure.

For primary sources in French, the digital service of the Bibliothèque Nationale in France offers a large, searchable range of scanned original editions for free download: http://gallica.bnf.fr.

HOLBACH AND HIS CIRCLE

There are few books on the Holbach circle and none of them recent, but for well-structured information and detail I would recommend Alan Charles Kors, *D'Holbach's Coterie: An Enlightenment in Paris* (Princeton, NJ: Princeton University Press, 1976), as well as Max Pearson Cushing, *Baron d'Holbach: A Study of Eighteenth-Century Radicalism in France* (New York: B. Franklin, 1971). Also of interest are René Hubert, *D'Holbach et ses amis* (Paris, 1928); C. Avezac-Lavigne, *Diderot et la société du baron d'Holbach* (1875; reprint, Geneva: Slatkin, 1970); and S. F. Genlis, *Les Dîners du baron d'Holbach, dans lesquels se trouvent rassemblés sous leurs noms, une partie des gens de la cour et des littérateurs les plus remarquables du 18e siècle* (Paris, 1822).

WORKS BY DIDEROT

Prolific and versatile, Diderot published an eclectic range of works, of which only his fiction and selections from the *Encyclopédie* are widely available. For French readers, I recommend the excellent collection of Diderot's (almost) complete works edited and annotated by Laurent Versini, and published in five volumes by Robert Laffont in Paris, 1994–1997.

Here is a small selection of works in English translation:

Diderot, Denis. *Diderot on Art*. Edited by John Crow. New Haven, CT: Yale University Press, 1995.

———. *Diderot's Early Philosophical Works.* Translated and edited by Margaret Jourdain. New York: AMS, 1973.

———. *Diderot's Letters to Sophie Volland: A Selection.* Translated by Peter France. London: Oxford University Press, 1972.

———. *Jacques the Fatalist and His Master.* Translated with an introduction and notes by David Coward. Oxford: Oxford University Press, 1999.

———. *Memoirs of a Nun.* Translated from the French by Francis Birrell. New York: Knopf, 1992.

———. *Political Writings.* Translated and edited by John Hope Mason and Robert Wokler. Cambridge: Oxford University Press, 1992.

———. *Rameau's Nephew; and First Satire.* Translated by Margaret Mauldon. Oxford: Oxford University Press, 2006.

———. *This Is Not a Story and Other Stories.* Translated with an introduction by P. N. Furbank. Oxford: Oxford University Press, 1993.

WORKS ON DIDEROT

Arthur M. Wilson's biography *Diderot* (New York: Oxford University Press, 1972) is the most authoritative, most humane, and most enjoyable of a small group of serious works on the *philosophe*, though the relevant passages in Peter Gay's *Enlightenment* (see above) are also illuminating, as is P. N. Furbank, *Diderot: A Critical Biography* (New York: Knopf, 1992). For readers interested in Diderot as editor of the *Encyclopédie*, which features many of the same people as the present book, may I suggest my own *Enlightening the World: Encyclopédie, the Book That Changed the Course of History* (New York: Palgrave Macmillan, 2005). The more understated title of the British edition is *Encyclopédie: The Triumph of Reason in an Unreasonable Age* (London: Fourth Estate, 2004).

WORKS BY HOLBACH

Only three of Paul Henri Thiry Holbach's works are commonly available in English translation. I quote exemplary editions, but others exist, always teetering at the brink of going out of print: *Christianity Unveiled: Being an Examination of the Principles and Effects of the Christian Religion*, translated by W. M. Johnson (New York: Gordon, 1974); *The System of Nature*, 3 volumes (New York: Garland, 1984); and *Good Sense*, translated by Anna Knoop, Great Books in Philosophy (Amherst, NY: Prometheus Books, 2004). Holbach's relatively few extant letters (some of them in the original English) are collected in *Die gesamte erhaltene Korrespondenz*, ed. Hermann Sauter and Erich Loos (Wiesbaden: Franz Steiner, 1986).

The lion's share of the baron's huge output is available only in French, and often only in the original eighteenth-century editions, though all works are now available in scanned versions from the excellent Web site of the French Bibliothèque Nationale: http://gallica.bnf.fr.

WORKS ON HOLBACH

There is no comprehensive biography of the baron, and most works are either very specialized, out of print, or out of date. The most approachable in English is Max Pearson Cushing, *Baron d'Holbach: A Study of Eighteenth-Century Radicalism in France* (New York: B. Franklin, 1971). Other works include the following:

Harthausen, H., H. Mercker, and H. Schröter. *Paul Thiry von Holbach: Philosoph der Aufklärung, 1723–1789: Katalog zur Ausstellung vom 11. 6.–2. 7. 1989 auf Hambacher Schloss anlässlich des zweihundertsten Todesjahres*. Pfälzische Arbeiten zum Buch- und Bibliothekswesen und zur Bibliographie. Heft 15. Speyer: Pfälzische Landesbibliothek, 1989. (Exhibition catalogue in German.)

Naville, Paul. *D'Holbach et la philosophie scientifique au XVIIIe siècle*. Revised edition. Paris: Gallimard, 1967.

Sandrier, A. *Le style philosophique du baron d'Holbach*. Honoré Champion. Paris: Gallimard, 2004.

Vercruysse, J. *Bibliographie descriptive des écrits du baron d'Holbach*. Paris: Minard, 1971.

Wickwar, W. H. *Baron d'Holbach: A Prelude to the French Revolution*. London: Allen & Unwin, 1935.

DAVID HUME

Hume's great philosophical works, *An Enquiry Concerning Human Understanding* and *A Treatise on Human Nature*, as well as his *Dialogue Concerning Natural Religion*, are readily available in numerous editions. For those interested in reading about him, Roderick Graham's *The Great Infidel: A Life of David Hume* (Edinburgh: Birlinn, 2006) may serve as a useful introduction. James Buchan's beautifully written *Capital of the Mind: How Edinburgh Changed the World* (London: John Murray, 2003) provides the intellectual and cultural context of Hume's philosophical development.

JEAN-JACQUES ROUSSEAU

There are many translations and editions of Rousseau's *Confessions*, *The Social Contract*, *Discourse on Inequality*, and novels *Émile* and *Julie, or the New Eloise*. When it comes to biographies, however, many candidates are too admiring or even hagiographical for my taste. Maurice Cranston's three-volume biography—*Jean-Jacques: The Early Life and Works of Jean-Jacques Rousseau* (New York: Norton, 1983); *The Noble Savage: Jean-Jacques Rousseau, 1754–1762* (Chicago: University of Chicago Press, 1991); and *The Solitary Self: Jean-Jacques Rousseau in Exile and Adversity* (Chicago: University of Chicago Press, 1997)—is still regarded as the standard, while Leo Damrosch's *Jean-Jacques Rousseau: Restless Genius* (Boston: Houghton Mifflin, 2005) may be overestimating its subject's originality as a thinker but gives an excellent overview of his life and character.

NOTES

CHAPTER I

1. Jean-François Marmontel, quoted in Jacqueline Hellegouarc'h, *L'Esprit de société: Cercles et "salons" Parisiens au XVIIIe siècle* (Paris: Garnier, 2000), 17.

2. Quoted in Arthur M. Wilson, *Diderot* (New York: Oxford University Press, 1972), 16.

3. André Zysberg, *La monarchie des Lumières 1715–1786*, Collection "Points histoire" (Paris: Éditions du Seuil, 2002), 153.

4. Denis Diderot, *Jacques le fataliste*, quoted in Wilson, *Diderot*, 20.

5. Quoted in Wilson, *Diderot*, 31.

6. Ibid.

CHAPTER 2

1. Marie-Angélique de Vandeul, *Diderot, mon père* (Strasbourg: Circé, 1992), 15.

2. Charles Théveneau de Morande, *La Gazette noire par un homme qui n'est past blanc*, 1784, imprimé à cent lieues de la Bastille, 212, here quoted in Robert Darnton, *The Literary Underground of the Old Regime* (Cambridge, MA: Harvard University Press, 1982), 24.

3. Ibid.

4. Anonymous (Henri de Boulainviller), "Origine des êtres et especes, fruit d'une conversation retenue imparfaitement," *Rivista di storia della filosofia* 1 (1994): 169–192.

5. Denis Diderot, *Oeuvres*, vol. 4, *Esthétique et théâtre* (Paris: Laffont, 1997), 730–731.

6. Denis Diderot, *Pensées philosophiques*, in Diderot, *Oeuvres*, vol. 1, *Philosophie* (Paris: Laffont, 1994), 19.

7. Ibid., 20.

8. Denis Diderot, *De la suffisance de la religion naturelle*, in Diderot, *Oeuvres*, vol. 1, 55.

9. Jean-Jacques Rousseau, *Confessions*, here quoted in Maurice Cranston, *Jean-Jacques: The Early Life and Work of Jean-Jacques Rousseau, 1712–1754* (New York: Norton, 1984), 31.

10. Jacob Bicker-Raye, *Het dagboek van Jacob Bicker Raye 1732-1772*, eds. F. Beijerinck and M. G. de Boer (Amsterdam: H. J. Paris, 1935), 122.

11. Quoted in Brunet, *Les physiciens hollandais et la méthode expérimentale en France au 18e siècle* (Paris, 1926), 93.

12. Letter from Thiry d'Holbach to John Wilkes, August 9, 1746, in Paul Thiry Baron d'Holbach, *Die gesamte erhaltene Korrespondenz*, ed. Hermann Sauter and Erich Loos (Wiesbaden: Franz Steiner, 1986), 9.

13. Julien Offray de la Mettrie, *L'Homme machine* (Paris: M. Solovine, 1921), 143.

14. Ibid., 183.

15. Ibid., 189–190.

16. Julien Offray de la Mettrie, *Discours sur le bonheur*, ed. John Falvey, Critical Edition (Banbury: Voltaire Foundation, 1975), 160.

CHAPTER 3

1. All quotations from Bayle's *Dictionnaire* are from Pierre Bayle, *Historical and Critical Dictionary: Selections*, trans. Richard H. Popkin (Indianapolis: Hackett, 1991).

2. Pierre Bayle, *Pensées diverses* (Rotterdam, 1683), vol. 1, 4.

3. Ibid., vol. 1, 6.

4. Ibid., vol. 1, 12.

5. Ibid., vol. 2, 296.

6. Denis Diderot, "*Pensées philosophiques*," in Denis Diderot, *Oeuvres*, 5 vols. (Paris: Laffont, 1994–1997), vol. 1, 38.

7. Denis Diderot, "*Lettre sur les aveugles à l'usage de ceux qui voient*," in *Oeuvres*, vol. 1, 167.

8. P. Bonnefon, "Diderot prisonnier à Vincennes," in *Revue d'histoire littéraire de la France* (1899), vol. 6, 203, cited in P. N. Furbank, *Diderot: A Critical Biography* (New York: Knopf, 1992), 47.

9. Jean-Jacques Rousseau, *Discourse on the Arts and Sciences* (London: J. M. Dent, 1923), 131.

10. Denis Diderot, "Encyclopédie" in Denis Diderot, Jean Lerond d'Alembert, eds., *Encyclopédie des arts et métiers*, vol. 5, 635.

CHAPTER 4

1. Vincent de la Chapelle, *Le Cuisinier moderne qui apprend à donner à manger toutes sortes de repas, en gras et en maigre, d'une manière délicate que ce qui en a été écrit jusqu'à présent* (The Hague, 1742).

2. Letter from Denis Diderot to Sophie Volland, July 25, 1765, in Denis Diderot, *Oeuvres*, vol. 5, *Correspondance* (Paris: Laffont, 1997), 506.

3. Georges-Louis Leclerc de Buffon, ed. and trans., Introduction to *Statique des végétaux de Stephen Hales* (Paris: Debure l'âiné, 1735), v.

4. Georges-Louis Leclerc de Buffon, *Histoire naturelle* (Paris: Imprimerie royale, n.d.), vol. 1, 12.

5. Denis Diderot, "*Pensées interprétation de la nature*," in Diderot, *Oeuvres*, vol. 1, *Philosophie* (Paris: Laffont, 1994), 564–565.

6. Denis Diderot, *Rêve de d'Alembert*, in Diderot, *Oeuvres*, vol. 1, *Philosophie*, 631.

7. Jean-François Marmontel, *Mémoires* (Paris: Mercure de France, 2000), 214.

8. Diderot, *Oeuvres*, vol. 5, *Correspondance*, 322.

9. Marmontel, *Mémoires*, 215.

10. Letter from Diderot to Volland, October 24, 1762, in Diderot, *Oeuvres*, vol. 5, *Correspondance*, 465.

11. Letter from Diderot to Falconet, September 1768, in Diderot, *Oeuvres*, vol. 5, *Correspondance*, 855–856.

12. Letter from Diderot to Volland, October 18, 1760, in Diderot, *Oeuvres*, vol. 5, *Correspondance*, 261–262.

13. Quoted in Francis Steegmuller, *A Woman, a Man, and Two Kingdoms: The Story of Madame d'Epinay and the Abbé Gallani* (New York: Knopf, 1991), 33.

14. Ibid., 40.

15. Rousseau in a letter to an unnamed correspondent, quoted in Maurice Cranston, *Jean-Jacques: The Early Life and Work of Jean-Jacques Rousseau, 1712–1754* (New York: Norton, 1984), 267.

16. Jean-Jacques Rousseau, *Confessions* (Paris: Le Livre poche, 1998), book 1, 176.

17. Ibid., book 1, 177.

18. Jean-Jacques Rousseau, *Oeuvres complètes*, vol. 12, *Émile* (Paris, 1792), 296.

CHAPTER 5

1. Quoted in Jonathan I. Israel, *Radical Enlightenment: Philosophy and the Making of Modernity, 1650–1750* (Oxford: Oxford University Press, 2001), 276.

2. Jean Meslier, *Oeuvres complètes*, vol. 1, *Testament*, ed. Roland Desné (Paris: Anthropos, 1970), 27.

3. Ibid., 15.

4. Ibid., 114.

5. Voltaire, "A, B, C!" in *Philosophical Dictionary*, vol. 2, 605, quoted in Peter Gay, *The Enlightenment*, vol. 2, *The Science of Freedom* (New York: Knopf, 1969), 527.

6. Peter Gay, *The Enlightenment*, vol. 1, *The Rise of Modern Paganism* (New York: Knopf, 1966), 122.

7. Voltaire, *Oeuvres complètes de Voltaire*, vol. 8, *Histoire de Jenni* (Paris: Desoer, 1817), 366.

CHAPTER 6

1. Michel de Montaigne, *Essais*, trans. Donald M. Frame (Stanford, CA: Stanford University Press, 1943), 786.

2. Letter from Denis Diderot to Sophie Volland, October 8, 1768, in Denis Diderot, *Oeuvres*, vol. 5, *Correspondance* (Paris: Laffont, 1997), 895.

3. Letter from Diderot to Falconet, May 15, 1767, in Diderot, *Oeuvres*, vol. 5, *Correspondance*, 731.

4. Paul Thiry d'Holbach, *Pièces inédites: Le Baron d'Holbach* (Paris: L'Amateur d'autographes, 1864), vol. 3, 75–77.

5. Letter from Diderot to Mme de Maux, April 1772(?), in Diderot, *Oeuvres*, vol. 5, *Correspondance*, 1105.

6. Ibid., 39–40.

7. Paul Thiry Holbach, *Le Christianisme dévoilé* (London, 1756), 45–46.

8. Ibid., 105–106.

9. Ibid., 64.

10. Ibid., 214.

11. Ibid., 233.

12. Quoted in William Wickwar, *Baron d'Holbach: A Prelude to the French Revolution* (London: Allen & Unwin, 1935), 62–63.

13. Letter from Diderot to Volland, November 21, 1760, in Diderot, *Oeuvres*, *Correspondance*, vol. 5, 320.

14. Letter from Diderot to Sophie Volland, September 22, 1761, in Diderot, *Oeuvres*, vol. 5, *Correspondance*, 352.

15. Letter from Diderot to Volland, May 1759, in Diderot, *Oeuvres*, vol. 5, *Correspondance*, 101.

16. Letter from Diderot to Guillaume Vialet, 1766, in Diderot, *Oeuvres*, vol. 5, *Correspondance*, 657.

17. Letter from Diderot to Volland, 1759, in Diderot, *Oeuvres*, vol. 5, *Correspondance*, 180.

18. Diderot, *Oeuvres*, vol. 5, *Correspondance*, 537–538.

19. Diderot, *Correspondance*, here quoted in Peter Gay, *The Enlightenment*, vol. 1, *The Rise of Modern Paganism* (New York: Knopf, 1966), 64.

20. Diderot, *Oeuvres*, vol. 5, *Correspondance*, 399.

21. Ibid., 191–192.

22. Diderot, *Le Rêve d'Alembert*, in Diderot, *Oeuvres*, vol. 1, *Philosophie* (Paris: Laffont, 1994), 873.

23. Ibid., 893–894.

24. Ibid., 917.

25. Ibid., 893.

26. Ibid., 907.

27. Letter from Diderot to Voltaire, in Denis Diderot, *Correspondance*, ed. Georges Roth, 16 vols. (Paris: Les Éditions de minuit, 1955–1970), vol. 6, 334.

28. Letter from Voltaire to Mme Saint Julien, December 15, 1766, in Voltaire, *Oeuvres*, ed. Garnier (Paris, 1876), vol. 44, 534.

29. Letter from Diderot to Volland, November 22, 1768, in Diderot, *Oeuvres*, vol. 5, *Correspondance*, 922.

CHAPTER 7

1. André Marmontel, *Oeuvres complètes* (Paris, 1819), vol. 1, 200.

2. Jean-Jacques Rousseau, *Confessions* (Paris: Le Livre poche, 1998), book 2, 23.

3. Denis Diderot, *Le Fils naturel*, in Denis Diderot, *Oeuvres*, vol. 4, *Esthétique et théâtre* (Paris: Laffont, 1997), 1112–1113.

4. Letter from Denis Diderot to Jean-Jacques Rousseau, March 14, 1757, in Diderot, *Oeuvres*, vol. 5, *Correspondance* (Paris: Laffont, 1997), 63.

5. Ibid., 64.

6. Rousseau, *Confessions*, book 2, 135.

7. Quoted in Maurice Cranston, *The Noble Savage: Jean-Jacques Rousseau, 1754–1762* (Chicago: University of Chicago Press, 1991), 75.

8. Quoted in ibid., 86.

9. Quoted in ibid., 98.

10. Letter from Rousseau to Voltaire, August 18, 1756, in Jean-Jacques Rousseau, *Correspondance complète de Jean-Jacques Rousseau*, ed. R. A. Leigh (Geneva: Institut et musée Voltaire, 1965), vol. 4, 81, quoted in Peter Gay, *The Enlightenment*, vol. 2, *The Science of Freedom* (New York: Knopf, 1969), 546.

11. Jean-Jacques Rousseau, *Oeuvres complètes*, vol. 12, *Émile* (Paris, 1792), 950.

12. Ibid., 954.

13. Jean-Jacques Rousseau, *Lettre à Monsieur d'Alembert sur les spectacles*, in Jean-Jacques Rousseau, *Oeuvres* (Paris, 1857), vol. 8, 21.

14. Characteristically, Helvétius doctors the quote by inverting it and leaving a line out. See Lucretius, *On the Nature of the Universe*, trans. Ronald Melville (Oxford: Clarendon, 1999), part 1, lines 130 and 132.

15. Claude-Adrien Helvétius, *De l'esprit*, trans. W. Munford (London, 1807), 27–28.

16. Ibid., 50.

17. Ibid., 172.

18. Letter from Diderot to Sophie Volland, October 15, 1759, in Diderot, *Oeuvres*, vol. 5, *Correspondance*, 172.

CHAPTER 8

1. Letter from Thiry d'Holbach to David Hume, August 22, 1763, in Thiry d'Holbach, *Gesamte erhaltene Korrespondenz*, ed. Hermann Sauter and Erich Loos (Wiesbaden: Franz Steiner, 1986), 18–19.

2. Roderick Graham, *The Great Infidel: A Life of David Hume* (Edinburgh: Birlinn, 2006), 264.

3. Ibid., 263.

4. Letter from David Hume to Adam Smith, August 9, 1763, in: David Hume, *The Letters of David Hume*, ed. J. Y. T. Greig, 2 vols. (Oxford: Oxford University Press. 1932), vol. 1, 483.

5. Graham, *Great Infidel*, 272.

6. Ibid., 498.

7. William Cole, quoted in ibid., 276.

8. Friedrich Melchior Grimm, *Correspondance littéraire*, ed. Maurice Tourneux (Paris, 1877–1882), vol. 5, 12.5.

9. Horace Walpole, *The Letters of Horace Walpole*, 6 vols. (London: Richard Bentley, 1846), vol. 4 226.

10. Ibid., vol. 6, 370.

11. Ibid., vol. 4, 298.

12. David Hume, *The Letters of David Hume*, ed. J. Y. T. Greig, 2 vols. (Oxford: Oxford University Press, 1932), vol. 1, 491.

13. Denis Diderot, *Oeuvres*, vol. 5, *Correspondance* (Paris: Laffont, 1997), 537.

14. James Buchan, *Capital of the Mind: How Edinburgh Changed the World* (London: John Murray, 2003), 61.

15. Ibid., 56.

16. David Hume, *My Own Life*, in *The Cambridge Companion to Hume*, ed. David Fate Norton (Cambridge: Cambridge University Press, 1993), 351.

17. David Hume, *A Treatise on Human Nature* (London: Penguin, 1984), 311–312.

18. Ibid., 312.

19. David Hume, quoted in Buchan, *Capital of the Mind*, 78.

20. Hume, quoted in ibid., 83.

21. Hume, quoted in ibid., 272.

22. David Hume, *The Natural History of Religion*, in *Dialogues and The Natural History of Religion* (Oxford: Oxford University Press, 1993), 182.

23. Ibid.

24. Hume, *Treatise on Human Nature*, 153.

25. Hume, *Letters*, vol. 1, 498.

26. Hume, *Dialogues Concerning Natural Religion* (London, 1779), 134, 142.

27. Hume, *Letters*, vol. 2, 93–94.

28. Edward Gibbon, *Memoirs of My Life*, ed. Georges A. Bonnard (London: Nelson, 1966), 136.

29. Letter from Diderot to Hume, in Diderot, *Oeuvres*, vol. 5, *Correspondance*, 813.

CHAPTER 9

1. Louis-Sébastien Mercier, *Panorama of Paris: Selections from Le Tableau de Paris*, ed. Jeremy D. Popkin and Helen Simpson (University Park: Pennsylvania State University Press, 1999), 30.

2. Ibid.

3. Lucretius, *On the Nature of the Universe* (Oxford: Clarendon, 1999), book 1, verses 63–71; my translation.

4. Ibid., book 2, verses 1090–1093; my translation.

5. Quoted in John Hill Burton, *Life and Correspondence of David Hume* (Edinburgh: William Tate, 1846), 196.

6. M. Mirabaud [Baron d'Holbach], *Système de la nature ou des loix du monde physique et du monde moral* (Amsterdam, 1770), 7.

7. Hubert, *Holbach et ses amis* (Paris: Delpeuch, 1928), 82.

8. Ibid., 80.

9. Ibid., 10.

10. Ibid., 194.

11. Ibid., 191.

12. Holbach, *Bon sens* (Amsterdam, 1772), 32.

13. Holbach, *Système*, vol. 2, 125.

14. Ibid., vol. 1, 45.

15. Ibid., vol. 1, 45.

16. Ibid., vol. 1, 48.

17. Ibid., vol. 2, 100.

18. Ibid., vol. 1, 72.

19. Ibid., vol. 1, 81–82.

20. Ibid., vol. 1, 81.

CHAPTER 10

1. Letter from Denis Diderot to Sophie Volland, July 18, 1762, in Denis Diderot, *Oeuvres* (Paris: Laffont, 1993–1997) vol. 5, 381.

2. Ibid.

3. Diderot, *Oeuvres*, vol. 5, 391.

4. Diderot, *Regrets*, in *Oeuvres*, vol. 4, 820.

5. Hume, *The Letters of David Hume*, ed. J. Y. T. Greig, 2 vols. (Oxford: Oxford University Press, 1931), vol. 2, 195–196.

6. Ibid., vol. 5, 328.

7. André Morellet, *Mémoires* (Paris, 1821), vol. 1, 131.

8. Abbé Galiani, *Correspondance* (Paris, 1881), vol. 2, 110.

9. Henry North Holroyd, Earl of Sheffield, ed., *The Private Letters of Edward Gibbon 1753–1794* (London: John Murray, 1896), 29.

10. Edward Gibbon, *Decline and Fall of the Roman Empire* (London, 1868), vol. 2, 247.

11. Letter from Sir James Macdonald of the Isles to Mrs. Elizabeth Montagu, Paris, April 11, 1764, in Elizabeth R. Montagu, *Mrs. Montagu, "Queen of the Blues,"* ed. Reginald Blunt (London: Constable, 1923), 97.

12. Gibbon, *Decline and Fall*, 34.

13. *Correspondence of the Late John Wilkes* (London: Richard Phillips, 1805), vol. 2, 35–36.

14. "Adam Smith's Correspondence," in W. R. Scott, *Adam Smith* (London: Oxford University Press, 1923), 298–299.

15. Letter from Diderot to Volland, October 7, 1762, in Diderot, *Oeuvres*, vol. 5, 457.

16. Laurence Sterne, quoted in A. H. Cash, *Laurence Sterne* (London: Methuen, 1975), vol. 2, 137.

17. Laurence Sterne, *Works of Laurence Sterne in one volume* (Philadelphia: Grigg & Elliot, 1843), 49.

18. David Garrick, *Letters* (Cambridge, MA: Belknap Press of Harvard University Press, 1963), vol. 2, 444.

19. Letter from Diderot to Falconet, July 1767, in Denis Diderot, *Oeuvres*, vol. 5, *Correspondance*, 745.

20. Denis Diderot, *Refutation d'Helvétius*, in *Oeuvres*, vol. 1, *Philosophie*, 855.

21. Denis Diderot, *Rêve d'Alembert*, in *Oeuvres*, vol. 1, *Philosophie*, 933.

22. Letter from Diderot to Volland, October 6, 1765, in Diderot, *Oeuvres*, vol. 5, *Correspondance*, 535.

23. Ibid., 536–537.

24. Ibid., 532–533.

25. Ibid., 533.

26. Letter from Diderot to Volland, December 10, 1765, in Diderot, *Oeuvres*, vol. 5, *Correspondance*, 568.

CHAPTER 11

1. Letter from Denis Diderot to Sophie Volland, Grandval, October 1, 1759, in Denis Diderot, *Oeuvres*, vol. 5, *Correspondance* (Paris: Laffont, 1997), 160.

2. Letter from Diderot to Volland, October 14–15, 1760, in Diderot, *Oeuvres*, vol. 5, *Correspondance*, 251.

3. Letter from Diderot to Sophie, Grandval, October 20, 1759, in Diderot, *Oeuvres*, vol. 5, *Correspondance*, 156.

4. Letter from Mme d'Epinay to Ferdinando Galiani, January 12, 1773, in Ferdinando Galiani, *Correspondance* (Paris, 1881), 166.

5. Letter from Diderot to Volland, September 28, 1767, in Diderot, *Oeuvres*, vol. 5, *Correspondance*, 774.

6. M. Mirabaud [Baron d'Holbach], *Système de la nature ou des loix du monde physique et du monde moral* (Amsterdam, 1770), 150.

7. Denis Diderot, *Jacques the Fataliste and His Master*, trans. David Coward (Oxford: Oxford University Press, 1999), 185.

8. Denis Diderot, "Jouissance," in *L'Encyclopédie*, vol. 8, 889.

9. Denis Diderot, *D'Alembert's Dream*, trans. A. W. Tanckock (London: Penguin, 1966), 174.

10. Denis Diderot, *Entretien*, in Diderot, *Oeuvres*, vol. 1, *Philosophie* (Paris: Laffont, 1994), 670–671.

11. Denis Diderot, *Salon of 1767*, in Diderot, *Oeuvres*, vol. 4, *Esthétique et théâtre* (Paris: Laffont, 1997), 632.

12. Letter from Diderot, November 3, 1760, quoted in Peter Gay, *The Enlightenment*, vol. 2, *The Science of Freedom* (New York: Knopf, 1969), 189–190.

13. Letter from Diderot to Volland, July 31, 1762, in Diderot, *Oeuvres*, vol. 5, *Correspondance*, 397.

14. Boyer d'Agens, *Thérèse philosophe* (Saint-Étienne, France: Université de Saint-Étienne, 2000), 34.

15. Julien Offray de la Mettrie, *L'Art de jouir* (Paris: Éditions du Boucher, 2000), 3.

16. La Mettrie, *L'Art de jouir*, 7.

17. Holbach, *La Morale universelle* (Amsterdam: Marc Michael Rey, 1776), xviii.

18. David Hume, *Treatise on Human Understanding* (London: Penguin, 1985), 22.

19. Holbach, *Morale universelle*, 68.

20. Montaigne, "Of Custom," in *Essays*, trans. Donald M. Frame (Stanford, CA: Stanford University Press, 1948), 83.

21. Letter from Diderot to Volland, in Diderot, *Oeuvres*, vol. 5, *Correspondance*, 357.

22. Quoted in Gay, *The Enlightenment*, vol. 2, *The Science of Freedom*, 188.

23. Letter from Diderot, August 16, 1759, in Diderot, *Correspondance*, vol. 2, 218, quoted in Gay, *The Enlightenment*, vol. 2, *The Science of Freedom*, 194.

24. Diderot, *Salon of 1769*, 420.

CHAPTER 12

1. Jean-Jacques Rousseau, *The Confessions*, trans. Angela Scholar (Oxford: Oxford University Press, 2000), 407.

2. Ibid., 388.

3. Jean-Jacques Rousseau, *Oeuvres complètes*, vol. 12, *Émile* (Paris, 1792), 221.

4. Jean-Jacques Rousseau, *Correspondance complète de Jean-Jacques Rousseau*, ed. R. A. Leigh (Geneva: Institut et musée Voltaire, 1965), vol. 8, 60–61.

5. Rousseau, *Oeuvres complètes*, vol. 12, *Émile*, 5.

6. Ibid., 358.

7. Jean-Jacques Rousseau, *Social Contract*, trans. G. D. H. Cole (London: Penguin, 1968), 3.

8. Jean-Jacques Rousseau, *Oeuvres* (Paris, 1857), vol. 3, 9.

9. Rousseau, *Social Contract*, 5.

10. Ibid., 8.

11. Ibid., 15.

12. Ibid., 29.

13. Ibid., 127.

14. Ibid., 36.

15. Ibid., 41.

16. Ibid., 41.

17. Ibid., 46.

18. Ibid., 96.

19. Rousseau, *Oeuvres complètes*, vol. 12, *Émile*, 774.

20. Rousseau, *Confessions*, 7.

CHAPTER 13

1. Cesare Beccaria, *Of Crimes*, trans. Edward Ingraham (Philadelphia, 1819), 31.

2. Ibid., 67.

3. Ibid., 50.

4. Ibid., 104.

5. Ibid., 105.

6. Ibid., 107.

7. Beccaria, *Opere*, vol. 2, 864, quoted in Alan Kors, *D'Holbach's Coterie* (Princeton, NJ: Princeton University Press, 1973), 108.

8. Arthur M. Wilson, *Diderot* (New York: Oxford University Press, 1972), 515.

9. Ibid., 515.

10. Ibid.

11. Quoted in M. Frasca-Spada and P. J. E. Kail, eds., *Impressions of Hume* (Oxford: Oxford University Press, 2005), 234.

12. Wilson, *Diderot*, 516.

13. Friedrich Melchior Grimm, *Correspondance littéraire*, ed. Maurice Tourneux (Paris, 1877–1882), vol. 6, 427–429.

14. Ibid., vol. 4, 241, here quoted in Kors, *Coterie holbachique*, 145.

15. Denis Diderot, *Réfutation d'Helvétius*, in Denis Diderot, *Oeuvres*, vol. 1, *Philosophie* (Paris: Laffont, 1994), quoted in Wilson, *Diderot*, 660.

16. Guillaume Raynal and Denis Diderot, *Histoire des deux Indes* (Amsterdam: Marc Michael Rey, 1770), vol. 3, 648–649.

17. Denis Diderot, *Observations sur le Nakaz*, in Diderot, *Oeuvres*, vol. 3, *Politique* (Paris: Laffont, 1996), 509.

18. Denis Diderot, "Sur les femmes," in Diderot, *Oeuvres*, vol. 1, *Philosophie*, 950.

19. Ibid., 953.

CHAPTER 14

1. Denis Diderot, *Essay sur les règnes de Claude et Néron*, in Denis Diderot, *Oeuvres*, vol. 1, *Philosophie* (Paris: Laffont, 1994), 1030.

2. Letter from Toussaint-Pierre Lenieps to Jean-Jacques Rousseau, quoted in Arthur M. Wilson, *Diderot* (New York: Oxford University Press, 1972), 500.

3. Letter from Friedrich Melchior Grimm to David Hume, quoted in Maurice William Cranston, *The Solitary Self: Jean-Jacques Rousseau in Exile and Adversity* (Chicago: University of Chicago Press, 1997), 159.

4. Letter from Rousseau to Hume, quoted in T. E. Ritchie, *An Account of the Life and Writings of David Hume, Esq.* (London, 1807), 160.

5. Letter from Hume to Hugh Blair, quoted in Ernest C. Mossner, *The Life of David Hume* (Edinburgh: Nelson, 1954), 512.

6. David Hume, *The Letters of David Hume*, ed. J. Y. T. Greig, 2 vols. (Oxford: Oxford University Press, 1932), vol. 2, 2.

7. James Boswell, *Life of Johnson*, trans. Charles Grosvenor Osgood (Princeton, NJ: Princeton University Press, 1917), 168.

8. Letter from Thiry Holbach to Hume, March 16, 1766, in Thiry Holbach, *Gesamte erhaltene Korrespondenz*, ed. Hermann Sauter and Erich Loos (Wiesbaden: Franz Steiner, 1986), 34–35.

9. André Morellet, *Mémoires* (Paris, 1821), 129.

10. Letter from Thiry Holbach to David Garrick, February 9, 1766, in Holbach, *Gesamte erhaltene Korrespondenz*, 32.

11. Ibid.

12. Hume, quoting Rousseau in his *Concise Account* (London, 1766), 52–54.

13. Hume, *Letters*, vol. 2, 29.

14. *A Concise and Genuine Account of the Dispute Between Mr Hume and Mr Rousseau* (London, 1766), 29–30.

15. Letter from Hume to Richard Davenport, July 15, 1766, in Jean-Jacques Rousseau, *Correspondance de Jean-Jacques Rousseau*, ed. R. A. Leigh (Geneva: Institut et musée Voltaire, 1969), 30, 528.

16. David Hume, quoted in Eliot Warburton, *Memoirs of Horace Walpole and His Contemporaries* (London: Colburn & Co., 1852), 269.

17. Anonymous, *Exposé succinct* (London, 1766).

18. Anonymous, *Un Pseudo-quaker défend Rousseau contre Hume et Voltaire*, unknown place, 1766, reprinted in Friedrich Melchior Grimm, *Correspondance littéraire,* ed. Maurice Tourneux (Paris, 1877–1882), 32, 516.

19. Hume to Blair, July 1, 1766, quoted in Mossner, *Life of David Hume*, 526.

20. Rousseau to M. Guy, *Oeuvres de Rousseau* (Paris, 1782), vol. 24, 387.

21. Grimm, *Correspondance Littéraire*, October 1766.

22. Voltaire, *Oeuvres de Voltaire* (Geneva: Institut et Musée Voltaire, 1968–1977), vol. 53, 492.

CHAPTER 15

1. Quoted in Denis Diderot, *Oeuvres*, vol. 5, *Correspondance* (Paris: Laffont, 1997), 76–77.

2. Denis Diderot, "Aguaxima" in *Encyclopédie*, vol. 1, 191.

3. Diderot, *Oeuvres*, vol. 5, *Correspondance*, 1109.

4. Ibid., 447.

5. Ibid., 495–496.

6. Denis Diderot, *Entretien*, in Diderot, *Oeuvres*, vol. 1, *Philosophie* (Paris: Laffont, 1994), 885.

7. Diderot, *Oeuvres*, vol. 5, *Correspondance*, 988.

8. Diderot, *Oeuvres*, vol. 5, *Correspondance*, 399.

9. Diderot, *Oeuvres*, vol. 1, *Philosophie*, 1119.

10. Ibid., 790.

11. Denis Diderot, *Réfutation d'Helvétius*, in Diderot, *Oeuvres*, vol. 1, *Philosophie*, 855.

12. Letter from Ferdinando Galiani to Louise d'Epinay, in Ferdinando Galiani, *Lettres de l'Abbé Galiani à Madame d'Epinay, Voltaire, Diderot, Grimm, le Baron d'Holbach . . .* (Paris: G. Charpentier, 1882), vol. 1, 230.

CHAPTER 16

1. Denis Diderot, *Correspondance*, ed. Georges Roth, 16 vols. (Paris: Les Éditions de minuit, 1955–1970), vol. 10, 15–16.

2. Letter from Denis Diderot to Voltaire, October 8 or 10, 1766, in Denis Diderot, *Oeuvres*, vol. 5, *Correspondance* (Paris: Laffont, 1997), 702.

3. Denis Diderot, *Éloge à Richardson*, in Diderot, *Oeuvres*, vol. 5, *Correspondance*, 158.

4. Louise d'Epinay, quoted in Arthur M. Wilson, *Diderot* (New York: Oxford University Press, 1972), 619.

5. Letter from Diderot to Sophie Volland, June 18, 1773, in Diderot, *Oeuvres*, vol. 5, *Correspondance*, 1180.

6. Georg Joachim Zollikofer quoted in Wilson, *Diderot*, 630.

7. Karl Lessing to Gotthold Ephraim Lessing, quoted in G. E. Lessing, *Sämtliche Schriften*, 25 vols. (Berlin: Göschen, 1886–1913), vol. 20, 287–288.

8. Grimm, quoted in Wilson, *Diderot*, 632.

9. Catherine II, quoted in Wilson, *Diderot*, 640.

10. Louis-Philippe Ségur, *Memoirs and Recollections*, 3 vols. (London, 1825–1833) vol. 3, 34–35, quoted in Wilson, *Diderot*, 641.

11. Letter from François Félix Dorothée Crillon to Jean d'Alembert about Diderot, quoted in Wilson, *Diderot*, 643.

12. Diderot, *Oeuvres*, vol. 3, *Politique* (Paris: Laffont, 1996), 508.

13. Denis Diderot, *Réfutation d'Helvétius*, in Diderot, *Oeuvres*, vol. 1, *Philosophie* (Paris: Laffont, 1994), 859.

14. Letter from Diderot to Volland, September 26, 1762, in Diderot, *Oeuvres*, vol. 5, *Correspondance*, 449.

15. Diderot, *Jacques le fataliste et son maître*, in *Oeuvres de Diderot*, Éditions Pléiades (Paris: Gallimard, 1951), 482–483.

CHAPTER 17

1. Louis-Antoine de Bougainville, "Mouillage à Tahiti," in *Voyage autour du monde* (1771), quoted in Richard Holmes, *The Age of Wonder: How the Romantic Generation Discovered the Beauty and Terror of Science* (New York: Pantheon Books, 2008), 4.

2. Denis Diderot, *Supplément au Voyage de Bougainville*, in Denis Diderot, *Oeuvres*, vol. 2, *Contes* (Paris: Laffont, 1994), 970.

3. Ibid., 970–971.

4. Ibid., 975.

5. Ibid., 976.

6. Ibid., 982.

7. Denis Diderot, *Essai sur la peinture*, in *Oeuvres de Diderot*, Éditions Pléiades (Paris: Gallimard, 1951), 1143–1144.

8. Diderot, *Supplément*, 987.

9. Jean-Jacques Rousseau, *Discours sur l'inégalité* (Amsterdam: Marc Michael Rey, 1755), 35–36.

10. Jean-Jacques Rousseau, *Oeuvres complètes*, vol. 12, *Émile* (Paris, 1792), 50–99.

11. References to ritual removal of one testicle among the Hottentots were a staple in travel accounts of the seventeenth and eighteenth centuries. Perhaps they should not be dismissed as legend altogether: Twentieth-century anthropologists such as Edward Evans-Pritchard have confirmed the ritual removal of one testicle among the Nuer. See E. E. Evans-Pritchard, *Nuer Religion* (Oxford: Clarendon, 1956).

12. Guillaume Raynal and Denis Diderot, *Histoire des deux Indes* (Amsterdam: Marc Michael Rey, 1770), vol. 3, 680.

13. Ibid., vol. 3, 698.

14. Ibid., vol. 3, 688.

15. Louis de Jaucourt, "Traité des nègres," in *Encyclopédie*, 16, 532.

16. Raynal and Diderot, *Histoire des deux Indes*, vol. 4, 167–172.

17. Denis Diderot, *Essai sur les règnes de Claude et de Neron*, in Diderot, *Oeuvres*, vol. 1, *Philosophie* (Paris: Laffont, 1994), 1197.

18. Letter from Ferdinando Galiani to Louise d'Epinay, May 18, 1776, reply from d'Epinay to Galiani, June 10, 1776, quoted in Francis Steegmuller, *A Woman, a Man, and Two Kingdoms: The Story of Madame d'Epinay and the Abbé Galiani* (New York: Knopf, 1991), 213–214.

19. Stacy Schiff, *Franklin in Paris* (New York: Henry Holt, 2005), 90.

20. Quoted in André Morellet, *Mémoires* (Paris: Mercure de France, 1988), 280.

CHAPTER 18

1. Letter from Paul Thiry Holbach to David Garrick, quoted in Max Pearson Cushing, *Baron d'Holbach: A Study in Eighteenth-Century Radicalism in France* (New York: Lanchester, 1914), 73.

2. Letter from Denis Diderot to Friedrich Melchior Grimm, June 9, 1777, in Denis Diderot, *Oeuvres*, vol. 5, *Correspondance* (Paris: Laffont, 1997), 1291–1292.

3. Louise d'Epinay, *Correspondance*, quoted in *Dictionnaire de Diderot*, ed. Roland Mortier and Raymond Trousson (Paris: H. Champion, 1999), 216.

4. Letter from Diderot to Grimm, 1781, quoted in Arthur M. Wilson, *Diderot* (New York: Oxford University Press, 1972), 701.

5. Denis Diderot, *Essai sur les règnes*, in Diderot, *Oeuvres*, vol. 1, *Philosophie* (Paris: Laffont, 1994), 1058.

6. Ibid., 967.

7. Ibid., 1107.

8. Ibid., 1029.

9. Letter from Diderot to Falconet, February 15, 1766, in Diderot, *Oeuvres*, vol. 5, *Correspondance*, 606.

10. Diderot, *Essai sur les règnes*, in Diderot, *Oeuvres*, vol. 1, *Philosophie*, 1029.

11. Ibid., 1035.

12. Seneca, *De brevitate vitae*, XIV, 1–2, in *Moral Essays*, trans. J. W. Basore, Loeb Classical Library (New York: Putnam's Sons, 1928), vol. 254, 333–335.

13. Quoted in Wilson, *Diderot*, 688.

14. Wilson, *Diderot*, 688.

15. Ibid., 711.

16. Ibid.

17. Quoted in Wilson, *Diderot*, 509–510.

EPILOGUE

1. Quoted in Nicole Bossut, *Chaumette, porte-parole des sans-culottes* (Paris: CTHS, 1998), 483.

2. Quoted in Daniel Brewer, *The Enlightenment Past: Reconstructing Eighteenth-Century French Thought* (Cambridge: Cambridge University Press, 2008), 108.

3. Letter from Denis Diderot to Mme d'Epinay, in Denis Diderot, *Oeuvres*, vol. 5, *Correspondance* (Paris: Laffont, 1997), 1085.

4. Jean-François de la Harpe, *Lycée ou cours de littérature ancienne et moderne* (Paris: Pourrat, 1839), vol. 18, 75.

5. Karl Vorländer, *Geschichte der philosophie* (Leipzig: Dürr, 1911), vol. 2, 214.

6. Friedrich Nietzsche, *Nachgelassene Fragmente*, in Friedrich Nietzsche, *Sämtliche Werke* (Munich: De Gruyter, 1999), vol. 13, 122.

7. Peter Gay, *The Enlightenment*, vol. 1, *The Rise of Modern Paganism* (New York: Knopf, 1966), 166.

8. Denis Diderot, *Le Neveu de Rameau*, here quoted in Peter Gay, *The Enlightenment*, vol. 2, *The Science of Freedom* (New York: Knopf, 1969), 190.

INDEX